Acclaim for JACK OLSEN's

Last Man Standing

"A great book." —*The Seattle Times*

"A telling narrative, beautifully written. . . . This is an extraordinary book about an extraordinary man."
—Martin Garbus, author of *Ready for the Defense*

"Jack Olsen descended into the hidden corridors of America's Gulag to tell the story of an innocent prisoner's fight for justice. . . . *Last Man Standing* is a moving, fast-paced and compelling book." —Kathleen Cleaver

"*Last Man Standing* combines dazzling, suspenseful narrative and superb investigative reporting into a truly stunning achievement. . . . A brilliant portrayal of the power of truth and the triumph of the human spirit. And a book you need to read."
—Andrew Vachss, author of *Dead and Gone*

"As compelling and thorough as any wrongful conviction book I have read—and I have read most of them. . . . Olsen's book goes where no other journalist has gone."
—Steve Weinberg, *Milwaukee Journal Sentinel*

"It's a riveting story that doesn't let up even after the last page is read." —*Booklist*

"Extraordinary." —*Essence*

JACK OLSEN

Last Man Standing

Jack Olsen is the author of thirty-one books and the winner of many awards, including the Edgar and the National Headliners Awards. A former bureau chief for *Time*, he has written for *Vanity Fair*, *Life*, *People*, *Paris Match*, *The New York Times*, and *Reader's Digest*. He lives on an island in Washington's Puget Sound with his wife and children.

Also by JACK OLSEN

Hastened to the Grave

The Climb Up to Hell

Salt of the Earth

Charmer

The Misbegotten Son

"Doc": The Rape of the Town of Lovell

"Son": A Psychopath and His Victims

The Bridge at Chappaquiddick

Night of the Grizzlies

Last Man Standing

The Tragedy and Triumph of Geronimo Pratt

JACK OLSEN

ANCHOR BOOKS
A Division of Random House, Inc.
New York

FIRST ANCHOR BOOKS EDITION, NOVEMBER 2001

Copyright © 2000 by Jack Olsen

All rights reserved under International and Pan-American Copyright
Conventions. Published in the United States by Anchor Books, a division of
Random House, Inc., New York, and simultaneously in Canada by Random
House of Canada Limited, Toronto. Originally published in hardcover in the
United States by Doubleday, a division of Random House, Inc.,
New York, in 2000.

Anchor Books and colophon are
registered trademarks of Random House, Inc.

The Library of Congress has cataloged the Doubleday edition as follows:
Olsen, Jack.
Last man standing: the tragedy and triumph of Geronimo Pratt /
Jack Olsen.—1st ed.
p. cm.
ISBN 0-385-49367-3
1. Pratt, Elmer Geronimo. 2. Black Panther Party—Biography. 3. Afro-
American political activists—California—Los Angeles—Biography. 4. Political
activists—California—Los Angeles—Biography. 5. Pratt, Elmer Geronimo—
Trials, litigation, etc. 6. False imprisonment—California—Case studies.
7. United States—Race relations—Case studies. 8. United States. Federal
Bureau of Investigation. I. Title.
E185.97.P73 O47 2000
979.4'9400496073'0092—dc21
[B] 00-029436

Anchor ISBN: 0-385-49368-1

Book design by Terry Karydes
Author photograph © John M. Harris

w w w . a n c h o r b o o k s . c o m

Printed in the United States of America
10 9 8 7 6 5 4 3 2 1

FOR
KATHLEEN RYAN,
HER MEMORY

And judgment is turned away backward,

and justice standeth afar off:

for truth is fallen in the street . . .

—Isaiah 59:14

LAST MAN STANDING

PROLOGUE: 1975

Stuart Hanlon steered his Toyota junkster under the barn-red towers of the Golden Gate Bridge on his way to visit a convicted murderer named Elmer Gerard "Geronimo" Pratt. The impromptu trip to San Quentin was the idea of a radical social worker and friend. "This guy needs some help," the woman had told Hanlon in a breathless phone call. "He's been in a cage for five years. He was a Black Panther leader, but they threw him out. His family's two thousand miles away and he's about as alone as you can get."

"What's he in for?" Hanlon had asked.

"Murder. But he didn't do it."

Driving north on Highway 101, the law student remembered a cynical line from a lecturer at Hastings College of Law: *There are four thousand inmates in San Quentin, and five thousand of them were framed.* He wished he knew more about the case. The fact that Pratt was a Black Panther leader was no recommendation. At twenty-five Stuart Douglas Hanlon tended to distrust authority figures of any color. "I've never met a leader who wasn't an asshole," he told friends. "Having power and having brains are two different things." His views had been reinforced by his own arrest on a charge of attempted murder of a police officer during the 1968 student riots at Columbia University, a charge that was quickly dismissed.

HANLON PARKED and walked along a winding path through a cheery garden court that only seemed to amplify the menace behind the walls. He wondered how his "Jewfro" would play with guards who favored brush cuts and flattops. At other penal institutions the staff glared at him as though he were smuggling contraband in his frizzy hairdo. Friends at law school dubbed him "Pigpen" and suggested that it was time to buy a few rep ties and shoelaces and take pruning shears to his hair. Soon he would be competing with polished young lawyers with station-wagon accents and blow-dried coiffures, and certain judges might look askance at his sartorial nonchalance. He remembered another law school truism: *Someday one of your clients will go to jail because the judge didn't like your tie.*

HANLON RODE a bench outside the San Quentin visiting room for two hours while chattering "Jailhouse Annies" fussed at the admitting officers. At eleven A.M. he was ushered into the narrow visiting room for prisoners in solitary confinement and directed to chair no. 4.

On the opposite side of a heavy-gauge metal screen, a light-skinned African American shuffled forward in Fu Manchu half-steps and lowered himself onto a metal bench. Hanlon's first reaction was that he was looking at a photo negative of himself. Both men had thick black moustaches, goatees and large hair.

Four other inmates arrived, each facing his own visitor. All wore handcuffs and belly chains. Hanlon asked, "Are you . . . Geronimo?"

The black man nodded. He seemed fidgety.

"I'm Stu Hanlon," he said, pressing his hand against the screen in a visiting room handshake. "I'm a law student. A friend said I might be able to help you."

Pratt frowned. Two whitish scars a little smaller than dimes seemed to come together on his forehead. "Hey, man," he began, then lowered his voice. "This isn't a good time. Maybe—"

Hanlon heard the scrape of metal on metal. Pratt's voice dropped to a hoarse whisper and his words became inaudible. He seemed more focused on the prisoner seated alongside him than on his visitor. Then Hanlon realized that an inmate farther down the row had slipped his chains.

"Don't do it!" a female visitor yelled.

The unshackled inmate tackled a guard who'd just entered the enclosure and slashed at his olive-drab jacket with a knife. As alarms blared, Geronimo Pratt flung himself between the two men and knocked the guard into a sitting position. He knelt on the officer's torso and thighs, pinning him to the floor. In the confusion it appeared that Pratt might be kicking at the prostrate guard's side, but Hanlon's view was partially blocked and he couldn't be sure. Then a team of officers burst in and everyone went down in a scrum of olive drab and prison blues, kicks, yells, whacks, curses and blood.

Before Hanlon and his fellow visitors were rushed from the area, the frightened law student saw a huge guard slam Pratt's head against the wall.

AT HOME that night Hanlon kept asking himself, What the hell happened? *What did I see?* He replayed the scene in his mind. He was sure he'd seen Pratt slide his husky body between knife and victim. But he'd also seen Pratt trying to hold the guard down.

Hanlon asked himself, What was Pratt trying to tell me? *This isn't a good time.* If he was in on the assault, why did he interfere? Or was I just seeing things?

He didn't sleep well.

HANLON WAS surprised when he was asked to appear as a defense witness at the disciplinary hearing in San Quentin's Adjustment Center, a secure area reserved for the most dangerous convicts. He told the blank-faced hearing officers exactly what he'd seen—and hadn't. No, he had *not* observed inmate Pratt attack Corrections Officer Michael Imm. Yes, it did appear that Pratt had helped to knock the guard to the floor. Hanlon told the officials that in his opinion Pratt might have saved Imm's life, but he couldn't be sure. It was Rashomon. There could be as many versions as there'd been participants.

He was ushered out before the verdict was returned.

A WEEK later Hanlon's request to revisit Pratt was denied by a guard at the reception desk. "Mr. Pratt is in a disciplinary cell."

"I'm his attorney," Hanlon explained. It was almost true. He was thinking about making Pratt his first client as soon as he passed the bar examination.

He was ushered into a small room reserved for legal visits. The guard slammed the metal door and told him to ring the bell when he was ready to leave.

Pratt materialized like a shackled ghost on the other side of a thick sheet of clear plastic. As the prisoner settled into his straight-backed chair, Hanlon spotted something shiny on the floor next to his foot. It was a large Afro comb. The teeth had been broken off and the edge sharpened. "Don't touch that!" Pratt yelled. "It's a setup."

Hanlon pushed the bell and an officer chugged into the room. "What's the problem?" he asked.

Hanlon pointed to the floor.

"Okay, okay," the guard said impatiently. "Hand it to me."

Pratt was shaking his head emphatically. Hanlon said, "I'm not touching it. Pick it up yourself."

"Give it to me. *Now!*"

The law student took a deep breath. "Go ahead and arrest me," he said. "I'm not touching that thing." The guard bent over and picked up the comb. Then he announced that the visit was over.

AT FIRST Geronimo Pratt hadn't known what to make of the earnest young man with the big hair. Perhaps he was the law student he claimed to be, but he could also be a plant. Whoever he was, he'd picked a bad time to acquaint himself with prison life. Visitors were a welcome relief from the tedium of the hole, but on this day racial tensions were running high, and an attack was planned on a guard who was rumored to be involved in a campaign to set up a black inmate for murder.[1] It was the latest skirmish in a running war between African American prisoners and their overseers. Each side considered the other fair game, and each side gave no quarter.

In solitary confinement since his first day in prison, Pratt had tried to remain aloof from the bloodletting. He'd made a life decision to avoid prison gangs and personal feuds. It was the only way to stay alive. Guards and inmates would be attacked from time to time and there was nothing he could do about it.

---

[1] A rumor that, like so many others in the paranoid atmosphere of the "hole within a hole" called the Adjustment Center, proved false.

The homemade knife had been wielded by Alonzo Brown,[2] a black revolutionary from Pennsylvania. In the upside-down prison culture, Brown was a figure of power and prestige; prisoners had named children after him. To speak against him or interfere with his planned attack would have been suicidal.

Pratt had felt almost relieved to be swarmed by the other guards and thrown against the wall. His last sight before falling had been the distorted image of the law student on the other side of the screen, eyes protruding, mouth open in shock.

IN THE AFTERMATH Pratt was grateful to the wounded guard for playing the deadly prison game with honor. Michael L. Imm, a fellow Vietnam veteran, prepared a report that seemed deliberately vague and ambiguous. "As the grill gate was opening," the young officer wrote, "I noticed that Brown's restraint belt was unbuckled and he was holding his hands over his stomach. I quickly closed the grill gate and reached for Brown's restraint belt at which time he turned to face me and by unfolding his hands he pulled out a knife. He then came at me with the knife in his right hand. I backed up toward the wall, peripherally observed the form of a black inmate who I cannot identify who grabbed me from behind and pushed me to the floor. I landed on the floor in a semi-sitting position with my legs outstretched and my back against the west wall. . . . Another black inmate who I cannot identify grasped my left shoulder and attempted to hold me while Brown kept stabbing at me with the knife. Grappling with Brown to avoid being stabbed, I managed to get to my feet."

The business end of Alonzo Brown's cloth-wrapped shank was a three-inch blade, sharpened on both edges, ground down from flat metal, perhaps part of a bed frame. Michael Imm was lucky; the heaviest blow had slashed his heavy Department of Corrections jacket and nicked his chest. He was also treated for cuts on his lip and wrist.

ON HIS third visit to the penitentiary Stuart Hanlon asked, "What was the ruling?"

"Guilty," Pratt answered through the slit.

---

[2] Pseudonym.

"Didn't the guard tell 'em you saved his life?"

"Nope. This is a war, man. If Mike Imm testifies that I helped him, I'm dead meat with the other inmates. It's a game. You follow the rules or they take you out."

Pratt said that the disciplinary committee had sentenced him to three more years in solitary confinement.

"Three *more*?" Hanlon said. He'd heard of difficult prisoners being sentenced to the hole for thirty days or even a few months, but three years? He asked, "How long've you been in the hole?"

"This is my fifth year. The hole isn't my main problem. My main problem is staying alive."

"You got a bed? A toilet?"

"The toilet's a hole in the floor. I got a bed now, but for a long time I slept on the floor. In my own—" His voice trailed off.

HANLON WAS unprepared for Pratt's story. The law student was the semihippified product of a middle-class home, a graduate of the Riverside Country Day School for Boys ("for rich Jewish kids," as he described it later) and Columbia University. He was the son of a gentle housewife, who was descended from Russian Jews, and a placid Irish Catholic father who taught math and English at the Dalton School for Girls in Manhattan. Hanlon had taken a course in penology and presumed that even in the worst holes in the worst prisons, inmates slept on bunks and were provided toilets. Yet Pratt didn't seem to be whining or complaining, just stating the facts. Hanlon wondered if four years in solitary had institutionalized him, brought him to that flat-eyed state of indifference that came over long-term prisoners.

Somehow Hanlon doubted it. There was still a fire in Pratt's brown eyes, a firmness to his motions and reactions. As their first lengthy discussion continued, the caged man made random references to Schopenhauer, Hegel, Spinoza and other philosophers, mispronouncing some of the names. His milk-chocolate skin seemed to glow with intensity as he spoke. At Columbia Hanlon had argued late into the night over the same deep thinkers. He found himself intrigued by the symmetry.

Considering that Pratt was living in a steel box, he appeared surprisingly fit. He explained that every morning he reverted to his army drill-sergeant role and led "cellisthenics" in the block. He looked to be a little below average height, maybe five-six or five-seven, but his shoulders were wide and his arm muscles rippled against the sleeves of his G.I. fatigue top. Hanlon thought there was a Yul Brynnerish cast to his features, a Eurasian touch. Or was it Byzantine? He thought, How silly that we call this man "black" or "Negro" or "colored." Pratt was a hybrid. His nose was on the thin side and slightly turned up at the tip, like Hanlon's. His dark-brownish hair was finely textured. When he saw Hanlon studying his hairline, he said, "Down home, we call this white man hair. I always wanted a big woolly-bully Afro, but my longest was an inch or two. My daddy's hair was straight. It's our blood—Irish, African, French, Cajun, Indian." He pointed to Hanlon's head and said, "What do you call that mess?"

Hanlon laughed. "It's my Jewfro," he said. "I'm half Jewish."

"Far out. And . . . half African?"

"My dad's Irish and my mom's Jewish."

Pratt grinned, showing perfect teeth. "You should call it a Mickfro," he said.

AFTER A few hours they were warned that their time was up. As Pratt clanked back into the shadows in his shackles, he called out, "Hey, Hanlon, check my file at the D.A.'s Office, will ya? My counselor says they brought some more charges against me."

"For what?"

He couldn't hear the answer.

THE YOUNG lawyer detoured to the nearby Marin County courthouse. As he walked across the courthouse parking lot, he felt a shiver despite the silvery California sun that bounced off the angled planes of the Frank Lloyd Wright building. Four years earlier, in this same parking lot, a seventeen-year-old black youth had tried to flee in a van carrying three accomplices and several hostages. In a firefight police sharpshooters killed the young man and two of his accomplices, but a judge's head was blown off and an assistant district attorney critically wounded. Hanlon walked where blood had ebbed into a storm drain.

In the records of the County D.A.'s Office he found a short notation about the visiting room stabbing case: "The reason Elmer Pratt will not be prosecuted is because bringing him to court would provide him with an escape opportunity and because he did not personally attempt to assault Mr. Imm."

Hanlon thought, Escape opportunity? Who are we dealing with here? Attila the Hun?

ON HIS next visit he asked, "Geronimo, how come everybody's so scared of you?"

Pratt winced. "Check my jacket, man. They wrote me up for everything except the Brinks robbery. Making poison darts. Rioting in court. Breaking out my homeys. Trying to hijack the prison school bus and kill a kid a day—cut off their heads."

Hanlon gulped. "Was any of it true?"

Pratt leaned into the speaking slot and began a defense of his innocence, ticking off his points with the metronomic precision of a trial attorney. In the end he apologized for his intensity—"But that's the way it was. The son of a bitches wanted to get me, and the son of a bitches got me."

"What son of a bitches are we talking about?" Hanlon asked.

"Everybody. The LAPD, the courts, the judges."

Hanlon asked where he could find the records on the case.

"You want to check me out?" Pratt sounded defensive. "See Johnnie Cochran."

"Who's he?"

"My lawyer in L.A. He's the only one I trust."

HANLON MET with Pratt's attorney in the backseat of a Rolls-Royce sedan on a Los Angeles street corner, an abrupt session that had been arranged by Cochran on the run. "We'll talk more tonight," he said rapidly. "I just wanted to shake hands with a friend of Geronimo's."

Hanlon took note of the lawyer's appearance: he wore his hair in a short natural and sported a hand-painted tie, highly shined shoes and creased pants. The law student observed a row of crystal glasses in the back of the Silver Shadow sedan. Cochran said, "That's my minibar. I don't drink. It's for my friends."

"Man," the ex-hippie blurted out, "you are *really* fucked up!"

Cochran laughed and said, "True."

Hanlon thought, This is two different ozones coming together, but in reverse. The black guy's got the Rolls.

THAT NIGHT they had a longer meeting in Cochran's office. "It all comes out the same," the lawyer said, beckoning toward stacks of files. "An innocent guy was found guilty. And I lost the case."

"Was it a fix?" Hanlon asked.

Cochran said, "When we were getting ready for trial, Pratt kept telling me that the whole thing was political. Said somebody just wanted to neutralize him and the Black Panthers. I kept asking, 'Who's *somebody?*' He kept saying, 'I wish I knew.' "

"That's about what he told me."

"I said, 'Son, you've got a vivid imagination.' I told him I'd won ten straight murder cases and he would be the eleventh. I said, 'We've got the facts and the D.A.'s got nothing.' So this college kid says, 'You're wrong, Cochran. We got to find out what's behind all this, or I'm going to prison.' Well, he was right and I was wrong. Now he's in his fifth year in solitary and I'm still losing sleep."

Hanlon asked, "No question he's innocent?"

"None. The guy is a victim of a frame-up that goes so high it's scary. I wouldn't be surprised if the FBI was involved."

"What's the proof?"

"That's the problem."

Hanlon shook his head. "How can I help?" he asked.

Cochran peered across his polished walnut desk. "Learn everything you can about the case. Learn about Pratt, who he is, where he's coming from, *everything*. Research the law and help me find new issues. We've got to get this guy out while he's still alive."

The Pratts of Morgan City

The patriarch, Enoch "Jack" Pratt Sr., was a stumpy little drayman who sifted the Morgan City dump and hauled his collectibles ninety-nine miles to New Orleans in rattly old trucks that bore the inscription "Jack Pratt & Sons." He drove his trucks till they were almost junk themselves. Before school and after school, on Saturdays and even on holidays, he drove his sons just as hard.

His youngest son, Geronimo, born Elmer Gerard, could never shake the smell of burning trash from his nostrils. "Daddy taught us to be tough, *made* us be tough," Pratt said years later. "Me and my three brothers, we worked in that fire and smoke till we near dropped, baled up rope, rags, newspapers, ripped the lead plates out of batteries, raked hot ashes for coat hangers and wire springs and bolts. We'd lash up the heavy stuff with chains, mash the fifty-five-gallon drums, drive over bedsprings to flatten 'em. Used sledgehammers, double-bladed axes, crowbars, acetylene torches. We could break the welds and chop up a car in an hour. Used wire cutters to strip insulation off house wire till it was top-grade pure metal. We sorted yellow brass, red brass, pewter, nickel, aluminum, tin, carbon. Daddy would drive the stuff home from the dump and store it in our yard six, eight feet high. Then we'd load up and head for New Orleans."

The Pratt family's first washing and sewing machines came from the dump, as had an upright Stromberg-Carlson radio and a black-and-white TV. Jack Pratt's sons rode bikes assembled from parts. "That's where I got these leg muscles," Geronimo explained. "Daddy put together an old Schwinn with balloon tires, one speed, no lights—gave it to me for Christmas. You had to be Charles Atlas to pump the pedals. My friends and I would race the white kids, and we weren't gonna lose."

WITH GERONIMO or one of his brothers riding shotgun, Jack Pratt would pull out of Morgan City at 2:00 A.M. to be first in line at Southern Scrap or Ed Levy & Sons or A. Marx in New Orleans. For miles they drove past whiskey-colored swamp water, cypress knees, palmetto, sawgrass, mangrove shrubs, accented by splashes of color from water hyacinths, crepe myrtle and azaleas. Jack Pratt shored up the sides of his truck with wooden beams, steel bed frames and other engineering improvisations so he could haul double loads. As the expeditioners crossed over the narrow Huey P. Long Bridge into New Orleans, the truck yawed and heeled alongside the railroad track that split the roadway down the middle. One day the brakes gave out at the highest point and Jack Pratt snubbed the truck against the guardrail for a mile, then pulled to the curb and replaced the linings with a used set he kept in back. Geronimo was always amazed at his father's way with metal. "Daddy didn't know what a socket wrench was. Didn't own a pipe wrench. Seems like he did everything with a hammer and a chisel. He taught us to harden our hands, use 'em as tools. After all my years in prison, you still can't hurt my hands with a hammer."

As they rattled along Highway 90, the father would say, "Well, son, I think we got about four ton on the truck. At thirty-nine bucks a ton, how much that gonna be? C'mon, gimme that answer right fast!" When Geronimo hesitated, his father would say, "Just multiply four times forty, son, and subtract four."

TRAVERSING THE dank Atchafalaya Basin, Jack Pratt sometimes pulled to the shoulder while one of his sons jumped out to retrieve a treat that had slithered or hopped or lumbered from the swamp. In the junkyards on Carondelet or Tchoupitoulas Street, fellow devotees of the trash art would ask, "Whatcha'll boys brought us today, Jack?"

"A coupla nice rabbits and a snappin' turtle," Jack Pratt would reply, or, "A pound of meat that used to be a possum." No one wanted to miss out on a serving of fresh wild meat that the junk dealers seared on cracked iron stoves that might have come from Gertie Yost's plush whorehouse on Esplanade Avenue or an antebellum mansion in the Garden District.

WHEN THE last coil of copper had been weighed out and the last thumb of spun brass chucked into its proper bin, Jack Pratt would steer his truck toward the used-clothing stores on South Rampart Street, his favorite place on earth, to begin a friendly ritual he called "haggling with the Jews." His closet held a row of neatly pressed suits, and his dress shoes were always buffed to a high shine. If his sons didn't show the same care, he buffed their behinds with the fan belts that he kept around the house for negotiating purposes.

The trash picker was idolized by his seven children. "He was a street-corner kid," Geronimo remembered. "He was the wretched of the earth, raised in Storyville in New Orleans and the back streets of Morgan City. Daddy was a high yellow with white people aspects. A lot of European features and some Indian, too. He was a great dancer, a ladies' man, but hard as oyster shell. Back when the Klan was active, he had his own gang. Whites asked his permission to cross the tracks. We had a reputation: 'Nobody mess with the guys from Across the Tracks.' White folks called him Mr. Jack."

AFTER SHOPPING on Rampart Street, Jack Pratt would drive to the French Market to bargain for the best price on okra, celery, peppers, cress and watermelon. His last stop was always Schwegmann's supermarket, where he would stock up on Snickers bars. His wife Eunice sliced them into seven parts for her children's desserts.

On the return drive southwestward, the port of Morgan City would come into sight as a broken line of cranes and derricks marking the edges of a tidal backwater named after steak: Bayou Boeuf. Barges settled deep in the water under the weight of oil rigs lying flat on their decks. Stevedores worked in the pale bluish light of mercury vapor lamps. Out in the Gulf, guttering yellow flares marked offshore wells. The Pratt truck rattled past storage lots and marshaling yards, past Bluewater Rubber and Gasket, Hercules Wire Rope, ABC Bait Co., God's Way Church. The window of Mr. Lucky's Club featured a half-naked woman in neon, legs and breasts flickering enticingly. A sign said, "Hello, we've been waiting for ya."

With one of his sons stretched out asleep in the passenger seat, Jack

Pratt would steer west on Highway 90 past the landlocked shrimp boat *Stella Maris,* plying the waves on the median strip for the benefit of tourists, then make a hard left and sound his horn like a riverboat captain in an old movie. In later years Geronimo Pratt, unable to sleep from persistent shrapnel pain, still heard the horn of his earliest childhood. "That meant Daddy's coming! Everybody run out in the backyard to see what he brought. Oh, what a time. What a time."

THERE WAS a lived-in quality to the black enclave known as Across the Tracks. After rain a sharp salty calcium scent rose from scattered gray mounds of oyster shell. Shotgun houses rested on stilts or bricks against the floods that welled up from the nearby confluence of the Atchafalaya River and Bayou Boeuf. Some of the walls were chinked with animal hair, river mud and Spanish moss, a mix that dried as hard as concrete. When these houses finally began to collapse, these "bousillage" walls fell last.

Most of the residents of Across the Tracks lived in sagging double-wides and weather-stained frame and cinder-block cottages with canted one-hole outhouses. Morning glories bloomed atop abandoned machinery rusting on the levee. The neighborhood saloon was the small unpainted Beer Garden at Second and Union, later renamed the Kick-'Em-Out. Until a black man gained ownership, African Americans were served through a slot in the wall.

Next door was a one-chair tonsorial parlor run by Jimmy Harris, a hawk-nosed part-Creek. The barber was an elongated version of Jack Pratt and brooked no sass. Above a nest of hair clippings that he swept under a narrow wooden bench polished to a gloss by thousands of posteriors, a sign advised, "The world's gonna end by the 25th please pay me now so that I won't hafta search all over hell for ya." On Saturday mornings Mr. Jimmy recounted battle stories from World War II as he scissored and razored his customers. He was the first man Geronimo Pratt ever heard use the term "civil rights."

THE PRATTS' frame bungalow, a block from the levee, consisted of four ten-by-ten-foot rooms sheltered by a corrugated tin roof that rattled like stage thunder during storms. After every hurricane there were fresh leaks, and the children caught the water in jars and pots. The house fronted on a bumpy old alley called Arkansas Street, unpaved, potholed and regularly scoured by floodwaters and floating debris. Some whispered that a black man had been lynched from a hanging tree that had since disappeared into the Pratts' woodstove. As unofficial mayor of Across the Tracks, Jack Pratt discouraged such talk, but he couldn't keep some of his neighbors from referring to Arkansas Street as "Death Alley." His scholarly wife, Eunice, the clan matriarch, banned the morbid name from her domain and declared the lynching to be mythology.

NOW AND then a carping historian would express regret at the city fathers' decision to name the place after an early benefactor named Charles Morgan instead of opting for something Gallic in the style of neighboring towns like Paincourtville, Thibodaux, Labadieville, Breaux Bridge, Pierre Part and Napoleonville. But "Morgan City" stuck and the town became known as a dolorous Eden where it took an energetic act of will to go hungry. Crawfish popped out of backyard burrows and begged to be boiled and decapitated and served in steaming bowls of étouffé and bisque. Residents dined on dishes that outlanders couldn't pronounce: *cochon de lait, couche couche, sac-à-lait, mirliton, maque choux*. "Never mind how it's spelt, just eat!" Jack Pratt snapped at relatives and visitors.

EUNICE PETTY Pratt, the drayman's lifelong mate, was his opposite in almost every way: a sweet, spiritual, cultured and superstitious woman, dark mahogany in color with straight black hair, a tiny waist and a petite shape that she modestly adorned in light purples and blues. She called herself a gumbo Creole, a bayou euphemism for mixed ancestry. She was born a Catholic and descended from slaves, *passants blancs* ("passing as white"), West Indians, a blue-eyed Irish grandmother, a great-grandfather who was manumitted from a sugar plantation in the 1840s, and various Indian tribes. Eunice's father, John Petty, the first black oysterman in Morgan City, had emigrated from the Caribbean to the Bayou Barataria backwaters where Jean Lafitte once moored his pirate ships. Eunice's self-educated mother started the first school for Morgan City's African American children. Two of her three daughters became college graduates.

Eunice was the third. She married Enoch "Jack" Pratt as a young woman and devoted her life to her family. She spoke excellent English mixed with Creole, a little French, and some Latin she'd learned in church. Her spiritual life was a mix of Roman Catholicism, random beliefs that went back to slave days, and a soupçon of Quedo or voudoun (locally pronounced "hoodoo"). Her husband converted to Catholicism for Eunice but was seldom seen inside the walls of the black Catholic church, Holy Eucharist. Whenever she importuned Jack to join her at mass, he would revert to his own theology: "Bible say, 'I am the church.' I, Eunice. *Me!* The presence of God in *me* is the church, not some drafty old church building where the preacher's trying to screw every woman in town."

SOMETIMES HER children found Eunice kneeling in front of a candle and chanting in a tongue they couldn't understand. No, she said, she wasn't speaking in tongues, like the Pentecostals. She was just repeating a liturgy passed down from her ancestors all the way back to the Caribbean and West Africa—she wasn't sure exactly where. She drilled her sons in their responses as altar boys: *Sicut erat in principio, et nunc, et semper, et in sacula saculorum.* . . . When they misspoke, she disciplined them with peach tree switches that she made them cut and peel.

Eunice thanked God repeatedly for the miracle he'd wrought on little Gerard. After the other children had begun teasing him for having "wheelbarrow" legs, she asked for guidance from Saint Gerard, the boy's patron saint, and Saint Jude, the patron saint of impossible causes. Night after night she rubbed the child's bowlegs while she chanted and prayed. When they began to grow straighter, she arranged a novena of thanks. Through the years the healing event became known as an overnight miracle, but the party of the first part wasn't so sure. "I think it took a little longer," Geronimo recalled. "And my legs never really straightened out. I was the only one in the family who ever questioned what Mama believed. She was so strict and devout, we kids couldn't understand why the pope didn't canonize her. I never told her about the day I cursed God to see if he would kill me. It was storming hard, thunder and lightning, and Mama had just whupped me for taking a sip of the church wine. I looked up and said, 'Go on, God! Go on and kill me if you there!' Repeated it over and over. Nothing happened, so I yelled the first curses of my life: muthafucka, son of a bitch, Jesus Christ! Blasphemed till I was hoarse. So then I began to doubt God because he didn't kill me. I'm saying, 'You flunked the test! You not up there!' But I was still thinking . . . he's *some*where."

ELMER GERARD PRATT was born in the shotgun cottage on Death Alley on September 13, 1947, the couple's eighth and last child (one son died).

Eunice wanted to name the baby after Saints Francis and Gerard, but her oldest son, Charles, protested that "Francis" sounded too feminine. Throughout his childhood the boy was called Gerard, except when his mother summoned him off the street with a pungent "Elmer *Geeeeee*" that some said could capsize a shrimper in the Gulf.

The four sons—Charles, Gerard, Timothy and Jackie—shared one lumpy bed. The three sisters slept together in the next room and the parents in the alley-front room. At night the boys would sneak into the yard, listen to cicadas and check to see if the moon was holding rain. They fell asleep to the chuff of tugboats herding barges on the Intracoastal Waterway; their father said that one of those diesel boats could push Avoca Island all the way to Key West. Helicopters chattered constantly, hauling oil rig supplies and personnel. An hour or so after midnight the Southern Pacific's train no. 1, the Sunset Limited, rattled windows as it rumbled west on its single track two blocks from the Pratt house. With fifteen thousand inhabitants, Morgan City was only a flag stop for the great express.

Every morning the family awoke to the bells of the nearby Sacred Heart Church, where their color made them unwelcome.[3] Geronimo recalled his family's church of choice, Holy Eucharist: "Father John Hartman was our priest, a white Josephite from Brooklyn. The Josephites were the church's shock troops, working in the social jungles. He preached love, and we gave it right back. At night he put on an eyeshade and played poker. At one mass he noticed some poor whites sitting in one corner, said, 'I want you all to move up and sit with the rest of us.' That was the first act of public integration in Morgan City."

AFTER A typical breakfast of beef liver, grits and milk, the children attended their all-black grammar school and then repaired to the hot ashes and scorched rats of the dump. At home Eunice Pratt continued their educations. "Mama recited as she was doing the ironing," Geronimo's sister Jacqueline recalled. "Over the hill to the poorhouse. Noah built the ark. She

---

[3] There was no set rule, but the priests made their preference clear. One day in the late 1950s Charles Pratt, then a student at UCLA, came home on vacation and went into the white church to go to confession. "I was at the altar doing my penance when the priest walked up behind me and cleared his throat. He walked to the door and slammed it behind me. It was one of the things that made me gravitate away from my Catholic upbringing."

made us recite Shakespeare, Plato, Longfellow, Confucius. We read African American writers—Langston Hughes, Richard Wright, Willard Motley. We put on plays in the kitchen. Mama wrote and produced. Had us memorizing *all* the time. Wouldn't let us split a verb! By the time we grew up, we barely had our southern accents."

RACE HAD seldom been an issue in Morgan City, perhaps because there'd been so much interracial coupling that many of the "white" residents were related to *passants blancs* or were passing themselves. On pain of harsh punishment none of the Pratt children used racial pejoratives, even in the most violent disagreements. In prison, where words like "nigger" and "redneck" were in common currency, Geronimo Pratt avoided them and counseled others to do the same. "I wasn't brought up thataway," he explained. "Mama gave us the good side of the Germans, the Jewish people, the Scottish, the Irish, everybody. Mama said, 'Always remember: the black folks didn't end slavery. *Whites* did!' She said, 'Read your Bible about the white martyrs.' I asked her what color was Mr. Shakespeare. She said, 'Mr. Shakespeare was *human* color.' "

Racial violence was rare. When Geronimo was nine or ten, he and a classmate were swimming at "the Point," where the tidal surge and the river met in rips. A group of white boys threw rocks, and the classmate was hit in the forehead. Three days later little Geronimo watched in shock as a fisherman unraveled the body from his trotline. "He was a very dark boy, almost black, but the crabs nibbled off his skin and turned him bluish white. River shrimp stuck to his fingertips. The skin on his stomach was so thin you could see his insides. It was a terrible, terrible thing, but we didn't think of it as racial. We just thought it was cruel. It could've been black kids that threw those rocks. That's the way we saw things."

EUNICE PETTY PRATT was aware of the pressures that had shaped her husband's attitude about sex and race, but she kept the information from her children till he was gone. Then she told them, "Your daddy cooked on paddlewheel workboats, but he quit when he saw how the crew disrespected black women."

Older brother Jackie Pratt pried out the details and related them later: "One day Daddy came out the galley as his boat was getting ready to dock.

One of the white guys was mouthing off about splittin' a black oak, changin' his luck, trash like that. The black whorehouse was a blight on our neighborhood, just a few blocks from our house. Daddy came up on deck with a cleaver and said, 'Look, you're gonna stop talking like that about black women. I'm *married* to a black woman. You don't hear me saying nothing about white women, do ya?'

"Here's a little guy, five-seven, hundred and forty pounds, standing up to that whole crew. When they docked, Daddy collected his pay and quit. That's what made him an independent drayman. He taught us kids not to take anybody's crap. Mama always reminded us, 'That's the kind of man raised you up. That's why not a *one* of you can see injustice and not do something about it. Thank your daddy for that.' "

ON THE muggy day after Palm Sunday in 1960, twelve-year-old Geronimo Pratt was walking home from mass with his mother, brother Tim and sister Emelda. Sister Jacqueline, the organist, was still in church, rehearsing the next day's music. The three other Pratt children had gone west, Charles to graduate from UCLA and work with computers, Jackie to enroll at California State University at Los Angeles and sister Virginia, an honors graduate of Southern University, to teach in the L.A. ghettoes.

Eunice was the first to spot Jack Pratt lying on his side near the chicken coop. A split bag of dried corn lay by his outstretched hand. Chickens clucked around his body. She dropped her missal, lifted him into a sitting position and then lowered him. "Emelda," she said in a soft voice, "call the ambulance."

The sight of their omnipotent father lying among the chickens was more than his sons could comprehend. Geronimo stood frozen, and Tim slowly shook his head.

"Timothy," the mother said, still speaking calmly, "get some salt."

Geronimo helped his mother arrange the drayman on his back and watched as she sprinkled salt into his mouth till he gulped and began to breathe. Then they formed a circle around his body and prayed.

The stricken man was driven to a Morgan City clinic in a hearse that also served the African American community as an ambulance. A doctor told Eunice, "He's had a very severe stroke. His chances are minimal. He'll have to go to Charity Hospital."

Eunice arranged herself in the back of the hearse for the three-hour drive to New Orleans. Before she pulled the rear door shut, she instructed her children, "Pray your rosaries."

CHARLES, JACKIE, and Virginia Pratt arrived on the first plane from Los Angeles to join in the vigil. Their father lay in a public ward with a dozen other patients, most of them terminal. For days he neither moved nor spoke. His children sat in upright chairs, their beads clicking through their fingers. Almost every night a patient died, and the brothers helped to wrap the bodies and deliver them by gurney to the hospital morgue. One morning Jackie was awakened as an old man fell dead across his knees.

Jack Pratt was pronounced dead three times. Then one day he began to mumble, but not even Eunice could understand him. After a few months he was returned to Across the Tracks in the same hearse. Under his wife's care he began to walk with a crutch, dragging a leg, one arm limp. He learned to say a few words. He sat in the sun on the weather-beaten back porch and stared at his loquat tree, his anvil and leftover collection of junk. One day he hobbled a few feet toward the river. The next day he walked farther, and the family members offered thanks for answered prayers. Then a neighborhood boy laughed at him, and he took a seat in the parlor and never walked again. The Pratts of Morgan City were now a matriarchy.

THE IMMEDIATE problem was money. The junkman had made his share but handed out more. All seven children were college-bound or had matriculated, and their parents were approaching sixty. The house was sagging; the porous roof had barely withstood the last hurricane, and Jack Pratt & Sons was defunct.

Timothy and Geronimo scrounged lumber and cinder blocks to erect a bungalow for their parents on an adjacent plot. Virginia helped with the financing. "We didn't know masonry or carpentry," Geronimo recalled. "All we knew was to make the sides higher and higher. Redid the roof four times before we got it right. Took us three years, but it'll stand a long time. There's a statue of the Virgin in front and a rosebush behind."

After school he scrounged for cash. "I shot rabbits and coons and sold the meat—that's how I bought Mama a nice hat for Christmas and my first pair of leather shoes. I got two dollars for coons, one-fifty for rabbits. I sold nutria pelts and the gators' meat. My daddy'd taught me to jump on backs and thump 'em hard in the throat."

Instead of burning their fingertips at the dump, the Pratt children chilled them at Mr. Ben's Freezer at the end of Arkansas Street. "Mr. Ben blew his siren when boats came in to unload, and everybody'd go running to get in line and head up the swimp. That's what they're called in Morgan City: *swimp*. Channel catfish swam under the docks; it was nothing to catch a dozen on a handline. I'd skin 'em and sell 'em to the white people across the tracks—a nickel a fish, ten cents cleaned."

AS HE entered his teens, Geronimo refused to cross to the other side of the street when he saw white girls approaching, but he tried not to give offense by ogling them or making remarks. It seemed to him that most whites acted the same; he considered it "showing mutual respect."

He was aghast when a summertime friend, son of a migratory fisherman, said hi to a fourteen-year-old white neighbor while playing football on the levee with Geronimo and his brother Tim. The girl threw them a hard look and ran off. Geronimo knocked the offender flat and said, *"Man, we don't do that here!"*

The boy said, "I didn't do nothin' wrong."

"Listen, man, we got this agreement in our neighborhood. We don't disrespect whites and they don't disrespect us. You're outa line, man."

An hour later Geronimo and Tim were playing in their backyard when the girl's father barged into their house and screamed racial epithets at their father in his wheelchair. Police arrived, handcuffed the brothers and took them to the station.

The white father and daughter berated the Pratt boys at the booking desk. "Hold on," Geronimo said. "Please. My brother and I didn't do nothin'."

"You whistled at my daughter," the man said.

"She say that?"

The girl nodded and pointed at Timothy.

"If you say that about my brother," Geronimo said, "you're a damn liar."

The father cocked his arm and a policeman intervened.

Timothy spoke up. "What's me and Gerard charged with?" He was remembering something his sister Virginia had told him: *Slavery isn't dead, Tim. It's just changed form.*

"Assault," the booking sergeant replied.

"For playing on the levee?"

"For whistling at a white girl. Making smart remarks."

Timothy asked what charges would be brought against her father. "He ran through our house without knocking. Disturbed my daddy in his wheelchair. I believe that is called trespassing."

The cop locked the young malefactors in a cell next to the K-9 kennel.

All night long Tim sat on the hard bench and prayed, his first instinct in times of trouble. Geronimo was more puzzled than angry. "Imagine that," he muttered to his brother. "We didn't say a word and we end up in jail. *Imagine that.*" He still blamed the fisherman's son.

The brothers were released in the morning after the police chief checked the booking sheet and learned that his cells were holding two of his friend Jack Pratt's offspring. He chauffeured the boys home in his personal car. Eunice Pratt walked to the complaining girl's house and warned her father that the next time he entered the family residence without knocking, he would be met by something a little stronger than First Corinthians.

DISCUSSING THE painful memory later, Geronimo explained, "I didn't blame the police; I blamed the other boy. That's the way I was conditioned. Going to jail was a learning experience, but I didn't learn nothin' from it. Color consciousness crept up on me and the other kids. We knew nothin' about black rage, wouldn't've understood a concept like that. Black rage? About *what*? We were happy. No kids ever got more out of life. Respected ourselves, our family, our neighbors, got along, worked and played. Until the Klan hurt Timothy. Then everything changed."

IT WAS Halloween night, and Geronimo Pratt was LaFitte the Pirate. "We were trick-or-treating on the other side of the tracks—me, Tim, my buddy Kaydoe Delco. We didn't know that black kids had jumped some white kids and taken their candy a few blocks away. A Klan family started a search-and-destroy. When their car drove up on us, we started running. I jumped a ditch and heard screams behind me. They'd caught Tim.

"I knew I had to go back and help my brother, but I was scared. So I went back in slow motion." He stopped to rub his eyes. "Still bothers me after all these years, what I *didn't* do. Tim was on the ground being beat up and I was shaking like a baby. I knew I could reach my brother faster, but . . . I was fifteen. The closer I got, the louder Tim screamed. They were pounding his head on the street. 'Nigger' this and 'nigger' that. I recognized the white man, his grown sons and another big white dude. My daddy always told us they were a Klan family.

"I pulled out my costume knife, an ugly plastic thing I found on the dock. Then I heard this *whomp whomp,* footsteps pounding up behind me. It was my big brother Jackie. He knocked my knife into the gutter and kept right on running toward Tim. Neither him nor Daddy ever backed down for nothin'. Right behind Jackie came Big Boy Pack, Kaydoe, then my sister Emelda and Mama. My sister Virginia finally caught up to the rest of us. She was waving one of Daddy's .44s with two hands. Ginny was the Harriet Tubman of our family.[4] She stopped and took dead aim, and the next thing we saw was dust and taillights.

"Tim was out cold. Mama put her ear to his mouth and cradled his head. When she stood up I saw a line of blood down the front of her dress. It was a long time till the hearse came to take my brother to the hospital."

TIMOTHY PRATT appeared normal when he returned home, but soon epileptic seizures began, first every few weeks, then more often. At school, where he'd been a leader, he suffered violent headaches and frequently had to be excused from class. "My brother made a full recovery, earned a master's degree and became a successful teacher," Geronimo recalled, "but it took him years to get over what the Klan did to him. His last couple years in high school, he was a big handsome guy with no confidence at all. Shy around girls. He knew he might fall down any minute and bite his tongue till it bled. A couple of times when we knelt in church alongside the priest, Tim jumped up and started sprinkling holy water without realizing what he was doing. Once he took the censer, so golden and beautiful, and wandered around the church with it. Mama would stop him. People would watch. We had to be so patient. Later he had no memory of what he did.

"I loved my brother and he was a constant reminder to me about cruelty and injustice. For a while I was obsessed with getting even, but how

---

[4] Harriet Ross Tubman was a runaway slave who was active in the Underground Railroad and became known as "the Moses of her people."

does a kid fight the whole damned Ku Klux Klan? The night they beat up Timothy, Elmer Gerard Pratt moved to another plane. I didn't stay enraged, I didn't even stay bitter, but I became *aware*."

AT MORGAN City Colored High Geronimo found a temporary outlet in football. His siblings had distinguished themselves as honor students, chorale members and cheerleaders.[5] Geronimo was a sophomore when the football coach saw the boy launch a pass that traveled fifty yards. Soon the baby of the Pratt family was starring at quarterback. "We played Franklin Colored High, Thibodaux Colored High, every colored high in south Louisiana. We didn't mind being called colored. That's what we were."

Pratt graduated in 1965 with a B average, a full grade below his studious older brothers and sisters, and entertained feelers for football scholarships to Southern University, alma mater of his brother Tim and sisters Jacqueline and Virginia, and to Grambling University. But the African American elders of Morgan City had other ideas. "In my teens I heard these guys talking down at Mr. Jimmy's barbershop or late at night on our porch or hangin' outside the Kick-'Em-Out bar," Geronimo recalled years later. "I didn't pay much attention. Everybody called 'em the elders and they set the tone in Across the Tracks. They'd talk about black people being killed and thrown in the river, sent to Angola Penitentiary for raping white women that they hadn't even touched, uppity niggers being tarred and feathered and run outa town."

The men known as elders included the barber Harris, the retiree Joe Ruffin, who liked to say, "I'd rather die on my feet than live on my knees," a bootblack named Bud Dudley, who wore a suit and passed out candy, and solid citizens Geronimo knew only as Mr. Aloysius, Mr. Campbell, Mr. Chim, Mr. Forest and Mr. Valentine.

"The elders never came right out and told you what to do, but they advised *strongly*. You wouldn't dream of going against 'em. If I was about to do something stupid, Mr. Joe Ruffin would whup me, then deliver me to

---

[5] The school was underfinanced, understaffed and mired at the level of its weakest students. The oldest Pratt son, Charles, who was valedictorian the year after sister Virginia's graduation as salutatorian, said later, "I graduated first in my class, but I'd never heard of physics, trig or chemistry. I had no foreign language. I read one book in high school and it was *Huckleberry Finn,* which none of us understood. We read comic books in class. I had to take dumbbell English to get into UCLA."

Mama for another whuppin'. Our whole neighborhood ran like that. We had no police protection; our cops were the elders. When they settled a dispute, it was *settled*. They made us say yes sir, no sir, taught us manners and common sense. We had reverence for the elders."

IN LATER years, when Geronimo found himself with unlimited time to study black history, he was able to trace the system of elders back to the 1920s and the revolutionary Marcus Garvey. "He created a military protectorate called the Legionnaires that was so organized it would blow your mind. One of my uncles was a Legionnaire. They organized throughout the South. It was simple self-defense against the Klan that was burning churches, preaching hate. Before that, black people had always rallied behind our preachers, but they were old men living in the past, loved everybody, shuffled off to City Hall with hat in hand. Yas suh, Mr. Whitey. No suh. The Legionnaires were more like army troops. In Louisiana they went under the name Deacons for Defense and Justice. They actively fought the Klan but they were outnumbered so they had to work quietly. You heard about all the churches burnt by the Klan, all the children burnt to death, but you never heard some of the retaliations the Deacons did in return. A lot of Klan never knew what hit 'em. I was born into this tradition of militance and secrecy, but I stayed asleep for a long time. Our elders reached back to the Legionnaires in a straight line. They weren't just a bunch of old black dudes sitting around telling lies. They were our underground, our soul and backbone. Those who knew about 'em didn't say, and those who said didn't know. When the elders told you what to do, man, you did it!"

THE DAY before high school graduation ceremonies, Geronimo Pratt and some of his friends received their marching orders. "Right there in Mr. Jimmy's barbershop, the elders laid it out. Some of the things they told me I already knew, some I hadn't caught up with. I knew about Malcolm X being killed. I knew about Freedom Summer, when three civil rights workers were murdered by the Klan in Mississippi. I knew about the marches and the murdered white preacher from Boston. I knew about the police using dogs and fire hoses on women and children. But I didn't know about the little girls incinerated in the church in Birmingham. I didn't know that the Klan killed a civil rights worker from Michigan for giving a ride to a black man. I didn't know about the Alabama state troopers that shot down Jimmie Lee Jackson, or the seminary student who was cut in half by double-ought buckshot from a white deputy sheriff in Alabama, or a whole bunch of other killings by the Klan and the cops."

And he didn't know about the specific incident that had caused the alarmed elders to call the local blacks together. A few days earlier Sheriff's Deputies Oneal Moore and David Creed Rogers had been driving on Route 21 in Washington Parish, a KKK stronghold north of Morgan City, when hooded men in a pickup truck opened fire. Moore died; Rogers lost an eye. Their offense appeared to be that they were among the first African American deputies to be commissioned in Louisiana. The Deacons for Defense and Justice immediately sent patrols to protect black citizens. Locals knew the identity of the killers but the white leaders swore they would never be prosecuted.[6] Wholesale killings were predicted.

After the elders finished relating their horror story, Geronimo asked, "How come I never read nothin' about that in the papers?"

Mr. Jimmy Harris told him, "Son, there is a *lot* of things you didn't read about in the papers."

Later Geronimo recalled, "By the time the elders finished amping me up, I was ready to take on the whole KKK single-handed. I said, 'Tell me what to do.' Mr. Elmo explained that the black community needed trained men to help protect our people. In the years after World War II and the Korean War there'd been a good supply of black veterans skilled in munitions, perimeter defense, sandbagging, riflery, hand-to-hand combat, stuff like that. But the older guys, like the Guidrys, Nanny Boo, Mr. Jimmy Harris himself and some of the other elders, they were losing their zest. We had to develop a new generation of black warriors or the Klan was gonna overwhelm us. They were *already* overwhelming us.

"I knew if I went in the army I'd be leaving Mama to cope with Daddy, but my sisters would help out and so would everybody in the alley. Nobody was ever gonna abandon Daddy. Our neighbors used to ask, 'Can I push his wheelchair, Miz Eunice?' 'Can I drive Mr. Jack to the store?' I planned to send my army paycheck home every month, every penny I didn't need. I knew they'd get by."

At 1:00 P.M. on the day after the meeting in the barbershop, Pratt entered the Greyhound station by the required side door to wait for the bus

---

[6] Thirty-four years later the case was still open.

they called the Blue Dog. In a brown fiber suitcase salvaged from the dump, he carried his Bible, a change of underwear and a toothbrush. He was on his way to the army recruiting office in New Orleans.

BACK HOME, Eunice Petty Pratt tried to come to grips with her latest loss. Geronimo would be the first of her offspring to turn away from a college education, a troubling thought.

In her dime-store notebook she printed the title of her entry in capital letters: MOTHER I AM GOING TO JOIN THE ARMY. "How vividly do I recall these words," she continued in her neat Catholic-schoolgirl penmanship. "I looked into the corner at the chair where my baby sat. . . . My baby joining the army. I grieve over my baby. I thought, 'My little baby a soldier!' . . . He slipped away quietly to catch the bus after insisting that I would not accompany him to the station. My heart went on with him, as well as my prayers. 'Oh God,' I cried, 'please help him. Go with him all the way. Help him to make a man of himself.' "

Soldier's Medal

At Fort Polk, Louisiana, the seventeen-year-old quarterback was issued dog tags, given shots and a physical examination and appointed trainee platoon sergeant. In Washington President Lyndon Johnson was preparing to sign a voting rights act. White supremacists were threatening to torch polling places and kill blacks. African American students at Cornell University were gearing up for armed insurrection. Geronimo's big brothers Jackie and Charles wrote from Los Angeles that the ghetto called Watts was afire in the "Burn, Baby, Burn" riots.[7] The Los Angeles Police Department crushed a series of student rebellions and engaged in a bloody battle with anti–Vietnam War demonstrators at the Century Plaza Hotel. Racial tension was high, and many blamed it on black militants.

GERONIMO WAS in his second month of basic training when he learned that Timothy and Virginia were heading for the Los Angeles battle zones, Tim to observe and Ginny to resume her work with children. The trainee's first thought was of his mother. "Mama, I can't stop thinking about you all

---

[7] Thirty-four died, one thousand were injured and damage totaled $200 million.

alone with Daddy," he wrote. "How can you do this by yourself? Oh, Mama, should I come home to help you?"

Eunice wrote back that she was doing fine but it was obvious that her youngest child was not—"You're homesick, just like every little boy who leaves his mamma."

Geronimo tried to overcome the dread illness by concentrating on guns, armor, reconnaissance, field tactics and the skills that might help to protect his parents and the other black people of St. Mary Parish if race warfare broke out. Five months after leaving Morgan City he completed paratrooper training at Fort Benning, Georgia, and pounded his wings into his bare chest. "In those days you did it to yourself. Man, the blood run! The army sent me to the 82d Airborne, strike troops. We were on orders for Vietnam."

En route to the Far East, Geronimo was granted a three-day pass in Los Angeles and called on his older brother Jackie, attending Cal State. "He was up for anything!" the older brother recalled years later. "Our country did a good job of preparing that young man for war. He said, 'Man, I am *ready*!' He wanted to save his country, the world, wanted to save his people back home. I couldn't believe the change."

SIX MONTHS after Pratt and his fellow troopers engaged in their first firefight in the Central Highlands, they were arrayed in a defensive perimeter around a group of battered tanks just off the Ho Chi Minh Trail. "We were barely dozing when we heard a chopper warming up to take off. Somebody started cussin', 'Goddamn son of a bitch, that fuckin' Chinook's gonna blow our fuckin' tents down.'

"I looked up. It was a medevac mission, taking out our wounded. The chopper wasn't airborne for a minute when it flew straight into the side of Titty Mountain, three hundred meters away. I ran through our perimeter, not even thinking—no rifle, no helmet, no brains. All I had was my radio. Those medevac guys were already wounded. They must be hurting bad.

"I went the last few yards hand over hand, almost straight up. The chopper was broke in half and guys were screaming. The air was saturated with aviation gas and somebody down below was shooting off flares. I called in, 'Tell them fools to quit those flares! You're gonna fry us up here.'" The helicopter's tail section was already ablaze.

His citation read:

Pfc. Pratt, disregarding his own safety, entered the burning aircraft. Aware of the possibility of enemy activity in the area and the likelihood of an explosion in the helicopter, Pfc. Pratt made repeated trips into the aircraft until all five occupants had been removed and taken a safe distance from the flaming wreckage. His heroic and selfless action, at the risk of his own life, is in keeping with the highest traditions of the military service and reflects great credit upon himself, his unit and the United States of America.

Geronimo was promoted to squad leader and awarded the Soldier's Medal, but before he had a chance to pin it on, he was wounded. "We were patrolling in Jeeps, cleaning out pockets of VC in the Central Highlands. Sergeant Maddox was in the point vehicle, kicking ass as usual, and I was right behind. He was our protector, our John Wayne, a white guy from Arkansas with fourteen years in. There was no racism around him—anybody said the n-word, he'd've whupped their ass.

"We drove around some trees and I heard an explosion. The lead Jeep flew straight up in a cloud of smoke. The rest of us took cover, waiting for the ambush. After a while we went forward and found Sergeant Maddox and two troopers. Between the three of 'em, there wasn't much left. The only whiteness left on Sergeant Maddox was around his eyes. I could see his brains. That killed me. I thought I would die from that sight. His skin looked like burnt toast. The ugliness of it. The indignity. I just couldn't understand.

"They medevacked the bodies out and we mounted up. Now I was on the point. I ordered the men to sandbag the floors of our Jeeps in case we hit another land mine. Four hours go by and all of a sudden I'm ten feet in the air. I know I'm a basket case or I'm dead, one. I fell into a thick bush, shrapnel up my ass, in my hips and thighs. My gunner and my driver had broken legs. I pulled 'em out and called in another medevac unit. The medics said the extra sandbags saved our lives. At the field hospital they were gonna drill a hole for a colostomy bag, but I took some Demerol and went back to my unit a few weeks later. I was more comfortable with my friends. It hurts me to think that some of them came home without arms or legs or their heads messed up, not much better off than Sergeant Maddox. White *and* black. Someday I want to go to the wall in Washington and say a prayer for his name, say a prayer for all of 'em."

BEFORE HIS nineteenth birthday Pratt had made sixty-four combat jumps and was wearing the Purple Heart and the Air Medal. "I did a lot of infiltration, long-range reconnaissance, night LPs—listening posts. I'd go out with a radio and a couple grenades and call in situation reports. I got so I almost enjoyed it, just me and the rats and Victor Charlie. In my first twelve months in Nam there was hardly a day my unit wasn't in a firefight. One morning I woke up and found the guy in the next tent with his throat cut—a visit by the V.C. It was a look at my future, but I didn't know it at the time. Sergeant Jones got hit—he was a black preacher that everybody loved—and I could see daylight through the hole in his head. I watched my best friend's head blown off by an AK-47. I stepped on punji stakes that were dipped in shit, got infected, took some antibiotics and went back to the line. A grenade fragment caught me in the left upper arm. Surgeons couldn't get the metal out. I was overrun twice, had a flare blow up in my face. But nothing, *nothing* ever touched my mind. I had a job to do in Vietnam. And I had a job to do when I got back home."

AFTER THE fierce mountain guerrillas known as Montagnards made him an honorary trooper, Pratt became lost in the jungle for three days, out of touch with his unit. Word reached Morgan City that he was missing in action. Back home, Eunice Petty Pratt wrote in her notebook: "I keep on praying. I am still hoping and praying that the good Lord will bring our baby back home safe and sound, and a much holier man. Who knows? He may even dedicate his life to God."

When she heard that her son was safe, Eunice was so relieved that her writing turned uncharacteristically jingoistic: "We are on a war path. The Devil's Army against our Lord's. As for us, God is our Captain and we are marching on to victory."

IN THE summer of 1967 Sergeant Elmer Pratt was rotated home to a country torn by the worst urban riots in U.S. history. African Americans were rising against ghetto conditions in Los Angeles, Baltimore, Newark, Chicago, Cleveland, New York, Detroit and Phoenix. Malcolm X had set the tone in a speech to black students from Mississippi:

You'll get freedom by letting your enemy know that you'll do anything to get your freedom; then you'll get it. It's the only way you'll get it.

When you get that kind of attitude, they'll label you a "crazy Negro," or they'll call you a "crazy nigger"—they don't say Negro. Or they'll call you an extremist or a subversive, or seditious, or a Red or a radical. But when you stay radical long enough and get enough people to be like you, you'll get your freedom.

Pratt's unit settled in at Fort Bragg and he was assigned to drill Green Berets. "I had no love for the army, but I'd made good friends." He thought himself indifferent to military pomp and ceremony, but at an awards ceremony he was curiously touched. "We didn't even know our company commanders that well, but the idea that they would take the time to honor me for the few things I did—I was really touched by that. Water came to my eyes, I ain't gonna lie. My platoon was really trippin' when the major pinned on my medals. I felt like my own little war was over, and I'm waiting for word from the elders. I'd done my year in Nam, already got my combat patch, made buck sergeant, got me a girlfriend off the post, lived in a brick house, drove a '65 Ford Fairlane drop-top. The life of Riley. Twenty years old and dumb as a stump."

His unit was sent to Detroit to put down a race riot that had cost dozens of lives and threatened to destabilize the city. "I hated that duty. We all hated it. Man, we were the 82d Airborne. Trained paratroopers! They took away our dignity as soldiers. One month we're risking our lives for our country, and the next we're getting ready to fire on our own people. I knew if the order came I couldn't obey it.

"One day some black paratroopers started firing at white National Guardsmen. Grenades, machine guns—a pitched battle. The army hauled our asses outa there and hushed it up. Back at Bragg I got word from the elders: *come home now.* I didn't mind. Mama was alone with Daddy and I worried about them. Before I could finish filling out my resignation papers, things turned bad in Nam. Lyndon Johnson withdrew the early-out option and me and my unit were ordered back. My brother Tim was so pissed he wrote Johnson, accused him of going back on his word, said there were all kinds of young bloods he could send, not his brother Gerard, who was wounded twice. Somebody in the Pentagon wrote back that the president had no choice.

"We flew to Danang, right into the middle of the Tet Offensive. We had to retake Hue City twice. I caught shrapnel in my upper arm and went blind for a while." His permanent medical record listed "grenade fragments lodged in buttocks and upper arm, intermittent scotoma and blurred vision."

ON THIS second tour the war looked an even darker shade. "I saw things I didn't used to notice. One day I was charged by a V.C. soldier with a bayonet. I shot him at close range and saw his face fly off. I began having nightmares about it, but in the nightmares my weapon didn't fire and I'd wake up screaming just as he started to stick me in the throat. I began to see faces of people I'd killed. I'd always been bothered by the cowards that couldn't win a fistfight in a ladies' toilet but got off on bullying the Vietnamese, kicking, terrorizing, killing. Women and children, it didn't matter. After I was made platoon leader I saw two white guys, privates, raping a V.C. nurse. I hit one in the head with my rifle butt. Later on, I caught two of my guys trying to hang an enemy soldier. Had a rope around his neck, threw it over a tree. They were pulling him up when I turned the corner. You can imagine what I thought, being black and from the South. I said, 'Hey, man, you crazy?' They said, 'Motherfucker had a grenade.' I was angry at our officers for letting things like this happen, but they'd say, 'Hey, we're at war. Guys lose their tempers. We can't watch 'em every second.' I said, 'Why not?'

"After a while I began to see the war as another kind of racism. In boot camp and advanced infantry training all we ever heard was 'gooks,' 'Buddha-heads,' 'slopes,' same way our daddies heard 'Krauts' and 'Japs.' You got to make people subhuman before you kill 'em. I saw things I don't want to remember. I *did* things I don't want to remember. That second tour was a bad time."

PRATT WAS sitting on a bunker outside Hue City in April 1968 when word crackled over Armed Forces Radio that Martin Luther King Jr. had been killed. "Hey," he said aloud, "what's happening back home? *What's going on?*"

Later in the day he heard a black activist named Bobby Seale in a radio interview. "You darn right we respect nonviolence," Seale said. "But to sit and watch ourselves be slaughtered like our brothers, we must defend ourselves, as Malcolm X said, by any means necessary." Seale was identified as one of the founders of the Black Panther Party for Self-Defense. Geronimo wondered what that was all about. He'd never run into any Panthers, black or otherwise.

WHEN HE was rotated back to Fort Bragg for the second time, he was contacted by Mr. Elmo and the other elders. "They made it very clear what

I needed to do. Everybody was expecting a race war. They told me my people needed me at home."

Two months later he was in Morgan City with an honorable discharge. So were most of the "homeys" who'd ridden the Blue Dog to the recruiting office in New Orleans. "Tony Delcour came back. Frank Francis, Larry Mays and Jessie Wayne Bradford made it. Some of my other friends were shot up pretty bad."

Geronimo had served one month less than three years, mostly in combat. His big brother Jackie exulted: "We prayed him out!" An ad appeared in *Abundant Living Magazine*:

> I would like to express my thanks to God the Almighty Father, and the Blessed Virgin Mary, and all the Saints to whom I prayed for the safe return of my son from Viet Nam. Please publish my everlasting gratitude. Eunice Petty Pratt.

Geronimo stayed home in Across the Tracks through the summer of 1968, consulting with the elders and adding some touches to the cinder-block cottage he and Timothy had built for their parents. The epileptic older brother was still attending Southern University in Baton Rouge, and he craved Geronimo's company. "I'd always loved my little brother," Tim wrote later, "and seeing him alive after Vietnam filled me with a love that I did not think I could possibly ever have for any human being, other than Mama. I begged him to enroll at Southern. But a weird thing happened before he decided. As he and I were driving in his car, we passed a fire station where white folks were having a barbecue. When they saw us, they began to call us all sorts of racist names. We drove on by and did not talk about the incident, but I felt that any chance I had of convincing him to remain in Louisiana was lost."

IN AUGUST one of the Morgan City elders advised Geronimo that he intended to put him in contact with a Los Angeles organization called the Black Panther Party for Self-Defense. The elder was related to a Los Angeles African American who was related to a Panther leader named Alprentice "Bunchy" Carter, also from Louisiana. "Those Panthers got some good ideas," the elder told Pratt, "but they need help organizing and defending themselves against the cops. You could do 'em a lot of good."

A FEW weeks later Geronimo's pretty sister Emelda, a brilliant mathematician like their father, declared her summer vacation over and announced that she was ready to return to her classes at California State University at Los Angeles, where she was working toward a master's degree, dating the football star Mel Farr and rolling out pie dough for the Fantasy Bakery on the midnight shift.

"I'll drive you to L.A.," Geronimo said. "There's a dude out there I'm supposed to meet."

He and the bank shared ownership of a 1967 Pontiac GTO two-door convertible, white over red, and he spent much of his time waxing and polishing. "Just one problem," he told his sister. "We got to go by way of Fort Bragg so I can say good-bye to my girlfriend."

"Fort Bragg?" Emelda said. "We're going from Morgan City to Los Angeles by the *hypotenuse?*"

Sister and brother kissed their parents good-bye and began their triangular tour by driving hundreds of miles through the heart of the South. Both were disheartened by the decrepit dwellings inhabited by blacks. "I thought the slave houses were all torn down," Geronimo said.

They spent two days in Fayetteville, visited friends in Washington, then headed west to Chicago. Geronimo drove fast, reveling in his freedom as a civilian with a hot new car, no second lieutenants to order him around and no incoming mortar fire. "What the hell," he told his sister as they drove through anthracite country on the Pennsylvania Turnpike, "I got a little vacation time coming. I'll take you to your school, see what I can do for this Bunchy guy and drive back home."

Brother and sister pulled into Chicago the day of the police riot that stained the city, its mayor and the 1968 Democratic National Convention. Geronimo was profoundly affected. "I saw the cops swinging their batons and the helicopters dipping down and it almost made me flip out. I'd just left a place where gunships fired into hamlets. To me it was a sign of oppression. I began to transfer that into this. I think that's when I really began disliking cops. I knew how they thought, how easy it was for low-ranking authority figures to lose their balance and control. I saw it every day in Nam. The strong preying on the weak, that's bad. The weak preying on the weak—that's the worst. I was glad to get out of Chicago."

Another War

On the sixth of September 1968, Emelda and Geronimo Pratt crossed into California on Route 66 and into racial conflict unlike any they'd ever encountered on the bayou. After dropping Emelda off at Cal State, Geronimo spent a few days catching up on his siblings. Virginia was teaching at Markham Junior High. Charles had worked his way through UCLA as a house painter and janitor, taken a master's degree in qualitative data analysis at the University of Southern California and was employed by Systems Development Corporation in Santa Monica. Jackie was finishing up at Cal State and working part-time as a bookbinder.

Three days after arriving in Los Angeles Geronimo met Bunchy Carter. "He was somebody you took to right away. Bunchy was like my father, my brothers, like Sergeant Maddox. *A man.* I'll always miss Bunchy."

Alprentice "Bunchy" Carter was founder of the Southern California chapter of the Black Panther Party for Self-Defense (later shortened). After a bout of polio as a child in his home town of Shreveport, Louisiana, he'd gone to Los Angeles with his mother, Nola Mae, and enrolled in a therapeutic dance class. He appeared in a *Little Rascals* episode and had a brief career as a middleweight boxer. For a few years he was a member of the five-thousand-member Slauson gang and became the leader of its most violent arm, the Icepick Gang. By the time Geronimo met him, Carter had already served a sentence for robbery at Soledad State Prison, where he came under the militant influence of the Black Muslims and Malcolm X. Now, at twenty-six, he was living with his mother in the heart of the South-Central ghetto. A colleague described him as "an uncanny composite of artist, street nigger, poet, and revolutionary." He was also a natural leader with scalding contempt for the dashiki-clad students who strutted around the UCLA campus quoting Kwame Nkrumah. In 1967, a year before Geronimo's arrival in Los Angeles, Carter had started the Southern California branch of the Black Panthers after becoming acquainted with Minister of Information Eldridge Cleaver in prison.

In a study made years later the Reverend James McCloskey of the Centurion Ministries described the trizophrenic nature of the Los Angeles group. "There were three faces or sides to the LA-BPP under Bunchy's leadership. They were political, military and 'underground.' The political tried to win the hearts and minds of the people; the military gathered a wide variety of weaponry and made fortifications for the 'revolution' and battle against the police and rival black organizations; and the underground consisted of criminal armed robberies against businesses and banks to 'liberate' money for personal and organizational use (in addition to the funds received from the very wealthy liberal white benefactors such as Jane Fonda and Jean Seberg).

"Bunchy's underground operatives were drawn and selected only from those who he knew well over the years from the streets and gangs of Los Angeles. This was a secret operation entrusted to only those tested on the streets of L.A. These people had come up from the streets and gangs, and had graduated from street crime to armed robbery of businesses. Bunchy's underground did not rob individual people for a few dollars or credit cards. They robbed institutions, not individuals . . . Bunchy kept the 'underground' side separate from the political and military side."

BUNCHY CARTER immediately saw Geronimo Pratt's value to the military face of the organization. The local Panther leader had always deplored the war in Vietnam—"Why should the black man fight the yellow man for the white man?"—but he admired Pratt for his courage in battle. The street fighter and the war hero eased into a friendship, and Bunchy assigned his young colleague a new name: Geronimo ji Jaga, which he explained meant "Geronimo of the Jaga," a tribe of feared African warriors.

In prison later, Pratt had fond memories of their close relationship.

"Bunchy was a striking dude, slender, with big round molasses-colored eyes, a woolly-bully natural and a thick black moustache. He had a mean look but a gentle side, too. Whenever somebody sang the Panther anthem, you could see how it touched him. He spoke the Queen's English. He was always fighting off the ladies and offering me his rejects, but they didn't take to me. I still said *puh-KON* for pecan, *marra* for mirror, *sayup* for syrup, *axed* for asked. He gave me speech lessons because he didn't want me embarrassing myself when I spoke. People would giggle and laugh, and it made me stick out. Ladies broke up. It was always, 'Say what? Hey, dude, where *you* from?' Bunchy taught me adjectives, adverbs, gerunds, participles. My sister Ginny was teaching English and she tutored me, too. I didn't improve a whole lot, but at least I could be understood."

PRATT SOON abandoned his plan to double back to Morgan City. It would always be his home and someday he would return, but Charles, Emelda, Jackie and Ginny ganged up on him and talked him into enrolling in UCLA's High Potential Program, majoring in black studies and political science with minors in linguistics, history and sociology. The program was limited to fifty minority students.

"Great!" he reported sarcastically when he returned from his first classes. "I always wanted to know about the Ashanti wars."

Bunchy Carter was already in his second year in the High Potential Program. The two young Louisianans spent so much time together that Geronimo began serving as the Panther leader's ex-officio bodyguard. "They were called the Black Panthers for Self-Defense, and that word 'self-defense' is all I needed to hear. It's what the elders kept telling me. Who'll defend the black man if he won't defend himself? The hair stood up on my neck when Bunchy read me a line from *Invisible Man* by Ralph Ellison: 'Live with your head in the lion's mouth.' Bunchy said, 'Even better, *be* the fucking lion!' He turned me onto writers I never heard of: Jean Toomer, Zora Neale Hurston, Countee Cullen, Claude McKay, Nella Larsen, folks who weren't afraid to take racial issues head-on. Man, it was a new world! He made me read Che Guevara, Chairman Mao, Cleaver's *Soul on Ice,* James Baldwin, Frantz Fanon, Malcolm X, Lenin, Hegel. I fell in love with books. Bunchy was deliberately propagandizing me, indoctrinating me. I *knew* that! I ate it up."

IN PRATT'S first semester at UCLA the two friends sat up late every night talking philosophy and politics with black intellectuals. At first he questioned the concept of using force of arms to bring about racial equality, a keystone of the Panther program. Bunchy argued that no Panther wanted to take to the streets and gun down whites, "but before we gain equality, we got to regain our dignity. There's a lot of dignity behind an M-15."

In the daytime the new friends cut classes for pistol and rifle practice in the desert, and Geronimo drilled Bunchy and some of the other Panthers in weaponry. At night they began attending rallies for the imprisoned Panther leader Huey P. Newton and listening to "Fuck Governor Reagan" speeches by fellow students. "We went to rallies where you half expected to see somebody sling a grenade. But Bunchy kept things cool, taught us how stupid it was to hate all whites just because of a few. Some fool would talk about putting sharpshooters on our roofs and picking off squad cars. Bunchy would say, 'Hey, jive motherfucker, we *de*fend against cops; we don't *off*end. We don't punch, we *counter*punch.' Bunchy quoted Eldridge Cleaver: 'In their rage against the police, against police brutality, the blacks lose sight of the fundamental reality: that the police are only an instrument for the implementation. . . .' Bunchy taught us, 'If somebody sics a killer dog on your mama and kills her, are you gonna spend the rest of your life trying to kill that dog, or are you gonna deal with the dog's trainer?' He said, 'Remember, the cops are lumpen proletarian, like us. There's assholes in the Panthers, too. You got to learn to pick and choose before you stigmatize people. Otherwise you end up as stupid and prejudiced as they are.' "

Not every Black Panther agreed, and the organization was already splintering into warring factions, a process accelerated by J. Edgar Hoover's FBI. A year before Geronimo's arrival in Los Angeles, "the Director" had proclaimed the Black Panther Party for Self-Defense "the greatest threat to the internal security of the country" and authorized electronic eavesdropping. Armed with inside information, agents found it easy to set one Panther against another. Through its existence the BPP had always been an amalgam of young and angry African Americans, many of whom, like Pratt, still didn't know their own minds. Some were genuinely committed radicals, some genuinely committed troublemakers. They were the angry, disenfranchised, conflicted, suspicious, insulted and traumatized descendants of six generations of slaves. They were both roguery and a reaction to roguery, their agenda a mix of black rage, black pride, radicalism and idealism, some of it as rational as a train wreck.

MOST OF Eunice Petty Pratt's offspring were dubious about the revolutionary group and tried to warn Geronimo away. His older brother Timothy quoted the statement by Malcolm X that "you cannot lead people who are not ready to be led" and added his own opinion: "And I certainly don't believe that African Americans are ready to revolt."

Geronimo replied with another quote: "If somebody goes upside your head, knock him on his ass."

"Who said that?" Tim asked.

"Daddy."

Sister Jacqueline, as pious as their mother, advised Geronimo to apply his youthful energy and idealism to more conventional activities. " 'Gerard,' I told him, 'you're not like those Black Panthers. They're mostly from cities; you're not. They're angry; you're not. Why can't you do something else to benefit our race? Doctor? Lawyer? You're too *smart* to be a Black Panther.' But he'd come straight from Vietnam, a young kid, still not thinking clearly. His blood was running hot and he was influenced by his brother Jack, and Jack was as militant as those other Louisiana boys, Bunchy Carter and Eldridge Cleaver. There was no way my thinking was gonna prevail."

AFTER GERONIMO entered UCLA in September 1968, his life began to spin out of orbit so wildly that in later years he was barely able to distinguish one upheaval from the next. Shortly before his enrollment three Panthers had been killed and two officers wounded in a shoot-out involving a traffic stop. "Everybody was buzzing about that case. The fourth Panther was tried for assault with intent to commit murder, and a jury acquitted him in two hours. Bunchy and me, we were happy about that verdict. Seems like we went from one hot incident to another. So much was going on, I felt like I exchanged one war zone for another."

A few months after his arrival in Los Angeles Pratt had become bonded to the Black Panthers through Bunchy Carter and his coleader, John Huggins, a graduate of the genteel Boston Latin School whose personal slogan was "educate to liberate." The two Panther leaders introduced him to members in Los Angeles and Oakland and briefed him on party plans and goals. Soon the ex-sergeant from the bayou country was serving breakfast to ghetto children, distributing clothes, helping to set up a program of sickle-cell anemia testing, repairing plumbing for seniors, arguing for the introduction of black history courses. Like his sisters and brothers, he was a quick study and was soon teaching informal classes of his own: political education, personal hygiene, the anthropology of racism. He also helped to familiarize the L.A. Panthers with their growing arsenal—Winchester rifles, AR-18s, M-1 carbines, M-15s and M-16s, shotguns and pistols and grenade launchers, a .55-caliber antitank gun and an old crossbow that looked like something that might have been assembled at the Morgan City dump.

IN MID-DECEMBER Pratt flew to Oakland to attend a series of Central Committee meetings about local racial problems, including a black students' strike that had shut down San Francisco State College. In Oakland the Panthers and the police department were locked in warfare. Geronimo learned about the "soul breaker" cells that city jailers maintained for difficult prisoners. It was said that no one except cofounder Huey P. Newton had ever lasted more than two days in the cells before turning into a slobbering wreck. Each unit consisted of four black walls and a rubber floor. There was no light, no toilet, no bed, no sound and, after a while, no up or down. "They use those cells to create snitches," one of the Oakland members explained. "By the time a dude spend an hour in there, he'll rat out his mama."

At meetings during Geronimo's week in Oakland he spoke eloquently about heroin-addicted soldiers in Vietnam and suggested that known users be expelled from the party. "When I got back to L.A., Bunchy said he'd heard cool things about me. He also told me that the cops shot a black kid in Watts and killed a nine-year-old for stealing a candy bar. Things were turning bad. But the worst was what happened to Captain Franco."

Six days before Christmas 1968, Franco Diggs, leader of one of Bunchy Carter's underground cells and a BPP elder statesman at forty, had been found lying faceup on a South Side sidewalk with three bullet holes in his head. Geronimo was stunned; Captain Franco had driven him to the Los Angeles airport in Pratt's red and white GTO for the flight to Oakland.

The angry Carter blamed the Los Angeles police for the death of his old comrade from the Slauson gang days. By Panther calculations a total of sixty black citizens had been killed by Los Angeles police in 1967 and 1968, and twenty-five were unarmed.

Harassment

In the first months of 1969 the LAPD's Urban Counterinsurgency Task Force—known as the Panther Unit—stepped up its program of stopping Panther cars and rousting the occupants. Party documents were thrown into gutters. Bundles of the newspaper the *Black Panther* disappeared in sewers. Police would order a driver to the curb, break his taillight, then stop him a few blocks away for defective lights. Panthers were arrested on suspicion of crimes ranging from reckless driving to murder and held in the labyrinthine 77th Division station, oldest in the city,[8] where they were interviewed, photographed and had their names added to intelligence files as high-risk offenders. At night officers shuttled detainees from precinct to precinct so they couldn't be bailed out. Sometimes the arresting officers drew their guns, ordered their victims to their knees and fired random shots into the ground or over their heads.

One member of the Panther Unit openly bragged to a party leader that he fired a thousand rounds of practice a day "so I can be sure to kill niggers like you." When a pregnant Panther dared a policeman to pull the

---

[8] The building was built in the 1920s and was already in an advanced state of disrepair when Raymond Chandler used it as a setting in his 1940 book *Farewell, My Lovely.*

trigger, he replied that he could shoot her in the stomach and "kill two birds with one stone."

Nor was Los Angeles the only city where confrontations between police and radical black groups were escalating. "Our people were getting massacred, and Bunchy ordered me to go around the country and teach self-defense," Geronimo recalled. "I went to the areas where there'd been marches and riots, Klan activity, where our people had been set on by dogs and fire-hosed till they dropped, and I taught 'em disciplined resistance. I talked in churches where children were firebombed. I met with teachers in schools where snipers had killed black students. I went into homes the Klan shot up with automatic rifle fire at night. I showed our people how to construct barriers, fortify buildings, handle guns, patrol a city nonviolently, read maps. I made 'em dig tunnels and use the dirt to fill up sandbags to line their walls. When the worst police raids began, this saved a lot of lives. Everything I taught was military preparedness, urban warfare, defensive structure, just what the elders sent me to the army to learn."

WHEN HE returned from this first cross-country trip, Geronimo found two FBI agents waiting at his doorstep. "They asked me a couple questions, I told 'em I didn't know nothin'. Before they left, the taller one said, 'I guess you know you're a dead man.' I said, 'Hey, I already died three times in Vietnam.' I was just shinin' 'em on. They gave me a look and left."

Geronimo reported the confrontation to Bunchy Carter and John Huggins. "Nothing new about this," Bunchy said. "FBI been on our ass from the beginning. They let the local cops do the dirty work, but they're always around."

The discussion turned to a pressing intraracial problem. Relations were strained between the local Panthers and a black organization called US (United Slaves), led by a brilliant student named Ronald Everett, a Baltimorean who had shaved his head, donned dark glasses, dressed in African garb, affected an English accent and re-created himself as Ron Karenga. His followers called him Maulana, a Swahili word meaning "great teacher." A few of the Panthers engaged in their own brand of racism by deriding him as "Pork Chop" and his followers as "Karangatangs." Members of the US organization considered themselves strict black nationalists and took issue with the Panthers' demand for integration.

Lately the animosity between the two black groups had been worsening. "Looking back," Geronimo recalled, "you got to wonder why two

African American campus groups were fighting each other. What a waste! We *all* wanted freedom for our people. Seemed like we got further apart every day. There was a rumor that the LAPD and the FBI were trying to set us against each other, but years went by before we could prove it—and by then it was too late. The blood was already runnin'.

"We got anonymous phone calls, letters, insults, taunts. We found hate mail in our lockers at school—'Your girlfriend fucks Karenga.' You'd get a phone call: 'I just left US headquarters. Your wife's panties are on the wall.' Of course it was bullshit, but after the third or fourth report you begin to wonder. We found out later that the United Slaves were hearing the same things about us. Right after New Year's 1969 the situation turned real bad. Karenga and US were trying to control the black studies program at UCLA, and Bunchy and John Huggins were arguing that the issues should be settled by vote. It was an honest disagreement, like college kids have all the time. There was a campus rally the night of January 16. Fistfights broke out. You couldn't hear the speakers over the boos."

JUST AFTER noon the next day, January 17, Geronimo was visiting an injured Panther in the UCLA Medical Center when a woman burst in and reported that Bunchy Carter and John Huggins had been shot in Campbell Hall. He ran across the campus but was stopped by police at the entrance. Hysterical onlookers told him that the two Panther leaders had been walking out of an acrimonious meeting of the Black Students Union when US officers opened fire.[9] Huggins and Carter fell so close that their fingertips touched. Frightened students trampled them as they fled from the building, and many jumped from windows.

Geronimo's first thought was of Huggins' wife Ericka and their two-week-old baby. As he was driving toward the black ghetto, he heard a news report: the UCLA students had been pronounced dead.

In the late afternoon traffic the drive took almost two hours. Geronimo tried to imagine Bunchy and John lying lifeless in the morgue and found the vision no more comprehensible than the sight of Jack Pratt lying on his side between the anvil and the chicken coop. For a long time he'd known that Bunchy was no pious seminarian. His Icepick Gang had

---

[9] Decades later, when it no longer mattered, Geronimo learned that the earliest reports were incorrect. It was John Huggins who'd fired first.

been named for its leader's weapon of choice. Bunchy might even have killed a few men in gang fights. Well, so did I, Geronimo told himself. What was Vietnam but a gang fight? He was my friend. I loved him like a man.

When he arrived at the Huggins apartment near the Hollywood Park racetrack, policemen with drawn guns ordered him to lie facedown on the driveway. A shotgun barrel dug into the side of his face.

He heard one of the officers banging on the door and called out, "There's nothin' but women in there, man!"

The cops led four females and a screaming infant from the apartment. Other officers went inside and confiscated what they later described as "Panther guns."

On the way to the 70th Precinct station a plainclothesman told one of the women, "You're the oldest whore of the pink pussies, so you must be the one with the biggest hole." At the station the women were ordered to remain shackled together, even while using the toilet. Ericka Huggins nursed her daughter, but after the women were informed that they were being held for conspiracy with intent to commit assault with a deadly weapon, the baby was taken away. A sergeant explained that they'd been tipped off that Pratt and the others were bent on revenge against the US, and the police had sped to the Huggins place to intercept them and head off "a retaliatory bloodbath." Geronimo and two other unarmed males were arrested on the same charge.

ACROSS CENTRAL Avenue from Panther headquarters, police emerged from behind a building facade and arrested every African American in sight. They confiscated ammunition, medical supplies, Panther literature and propaganda, gas masks, address books and marijuana. By midnight nearly a hundred Panthers had been herded into paddy wagons, driven to Los Angeles County Jail, booked, fingerprinted, run through showers, sprayed for bugs and locked into seven-by-eight-foot maximum-security cells. Police confiscated party files and pored over boxes of information—driver's licenses and license plate numbers, unlisted phone numbers, names and addresses of financial supporters like the actresses Jane Fonda and Jean Seberg (who used the code name "Aretha" on her checks) and prominent Hollywood citizens. The LAPD's war against the Panthers was now fully engaged.

AT THE jail Geronimo's emotions flickered from embarrassment to rage. "I hadn't been in a cell since Johnnie Lee Emerson talked up to a white girl. One of the jailers told me to lean over and spread 'em. I said, 'Huh? For what?' He said, 'None of your fuckin' business.' It wouldn't be the last time a guard asked me to spread, and I would never do it. Didn't take me long to learn that a lot of those jailers and prison guards and other people in authority were the same kind of son of a bitches I had in my platoon, the ones that were empowered beyond their own ability to handle it. I'd stopped that kinda shit in my platoon and now the cops were doing it to my people in Los Angeles. I felt ashamed."

After seventy-two hours all charges were dropped for lack of evidence, and Geronimo and his friends were freed in time to learn what had happened at John Huggins' funeral in his native New Haven, Connecticut. Huggins' parents, a Yale steward and a librarian, had planned a dignified low-key service. FBI agents entered the church to shoot pictures of the body in its open casket. At the door another agent photographed mourners. The lawmen departed after copying the names on the sign-in log.

THE LOS Angeles funeral for Bunchy Carter threatened to be an explosive affair. The city was waterlogged by the longest sustained rainfall in a century. Yellow-slickered patrolmen ringed the crowd while men in dark suits snapped pictures. Under a canopy of umbrellas, thousands of mourners filled the ghetto church and overflowed into the street. Twosomes and threesomes passed through the crowd singing the BPP anthem as a dirge.

Along the walls of the church, Panthers stood at attention in their black berets, powder-blue shirts and black leather jackets. Plainclothesmen from the Panther Unit took notes as party Chief of Staff David Hilliard eulogized his colleague. A preacher based his sermon on how Moses had delivered his people from bondage after killing an Egyptian soldier who was beating a slave to death. Geronimo thought, How many times have I heard Mama tell the same story?

At party headquarters that night he was besieged by angry and confused Panthers. Jackie Pratt recalled, "People were coming to my brother: 'What're we gonna do? Geronimo, we're looking to you, man. *What're we gonna do?*' He put them off as long as he could. He'd say, 'I'm just a country boy from Louisiana. Don't ask me.' But they didn't know where else to turn."

With his friend Bunchy Carter dead, Pratt tried to focus his anger on the police, but he was also disturbed with himself. He thought about leaving college and returning to Morgan City to help his mother and father. He had no taste for more combat, whatever the cause. He might even join his brother Timothy at Southern University in Baton Rouge, a safer place than the battlegrounds of UCLA, even for quarterbacks. He was sick of fighting racial wars in an unaccustomed setting a world away from home.

Driving While Black

As police pressure increased, so did Geronimo's need to stick by his fellow Panthers. The members were tailed wherever they went; suddenly the chronically underfinanced LAPD seemed to have inexhaustible resources. Pratt's red and white GTO convertible, nicknamed the Goat and borrowed by BPP functionaries as needed, was stopped so many times that it was re-painted blue in order to throw police off.[10] At one time or another, officers impounded the Panther car, stripped it, ran it up a telephone pole, smashed its signals, poured sugar in the gas tank and pitched the seats into the street.

One drizzly night police aimed their pistols at a three-week-old Panther baby and jacked shells into the chamber of their shotguns as they ordered the six occupants out of the car. "What's this about, Officer?" Geronimo asked.

"It's about a possible murder," the cop answered.

Fellow Panther Roger "Blue" Lewis was flung to the ground, choked,

---

[10] Local police had a reputation for enforcing the offense known as DWB (driving while black). Once they stopped Johnnie Cochran in Hollywood, ordering him out of his car at gunpoint and terrifying his two young children. The two officers apologized when they learned he was an assistant district attorney.

and kneed in the groin. At the precinct a sergeant extinguished a cigarette on his arm.

After three hours friends and relatives began arriving at the station, alerted by a Panther backup car that also had been stopped by police. A sergeant told the new arrivals, "I wouldn't put it above you people to blow up a police station. So for reasons of division security I'm gonna have to ask you to leave."

By midnight everyone had been released, and the murder charges were never mentioned again. A few days later two policemen wrestled Geronimo to the ground as he walked out the front door of Panther headquarters. One yelled in his ear, "Why'd you draw a bead on me from that window?"

"I didn't," said the disgusted Pratt, "but maybe I should've." He was released after an exchange of angry looks.

When Geronimo attempted to shuttle UCLA students to the ghetto to help in the Panther programs, police curbed his car, took names and ordered the students back to campus. "We were okay on the Santa Monica Freeway, but as soon as we hit the city streets the cops would pull us over. One day I was carrying a bunch of black students to distribute used clothes in South-Central. Cop makes 'em get out and put their hands against the car. I said, 'What's the charge, Officer?' He stopped to think. Then he said, 'Too many blacks in one car.' "

Pratt began logging the stops but quit when he reached fifty. His dormitory room was burglarized twice and regularly searched. He wondered how many listening devices had been planted in his walls, in his GTO, in his relatives' houses where he sometimes overnighted for peace and privacy. L.A. police and FBI agents searched the homes of his brothers Jackie and Charles and interviewed his sister Virginia. A dozen officers in black and white squad cars raided his sister Emelda's place while Geronimo was visiting. She tried to explain that she was putting herself through college as a night-shift baker and had no connection with the Panthers, but they ransacked her two rooms.

WHEN GERONIMO assigned young Panthers to shadow their shadowers and report acts of harassment to police officials (an admittedly provocative technique that had caused bloody confrontations in Oakland), desk sergeants refused to take their complaints. One of the young Panthers was told to back off or "you'll find yourself cleaning our shitters."

Even in the Deep South, Geronimo had never seen such pressure. "The cops were like an occupying force. To them we were a lower form of life. They thought we wanted to take over Los Angeles by brute force, kill the men and rape the women. It was a time-warp thing, all the way back to the frontier days. We were the Indians."

Surveillance cameras appeared across the street from Panther headquarters. BPP members took time off from school or work to defend themselves against petty charges in the lower courts, where judges seemed predisposed to believe police testimony ("He pulled a knife on me, Your Honor . . ." "He tried to run me down with his car . . ."). A standard technique was to wrench ignition wires loose or remove distributor caps to disable Panther vehicles. Legitimately parked cars would be ticketed and towed to the city pound. The party's limited treasury became drained. Fund-raising fell off after police confronted financial supporters at Hollywood rallies and ripped up donation checks. Panthers were arrested for selling the party newspaper on street corners without the proper licenses, their stocks confiscated. Children who took part in the free breakfast program had to make their way past uniformed policemen to enter the ghetto buildings.

When the police weren't disrupting and harassing, they were ridiculing and taunting. "Jungle bunny" became the favorite epithet, replacing "spade," "dinge," "jig" and "jigaboo" (although the universal "nigger" never went out of style). Two Metro Squad members idled away their evenings by riding up and down Central Avenue wearing foot-high Afro wigs and bright dashikis and yelling "Power to the People!" through a high-powered bullhorn. On one of her frequent trips to jail, a female Panther noticed a banner on the wall of the booking room: "PIGS 11—PANTHERS 0."

If it was a game, it soon turned deadly. A delegation of California Panthers had already unnerved police by appearing in public carrying rifles and side arms, their legal right until the law was changed. While Panther children marched up and down chanting, "The revolution has come, it's time to pick up the gun," national BPP leaders instituted a firm policy about firearms: no concealed weapons, no gunfighting or cowboy antics. But every member was expected to practice self-defense for himself and his family, and each household was required to have at least one loaded shotgun. "If the cops attack, we'll go down firing," one of the leaders told a reporter.

Later Geronimo Pratt was asked in court to define "self-defense" in the Panther context. "It was based on the principle from an older organization that if a nation fails to protect its citizens," he testified, "then they cannot condemn those who take up the task themselves, and in light of what was happening in the early part of the 1960s, no one was really protecting the black people and we had to protect ourselves. That's the basic principle of self-defense." He repeated a Malcolm X declaration that he'd first learned from Bunchy Carter: "We should be peaceful, law-abiding, but the time has come to fight back in self-defense whenever and wherever the black man is being unjustly and unlawfully attacked," to which Carter had always added, "We may suffer, we may die, but even if we don't regain our freedom, we'll regain our dignity."

Deep-Seated Hatred

In April 1969, three months after the deadly shoot-out in UCLA's Campbell Hall, Eldridge Cleaver's handsome wife Kathleen phoned and asked Pratt to fly to Oakland for an important meeting. There he was informed that Bunchy Carter had left a taped message naming him as his successor in Southern California. Geronimo demurred at the top of his lungs. "I was so mad! I said, 'I can't explain it to y'all, but I don't want the job. I'm not from California. I don't even *like* California.' They told me I was now on the Central Committee and the First Cadre, the highest decision-making body. They made me deputy minister of defense of the whole damn BPP and told me to take command.

"Some of my Panther friends were waiting for me when I got back to L.A., and they said, 'Brother, if you split for Louisiana, we're jumpin' your ass right here.' Long John Washington said, 'You wanna duke it out with the six of us?' I got in touch with the elders in Morgan City and they said they needed military guys more than ever. They told me to use my own judgment. I decided to stay in L.A. for a month or two, at least till the Panthers could find somebody else to take over. Next thing I knew, I heard that Julio Butler's nose was out of joint. He expected to succeed Bunchy. Julio and me, we never got along. He was an old guy, about forty, a high yellow with big lips, chunky body, greasy hair. He thought of himself as a sharp dresser, but his clothes always looked a size too small. He had a smug, snooty, snotty expression—superior, condescending. My brother Charlie took one look at him and said, 'That guy's a snitch.' I should have thrown Julio's ass out of the party right then and there. Charlie was seldom wrong about things like that. Whatever the dude was, he was a problem. But who could have guessed how big?"

JULIUS CARL BUTLER, also known as Julio, Mama and Mother, was an ex-marine sergeant, former Los Angeles County deputy sheriff and nominal head of BPP party security in Los Angeles. Most of his official activities took place in his own fief on the Westside of Los Angeles, a largely white section where Panther presence was weak. Butler was an unlikely racial activist, a strong-arm man who liked to refer to himself as "the mayor of Adams Boulevard."[11] He'd retired as a deputy in 1960, joined the Panthers in 1968 and now ran a hairdressing business in the West Adams–Crenshaw neighborhood. His business card advertised "Mr. Julio, cosmetologist and micro-trichologist. Scientific hair care and micro-analysis with all phases of cosmetology. Coiffures la dames." With his goatee, heavy brows, full lips and gleaming wavy hair, the ex-deputy had something of the look of a Harlem bandleader in a 1930s movie.

WORD CONTINUED to trickle into Panther headquarters about Butler's angry reaction to Pratt's elevation to Southern California leader. As an investigator[12] reported later: "It didn't help matters that Pratt was twenty-one years old (fifteen years younger than Butler) and new to the organization and was a complete outsider who was from rural Louisiana, not urban Los Angeles, and had no established track record within the party in any area of operations. Butler decided to run his own operation from the Westside and defied any authority coming from Pratt and his inner circle of lieutenants. Butler felt that Pratt was incompetent and totally unqualified to

---

[11] A few sagging mansions remained from the 1920s and 1930s when the upscale neighborhood had been home to silent-film luminaries like Roscoe "Fatty" Arbuckle.

[12] The Reverend James McCloskey of Centurion Ministries.

lead. Butler considered his people to be far better qualified and trained to do the work of BPP. Pratt and Butler clashed time and again. . . ."

Geronimo had to deal with the Butler problem shortly after his return from the April meeting in Oakland. "Julio accused a kid named Bobby of gutlessness. He ordered Bobby to go out and find a dog or cat, bring it back and cut its throat. The brother was only sixteen, seventeen years old, and when he couldn't find the right animal, Julio knocked out his front teeth. We had a few words about that."

Not long afterward, Pratt rushed to Butler's upstairs apartment in response to an emergency call from a mutual friend. "Julio was pounding on one of our recruits, a high school kid named Ollie Taylor. Julio was always jacking people. The boy's eye was shut, his face was bloody and some of his teeth were knocked out. I looked over in the corner and saw his schoolbooks. Made me feel bad. I apologized and told him we'd pay his medical bills. Then I took Julio in the other room and said, 'Panthers don't do each other like that.' I told him he was under house arrest and he wasn't security chief or a section leader anymore. He was drinking Bacardi rum. He said, 'You're making a big mistake, Pratt.' "

Prodded by an uncle with police connections, the injured Ollie Taylor made a formal complaint to the authorities, and Pratt, Butler and three other Panthers found themselves charged with assault with a deadly weapon, kidnapping and false imprisonment. Two days later an old friend in Morgan City tipped Geronimo that FBI agents were asking about him in St. Mary Parish.

Pratt and his colleagues viewed the arrests as more police harassment and vowed to fight to the end in court. But Julius Butler took a more relaxed approach. He told confidantes that he intended to plead nolo contendere to all four counts, serenely running the risk of a penitentiary sentence. A judge put him on three years' probation and ordered him to pay a $200 fine and restitution. Geronimo and the other accused Panthers fought the charges and won.

"I LOOKED at how it all went down," Geronimo recalled, "and to me it spelled r-a-t. I couldn't prove Julio was a police agent, but I was sure enough to make my move."

He'd already ousted Butler as section leader and chief of security. Now, with his new power as deputy minister of defense and leader of Southern

California Panthers, he expelled the hairdresser from the party. Headquarters approved the ouster.

When the expulsion was reported in the *Black Panther,* word came back that the enraged Butler had sworn revenge. As investigator McCloskey reported later, "This expulsion by the young upstart outsider Pratt humiliated him in front of his own men and the entire community where he'd lived his whole life. . . . Some of Butler's former associates and squad members told me that Butler has an unnatural but deep-seated hatred for Mr. Pratt."

The loathing was more than a personality conflict. "No wonder he was enraged," the investigator reported. "As head of the L.A. Panthers, Julio would've been the most valuable police informer, the king snitch. One Panther told me that Julius wanted to kill Pratt with his bare hands." Instead, he used a subtler weapon.

Jail Time

For most of Geronimo Pratt's first full year as Southern California Panther leader, his time was spent raising bail or appearing in court for himself or others. On the night of April 12, 1969, his GTO was pulled over and searched again. He seldom drove the Goat anymore; the deputy minister of defense was more likely to be seen in a blue Volkswagen or other cars borrowed from friends.

This time the police report said, "Officers observed a white coat lying in the front seat of the vehicle covering some objects. The officer picked up the coat and observed a brown paper bag with a metal pipe sticking out of the bag and the end of the pipe was a 6-inch fuse. This pipe appeared to be a homemade bomb. Found 12-in metal pipe w/caps on both ends and a 6-inch fuse extending out end of one and other bombs and blasting equipment, blasting caps, live ammo, instructions on how to make a home-made bomb in handwriting. . . . Also 45 cal automatic, 38 revolver."

Pratt described the report as "pure fiction" and explained that the highly visible GTO was the last car that any Panther would have used to haul contraband.

AFTER THIS latest stop Geronimo was bemused by an offer of round-the-clock protection from a woman. "I'd never had a bodyguard. When they named me to the Central Committee, Bobby Seale and David Hilliard offered me security. I told 'em, 'Hey, I'm my own bodyguard.' Then this cool-looking sister, nineteen years old, big, rangy, waltzes into headquarters, says, 'How do you do, Mr. Pratt, I'm Saundra Lee. Call me "Red." I'm your bodyguard.' I says, 'Say what?' I'm laughing! I told her, 'Hey, baby, I *train* bodyguards!' She pulls up this denim skirt and shows me a .25-caliber automatic in her black panties. I'm breaking up! A peashooter! She says, 'Don't underestimate this weapon, Mr. G. It already put several cats to sleep.' Sticks the barrel in my face, says, 'You're not so tough. I'll *kill* you.' She says, 'You jive son of a bitch, you think I won't do it?' I laughed louder. She told me later, 'The second time you laughed, that's when I decided I *want* this mother.' Me, I just figured, This chick is crazy, and ushered her out.

"I asked around and found out she had a history. I mean, a *history*. Her mother sent her to good schools, gave her everything. She was number one in her high school class when she discovered her mama was a 'ho.' Red took it hard. She was gang-raped at thirteen, became a hooker herself, went up to San Francisco, rejected her pimps and became a 'stud broad'—an independent who goes both ways. She was sixteen by then. Goes east, ends up as the madam for a guy in the Cosa Nostra and begins shooting up heroin. At that time the Panthers were rounding up drug dealers and pimps and trying to straighten 'em out. A couple of our people found Red in a gutter, no veins left, shooting up in her tongue. They dried her out and found out she was so smart she made 'em all feel stupid."

THE COUNTRY boy from Atchafalaya swamp country was more surprised than anyone when the rehabilitated Saundra appeared at Panther headquarters to attend his night classes in guerrilla warfare and area defense. Soon she was visiting his bedroom and telling him to sleep in peace—"nobody gonna bother yo' ass while Red's around."

He returned from a trip to Chicago to find a marriage certificate hanging over his bedroom door. She said, "Now lemme see you reject me as a bodyguard! We're legally married!"

Geronimo pretended that the license was valid. "Everybody else thought I was married to her. So we acted like we were." In time, Saundra became one of the best-loved Panthers, a cliché "whore with a heart of gold," and Pratt developed a genuine affection for the woman known as his wife.

IN THE last months of 1969 the internecine warfare with the United Slaves organization seemed to subside. "That fratricidal crap only lasted four or five months. Ron Karenga and us Panthers, we finally wised up and stopped fighting. We were pretty sure where the nasty letters and phone calls were coming from. We were stupid for a while, but we weren't gonna be stupid forever."

The Panthers could tell they were under steady surveillance from buildings on Central Avenue. Geronimo redoubled his efforts to fortify the headquarters, a rickety old brick and wood structure whose primary means of support was the buildings on either side. "Every trooper has a horror of being overrun. When somebody tries to take your position, the first thing he does is lay down a barrage, open up holes in your defense, make you vulnerable. I wasn't gonna let that happen. The cops had already shown what they would do. They fired shots into our national headquarters in Oakland. How were we supposed to react? Paint bull's-eyes on our ass? We *had* to defend ourselves. So we started using sandbags. Whenever our people were late for political education classes or didn't sell enough Panther papers or got caught with drugs, I made 'em dig tunnels in the basement and fill sandbags with the dirt. Now if the situation got out of hand, we could use those tunnels to duck out of the line of fire. We stuffed sandbags in the panels behind our walls, below our ceilings, up under our roof. We put up *tons* of dirt. It was all defensive structure. No bullet was gonna penetrate three-foot walls."

ON DECEMBER 4, 1969, fifteen months after Pratt's arrival in Los Angeles, word came from Chicago that plainclothes police, armed with a floor plan provided by an FBI informer, had kicked in the front door of a Panther apartment at 4:40 A.M. and killed Illinois leaders Fred Hampton and Mark Clark. Four other Panthers and one policeman were wounded.[13] The

---

[13] A federal grand jury inquiry confirmed that all victims, including the wounded officer, had been hit by police gunfire.

twenty-one-year-old Hampton had been shot in the head at point-blank range. One of the weapons used by police was the famous "Tommy gun," long a part of Chicago's tradition of violence.

"You're next," Geronimo was warned in an anonymous call. "You and your ho."

On advice from Panther headquarters in Oakland, Pratt and Saundra began sleeping in safe houses. "Me and Red, we're not afraid of dying," he told Long John Washington and Blue Lewis, "but we're not gonna die like Fred and Mark. We're not gonna die like dogs."

Incoming

In the stillness of predawn on December 8, 1969, four days after the deadly Chicago raid, thirty-nine L.A. policemen and FBI agents in bulletproof vests, black jumpsuits, black boots and black baseball caps quietly took positions around Panther headquarters at Forty-first and Central. Another three dozen officers waited around the corner. In the police version of the raid, four cops with a battering ram were met with a fusillade of gunfire as they tried to break down the steel-plated front door. Three fell, one critically wounded. (All casualties recovered, including the critically injured Sergeant Edward C. Williams, who had been hit in the chest, groin and finger.)

Inside the building the occupants awoke to a warning from Melvin "Cotton" Smith, who explained later that he just happened to be looking out a front window. Some of the Panthers claimed later that Smith shouted, "The pigs are coming in!" and that he grabbed a rifle and began firing from a fortified upper window.

In the ensuing gunfight five thousand police rounds struck the brown brick walls of the building, most of them burrowing harmlessly into Pratt's sandbags. Tear gas canisters, fired from grenade launchers, bounced off heavy metal grilles and clanked back on the street. Frustrated commanders ordered a dynamite charge dropped from a helicopter. It rearranged some sandbags but caused no damage.

Four hours into the mini-war, two hundred officers were on the scene, firing assault weapons from squad cars, armored cars, dark blue trucks and an olive-drab personnel carrier borrowed from the National Guard. Fire trucks, their low-throated engines idling, waited at nearby intersections. Reporters and cameramen huddled behind sawhorses at the edges of the battle zone and were joined by mobs of curious neighbors, coughing in the blue haze. A dog loped onto the battleground, yelped and ran off. Two and a half blocks from the epicenter of the violence, a patrolman felt a tug and found his pea jacket collar holed by a stray round.

At 9:45 A.M., five hours after the opening shots, police glimpsed a flash of white in a window and held their fire. A few minutes later a nineteen-year-old Panther named Renee Moore staggered out the front door waving a white flag. Her yellow dress was ripped, revealing a bra caked with dirt. She was followed by eleven disheveled Panthers with their hands on their heads.

"Walk down the sidewalk," a policeman with a bullhorn ordered. "One at a time."

Moore yelled to reporters, "We gave up because it's not the right time. We'll fight again when the odds are more in our favor." She was cut and bruised but not seriously hurt. Roland Freeman had been shot in both arms, Tommye Williams in both thighs, Wayne Pharr in the chest, arm and wrist. As Pharr staggered to the street under the sign FEED HUNGRY CHILDREN—FREE BREAKFAST, he called out, "Tell Mother I love her. Tell Sharon I love her." Six Panthers had been wounded.

IN A house a mile away, in the heart of the South-Central area just off Broadway, Geronimo Pratt and Saundra "Red" Lee were asleep in a rear bedroom when police broke through the door. In the first LAPD version of the incident, "Officers identified themselves, told defendant not to move. Defendant made movement toward floor under bed. At this time a sergeant fired a shotgun over defendant's head. Defendant then froze in his position and was taken into custody and handcuffed." According to the police report, a loaded .357 Magnum was found under the bed.

"They handcuffed us and marched us down the street naked," Pratt said later. "We looked like slaves on a gangplank."

He was charged with conspiracy to commit the assault and murder of a police officer. Saundra protested her innocence, but while she was being held on suspicion, police ransacked their apartment and turned up an old photograph of her posing with a submachine gun. Based on the picture, she was charged with possession of an illegal weapon.

FIVE THOUSAND African American citizens mounted the steps of City Hall to hear Panther spokesmen denounce the police raiders as fascists who'd fired on a houseful of men and women on the slimmest of pretexts and for the oldest of reasons: racial hatred. Later the group joined other demonstrators at the Hall of Justice, where speakers with bullhorns charged that Police Chief Edward M. Davis had assumed dictatorial powers in his zeal to drive the Panthers from town. A black politician, State Senator Mervyn Dymally, called the raid part of "a national plan for police repression." Packs of students roamed in and out of the area, throwing rocks and bottles at squad cars and raising their fists in the Black Power salute. Police snipers were positioned atop four divisional stations and the police administration building but fired no shots.

IN THE next few days so many demonstrations were held in the South-Central and Watts ghettoes that a deputy police chief, perhaps remembering the buildup to the "Burn, Baby, Burn" riots of 1965, complained publicly, "We're being whipped by a propaganda warfare." At a press conference Acting Police Chief Daryl Gates explained that the raiding party had anticipated felonious resistance because of a Panther doctrine that "unwarranted entry would be met with armed resistance." Governor Ronald Reagan called the raid "a tragic and deplorable thing . . . but it is clear that the Black Panthers have made their policy one of violence and outright revolution." According to Reagan, the biggest victims of the BPP were "the overwhelming majority of the black community."

TWENTY PANTHERS from three locations appeared before a Municipal Court judge in their jailhouse sandals and orange jumpsuits to face charges including conspiracy to possess illegal explosives, assault and attempted murder. The judge proclaimed the Panther resistance "armed anarchy" after a prosecutor charged that the BPP stood for revolution and the murder of lawmen, backing up his claims with 106 exhibits, including twenty-eight weapons taken in the raids. The judge frowned as he perused the blood-thirsty Panther literature; party propaganda had always been heavy on bluff and bombast.

"Even if we ignore the material in the documents," the judge said, "the condition of the premises . . . and the bombs and armament would lead anyone, even a casual visitor, to believe illegal activities were planned. They didn't have to stay there. They were under no misapprehension about what was going on there. . . . They were acting in concert with party discipline."

Panther lawyers argued that the defensive fortifications were justified by recent history, including the killings in Chicago and police raids in other cities. They called the search warrants illegal and "an excuse to raid the building," and characterized the arrests as political persecution and part of a conspiracy to destroy the party. Attorney Charles Garry called for an investigation by Congress and said he would bring the matter to the attention of the United Nations. The judge ordered the defendants bound over for trial.

IN THE days following the shoot-out the Black Panther Party found itself vigorously defended by mainstream African Americans for one of the few times in its three-year history. The Congress for Racial Equality demanded an investigation "of the death of 28 Black Panther members killed in clashes with the police since January, 1968."[14] The Southern Christian Leadership Conference complained of "a calculated design of genocide." The Urban League and NAACP joined in the protests. Julian Bond, a charismatic black legislator in Georgia, charged that "the Black Panthers are being decimated by political assassination arranged by the federal police apparatus."

The *New York Times* took up the theme by referring to a growing concern that "the Federal Administration has had a hand in the recent wave of raids, arrests and shoot-outs." The newspaper blamed President Richard Nixon's administration for creating a climate of opinion producing "a virtual open season . . . on the Panthers." *Newsweek* asked, "Is there some sort of government conspiracy afoot to exterminate the Black Panthers?" *Time*

---

[14] The number was incorrect but became widely accepted. In a study commissioned by *The New Yorker* many years later, the respected investigator Edward Jay Epstein determined that ten Panthers were killed by police, some while posing a mortal threat to the officers who shot them.

referred to "a lethal undeclared war." Even the understated *Christian Science Monitor* mentioned "a growing suspicion that something more than isolated local police action was involved." Eventually all would be proved correct.

FEW SUCH protests were heard in California, where the ultraconservative *Los Angeles Times* echoed J. Edgar Hoover's pronouncement that the Panthers were the biggest threat to America's peace and security. On June 21, 1970, under a five-column headline on the front page, the *Times* claimed that the "Black Panthers and police are fighting a battle in South-Central Los Angeles that has shadows of an International Communist movement. . . ." The article warned that "the Panthers have trained at least 100 young men and women in guerrilla warfare, including sabotage, handling machine guns, hand grenades and other weapons." It quoted an anonymous woman: "For a long time I thought the Panthers were right in what they said, but I just wasn't willing to pick up a gun and shoot somebody or die." An unidentified police officer claimed that he'd been approached by a boy about four or five years old who spoke "in unprintable, obscene language imitative of the Panthers. . . ."

The inflammatory article gave particular attention to the twenty-two-year-old Southern California Panther leader:

Geronimo is what many feared would be a disastrous byproduct of the Vietnam war, a black man trained as a soldier who returned home to turn his skills against the Establishment. Pratt, a paratrooper, says he was trained as a guerrilla fighter and an assassin and at one time taught Green Berets. In Vietnam he was dropped behind enemy lines to kill village chiefs cooperating with the Viet Cong, he said.[15]

According to the *Times,* the trained assassin and his Black Panther Party "hoped to immobilize the police by making them afraid to enter the ghetto, to make South-Central Los Angeles a 'liberated territory.' " Overall Panther strategy, according to the newspaper's blind sources, was "to create several pockets of 'liberated territories' across the country and then form an alliance with the Chinese, North Vietnamese, North Koreans, Africans

---

[15] Pratt hadn't been interviewed by the *Times* or any other newspaper. Later it was revealed that the provocative information originated with an LAPD public information officer.

and other nonwhite people for mutual protection. . . . Eldridge Cleaver . . . is said to be negotiating for that treaty with foreign countries."

LOCKED IN the bowels of the overcrowded Los Angeles County Jail, the perplexed Pratt and his fellow militants awaited courtroom proceedings in which they would eventually be acquitted of all but a few charges. Their lawyers filed a $10-million lawsuit alleging that in a single year the LAPD had engaged in fourteen assaults against the Panthers, ten beatings, fifty-six false arrests, nineteen "stop-and-frisk" traffic stops, eighteen "humiliating treatments," twenty-one search-and-seizure missions without cause, nine incidents of mistreatment of Panther prisoners and nine incidents of destruction or theft of property.

From their first hours inside the antiquated jail, the Panthers butted heads with guards and administrators who seemed to Geronimo to be as racially biased as any member of the Ku Klux Klan. Some of the deputies taunted the prisoners and tried to provoke fights. "Panthers?" one of them said behind the safety of heavy wire grille. "You look more like pussies to me." Two guards strutted up and down the cellblock loudly repeating: "What kind of things live in cages? Animals in a zoo. They must be animals—and we must be zookeepers."

A black inmate told Pratt, "These fucking deputies figure if we fight with each other we're too busy to fight with the staff."

Geronimo watched as three guards dragged a gray-haired African American along the corridor and beat him with truncheons and saps. In the corner of a recreation room, Pratt saw two inmates double-team a puny young black who was shaking from drug withdrawal. A tittering guard called out from the other side of the screen: "Stick him good, man!"

Geronimo turned away as one of the attackers started to unbutton his pants. In his mind's eye he saw Vietnam again: children sodomized in their cots, women forced to their knees, husbands and fathers pistol-whipped when they dared to object. That night he passed word to his Panther colleagues. "The damn guards are acting like slave masters. We got to do something."

When word went out that Pratt planned a reprisal, deputies struck first by claiming that he'd tried to stab one of them with a pencil. Geronimo represented himself in court and was acquitted of a felony charge of assault.

Guards began patrolling the cellblocks in threes, then fours. Whenever a deputy abused an older or weaker prisoner, Pratt or another Panther lodged complaints, and if no charges resulted, they tried to mete out their own punishment. The most vicious deputies were attacked with fists and homemade weapons. The jailers responded by cramming the dissidents into a holding tank that was so crowded they had to stand.

A group of desperate young prisoners planned a mass escape, and Geronimo felt sympathic. "Their lives were definitely in danger. They were gonna go out through a window, use a rope and pulleys to reach a truck across the city street and make their way to the parking lot. There was seventeen of 'em, young Panthers, *my* Panthers. They had mothers and fathers, wives, kids."

An informer tipped a deputy. "At two in the morning the sheriff of L.A. County, Peter Pitchess, entered the cellblock with fifty deputies with gas masks and guns. We were all in our box trying to sleep when the lights came on. Deputies were lined up every two or three feet along the tier. They threw me in Sirhan Sirhan's old cell in the hole to separate me from the rest of my Panthers. At least I had my own toilet then. Sirhan had a little stove for preparing his food, 'cause everybody wanted to kill him for assassinating Bobby Kennedy and the guards had to keep him isolated. It was isolated, all right. I had two weeks of it: no books, TV, magazines."

ON FEBRUARY 6, 1970, two months after the police raid on Panther headquarters, jailers entered a holding tank where Pratt and four others awaited transport to court and began laying about with batons and blackjacks. Geronimo led the counterattack. "The guards made a tactical mistake. There was six of 'em and they got in each other's way. Some of 'em ended up clubbing each other. We whipped their ass in hand-to-hand combat, knocked one cold, broke some arms and legs. I wasn't ashamed or sorry. It was a setup, an ambush. We defended ourselves."

After the fracas the guards refocused their anger on the Black Panther leader. "Twenty-four hours a day they'd come into my cell and jump me. When I fought back, they filed assault charges. Some of those times I might've been beat to death except that the Vietnam vets on the staff intervened. They knew I'd been a soldier, so they tried to cut me a little slack. After three or four weeks of this, an undersheriff came in and asked if we could negotiate. He said, 'If you back off, we'll back off.' I said, 'Why run your mouth? Just do it.' After that, things improved. I thought about a Frederick Douglass quote I got from Bunchy: 'Power concedes nothing without a struggle.' "

At San Quentin years later, a gnarled old prisoner hugged Geronimo and said, "Thanks for what you boys did at the L.A. Jail. Everything changed after that. First time a white guard ever called me 'Mister!' I wasn't used to all that respect."

On the Road Again

At last Geronimo was freed on bond, and Huey P. Newton ordered him to go underground to help build Panther defenses and open up what Newton called "a revolutionary infrastructure" around the country. The BPP cofounder was facing manslaughter charges himself and becoming increasingly irrational. Some blamed the drugs that eventually destroyed him; some blamed the constant pressure by authorities and his widening split with the Eldridge Cleaver wing. Like his own hero, Bunchy Carter, Pratt leaned toward the Cleaver faction, but he accepted Newton's order without complaint and took to the road. In Philadelphia, New Orleans and Seattle he taught Panthers how to protect themselves from police raids like the ones in Chicago and Los Angeles. A Panther who later became a journalist credited Geronimo in print with saving dozens of lives. "If he hadn't come to Philly and made us stop jiggling and acting complacent—he said, 'This ain't no joke!'—and made us dig tunnels and put up sandbags, Frank Rizzo [police chief and later mayor] would've exterminated us. A lot of good men are alive today because of Geronimo."

After Philadelphia, Pratt traveled to New York, New Haven and Newark, then swung south to Winston-Salem, Atlanta, Birmingham and other cities in the so-called Black Belt. He was distantly aware that he was missing court dates in Los Angeles, but he intended to put off facing the

charges against him as long as possible. He regarded every count as fraudulent; some had already been dismissed by judges who saw through the
LAPD program of harassment. He didn't feel like an outlaw or a criminal;
he felt like a worker doing a job. When a friend informed him that the *Los
Angeles Times* was reporting that he jumped bail, he said, "Well, that's their
way of looking at it." Establishment justice could wait.

IN THE hottest part of the summer of 1970 he reached New Orleans,
where blacks and rats shared living quarters in housing projects that had
been built to improve their lives. His brother Timothy wrote later: "Gerard
seemed obsessed about the way our people had to live in New Orleans. I
think it had something to do with all those trips we made with Daddy as
young men and boys. Everybody knew the Desire Housing Project was the
worst. From their windows the residents could see and smell the muddy
Mississippi. It was as poor as most third-world countries. There were more
people per square mile than in any other place in the United States. All of
the pathologies that accompany poverty and despair—serious crime,
teenage pregnancy, unemployment, functional illiteracy, dropout rates, tru-
ancies, etc.—were extremely high. The people of the Desire Projects were
truly desperate."

ON A steamy Monday afternoon in the ghetto, Geronimo got word that
his father was dead. Stressed and upset, he reached Morgan City in time to
disrupt a scene in the church where he'd served as an altar boy. "The
Rosary was finished," his brother Jackie recalled. "The priest had left, and
we were sitting around reminiscing—Charles, Tim, Emelda, Ginny, Jacqueline, me and Mama. All of a sudden Gerard bursts through the doors. He
glanced at the coffin and saw the rosary beads in Daddy's hands where
Mama had put 'em. Daddy always took a dim view of religious ritual, so
Gerard said, 'You dumb-asses! You got my daddy on *dis*-play? You're not
worthy of sitting here with my daddy.' Then he was out the door.

"When we got home from the wake, Gerard was sitting in Daddy's favorite old rocking chair. Jacqueline started yelling—'Gerard, you listen to
me! We don't need that Panther stuff at a time like this! We don't need some
fool cursing and defiling our church.'

"Mama turned to Jacqueline and said, 'Sit down, child. Leave your
brother alone.' Mama took a seat on the couch and said in her soft voice,

'Do y'all know why Gerard is a Black Panther? Do you have the slightest idea? It's directly because of your daddy.' Gerard, he kept on rocking. Mama said, 'It's because of what your daddy taught him, the way your daddy lived, the example he set. Not a one of you would be what you are today if it wasn't for your daddy. Gerard? Look at me, son. That's true of *you* most of all. You're more like your daddy than anybody.' "

For the first time Geronimo looked up. His eyes glistened, but he didn't speak. With his brothers and sisters, he listened as Eunice Petty Pratt related the full story of their father's life for the first time, from his fatherless childhood through his days in Storyville to his days as a paddleboat cook and drayman. "She talked for three hours," Jackie said. "Told us things we never knew. We sat there like little kids, Gerard no different. When she was finished, we were a family again."

GERONIMO FELT guilty about not visiting his father in the old man's final year. Maybe I should have spent more time at home, he admonished himself. Maybe I should have been the one who wheeled Daddy up and down the alley, talked to him, read to him. What'll Mama do now that she's all alone?

He immersed himself in his work, returning to New Orleans to help start a new BPP unit, then headed to Mobile, Memphis and Shreveport to talk to black groups about self-defense. He'd lost track of his pending hearings. But the Los Angeles Police Department hadn't.

PRATT WAS contacted by his fellow Panther Melvin "Cotton" Smith and advised that Huey Newton had ordered both of them to a meeting in Marshall, Texas, 150 miles east of Dallas. The theme would be unity—"No more bickering," said Smith, who seemed to be recasting himself in the role of Pratt's friend and sidekick. "No more Cleaver faction, no more Newton faction. No more East Coast and West Coast. We all just Panthers, going in a new direction. Us against the pigs."

When Newton failed to appear at the Texas rendezvous, Geronimo was puzzled. "Everything at that point became very weird to me," he testified later. It was time to return to Los Angeles, get back to work in the ghettoes, reunite with his girlfriend Saundra and his Panther brothers. But Cotton Smith urged him to stay put. "Huey'll show up," Smith told him. "There's just some little mistake. You know Huey."

Yes, Geronimo thought, I know Huey. He's been a hero and an inspiration, but right now he's out on bond on a manslaughter rap and spending Panther funds on cocaine, one of the BPP's strongest taboos and grounds for immediate expulsion. Every member knew what was going on but none knew what to do about it.

Pratt tried to contact the supreme commander in Oakland but couldn't seem to connect. "Huey's out of town," a female voice reported. "We don't know exactly where."

Three more days passed before Cotton Smith said he'd finally reached Newton and had been ordered to deliver Geronimo to a BPP safe house in Dallas. As soon as they arrived, Dallas police arrested them on federal UFTAP (unlawful flight to avoid prosecution) warrants. In the jail at 500 Commerce Street Pratt exchanged his brown polyester leisure suit, open-collared shirt, charcoal-colored boots and dark brown leather cap for a bright orange jumpsuit that reeked of disinfectant. He was placed in solitary confinement, "the hole." He wondered what happened to his friend Cotton. The police had rushed him off to another part of the jail.

ON HIS second day of confinement Pratt was visited by an FBI agent who acted as though he were the bearer of good tidings. "Read this," he said, and handed over a copy of a document on Panther stationery. On page one Geronimo saw pictures of himself as a civilian in dark glasses and as a soldier wearing a steel helmet, combat infantryman's badge and paratrooper wings over a U.S. Army patch. The top line read: ON THE PURGE OF GERONIMO FROM THE BLACK PANTHER PARTY.

Pratt blinked as he read a statement from Huey Newton charging him with "44 flagrant violations of our Party's principles." Newton had written: "His devotion and allegiance was still to the ways and rules of the Pig Power Structure. . . . He is as dedicated today to that Pig Agency as he was when he was in Vietnam, killing innocent Vietnamese women and children on various 'search and destroy' missions."

The astonished Geronimo found himself described as "a jackanapes," "pig," "raper of black sisters," "renegade" and "snake" who'd committed the cultural offense of purchasing Christmas presents ("Christmas being the high holiday of the pig capitalists"), threatened to assassinate the Panther supreme commander and other party leaders, used official funds "to purchase alcohol and narcotics for the purpose of indulging himself and his stupid cohorts in nightly bourgeois, orgiastic revelry's," revealed innermost secrets, attempted to organize "a counter-revolutionary little rebel roving band" and violated "the masses of people themselves."

The polemic concluded: "Let it be known, then, that Geronimo (Elmer Gerard Pratt), his wife Sandy Lane Pratt or Saundra Holmes or 'Red' (who worked in concert with him) are forever purged and expelled from the Black Panther Party. Any Party member who attempts to aid them or communicate with them in any form or manner shall be considered a part of their conspiracy to undermine and destroy the Black Panther Party. ALL POWER TO THE PEOPLE!"

Geronimo's first reaction was that Newton had finally lost his mind to drugs and had written the pronouncement in a mental ward. But after sober thought he came up with a more realistic scenario: he was the latest victim in the old East-West Newton-Cleaver feud, a fight that had escalated to the point where Cleaver supporters tried to assassinate Newton by blowing out a brick wall at the San Francisco Panther office.

In such a charged atmosphere no one could please both sides. Like Bunchy and John Huggins and Long John Washington before him, Pratt had backed Eldridge while trying not to alienate Huey. In the past this confused allegiance might have been a minor annoyance to the Newton forces, but apparently it was now a capital offense.

DAYS PASSED as Geronimo spent his jail time writing inspirational letters to fellow Panthers and friends. He still mourned the loss of Carter and Huggins, and he wrote a friend in a newly florid style: "The example set by John and Bunchy serves as an illuminous flame in a dark path that has many twists and turns. Without it we surely would be like blind men groping in the dark. . . . We will halt the rotation and orbitation of this planet, seize the time, and have our say on anything or anyone that gets in the way of our freedom. If I were not to reach our goal, then color me a radiant red, dead, with a bullet in my head."

He was in no hurry to return to the city where he'd spent so much time posting bond and looking over his shoulder. No one came to visit him in Dallas, and his requests for information were ignored. He tried to reach out to Saundra in Los Angeles, but his entreaties went unanswered. He remained bewildered about his expulsion from the BPP. What happened to my friends? he asked himself. What happened to my Panthers? We were tighter than I'd ever been with my platoon in Vietnam—and now I'm a pig and a traitor.

He wrote an anguished note to another colleague: "No one in Oakland has even tried to contact me about the matter—we're still trying to figure out the root cause. . . . David Hilliard was (I thought) closer to me than any of my blood brothers and he's the main one who upset me so. . . . I sent him reports and tried to call, also I had my lawyer to deliver some messages. All this to no avail."

A jailer informed him he was being held incommunicado at the request of the LAPD's Criminal Conspiracy Section, successor to the department's notorious "Red Squad." He learned later that the CCS had been searching for him for months—"they were told I was with Eldridge in Algiers, in Moscow, Paris, Nairobi, or I was in South America with Che Guevara. That was the first time I began to realize that the cops thought I was a whole lot bigger than I really was. They'd built me into a world-class revolutionary."

SOMEONE ALERTED Pratt's Dallas jailers that the rabble-rousing inmate needed special attention. "They beat me so bad they had to take me to Parkland Hospital, the same place where President Kennedy was pronounced dead. Then they threw me in the tank with about eight guys, including a black dude named Trainwreck. He was maybe six-four, two-sixty, had a big dent down his forehead. First thing I saw was Trainwreck trying to rape a little brother with a greased-up broom handle. It was as bad as anything in Nam. The boy kept screaming and Trainwreck kept trying to shove this broom handle up his butt, kissing him on the ears, slobbering, holding and choking him at the same time. I said, 'Hey, man, leave that kid alone!' We fought for an hour, just me and Trainwreck, and I wore his ass out. After that I began to get some respect from the prisoners. Word went out, 'Lay off Pratt.' A couple of Panthers were thrown in the tank and told me things were bad on the outside. 'Since you left, we slidin' downhill. Party's breaking apart. Cops sent in so many snitches, you're afraid to talk to *anybody*.' "

AFTER TWO months in the Dallas Jail Geronimo was returned to California by the point man on his case, Sergeant Raymond Callahan of the LAPD. In Los Angeles Pratt immediately came under investigation for a laundry list of unsolved crimes: the theft of guns from the Camp Pendleton Marine Base, an unsolved robbery in Alabama, the infamous Tate-LaBianca murders in Hollywood and other open cases.

At first he was held in solitary confinement in the "glass house" in Parker Center. The unsprung metal rack was hard on his bad back. He slept for five or ten minutes at a time but only when exhausted. He dreamed about torched villages, roasted flesh and eyes pecked out by crows; snakes, rats, leeches, spiders, ants and lice. A jail psychiatrist diagnosed his sleep problem as "excessive anxiety and nervousness" complicated by the "harassment and intimidation" by jailers, and put him on the tranquilizer Librium.

Needle fragments still pierced his intestines, causing alternating bouts of constipation and diarrhea. For all his desensitizing army experience and bivouac training, he still felt embarrassed when guards walked past his cell as he strained over the hole in the floor. Some stopped and peered in. "I'm not putting on a damn show!" Pratt snapped at a crew-cut young deputy.

The guard observed that he had a cute little ass.

A FEW days after the return from Dallas Geronimo appeared in Los Angeles Superior Court in clogs and chains to hear himself arraigned for first-degree murder and conspiracy to murder police officers in the raids on December 8, 1969. He wasn't surprised about the charges. During the police campaign against the Panthers he and his colleagues had often been arrested on suspicion of murder; when the legal holding period expired, the charges were dropped. But this time the charges hadn't been brought by cops. They'd been brought by the Los Angeles County district attorney.

"What the hell is this 187 P.C. crap?" he asked his lawyer, Luke McKissack, after the hearing. "Who'd I murder now?"

The attorney riffled through the court papers and asked if he remembered the tennis court shootings in Santa Monica on December 18, 1968.

"I was in Oakland then."

"Can you prove it?"

"Easy."

"The police report says your car was seen in the neighborhood."

"My little GTO? I left it with a couple of Panthers—Franco Diggs and Bunchy."

"Can you prove that?"

"Yep."

The lawyer said there didn't seem to be anything to worry about.

FOUR CRUISERWEIGHT deputies transferred Pratt to the new Los Angeles County Jail after the arraignment. Who am I? he asked himself. Superblack? Why do I need a thousand pounds of guard?

Inside his cell he held out his wrists so the handcuffs could be unlocked. A blow across the back of his neck sent him sprawling. One of the deputies said, "Boy, you killed a white woman."

When Geronimo tried to stand, he was slammed against the wall. He landed a two-handed chop before he went down in a flurry of punches and kicks. He awoke naked and alone. A guard told him he'd been sentenced to "BAAC" (bare ass and concrete) indefinitely. He would be fed bread and water twice a day.

WHILE HE was recovering from his injuries, Pratt heard from McKissack. "This 187 P.C.?" the lawyer said. "The D.A. is serious, Geronimo. You were secretly indicted in December. Several witnesses testified. One of 'em said you confessed to the tennis court murder three or four times."

"I confessed?" he said. "To who?"

"Julio Butler."

FLASHBACK: Murder Most Foul

At 8:00 P.M. on December 18, 1968, two years before Geronimo Pratt was arrested in Dallas, Barbara Mary Reed had watched nervously as two light-skinned black men entered her store. A short, elderly shopkeeper, she owned and operated the Lincoln Hobby Center on the busy corner of Lincoln Boulevard and Broadway in Santa Monica. She was alone and about to close. The taller of the two men moved to the back and studied the rare-coin cases. The other went to the storeroom and peered inside.

She felt relieved when they drifted toward the front. "May I help you?" she asked.

The shorter man said he needed materials to build a dollhouse for his wife. "Oh, I don't carry that," she said.

He said, "Is there any reason why you won't sell it to me?"

"I *can't* sell it to you," she answered. "I don't stock items like that."

She walked behind them as they left, locked the door and reversed the sign in the window from "Yes we're OPEN!" to "Sorry we're CLOSED." As she watched, the pair walked north, then stopped. One of the men returned, jiggled her door and yelled, "Let me in!"

A pearl-handled pistol glittered in his right hand. She stepped backward and dialed police. When her husband arrived a few minutes later to drive her home, the intruders were gone. He told her that he'd seen two black men walk to the Radio Shack parking lot a block north and disappear.

IT WAS a clear night, the temperature in the forties, subarctic weather for Santa Monicans, and Kenneth Crismon Olsen, thirty-one-year-old head of the English department at Belmont High School, looked forward to a few sets of tennis with his ex-wife Caroline. The Olsens were divorced but discussing reconciliation.

He parked on Wilshire Boulevard at the Lincoln Park tennis court, four blocks from the Lincoln Hobby Center, and accompanied Caroline to the center court. Both were dressed in tennis whites, V-neck pullovers and white tennis shoes. Kenneth set his gear on a bench, and Caroline, a twenty-seven-year-old second-grade schoolteacher, laid her purse alongside and fished for a quarter to activate the coin-operated light switch.

Olsen saw that she seemed to be having trouble with the meter. As he walked over to help, he spotted two figures entering the enclosure. He wasn't concerned and barely registered their arrival. He dropped the coin into the slot for thirty minutes of playing time and watched the shadows turn to incandescent green, white and black. As he walked back toward the bench with Caroline, the men approached. He saw that they were armed.

"All right," one of them snapped, "hands up!"

The robbers mumbled between themselves, and the same man said, "Yeah, hands up! *Now!* We want your bread."

Caroline pointed to her white Naugahyde purse on the bench. Kenneth removed the black leather wallet and car keys from his racket bag and handed them over.

"Eighteen bucks," the talkative robber said. "That ain't enough." Olsen said he had more money in his car.

"Turn off the lights."

Olsen said the switch was on a timer and couldn't be turned off. "You'll have to shoot them out if you want them out."

"Get down," the robber said. "Lay down and pray!"

With their noses to the tarmac the couple heard a few receding footsteps, then silence. Olsen looked up and saw that the two men were standing six or eight feet away. As he watched, they turned and raised their guns. A volley of shots rang out and slugs tore into his body.

Caroline moaned as the gunmen ran out the exit to the street. Ken asked, "Are you okay? Can you move?"

He tried to help her up but she seemed paralyzed. Bleeding from a head wound, he realized that he had to get help before he fainted. He staggered across the street to the Broken Drum restaurant.

"We've been shot," he gasped to a waitress. "My wife is on the tennis court and she can't move or speak. Please—help us." Then he collapsed.

BACK AT the hobby shop, Santa Monica Patrolman Richard Plasse was taking a report from Barbara Reed when an emergency signal crackled over his police radio: "Shots fired at the Broken Drum. Victim down."

Plasse radioed a Code III ambulance request and sped to the nearby restaurant. He found a man spattered with blood from his face to his bare muscular legs. His head was swathed in a blood-flecked towel. The man pointed in the direction of the tennis courts and said, "My wife's been shot."

The patrolman ran across the street and saw a woman lying facedown, her hands doubled over her midsection. "Why?" she was moaning. "Why? *Why?* We gave them the money."

Barely conscious, the woman described the gunmen as black, about twenty-five years old, five-eight to five-nine, weighing about 140 pounds.

DOCTORS AT Santa Monica Emergency Hospital found two bullet wounds in Caroline Olsen's lower chest and an exit wound in her back. A slug remained in her body. She was listed in critical condition. Kenneth Olsen had suffered a broken thumb, a wound to his right forearm and crease wounds on his stomach and forehead. He was listed as satisfactory.

PATROLMAN PLASSE and a homicide detective team converged on the tennis court and found three .45-caliber shell casings and three spent slugs. Players at the Santa Monica Chess Club, less than one hundred feet from the scene, told the officers that they'd heard what they thought were firecrackers or backfires. Another witness said he'd heard gunshots and followed a man wearing a light-colored car coat as he ran from the tennis court area into the shadows. He described the runner as Caucasian. Two other men told the investigators that they'd been getting into their van when they saw two black men entering the Lincoln Park area. A few minutes later they heard five to seven shots and saw the men run from the park and get into a car, "possibly a 1964 to 1968 dark red, possibly blood red vehicle with a white convertible top . . . very clean and shiny . . . and a white license plate." The car had left tire marks as it accelerated north on Seventh Street.

AT THE hospital Kenneth Olsen told detectives that he'd seen the robbers at a distance of two to three feet. On the basis of his information, police listed suspect no. 1 as a clean-shaven Negro, about twenty-five years old, five-eight to five-nine, 140 pounds, with black hair and unknown eye color, "possibly dark," and wearing a "brown leather waist-length coat, suede possibly." Suspect no. 2 was described as a Negro, twenty-two or twenty-three, five-ten, 140, dark eyes, wearing a leather waist-length coat and light pants.

BARBARA REED provided sharper detail. The shopkeeper said that the taller man had been a six-footer, twenty-three to twenty-nine years old, "thin build, 155, medium complexion, very clean looking, narrow shoulders and hips, wearing dark pants and shoes, light tan or beige jacket, with loops hanging down on each side; wore a dark shirt or sweater underneath."

The shorter man, she told police, was twenty-three to twenty-nine, five-eight or five-nine, 145 to 150 pounds, "medium light complexion, clean looking, very trim haircut, black shoes, black or dark pants, Eisenhower-type jacket, light beige, rust or brown colored shirt or sweater underneath the jacket."

She helped a police technician to assemble Identikit composites of the shooters, and bulletins were prepared showing facial close-ups of two clean-shaven black men with short hair and no scars. Later Mrs. Reed explained that she was disappointed in the Identikit results on no. 2, the shorter man, because the technician didn't have a template small enough to match his thin mouth and nose.

CAROLINE OLSEN remained in a coma through Christmas and appeared to be recovering, but eleven days after the shootings she died of "suppurative peritonitis, with hemorrhage due to gunshot wound penetrating multiple viscera," as the coroner reported.

With the case upgraded to homicide, Santa Monica detectives faced the typical problems of an investigation involving cross-racial descriptions and identifications. They had little doubt that the killers were African American, but motorist Ralph Bryan's description of them as Caucasian suggested the possibility that the other witnesses were wrong or that a third man, a white, had been involved. The detectives realized they were dealing with impulse killers, amateurs, the maddest of mad dogs. There was no earthly reason to fire at victims who'd already been robbed and were prone on their stomachs. Every element of the crime, from the confrontation in the hobby shop to the shootings on the tennis court, spelled unreason and irrationality, probably caused by narcotics, liquor or both.

FOR ALMOST a year after the Christmas season of 1968, Santa Monica detectives kept Kenneth Olsen and Barbara Reed busy studying mug books and posters. Photos and information on similar crimes arrived from Modesto and Van Nuys and other California cities, leaving police to wonder if the tennis court killers might still be active. Reed never wavered from her insistence that she would be able to make a positive identification if the right photo turned up. But Olsen was a problem; in the trauma of losing the woman he loved, he seemed overeager for revenge. A Los Angeles deputy D.A., Ronald Carroll, later described the school administrator as "a little flaky" and said that the Santa Monica police "had little confidence" in his ability to make a positive ID.

DESPITE THEIR misgivings, detectives enlisted Olsen's aid after they received information on December 12, 1969, that the Van Nuys division of the LAPD was investigating a similar case. The police said that five days after a robbery, a suspect named Ernest James Perkins had returned to fire a shot at his victim. Now Perkins was in custody, charged with attempted murder, and a warrant was out for his suspected accomplice in the robbery, Stanley Vance. Santa Monica detectives sent for head-shot photos and rap sheets on the suspects.

A few days after the first anniversary of the tennis court shootings, Olsen was summoned to headquarters for the eighteenth time. His face lit up as he studied an array of mug shots and identified Perkins and Vance as the men who had murdered his wife. He said he would like to see them in a live lineup.

Police still hadn't tracked down Stanley Vance, but at 10:00 A.M. the day before Christmas they paraded the twenty-year-old Ernest James Perkins and five other young black men past Olsen as he sat behind a one-way mirror. This time the school administrator made a positive identification.

Detectives redoubled their efforts to find Perkins' crime partner so they could wrap up the case. But a routine check established that on the night of the shootings Perkins had been locked in a prison facility at Tracy, nearly four hundred miles north of Santa Monica. The police were reluctant to give up on a suspect who'd been selected with such certainty, and they drove to Tracy to examine bed-check records to see if Perkins might have been AWOL on the murder night. He and every other inmate had been marked present at a bed check. Kenneth Crismon Olsen had been confident, positive and wrong.

Accused

As the second anniversary of the tennis court murder approached, Santa Monica police all but gave up on the case. Hundreds of man-hours had been wasted on false leads. Repeated show-ups had produced nothing but misidentifications and confusion.

Then the LAPD's Panther Unit produced explosive new information. A Black Panther squad leader named Julius "Julio" Butler had named the Southern California leader, Geronimo Pratt, as one of the killers. A few days after Pratt expelled him from the party on August 5, 1969, Butler had written out his charges and turned them over to a police friend in a sealed envelope on which he'd scrawled "to be opened in the event of my death." Then he'd passed word to the FBI and the Panther hierarchy that he'd written "an insurance policy." His letter, he claimed privately, could put Panthers in the gas chamber and would be made public if he were ever harmed.

Semiliterate passages appeared to border on hysteria. "At the time of this writing I've been working and living under the threat of assassination by Local and National Leaders of the Black Panther. Namely Bobby Seale, (Chairman of the Black Panther Party) Elmer G. ('Geronimo') Pratt, (Dep. Minister of Defense, So. Calif. Area), John ('Long John') Washington (So.

Calif. Field Sec. Rank of Major), Rodger ('Blue') Lewis (Body-guard and Assasin, Rank of Capt.) Omar (In Charge of Goon Squad, Locally)."

Butler's letter spoke of "the party changing its direction" and of how he'd been "Relieved of all duties and official working capacities." He described an evening when "A Heat discussion grew out of the fact I still Refuse to Adhere to this New gang Like Direction and was order shut up, at which time Long John Drew a Rugers Black Hawk 357 Magnum and cocked it to full cock and pointed it at my Head, then Geronimo shouted several times 'shoot him, if you don't shoot him, I'll shoot you.' "

In his letter the hairstylist addressed the widespread rumors that he was a police agent and informer. "I heard 'Long John' state 'Julio is a pig. He is Receiving $1,200.00 per month from the C.I.A. and the Los Angeles Police Dept., That they Had evidence proving my badge number and Rank in the C.I.A. He also stated I was the one who killed Capt. Franco, and I was the man Responsible for the Deaths of 'Bunchy' Carter and John Huggins at UCLA And that the order was out to Kill me, to save the people's Liberation struggle . . . I've Continually Received calls by persons unknown 'such as you're a Dead man,' you know too much and must die."

Butler cited "the following reason I feel the Death threat may be carried out. Through Listening to Breggado conversation with these men, myself and other persons Have Reasonable cause to believe these persons were Responsible for Acts of murder they carelessly Bragged about. No. 1: Geronimo for the Killing of a White School Teacher and the wounding of Her husband on a Tennis Court in the City of Santa Monica some time during the year of 1968. No. 2: Geronimo and Blue being Responsible for the Killing of Capt. Franco (Black Panther Party) in Jan 1969 and constantly stating as a threat to me that I was just like Franco and gave them No Alternative but to 'Wash me Away.' "

The letter ended, "I can not Afford to testify to this in court because this Letter Represents the only Real Protection I have for my family. All the Above Statements are true and done by my own Hand, and of my own free will."

THE "INSURANCE letter" from Pratt's deadliest enemy remained unopened for months until it came to light in the course of a police internal affairs investigation. In normal times the note might have been considered the work of a vengeful crank and ignored. But the times were far from normal. For two years the LAPD had been fighting the Panthers, stopping BPP cars, bringing false charges, cannonading party buildings, arresting Panthers for cursing in public and jaywalking.

Los Angeles detectives immediately wrested the murder case from the Santa Monica police. The new ramrod would be Sergeant Raymond Callahan of the Criminal Conspiracy Section, working closely with the FBI. On a tip from an anonymous informer, Callahan sent an arrest team into the South-Central area to pick up a nineteen-year-old Panther named Tyrone Hutchinson, whose main connection with the case seemed to be the fact that he was six feet tall and built like a toothpick. Hutchinson was held for felony possession of marijuana and investigation of murder.

In a high-intensity session at police headquarters, Sergeant Callahan told the frightened Panther that he'd been positively identified as Geronimo Pratt's accomplice in the tennis court murder. Hutchinson responded with a positive ID of his own. He said he knew the real killers. They were his neighborhood homeboys Herbert Swilley and Larry "Dobey" Hatter, who were friendly with Julio Butler. Lately the young addicts had turned to increasingly flagrant crimes to support their heroin habits. In one narcotic rampage Swilley had attacked his mother, broken his girlfriend's nose and tried to drown his sister in the bathtub. Hutchinson told Callahan that the two muggers had talked about the tennis court murder and seemed pleased that their victims had cowered in fear before they were shot. The killers had mentioned the time, date and location but refused to discuss crucial questions such as who fired the fatal shots.[16]

The "Panther Unit" leader asked if anyone else had been present during the confessions, and Hutchinson named three other men who'd been in the Black Panther office at Eighty-fourth and Broadway when Swilley and Hatter, high on narcotics, swaggered in to boast of their murderous score.

Four days after his arrest Hutchinson was freed. In his official report Callahan described the Panther as "uncooperative." Police made no effort to interview the other witnesses to the Swilley-Hatter confessions. As private investigator James McCloskey reported years later, "Callahan did not pursue the Swilley and Hatter leads because he already had his case built against the notorious BPP leader Pratt and was now looking for the sec-

---

[16] Kenneth Olsen had reported that both robbers fired their weapons.

ond, taller suspect. New and different suspects were obliterated by his blind focus on Geronimo."

After failing to advance his case against Pratt, Callahan buried all references to Tyrone Hutchinson and turned back to his original eyewitnesses and his new star, Julio Butler. For someone dedicated to bringing down the Panthers and their leaders, this appeared to be more fertile territory.

ON DECEMBER 3, 1970, two weeks before the second anniversary of Caroline Olsen's death, a deputy D.A. ushered Butler before the Los Angeles County Grand Jury.[17] For the record the hairdresser declared that he was appearing against his will, then launched into hours of testimony against the leader who'd expelled him from the Panthers. In Butler's version of events, he and Pratt had been warm friends who freely exchanged innermost secrets.

He was asked if he'd seen Pratt "on a particular evening in December 1968."

"I did." Butler testified that Pratt had visited his shop in the company of another black man named Tyrone. Pratt had called him outside because of a fear that the hairdressing parlor might be bugged.

Before the deputy D.A. continued the questioning, he introduced a subject that later would become of crucial importance. "By the way," he said, "were you working for any law enforcement agency at that time?"

"No."

"Were you an agent of the CIA or anything of that sort?"

"No."

Butler identified a picture of the white-over-red GTO "Panther car" and claimed that the ex-paratrooper Pratt carried a .45-caliber semiautomatic in a shoulder holster or in his waistband "most of the time."

On the day after he'd been visited by Geronimo and Tyrone, Butler continued, he read newspaper accounts of a shooting in Santa Monica "and then I think it was later that evening or the next day I saw [Pratt] at the Panthers' office. . . . He said he had shot some people. He said it was in the City of Santa Monica and he was hot." Butler told the grand

---

[17] On the same day, the road warrior Geronimo Pratt was speaking at a meeting of Stokely Carmichael's Student Nonviolent Coordinating Committee in Atlanta.

jurors that several weeks later Pratt told him that he'd destroyed the barrel on his .45 and that Bunchy Carter had ordered him to get rid of the hot GTO.

AFTER BRIEFINGS about the suspected killer by the D.A.'s Office, Barbara Mary Reed and Kenneth Olsen told their own stories to the grand jurors. Each had already selected Pratt from photo lineups. Their earliest description of killer no. 2, the shorter gunman, was that he was five-eight or five-nine, with a light-skinned complexion and wearing a jacket. In the photo spread of sixteen young African American males shown to Reed, only three of the men were under six feet, as shown by the height markers next to their heads. Thus the lineup was effectively reduced to three. Of these, two were noticeably dark-skinned, unlike Pratt, and Pratt was the only one wearing a jacket. As attorney Stuart Hanlon was to say years later, "That was a photo lineup of one." Overzealous police and prosecutors had used similar techniques for years.

Reed told the jurors that she based her selection of Pratt on his face and jacket, which she now described as a "safari jacket." On the night of the killing, two years earlier, she'd referred to an "Eisenhower-type" jacket. The discrepancy, six or eight inches of length and major differences of style, went unexplained. When the deputy D.A. pointed out that Pratt had facial hair, Mrs. Reed answered, "Yes, but he was clean-shaven when he was in the store." She made no mention of a widow's peak, which she'd described to police earlier, perhaps because no widow's peak or other unusual hair characteristics appeared on the Identikit she'd helped to assemble at the time of the killing. Nor did she mention facial scars. Since childhood, Geronimo Pratt had had two conspicuous chicken pox scars on his forehead.

IN HIS own testimony Kenneth Olsen made it seem as though he'd never been certain about his identification of Ernest James Perkins, contradicting his positive ID for the Santa Monica police. The school administrator had been shown some five hundred photographs of young black men before selecting Pratt. Almost as though he'd been briefed on the suspect's biography, he made a point of stressing the gunman's "military" bearing. "I mean, he may not have a military background, I am just saying there was a very commanding . . . he sounded like he could have been a drill instructor or something, I don't know." Pratt had been a drill instructor at Fort Bragg. The witness seemed to know his subject.

ON THE basis of the information provided by Butler, Reed and Olsen, the grand jury returned a sealed indictment charging Elmer Gerard Pratt with the murder of Caroline Olsen, assault with intent to commit the murder of her husband and additional counts of robbery and conspiracy. This was the indictment that was opened in Superior Court when Sergeant Ray Callahan returned Pratt from Texas. It had been sealed for two months.

Disorder in the Court

Before he could defend himself against the murder charge, Geronimo Pratt had to appear in court in the original conspiracy case, a grab bag of seventy-two counts that had been brought against him, his common-law wife Saundra, and eleven other Panthers after the raid that destroyed their Central Avenue headquarters. The tennis court murder case would have to wait its turn; the new and mysterious charges were bothersome, but Geronimo expected the matter to fade away as soon as the D.A. verified that he'd been in Oakland on the night of the shootings and could call a dozen witnesses to prove it. Besides, what jury would believe the likes of Julio Butler?

From the first sharp rap of Superior Court Judge George Dell's gavel, it became clear that the District Attorney's Office planned a show trial that would damage the Panthers' image, if not finish them off. In his opening statement a deputy D.A. promised to prove that Geronimo Pratt and his henchmen had stockpiled weapons, conspired to kill lawmen and lured the police into a murderous firefight.

The defense, including Pratt's new lawyer Marvin Zinman, responded that the LAPD had subjected the Panthers to a two-year campaign of harassment in a deliberate attempt to provoke a serious incident, and that the Panthers had fortified their headquarters in anticipation of the same type of midnight raids that had resulted in Panther deaths in other cities. As

Johnnie L. Cochran Jr. said in his opening statement on behalf of his client Willie Stafford, "We will show that the LAPD got exactly what it asked for. They attacked, the Panthers defended. That's called self-preservation. It's the oldest rule of nature."

FROM THE first testimony it was clear that the state's case would be built on inside information. In the racial crucibles of Watts and South-Central L.A. it had never been difficult for police to develop informers. In exchange for information, deals were made with prosecutors, charges reduced or dropped, records expunged, favors granted. Members of street gangs were quick to "drop the dime" about a rival group's activities. Certain disenfranchised blacks would "snitch off" their best friends for a twenty-dollar bill or a pat on the back.

Zinman, Cochran and their fellow defense attorneys found their defense sabotaged by witnesses and prosecutors who seemed to know their every strategy in advance, a crippling liability in any litigation. "Sometimes, it seemed that they could read our minds," Cochran wrote later. "Maybe, I thought, they're that good; maybe they're just lucky. As it turned out, they were neither. They were the skulking beneficiaries of lawless treachery. . . . One of my co-counsels in the Panther trial was an FBI informant. . . . When he was confronted with his misconduct, [he] said he informed because he feared the Panthers were plotting to escape. His excuse was as contemptible as his conduct. Sadly, he would not be the last of his loathsome species I would encounter."

AS THE months dragged on in what would become the longest conspiracy trial in California history, the prosecution relied heavily on the marathon testimony of Melvin "Cotton" Smith, the police informer who'd steered Pratt into their hands in Dallas. Day after day the ex-convict rang variations on his central theme that the Panthers intended to start a revolution by killing "pigs." On Friday, July 23, 1971, five months after the tedious trial opened, he testified that the official BPP slogan was "Off the Pigs."[18] When he was asked to name Panthers who'd used the expression, he pointed into

---

[18] The official slogan was "Power to the People."

the courtroom and said, "I've heard every Panther in the room make that statement."

"I didn't know we had Panthers in the audience," Judge Dell commented. "Welcome, gentlemen."

The forty-two-year-old Smith told how Geronimo Pratt and his attack teams "used to go into the sewers at night and make maps trying to find 77th Station," their leader ordering his men to "find a place under there close enough to blow the place up." The informer told of serving on one such mission and wearing a mask against the sewer gas. Pratt, he said, led the subterranean party with a submachine gun. Sometimes the sewer mappers became lost under the city streets. Smith also described the digging of an "escape tunnel" that remained unfinished on the night of the police raid.

During a recess Pratt admitted to his lawyer, Marvin Zinman, that there'd been indifferent attempts at digging a tunnel to provide a safe haven from police firepower and to collect dirt for the sandbags that eventually saved their lives—"a defensive measure, like everything else we did." As for the sewer searches, he said, "What dumb son of a bitch would take a submachine gun into a tunnel? To shoot who?"

The lawyer asked Pratt how Cotton Smith had managed to insinuate himself into the party's inner circles. "I wish I knew," Pratt said. "He fooled me, fooled Bunchy, fooled everybody. He was a good liar, I guess."

Zinman reminded him of the old expression "When you lie down with dogs, you get up with fleas."

"Right on," Geronimo replied, "but you don't expect to get up with rats."

AFTER A weekend break Cotton Smith provided lurid testimony that appeared in the *Los Angeles Times* under the headline PANTHERS TAUGHT CHILDREN TO HATE POLICE. The ex-convict informer told of female teachers rehearsing children in lyrics like "Piggy wiggy, you got to go now. Oink, oink. Bang, bang! . . . They were taught to draw pictures of people killing these pigs . . . people sticking knives in them and shooting them." He told of his horror at seeing a seven-year-old boy playing with a pipe bomb at Panther headquarters. "I asked him what he was doing with it and since he didn't have any business with it, I took it away."

The star witness's most eloquent testimony concerned the raid on Panther headquarters. Neglecting to mention that he'd been acting as an FBI agent provocateur, he told the jury, "We were supposed to kill them at the door and then take our weapons and leave. When the people arrived there they didn't want them to find anything but dead pigs."

IN NOVEMBER, nine months into the trial, Pratt's attorney Zinman and Willie Stafford's attorney Cochran held a brief meeting with Pratt in the lockup. "Mr. Cochran just wanted to shake your hand," Zinman said. "You guys are a mutual admiration society."

Geronimo had watched Cochran in action and spoken highly of him in a conversation with his friend Stafford. "That guy's cool," Pratt had said. "I like the way he wears his natural—not afraid to look black. Most of these black lawyers are imitation whites."

Pratt was also impressed by Cochran's passionate advocacy. In court the aggressive young lawyer acted as though his own fate was on the line. Long after his colleagues had subsided, Cochran would remain on his feet, challenging witnesses, poking the air, demanding that his client be accorded his rights under the U.S. and California Constitutions, which he often cited line by line. When a deputy D.A. referred to Stafford as "Willie," Cochran jumped to his feet. "Are you referring to *Mister* Stafford?" he asked. Judge Dell had threatened him with contempt several times.

After a handshake in the attorneys' interview room, Geronimo learned that Cochran was born in Louisiana but had gone west on the Sunset Limited at the age of six. "My Creole uncle, Aristide Albert, was a pullman porter on that train," the lawyer said.

Pratt laughed and told him that fellow Panthers Bunchy Carter, Eldridge Cleaver, Huey Newton and several others had traveled the same route. "None of y'all knew it," Geronimo said, "but you passed right behind my house. Morgan City was only a flag stop. We used to say that's why they called it the Sunset *Limited*."

The ex-Louisianans discovered something else in common: both had been undersized high school quarterbacks. Cochran recalled the advice of his Los Angeles high school coach to the team's linemen: "The quarterback is like your mother. Don't let anybody get to him. Don't let them get in there and blindside Cochran."

"At Morgan City Colored High," Pratt said, "we had a different approach. *Run for your life!*"

The reminiscences were interrupted by the unexpected arrival of

Sergeant Raymond Callahan of the LAPD's Panther Unit. "We just identified a Jane Doe at the morgue," the Panther Unit leader told Pratt. "Your wife's dead. So's your baby." The body of the pregnant Saundra "Red" Lee had been found in a sleeping bag in a suburban gutter, shot five times, once through the stomach.

Cochran wrote later: "To the day I die, I will retain two memories of that awful moment—Geronimo's nearly imperceptible but successful struggle to retain his composure and the smirk that played across the detective's face."

TIMOTHY PRATT stood in for his jailed brother at Saundra's funeral services and recited a passage from "Black Mother," a poem that Bunchy Carter had written just before his death:

> Black mother, I must confess that I still live though you are not free.
> Forgive my coward's heart,
> The frenzy of the whole thing. Screaming, crying, Black Power . . .

In his cell Geronimo wondered if the increasingly narcotized Huey Newton and his cohorts had been behind the execution. Saundra, free on bail, had been a fervent supporter of Newton's enemy Cleaver and had served as a link between Geronimo and the exiled Panther leader. Until her last days she'd received death threats from the Newton faction.

THE *Los Angeles Times* continued its intense coverage of the Panthers under the headline PANTHER SLAYING MAY BE START OF CLEAVER-NEWTON SHOWDOWN. Moderate members of the feuding factions viewed the article as a blatant attempt to widen the schism. The same reporter who had once described Pratt as a trained "assassin" and "a disastrous by-product of the Vietnam war" now related a police theory that Newton's hit men had tortured Pratt's mistress while "trying to learn from her when Cleaver would be returning to the United States."[19]

---

[19] It was years before Geronimo learned the truth about the murder, and it turned out to be unrelated to the Cleaver-Newton feud. "Red's problems went back to her New York days,

ON MONDAY, November 15, talk of retribution was in the air, and court personnel on the eighth floor of the Hall of Justice were tense. Deputies with shotguns waited for riot calls. The Panther defendants entered the courtroom reluctantly after milling around in the holding tank for almost an hour. Newton's supporters were assigned to one table, Cleaver's to another. Just as the jurors were taking their seats, a Cleaver backer clubbed the nearest Newton supporter with a briefcase. The melee was on.

As Cochran, Zinman and a dozen other attorneys scrambled for safety, Judge Dell and the prosecutors backed toward the judge's chambers, open jackets revealing the side arms that were supposed to be banned in the courtroom.

The aggravated Pratt felt disappointed in his warriors and tried to hold them back. "These were *my* Panthers," he explained later. "My Panthers are supposed to be disciplined."

But when deputies waded in with shotgun barrels and clubs, he joined in the fight. "It was like nothing any of us had ever seen before," Cochran wrote later. "They began beating our clients, and, within seconds, the courtroom floor literally was awash in blood." Geronimo ended up prone on the prosecution table, a shotgun muzzle a few inches from his face.

A headline in the next day's *Los Angeles Times* informed readers: HUSBAND OF SLAIN WOMAN LEADS ATTACK. Elmer Pratt, the article said, "was charging after [Albert] Armour who had fled to the jury box when a deputy pointed a revolver at his head and yelled, 'Pratt, stop! Get back over there.'"

Pratt recalled later, "By then, the newspapers had trashed me so bad they could've accused me of the Lindbergh kidnapping and people would

---

long before we ever met. She'd worked as a madam and tricked with a Jewish guy in the mob. When she first hooked up with the Panthers, she gave us inside information about the New York crime families, how the mob pushed heroin into schools in Harlem, Bed-Stuy, Jamaica, Queens, names and dates about hits—*heavy* stuff. The Panthers had a strict no-drugs policy and we flashed our people in New York to run the Mafia out of our neighborhoods. The mob found out she'd violated their code of *omerta* and killed her trick with the big mouth. She told me there was a contract on her, too, but I said, 'Stick tight with us, baby, and you'll be safe.' Then I went to jail and she was defenseless. The LAPD tipped the mob where she was staying. A Mafia hit man executed her slow and easy, shot her in the arms, then in the leg, and then in the stomach. I guess she still wouldn't tell 'em what they wanted to know, so he shot her in the head."

believe it. I'm not even sure I hit *any*body. I just reacted, that's all. I *hate* to think of Panthers fighting Panthers. The cops always used the media to make us look like gorillas. They were better at propaganda than we ever were."

IN THE days following the brawl, Judge Dell clamped down on belligerents and attorneys. While waiting to enter the court, Pratt and the other prisoners were separated and chained. A sign was posted informing lawyers that "the bailiffs' first responsibility is courtroom security," a veiled warning that hostages would be on their own. Defense lawyers found their objections routinely overruled. Cochran was held in contempt for arriving late from lunch, an offense usually disciplined by a frown or a few words.

To worsen matters, race relations had been deteriorating in California courts and prisons following a bloody chain of events that started when a white guard killed three black convicts at Soledad Prison and inmates retaliated by pitching a guard to his death from an upper tier. After career criminal George Jackson was charged with the murder, his teenage brother Jonathan tried to break him out of prison and turned the San Rafael County courthouse into an abattoir. Not long afterward, George Jackson started a shooting war of his own that ended with the deaths of three guards and three prisoners, including himself. African American convicts hailed Jackson as a martyr and mounted rebellions in San Jose, Dallas, Boston, San Antonio and other cities. The bloodiest uprising came in September 1971 at Attica in upstate New York, where thirty-one prisoners and nine guards died in the worst riot in American prison history. The Los Angeles Hall of Justice wasn't the only place where courtroom personnel began to carry guns.

ON THURSDAY, December 9, 1971, three months after Attica, Johnnie Cochran nodded to his parents in the courtroom and began his final argument on behalf of his client Stafford. Preparing his remarks the night before, he'd decided to jettison the flowery formalities that he'd been taught at Loyola Law School. He had mixed feelings about the lead prosecutor, Ronald M. "Mike" Carroll, whose case relied so heavily on turncoat information from the underworld. This jury was markedly different from the typical white middle-class Los Angeles jury; it consisted of two whites, six African Americans, three Chicanos and an Asian American. One of these jurors, Cochran told himself, is bound to have street experience with cops and informers and be skeptical of their motives. He'd already seen suggestions of doubt in their facial expressions.

He began his closing comments with an evisceration. He described Cotton Smith's lifetime of crime, outlined his duplicities and drubbed him with epithets like "lower than a snake," "Uncle Tom" and "a flunky for the prosecution." Smith, he said, would never be anything but a mugger and a thug, his chosen professions, and such criminals often curried favor with lawmen. Hence Smith's enthusiasm for "ratting out" his former Panther colleagues and his inclination not only to involve himself in Panther action but to initiate it and push it to extremes.

"There's a word for that kind of person," Cochran said. "I don't know if I can pronounce it. *Agent provocateur.* You don't need to look it up. Just look at Mr. Melvin 'Cotton' Smith. He's the definition."

Cochran ridiculed the informer's claim that the Panthers planned to kill cops to jump-start a black revolution. "How many L.A. police officers did these bloodthirsty Panthers kill?" he asked. *"Zero!* If all these mad dogs were running around looking for cops to kill, how come they never killed a single one? Never sniped one from a rooftop. Never blew up one of their squad cars. Never . . . killed . . . one." He paused, then said, "Some killers. Some revolution."

Near the end of his summation, Cochran turned toward the prosecution table and his white adversary Carroll. He accused the deputy D.A. of joining forces with the criminal Cotton Smith in a "callous disregard for the rights of the defendants." Cochran reminded the jury that throughout the trial Carroll had spoken contemptuously of the Panthers' social programs and suggested that they were nothing but a cover for violence. "Mr. Carroll is somewhat happy with the status quo and doesn't want a change," the black lawyer said. "I can understand some of the things that Mr. Carroll can't, and I ask you to consider your own experience in weighing the credibility of all the testimony."

Judge Dell broke in with a charge that Cochran was using "borderline tactics." When he tried to continue, the judge said, "That is unworthy of you, Mr. Cochran."

But Cochran considered race to be at the heart of the conspiracy case and refused to subside. Later the other defense lawyers took up the theme, and one outdid Cochran in his own final argument. Attorney James Gordon called the officers in the raiding party "racists who went to the headquarters under false pretenses and then lied in court." He told the jury, "If you find the defendants guilty, you are exonerating the police action and setting a precedent . . . that the doorway of the people in the ghetto can be kicked down at will."

The crusty Judge Dell waited till the jury began deliberations and motioned the defense attorneys, most of them African Americans, to the bench. "You gentlemen have been entrusted by the court with this appointment," he said, "and you have failed in that trust. I'll never appoint any of you attorneys again."

Cochran was more concerned about the opinion of his beloved mother and his church deacon father. "I'm very, very proud of you, son," Johnnie L. Cochran Sr. told him after the courtroom emptied out.

Hattie B. Cochran gave him a maternal hug and said she would never forget his eloquence. "You said what needed to be said."

They laughed together when a courtroom habitué shook Cochran's hand and said, "You nailed it, Johnnie. This whole thing is about color. There wouldn't even be a case if these guys were called the White Panthers."

IT TOOK the jury eleven days to reach a verdict on the seventy-two counts. Cochran wrote later, "I never had heard so many 'not guiltys' in my life." The Panthers were acquitted on the most serious charges, but Geronimo Pratt, Willie Stafford and seven others were found guilty of the rare charge of conspiracy to possess illegal weapons. Pratt's attorney, Marvin Zinman, was exultant. "It shows the jurors believed the police were the aggressors," he told reporters.

Deputy D.A. Carroll claimed victory and told reporters, "This is the first time in the United States a conspiracy charge of any kind has been returned against Black Panther defendants."

Judge Dell congratulated the jurors on their coolness. He referred to the melee in the courtroom and noted that "a jury under these circumstances might have been stampeded and found everyone guilty." He said that the final verdict was "not very different from the one I would've reached."

Two weeks later, after the Christmas and New Year's holidays, Geronimo Pratt was sentenced to five years imprisonment. He'd been held in solitary confinement in the Los Angeles County Jail for a year, ever since his return from Dallas, and a murder trial in the Santa Monica tennis court case still lay ahead.

Enchained

Locked in the hole without TV, radio, newspapers, a flush toilet or any contact with the outside world, the bored Pratt asked permission to conduct classes on African history and culture. Every few days he would share the information that he'd picked up from his parents, his mentor Bunchy Carter and authors like Frantz Fanon, Langston Hughes and James Baldwin. He found he could get the black inmates' attention by opening with a tidbit of information he'd gleaned from Huey P. Newton, that the African city of Timbuktu was once the cultural center of the civilized world and "the Greeks took their gold all the way across the desert to Timbuktu to exchange it for information and books for their colleges in Athens."

He introduced himself to his students as "Geronimo ji Jaga," the ethnic name assigned by Bunchy but seldom heard in the Panthers, where he was known as G or Geronimo. "The inmates wanted to know where I got 'ji Jaga,' and I explained that it came from African history. One of the brothers said, 'Black history? I didn't know there *was* any black history.' I told him you had to know where to look. Some of the guys were hip that Geronimo was the name of an Apache chief, but I told 'em how Bunchy checked the etymology back through a dozen civilizations and found it started as a Nubian name, written in hieroglyphics. I taught that the Jaga tribe were fighters, mercenaries. Slave traders never messed with them—they were too rebellious, wild, suicidal. The few times the Jaga were caught, they killed themselves in their chains."

LIKE EVERY pedagogical Pratt from his maternal grandmother down through his mother and siblings, Geronimo had always enjoyed learning and teaching, and now that he was imprisoned with Hispanics he began boning up on old interests. Soon he was teaching Mexican history to Mexicans. He described how Emiliano Zapata had fought for the peasants and Pancho Villa had eluded the *federales* and how the earliest Mexican Indians had been oppressed first by the Spanish and then by their own leaders. "The more I talked about the indigenous peoples, the more attention the Hispanics paid. They began to lose their *Mexican*ness and concentrate on their *Indian*ness. Their indigenous spirits were coming out. Then I would tell 'em about the biggest body of indigenous peoples on earth: the human race— not including the guards. That always got a laugh."

But the cellblock educational sessions came to an end after a few months. Shackled, handcuffed and barefoot, Pratt was driven from Los Angeles to the state facility at Tracy, an admissions center where convicts were screened, tested and reassigned to prisons like San Quentin, Folsom and Tehachapi. His head and facial hair were shaved for lice. Now I'm cleanshaven, he joked to himself. Barbara Mary Reed is finally right.

Without explanation he was assigned to solitary confinement. At 4:00 A.M. on his first night, he was trying to sleep when he heard the electrically operated lock on his door click open. No guards were in sight. Two Latino prisoners padded quietly toward his cell from the far end of the dimly lighted corridor. Geronimo stepped out and walked toward them at the same deliberate pace. He'd never been in a penitentiary, but he knew that some of the Hispanic and black convicts were at war. If this was a setup, he intended to die fighting.

"Hey, man," he said, trying to brazen things out, "y'all got something for me to read?"

He saw the glimmer of a knife blade. There was no place to run. When the men were a few feet away, he decided that his only hope was to lunge for the shank. He was tightening his leg muscles when he heard a shout from one of the cells. He thought he heard *"conejo,"* the Spanish word for rabbit, then *"cabrones,"* the vilest insult, and then "no, no, *no!*"

The intruders halted. The mystery voice softened and said in a heavy Spanish accent, "Hey, bro, get your fockeen ass over here."

Geronimo stepped to the nearby cell and peered inside. A picture of Adolf Hitler adorned the wall, bordered by swastikas and a cross. A small tea-colored man with a flowing black moustache reached through the bars and offered his palm. Geronimo looked around and saw the hit squad still frozen in place.

"I know you, man," the convict said. "You're Geronimo. I'm Juan Dominguez.[20] *Mucho gusto.*"

"How do you know me?" Pratt asked. "You been down to County Jail?"

Dominguez nodded and said, "You been set up, man. The guards open your door and somebody comes in and sticks you. But I'm not gonna let my people do you, man."

Geronimo said, "This is crazy. You don't even know me."

"I heard about the history lessons you giveen at County. Shotgun tol' me. You know Shotgun? He's an O.G."

"O.G.?"

"Original Gangster. *Muy malo.* Very dangerous. Hey, how the fock you know Mexican history?"

A door clanged at the far end of the corridor and four guards burst into the cellblock. "Okay, okay, lock it up!" they yelled. *"Lock it up!"* They motioned to the two men in the middle of the corridor. "Get back in your cells!" To Pratt the guards seemed to be putting on a show.

He slipped inside his own cell as the guards marched off with the two Mexicans. His door lock clicked into place.

---

[20] Pseudonym.

Desperation

A few months later Johnnie L. Cochran Jr. picked up his phone to hear the voice of his fellow Sunset Limited traveler. "Cochran," said Geronimo Pratt, "I need you bad and I need you fast. Those son of a bitches are gonna put me on trial for a murder I didn't do."

He explained that the court had appointed Charles Hollopeter of Pasadena to represent him in the tennis court murder case. Cochran knew Hollopeter by reputation: he was a respected member of the criminal defense bar, a successful attorney in his sixties. Pratt was lucky to get such high-caliber representation.

"Hollopeter's okay," Geronimo continued in a torrent of words, "but I want you to be my lawyer, too. I want you to be on my case. I saw the way you were with Willie Stafford. I saw you argue for him. I want you to argue for me like that. I love the way you argue, Cochran."

Cochran was in such demand that he'd had to ask his two busy partners in the firm of Cochran, Atkins and Evans to help with his caseload. Business was so good that he was planning to trade in his Cadillac El Dorado on a Rolls-Royce.

During the conspiracy trial he'd come to respect Geronimo Pratt. Willie Stafford also thought highly of the Panther leader and insisted that in the worst moments of the police crackdown, Pratt had continued to push the BPP's original social programs. "That guy don't have a mean bone in his body," Stafford had told Cochran. "I mean, he'll fight you if you cross him, but fighting isn't his game. I met some of his family; they're all into helping folks. That's just the Pratts."

COCHRAN CHECKED with Hollopeter and won his enthusiastic approval to join in the case. "There are things about this shooting that don't compute, Mr. Cochran," the older man said. "Maybe you can help me sort 'em out."

"Like what?"

"Well, the D.A. has two eyewitnesses: the wounded husband and a woman that runs a hobby shop up the street. Seems like their descriptions change every other day. I don't doubt their honesty, but I think they're being manipulated."

"Didn't they identify Pratt in a live show-up?"

"There wasn't any."

In Cochran's experience police and prosecutors held live show-ups when they were sure they had the right man but deftly bypassed the procedure if they were uncertain. Photo spreads and courtroom identifications were easier to manipulate.

Hollopeter said he also had concerns about the state's main witness, Julius Carl Butler. "Geronimo claims he kicked the guy out of the party because he's an informer. Says everybody knew he was a paid agent for the LAPD and the D.A. and probably the FBI. But I can't get the D.A.'s Office to admit it."

"Shouldn't that have come out in discovery?" Cochran said in a reference to the pretrial exchange of information and evidence.

"It should have, but it didn't. The prosecutor swears that Butler's clean."

"Who's prosecuting?"

"A deputy D.A. named Kalustian."

"Dick Kalustian? He was in my graduating class at Loyola."

"Good. Maybe he'll be more cooperative with you."

COCHRAN DROVE to the Hall of Justice and asked Kathleen Parker, the sixty-six-year-old Superior Court judge assigned to the case, to add his name as counsel for Pratt. He'd made many appearances in her court, and they seemed to have good rapport.

But this case would be different. "I didn't know it at the time," Cochran wrote a quarter century later, "but I had just crossed over into a twilight zone of deceit, dishonesty, betrayal, and official corruption whose darkest corners have yet to be illuminated."

He went from the judge's chambers to the Los Angeles County Jail for a sit-down with his new client, recently returned from the hole at Tracy. He found Pratt unusually agitated, his Creole drawl replaced by a jackhammer cadence and drive. "You know me and you know I didn't kill that woman," he blurted out before they'd finished shaking hands. He began a rambling disquisition to the effect that he was a marked man, somebody was out to get him, maybe the FBI, maybe the LAPD, *I can't sleep at night trying to figure it out they're framing me for murder Cochran you gotta help me, man. . . .*

"Geronimo," the lawyer said, gentling him down with a soft pat on the shoulder, "didn't you and I and Marv Zinman and a bunch of other guys just spend months and months proving who was out to get you and Willie Stafford and your wife and every other Panther? Didn't we *prove* it's the LAPD?"

"It ain't just the LAPD," Pratt said emphatically.

"Then who is it?" Cochran asked.

Geronimo shook his head. "I dunno, man," he said. "I—just—don't—know. Too many weird things been happening. Did you know I was set up at Tracy?"

"For sure?"

"Two Mexicans. Middle of the night. The guards were behind it."

"A race thing?"

"What's the difference? Dead is dead, Cochran. They had knives."

The lawyer was thinking that Pratt wasn't the first client who thought the universe was against him. The reaction seemed to hit accused men as soon as they donned jail clothes and heard a steel door slam shut behind them. Every day after that, they were pushed around and insulted and injured and controlled so much that they went a little crazy. Prisoners routinely turned on their own lawyers. It was a risk of the profession.

"Relax, friend," Cochran said. A deputy arrived to tell them that their time was up. "We've got a strong case. You may serve some time for that gun conviction, but you're not going down for murder."

TOGETHER WITH Hollopeter, Cochran decided to contact the high-ranking Panthers who could verify that Pratt had been in party meetings in Oakland on the night of the tennis court shootings. They called for assistance from the ad hoc Pratt Defense Committee, which consisted of Long John Washington, the Freeman brothers Roland and Ronald, several radical Los Angeles attorneys and their staffers and the defendant's oldest brother Charles, who'd quit his post with a computer company to throw his high I.Q. and financial resources into the battle to save his brother.

The defense committee members made several stabs at reaching David Hilliard, Panther chief of staff, and Bobby Seale, cofounder of the party and Huey Newton's second-in-command. When they couldn't get through, they thought they were having typical long-distance telephone problems. But after a week they realized they were being deliberately ignored.

At Cochran's request Pratt asked one of his Panther friends to find out what was going on. Two days later Geronimo phoned from jail: "Cochran? Forget about Seale and Hilliard and all those heavies in Oakland. Huey Newton issued another order: anybody who has anything to do with me is a running dog capitalist motherfucker and will be expelled from the party forever. Forever. I'm now a pariah."

"Well, other people must've seen you in Oakland," Cochran said.

"Small fry. Drivers, secretaries, flunkies, the ones that kiss Huey's ass. They would never challenge him."

"What about Kathleen Cleaver? Didn't you tell me she was in Oakland that night?"

"Yeah. Kathleen's cool, but she's in North Africa with Eldridge."

WITH THE murder trial set for March 1972, the defense attorneys sat down to consider the essential elements of the prosecutor's case, as revealed in preliminary statements and pretrial motions.

- Kenneth Olsen would identify Pratt as the shorter of the two gunmen.
- Barbara Reed would identify Pratt as the man who returned to her shop with a gun a few minutes before the nearby shootings.
- Julio Butler would testify that Pratt admitted complicity in the crime at least three times.
- A passing motorist would place a car that resembled Pratt's GTO at the scene.

• A forensics expert would affirm that markings on the murder cartridges matched markings on a gun that had been taken from the Panthers by police and might have belonged to Pratt.

The lawyers knew that the vague sighting of a red and white Pontiac
GTO with "whitish" license plates could be neutralized by witnesses who
would testify that Geronimo's prize possession had become a Panther car,
known as the Goat, and was driven by many others, including Julio Butler
himself. The prosecution's witness list showed that the forensics expert
would be DeWayne Wolfer, who was already under fire for his work in
other cases. That left two major problems: the eyewitnesses and the hairdresser.

Geronimo repeated to his lawyers that "everybody" knew Butler was a
paid informer for the LAPD. "Is the jury gonna believe a known snitch?"

Cochran told him, "We can't put 'everybody' on the witness stand. We
need convincing proof, the more specific the better. How'd he give himself away?"

"Aw, he was always egging us on, trying to get us to do stuff. Crazy
stuff." He paused. "Hard to explain."

"Exactly," Cochran said. "That's why it won't fly in court. We have to
prove that the guy's an informer, or he's gonna hurt us bad."

AT COCHRAN'S request, cocounsel Hollopeter contacted Deputy D.A.
Kalustian to ask if all evidence about the Pratt investigation had been
turned over to the defense under the rules of discovery. Once again Kalustian assured him that the answer was yes.

Cochran was baffled when Hollopeter recounted the conversation. If
Julius Butler was a police informer, the admission should have been included in the material that Kalustian had already submitted. Cochran
checked the discovery file again, but the hairstylist's name wasn't mentioned. Professional ethics and the rules of procedure mandated that
Cochran's old classmate play fair or risk his case and reputation.

Cochran remembered Kalustian as a bright, decent young student.
They were among forty survivors out of a starting class many times larger.
The late word on Kalustian was that he'd become a skillful prosecutor
whose legal talents were being wasted on picayune cases in Los Angeles
backwaters like Torrance. *People of California* v. *Elmer Gerard Pratt* was his

breakout opportunity. Cochran wished his old classmate well. He hoped he lost with honor.

His thoughts drifted back to Julius Butler. The man known as Mama and Mother was a businessman, a beautician, an ex–deputy sheriff, almost twice the age of the typical Panther. What did he have in common with the young hotbloods of the BPP? Cochran had sniffed out plenty of paid informers in his courtroom battles; they were a prime investigative tool of the LAPD, the FBI and the D.A.'s Office, especially in matters involving black defendants. To Cochran, Julius Butler had "snitch" written all over him.

But how could he prove it?

THE LAWYER turned next to the sticky problem of the courtroom identifications of Pratt as the killer. There were sure to be at least two finger-pointers and both would be positive. Such witnesses always were. *Do you see that person in this courtroom? Yes, sir! He's the man sitting right there.* Every member of the legal establishment knew that such IDs were essentially meaningless as instruments of truth. Who else would a witness identify in the courtroom? The lawyers? A bailiff? But the accusations were effective theater.

Cochran recalled that a friend, attorney Leo Branton, had attacked cross-racial identifications in winning an unexpected acquittal for the black revolutionary Angela Davis on charges of murder, kidnapping and criminal conspiracy. He phoned his old mentor and spent the next forty-five minutes taking notes on the latest scientific information about the effect of racial differences, hysteria and stress on eyewitness testimony. "You need some Ph.D.'s to testify," Branton concluded. "There's a lot of new data." He said he knew just the man.

The People Versus Pratt

The tennis court murder trial opened with a rancorous discussion in the judge's chambers. Bailiffs cited the melee in the conspiracy trial and insisted that the "ringleader" Pratt be kept in shackles and handcuffs for everyone's safety, especially theirs. "I was at that trial," Cochran said forcefully. "There was blood on the floor—and it came from our clients. The deputies were the ones with the guns and clubs."

Charles Hollopeter argued that visible restraints would prejudice their client in the jury's eyes. As a compromise, Judge Kathleen Parker, a thin-faced woman who wore her gray hair pulled sharply back, ruled that the defendant would be shackled whenever he was in the adjoining holding cell. In the presence of the jury he would be unchained.

AT 11:15 A.M. on Wednesday, June 14, 1972, Deputy D.A. Richard Kalustian stood up to make his opening statement. Before he could start, Cochran was on his feet. He'd spotted Barbara Mary Reed staring at Geronimo from the first row. He suspected that she was being prepped for the eyewitness identification. By the time she took the stand she would be able to describe every pore on the defendant's face.

"At the outset," Cochran told the judge, "we would make a motion to exclude any witnesses who may be present, save the investigating officer, Your Honor. I would ask that any witnesses present be excused."

The judge ordered Reed out.

KALUSTIAN'S CRISP opener lasted only ten minutes. The prosecutor maintained a countenance as grim as his material, his heavy black eyebrows, thick shock of black hair, full black moustache and hawkish nose producing a saturnine look that seemed to command the jury's attention. He retraced the steps of "Elmer Pratt and a man named Tyrone" from the Hobby Center to the tennis court to a car that resembled Pratt's GTO. He told the jurors, "The culprits were to remain unknown until August or September of 1970, when a certain letter was uncovered. A year previously, in August of 1969, at a time when Julio Butler was still a member of the Black Panther Party, a rift occurred between Julio Butler and other members of the party. His life was threatened. He decided that he would commit what he knew to paper. Among his many topics were the tennis court shootings. He delivered the letter to a community relations officer, Sergeant Rice, and asked [that] the letter not be opened at all. He felt it was an insurance policy."

But the letter was opened a year later at a police department disciplinary hearing, Kalustian explained, and "that's the first time, the first lead, in the case." Subsequently Kenneth Olsen and Barbara Reed identified Elmer Gerard Pratt from a series of mug shots; a forensics expert connected a gun believed to be the defendant's with the cartridges recovered from the tennis court, "and an indictment was returned. This is the people's evidence. Thank you."

HOLLOPETER AND Cochran waived opening statements, and Kalustian called his first witness: Barbara Mary Reed. In the middle of her dramatic account of events on the murder night, he asked, almost as an aside, "By the way, do you see in court the shorter of the two gentlemen that was in your store that night?"

The jurors watched attentively as she replied, "This gentleman on my left at the end of the table."

"Is that the gentleman in the striped shirt?"

"Yes."

Kalustian held his hand over Pratt and said, "The gentleman I have my hand over?"

"Yes."

"In looking at Mr. Pratt today," the prosecutor continued, "what is it about him that enables you to say that he was in your store on the 18th of December, 1968?"

The woman answered in slow, emphatic terms. "I remember his face thoroughly . . . exactly everything about his features. . . . Everything about him, his haircut, the shape of his head, his eyes." She said he'd had a "full head of hair and a widow's peak."

When Kalustian asked if she'd noticed "any marks on his face, or scars, or anything," the judge sustained Cochran's objection that the question was leading and suggestive. The prosecutor took another approach:

Q. You have indicated that when you were talking to Mr. Pratt, you were standing face-to-face talking with him. Is that right?

A. Yes. He was about the same height I am.

Q. And did you get a look at his face as you were standing?

A. Yes. I was face-to-face with the man, and what drew my attention to him, one predominant feature—well, indirectly a feature—was a scar on his forehead.

Q. Where was the scar?

A. Between his eyes on the lower part of the forehead, above the eyebrows.

Q. What was the shape of the scar?

A. Just an indentation of some kind.

Q. Well, was it a long scar?

A. More round than anything else.

A few minutes later Kalustian returned to the same subject. "Do you recognize anything about Mr. Pratt's face as you look at it now that was the same as the individual you saw in your store?"

"Yes," the woman answered.

"Tell us, please, what?"

"Well, as I said before, the scars on his forehead seemed to draw my attention. . . ."

Cochran made a note, "It's scars now? *Plural?*" He realized that the woman was improving her description as she testified. Every attorney was warned about this phenomenon in law school. It was called "filling in memory" or "evolution of testimony" and had sent many an innocent to prison.

Kalustian finished his examination by asking, "Is there any doubt in your mind as you view Mr. Pratt now that he was in your store at about eight P.M. on December 18th, 1968?"

The positive woman replied positively: "There is *no* doubt in my mind."

IN A lengthy cross-examination Cochran tried to point up a pattern of police manipulation of a witness who appeared only too glad to be manipulated. He led Mrs. Reed through descriptions of closed-door sessions in which she, the victim Kenneth Olsen, Panther Unit detectives and a deputy D.A. had sorted through stacks of pictures in which Pratt was the only short black man and the only one wearing a bush jacket. He showed that she'd been inconsistent about the killer's attire and facial hair and had originally failed to mention any scar or widow's peak. She was now as positive that his shoes had been tan as she'd once been positive they were black. She flatly contradicted some of her grand jury testimony, which had been equally self-assured and emphatic.

Nor did she ever seem bewildered or uncertain of her answers. She said she "couldn't remember" whether Pratt had a goatee or moustache (he was wearing both in court), then corrected herself and insisted that he'd been clean-shaven, bringing her testimony back in line with her original report. She denied that she'd told Santa Monica police that the gunman wore an "Eisenhower-type" jacket and now insisted that it was a "safari" or "bush" jacket. She explained with her usual certitude that the officer who'd taken her original statement must have misunderstood her. So had the police employee who created a composite at her direction within twenty-four hours of her exposure to the men in the hobby shop. Somehow police technician Margaret Morgan had omitted the scars, Reed testified, again referring to them in the plural.

Cochran marveled at the spectacle of a respectable middle-class shopkeeper busily distancing herself from a composite that she herself had generated. Malleable witnesses were a prosecutor's dream.

THROUGH HIS cross-examination Cochran deliberately kept his voice low. Jurors didn't like to see female witnesses bullied—except on TV—and tended to hold such tactics against the client. He said, "You told us earlier that one of the things that helped you remember this man was the fact that he had a scar above his nose, between his eyes. Is that correct?"

"Yes," she replied.

"Now, you never told Detective John Eckstein [the original investigating officer] about this scar on his nose at the time you talked to him in December of 1968, did you, ma'am?"

Mrs. Reed ignored the question and said, "I did [tell] Mrs. Morgan."

Q. The question was: did you tell Detective John Eckstein?

A. I don't remember if I told him, but I told her, because of the composite.

Q. Well, in the composite, did you—I'd like you to look at it again and see if you see any scar placed on suspect no. 2, over his nose. Do you see any scar there?

A. I told her, sir. Whether she put one there or not, I can't help it.

Q. There is no scar contained on this composite, is there?

A. No, but I definitely told her.

"You know what I don't understand?" Geronimo said to his lawyers after court adjourned at 4:20 P.M., somewhat late for a judge who was famous for her bobtailed sessions. "For two years my face was in every newspaper in town. It was on all the TV news shows, too—after the shootout, during the conspiracy trial and when they brought me back from Texas. And yet this woman didn't recognize me till the cops showed her a photo spread."

"I think she's very flexible," Hollopeter said. "*Too* flexible."

"You have to feel sorry for her," Pratt said. "She's just an innocent old lady that's trying to help the D.A. I don't think she's part of any conspiracy."

Hollopeter looked confused. "This woman is trying to send you away for life," he said, "and you feel *sorry* for her?"

"This is nothing new," Cochran said, visibly annoyed. "The poor woman looks at pictures for two years and can't identify a soul. Then the cops call her up and say, 'Come down and look at some new pictures.' They lay out a corrupt photo spread, she studies the faces with her husband and Ken Olsen, the cops drop some hints, and—*Hey, look! That's him right there!* Now she's got to help the prosecutor take the killer off the streets. The guy's guilty, isn't he? The cops said so."

AT 2:50 P.M. the next day, Fred Reed, Barbara's husband, told the court that he'd spotted "two male Negroes" jiggling the doorknob at the front of his store on the night in question, but he hadn't driven close enough to get a good look. He said that he lost sight of them as he circled the block and then saw them turn into the Radio Shack parking lot, where "one car there had a light top and a dark bottom." Asked directly if he was able to say that Geronimo Pratt had been one of the two, he answered without hesitation, "I can't say whether or not he was, no."

Cochran had started his cross-examination when Kalustian said, "Excuse me, Counsel. May I ask one further question?" He asked the witness how he'd known that the two men in the parking lot were the same pair he'd seen at the front of his store.

"Well," Fred Reed answered, "one of them had a safari jacket on."

Cochran jotted down "safari." In bed the night before, he'd reread the 244-page grand jury transcript. Fred Reed had described the shooter's apparel as "a light-colored windbreaker, a trench coat of some kind." Apparently the prosecution witnesses had been warned of the need for consistency, and "safari jacket" had been selected as their preferred description throughout the trial.

As though Kalustian sensed Cochran's cynicism, he quickly asked, "How do you know to call this a *safari* jacket?"

"Oh, the old movies," Reed replied. "You see these actors wearing jackets like that, and we call them safari jackets, I guess."

Kalustian said, "I see."

ON CROSS-EXAMINATION Cochran emphasized the sartorial revisionism in the hope that the jury would catch the scent of collusion; jurors were notoriously unfriendly toward rehearsed testimony. "Now you used this term 'safari jacket,' " he said to Reed. "You never mentioned anything about a safari jacket when you testified at the time of the grand jury, did you, sir?"

The witness said he didn't remember.

Cochran began a set of questions aimed at suggesting overly intensive pretrial rehearsal: Did you discuss this case with Mr. Kalustian prior to testifying here today? You haven't talked to him at all? Did you talk to him yesterday? Did you talk to your wife about her testimony yesterday? Didn't say a word to her about it? *She never mentioned anything to you?* . . .

Every question produced a terse "No." Cochran left the matter to the judgment of the jury and said, "I have nothing further of this witness at this time."

KENNETH CRISMON Olsen, a dark-haired man whose moustache and goatee flowed together in a perfect oval, took the witness stand, carefully spelled out his name and launched into a vivid description of the events of December 18, 1968. Once again Kalustian introduced the in-court identification almost offhandedly. Olsen had just finished quoting one of the gunmen as saying, "Yeah, man, this is a stickup. We want your bread, or we're going to burn you. Come on, put your hands up!" when Kalustian asked if he noticed either of the two killers in court.

"Yes, I do," the school administrator responded.

"Would you so indicate, please?"

"Yes." Olsen raised his hand and pointed. "The man sitting next to Mr. Cochran."

"The gentleman I have my hand over?"

"That's correct."

Cochran had a special reason for being contemptuous of the exercise. Three months earlier Kenneth Olsen had been escorted into the courtroom by an LAPD detective during a routine proceeding at which Olsen's presence was not required. Like Barbara Reed, the school administrator had appeared to be studying Pratt's face. Cochran had wondered at the time: Why are they giving him a preview?

AFTER THE day's proceedings, Cochran consulted with Pratt in the county jail's attorney room and found him on the edge of desperation. "I didn't kill this woman, Cochran," he said, shaking his head. "I wouldn't do that. It's not my style. This whole case is about something else."

The attorney said, "Oh, man. What is this about except this crime? You are innocent, but you're really being paranoid."

"You'll see. They're after me, and they're going to do whatever it takes to get me. . . ."

Later Cochran wrote:

As much as I liked and respected Geronimo Pratt, I refused to follow him into his never-never land of official plot and governmental conspiracies. Time to get back to work, I thought as I walked back to my car. Time to rejoin the real world. I had faith in the rule of law. . . . I trusted in the integrity of my old classmate, Richard Kalustian. He was a stand-up guy; we wore the same school tie. Geronimo Pratt and I were about to learn which of us was living in a dream world.

Guilt Feelings

In court the next day Geronimo was in slightly better spirits—Cochran had given him a pep talk about the way the justice system lurches along but usually reaches the right conclusion—but he wondered how many indignities and slanders he would have to endure and how long he would have to lie awake in the hole, waiting all night for the metallic click that meant he'd been set up for execution, again.

His attorneys had instructed him to think of himself as their cocounsel, to use his own wits and brains to help them analyze the prosecution testimony and develop fresh lines of attack. Hollopeter had handed him a pencil and a legal pad and advised him to take notes. But all Geronimo wanted to do was stare at the grizzly on the green California state seal and beam himself to a cloud. He felt alternately perplexed, hopeful, angry, disoriented, his emotions changing minute by minute. The central theme of his life had become: Who is out to get me? *Who is behind all this?*

He cringed as his name rattled across the well of the courtroom like incoming machine-gun fire. There were moments when he almost felt guilty. When Kenneth Olsen pointed him out, he felt as though he'd been hit with a sledgehammer. He wanted to scream: Not me, you stupid son of a bitch! *Not me!* Then he wanted to comfort the poor man and tell him he knew how it felt to lose comrades and lovers and how sad it was that he'd suffered so much and in so many ways. From earliest childhood Geronimo had never been able to hold a grudge. He wrote on his yellow pad: "Ken—brainwashed?"

WITH THE shooting victim on the stand, Cochran and Hollopeter decided to hold their objections to a minimum. No matter what the jurors thought about Pratt's guilt or innocence at this early stage of trial, Ken Olsen came across as a sympathetic figure. He testified that the police had shown him sets of pictures of possible suspects "seven or eight times," starting in Santa Monica Hospital the day after the shootings. He said he'd picked out some black men who were "similar" to the tennis court killers but had never made a positive ID. In December 1969, he said, he picked out "a person who had strong similar features." There'd been another lineup a few days later, and "I identified the person at the lineup that I had seen in the pictures, as such. And I told Detective Eckstein that while there was a possibility, I didn't feel I could really make an identification of that person, because I didn't feel, really, it was the person."

Kalustian abruptly turned to another subject as Cochran said to himself, Olsen sure used a hell of a lot of words just to say that he went to a live lineup but couldn't make an ID. What's the guy hiding? He scribbled, "12–69. No ID?"

The interrogation turned to the sixteen-picture spread in which Olsen had identified Geronimo Pratt, no. 13, the only one wearing a bush jacket. "I felt that this definitely did look and appear photographically to be one of the assailants," the school administrator testified, "and that while I didn't think I could make a positive identification from any photograph, and had expressed this to the police department, I felt that that was a picture of the person."

Kalustian asked, "Was this the first time that you felt that you had seen the person?"

"Yes."

Cochran recalled that Pratt had never appeared in a live lineup, a strange omission in a case in which eyewitness testimony was so important. After Olsen had made his pick from a selection of photos, wouldn't the next step have been to put the suspect in a lineup so the victim could identify a live human being and strengthen the prosecution's case? Every competent detective would have followed that simple procedure. Why not this time?

Kenneth Olsen continued his testimony in a firm voice, losing control only when Kalustian asked him to identify an emergency room photograph of his ex-wife Caroline. He winced and said, "Would you mind turning that photograph over?"

The prosecutor flipped the picture and said, "Sorry."

The direct testimony lasted a half hour and ended with Kalustian asking if there was "any doubt in your mind at this time that Elmer Pratt, the defendant in this case, was one of the two men on the tennis court in Santa Monica on December 18, 1968?"

His strong voice returning, Olsen said, "There is no doubt."

COCHRAN AND Hollopeter had decided that the courtly older member of the courtroom partnership would handle the cross-examination. A deputy D.A. had already characterized the grieving Olsen as "flaky," and the only living witness to the tennis court shootings had to be handled with care. Hollopeter took him through his story in a restrained manner, eliciting no startling contradictions. After Olsen admitted that he'd been "face-to-face with both of them probably two or three times," the lawyer asked if either of the gunmen had had a moustache.

"No," Olsen answered. "They were clean-shaven."

It was a crucial point. Nine or ten defense witnesses were prepared to testify that they'd never seen Geronimo Pratt without facial hair. He'd worn a moustache from age sixteen and a goatee off and on, even in the army.

Hollopeter asked, "Both men were clean-shaven?"

"Yes."

"You are absolutely certain of that?"

"Yes."

A trace of testiness crept into Olsen's voice when the lawyer pressed him about the killers' jackets. "Well, I was not, Counselor, concerned about the jackets with a gun in my face."

A few minutes later Hollopeter nailed down an important point for the defense.

Q. Well, now, when you got up within a few feet of the shorter man, you took a good look at his face, didn't you?

A. Yes, I did.

Q. Now did you see any unusual features or strange—

A. No.

Q. —Facial characteristics?

A. No strange facial characteristics.

Q. You were about two feet from him at one time?

A. Yes.

Q. You told us the court was brightly lighted?

A. That's correct.

Q. Did you see any scars on his face?

A. I didn't notice scars, no.

Hollopeter asked if there'd been anything unusual about the way the shorter man "walked or conducted himself." No reference had been made to Geronimo's bowlegs in the earlier statements by prosecution witnesses, and the defense lawyers wanted to see if memories had been enhanced on that point as they'd been on so many others.

"Very definitely," Olsen answered.

"What was that, sir?" Hollopeter asked politely.

"The fact that he held us up and then pumped bullets into us and murdered my wife."

Several of the jurors seemed affected by this repeated reminder of the horror of the crime.

Echoing Cochran's cross-examination of Barbara Reed, Hollopeter closely examined the school official about the Identikit composites. Olsen said he'd been visited in the hospital two days after the shooting by a police technician with "a kit of moustaches and eyes and so forth." By now both sides were well aware that the original composites bore little resemblance to the hirsute man sitting at the defense table, and Olsen provided the same explanation as Reed: the composites were faulty. "I didn't think they really were very good. . . . I didn't feel it really was anything but a very rough description, because those things just aren't people, that's all."

Hollopeter asked, "The artist drew that sketch according to your directions then?"

"Well," Olsen answered, "he drew it while he was interviewing me. . . ."

"What corrections did you make?"

". . . He showed me, and I made corrections. . . ."

"And you finally approved that one? Is that true?"

"Yes, because I didn't feel I could do any better."

Without being asked, the witness volunteered that "one of the most distinguishing things about Mr. Pratt is his intensive eyes."

Hollopeter asked, "Well, what is meant by intensive eyes?"

"Well, they are very piercing and very penetrating, and—"

"Are they wide-set, or are they narrowly set? Are they close together or far apart?"

"I'd say they are just—they are neither."

"Are they deep-set eyes? That is, sunk back into his head?"

"No."

"Are the eyes protrudent?"

Olsen seemed frustrated at his own inability to define what he'd meant by "piercing" and "penetrating." "Well," he said after a pause, "I didn't feel that there was anything in his eyes or in his face that was, that—I mean, he doesn't have a big scar, or he isn't built in any unusual way, but I can remember his face."

"Does he have any scars?"

"Not that I have noticed."

Hollopeter was pleased to elicit this second inconsistency about scars and said, "I have no further questions."

The Helpful Witness

At night in solitary confinement Geronimo kept reassuring himself that his case was going well, but he couldn't shake his feelings of guilt and shame. He remembered some of the insults leveled at him in Huey Newton's public denunciation: "snake who crawled into a baby's crib," "no longer a man," "disgraceful, counter-revolutionary, piggish, dog-like." Geronimo asked himself, Is that me? What made Huey so angry? *Could he be right?*

He remembered how often his mother had told him that people usually get what they deserve: "God sees to it." Was that what was happening? Were his courtroom ordeals some kind of payback, a balance, a reckoning for Vietnam?

He'd been transferred to the new Los Angeles County Jail and was enjoying the luxury of a bolted-down metal toilet instead of a hole in the floor. He no longer slept in his body wastes when the guards neglected to flush. But the attitudes of jail personnel hadn't changed. When his brothers Jack and Charles and his sister Virginia tried to visit, deputies sometimes turned them away or made them feel so uncomfortable that they left voluntarily. Ginny canceled a visit when she was ordered to strip for a body search. Jack and Charles were made to open their mouths while guards probed for narcotics. Even Cochran and Hollopeter had to wait for long periods. "Mr. Pratt isn't available right now. . . . You didn't call ahead. . . . Your papers aren't signed. . . ."

DAYS PASSED in wrangling over the admissibility of evidence. Kalustian argued that a .45 automatic, one of many weapons confiscated at John Huggins' house the day of the Campbell Hall killings, was Geronimo Pratt's personal side arm, and Hollopeter responded that it could have belonged to dozens of Panthers who frequented the place. Judge Kathleen Parker allowed the weapon into evidence.

"This is simply Tweedledum and Tweedledee," Hollopeter complained to the judge. When Kalustian expressed chagrin, Hollopeter responded, "I must say that I am aggrieved that Mr. Kalustian is chagrined."

WHEN THE word games were over, police officers and medical experts trooped to the stand to relate the bare facts of the killings. A witness told of seeing a car that looked like Pratt's GTO fleeing the scene of the shootings. LAPD Sergeant DuWayne Rice told of receiving an envelope from his old friend Julius Butler after "he stated to me that he was in fear of his life. He felt there was a contract out on him to kill him. . . . He said, 'In the event I am killed or if I die for some reason, I want you to take this, open it, read it and give it to my mother.' " Rice described Butler as "a pretty stable guy. He thinks pretty clearly and he acts in a very stable manner."

Soon the jurors had an opportunity to judge for themselves. Julius Carl Butler had given up his raffish image and now appeared in a funereal three-piece suit and professorial dark-rimmed spectacles. His voice was inaudible beyond the first row of spectators as he identified himself as a hairstylist who'd been in business for ten years as "Mr. Julio." Within a few minutes he was repeating the story he'd told the grand jury after Pratt had thrown him out of the party.

Early on the evening of the tennis court shootings, said Butler, "Pratt told me he was going out on a mission." Later that night, "he said that he'd shot some people." The next day Pratt pointed to newspaper headlines and said "that was the incident that he was talking about." A few days later Pratt "stated to me that he was the one that did the shooting, that shot the people, because Tyrone didn't shoot." Butler said he didn't know Tyrone's last name and hadn't seen him since Pratt had introduced him on the night of the "mission."

The hairstylist told the jury that his close friend Geronimo, not content with three admissions of guilt, later filled in details of the shootings. Butler gave the impression that he and Pratt were so close that they often engaged in intimate colloquys. In one of them Pratt had told him that the red GTO was "hid out."

Butler admitted that there'd been no earwitnesses to any of the incriminating conversations; it was his word against Pratt's. According to his testimony, Geronimo always carried a .45 semiautomatic, the same caliber as the murder weapon. Butler said that his good friend admitted changing the barrel to make it harder for police to connect his personal side arm with the killings.

At the defense table Johnnie Cochran hoped that the jury was sharing his growing sense of outrage. Not only had Butler suggested a friendly relationship that never existed; not only had he described the taciturn Pratt as a motormouth who beat a path to "Mr. Julio's Coiffures la Dames" to reveal incriminating secrets; not only had Butler put the alleged murder weapon in Pratt's hand, but now he was busily plugging one of the biggest holes in the prosecution's case. In pretrial proceedings a police forensics expert had testified that the striations on the murder slugs didn't match the rifling in the barrel of the weapon alleged to be Pratt's. Julio had solved that tricky problem in one swoop: *Geronimo told me he changed the barrels.*

In the recorded history of murder trials all the way back to ancient Greece, Cochran asked himself, has there ever been a more helpful witness? He's tied up every loose end! Surely the jury could recognize a story too convenient to be true. Cochran felt ashamed for his old classmate Kalustian. None of their Loyola law professors would have countenanced a case built on the testimony of such an obvious liar. Indeed, an opposite precept had been drilled into the students: the first obligation of every prosecutor was justice, not convictions. It disturbed Cochran that by calling Butler as a witness, Kalustian implicitly vouched for his probity. The beautician in the three-piece suit had provided gravitas without veritas. Cochran hoped the jurors noticed.

COCHRAN OPENED his cross-examination by asking Butler's age. "I'll be forty in August," the cosmetologist replied.

The attorney quickly turned to the relationship between the young Panther Pratt and the senior member Butler:

Q. In fact, you didn't like Mr. Pratt too much, did you?

A. I didn't have any feelings. I didn't know him.

Q. Well, you don't like him too much now, do you?

A. I guess the truth of the matter would be no, I don't care for him.

Q. . . . Would you say that you hate him?

A. I don't hate anyone.

Q. But you dislike him. Is that a fair statement?

A. I don't want him as a friend.

Q. Well, you dislike him. Is that right?

A. Yes, sir.

To Cochran's surprised satisfaction, Butler confirmed that Pratt had always worn facial hair—"a moustache and goatee. It wasn't much of a beard"—and identified an old photo of Pratt with a dense Fu Manchu.

"That's the way you remember him in November and December of 1968?" Cochran asked.

Butler said, "To my best recall." Then he added, "Let's put it this way: I don't remember ever seeing him without it." If Butler had been a defense witness, Cochran couldn't have asked for a better answer.

He turned to the matter of the white-over-red Pontiac GTO that had been spotted leaving the murder scene with one or two black men. "In fact," Cochran asked, "it is true, is it not, that a number of people of the party drove that vehicle? Isn't that correct?"

". . . Yes."

"In fact, did you ever drive the car?"

"Yes."

The first hint that the hairdresser would resist any suggestion that he'd been an informer came after Cochran asked if he'd served as a Los Angeles sheriff's deputy. "That's correct," Butler replied.

"And when you were working for the Black Panther Party, were you also working for law enforcement at the same time?"

"No."

"You had severed any ties you had with law enforcement?"

"That's correct."

"Have you at any time since leaving the sheriff's department worked for the FBI or the CIA?"

"No." The answer was emphatic.

Cochran left the subject for the moment and inquired about Butler's separation from the Black Panther Party. The man known as Mama testified that he'd resigned after a conversation with Bobby Seale, one of the founders. Cochran asked, "Were you ever disciplined by Mr. Pratt in April of 1969, with reference to Ollie Taylor at any time?"

Butler replied, "I was never disciplined by anyone."

Cochran asked if there'd been harsh words between him and Pratt about the schoolboy's beating. "No," Butler responded.

After several more questions Cochran decided to bring Butler back in the morning. He might even be useful as a defense witness on rebuttal, but not until more testimony had been adduced. Judge Parker adjourned court at 4:30 P.M. and ordered the attorneys to return at 11:00 A.M. Cochran said, "Your Honor, Mr. Pratt has requested leave of the court to make a phone call at his own expense to Louisiana, to his mother. He has received information that his mother, who is elderly, is ill."

The judge was halfway off the bench. Over her shoulder she said he could make the call "at his own expense, not to exceed ten minutes."

HIS HAND shaking, Geronimo phoned Morgan City and learned that his aging mother was mending after a brief bout of dyspepsia. She was in the healing hands of her oldest daughter Jacqueline, the church organist.

"What're you doing in court, baby?" Eunice Pratt asked in a weak voice that barely traveled over the phone lines. She was sixty-six now, and he was the baby of the family, a biographical fact that she never let him forget.

"Mama," he said, "it's nothing, sweet thing. Somebody made a little mistake, that's all. Soon as this is over I'm taking the Blue Dog home." He couldn't bear to tell her that he faced penitentiary time on the earlier gun conviction.

His mother promised to light more candles for him and request a novena. "I pray for you every day, son." His sister Ginny had told him that their mother also offered up Quedo mantras for his release—"she isn't missing any bets."

Eunice asked, "Do you still have your Bible?"

"Yes, ma'am," he said. He didn't tell her that he no longer opened it.

THE NEXT morning Cochran asked Julio Butler if he'd hit young Ollie Taylor in the mouth and knocked out some teeth. "That is incorrect," the witness replied with heat.

Cochran asked if the teenager "sustained some injuries. He was bleeding? His face was swollen? A towel was required to wipe up the blood?"

"That's correct," the witness said, but added in the same breath, "Pratt perpetrated the incident."

After Butler testified that he and Pratt had gone into Butler's bedroom with Taylor and a few other Panthers, Cochran asked, "During this conversation isn't it true Mr. Pratt reprimanded you for any action that you directed toward Mr. Taylor?"

A. No.

Q. He never reprimanded you?

A. No, sir . . .

Q. You never participated in any manner in any of these injuries?

A. I slapped Ollie Taylor.

Q. You never hit him with your fist?

A. No, sir . . .

Q. Do you recall a conversation with Mr. Pratt where he indicated to you that there had been some directive issued that there was not to be any fighting with any member of a rival organization or fellow Panther members?

A. That is a lie . . .

Q. He never told you you did wrong?

A. No, sir . . .

Q. At some point did you ever call the Central Avenue office and threaten to kill Mr. Pratt and his family?

A. No.

Q. Did you ever at any point direct any threats toward Mr. Pratt?

A. . . . I was prepared to protect my life, sir. . . . I was prepared to use whatever force was necessary. . . .

Q. Well, if you dislike him or were paranoid enough to shoot him, are you paranoid enough to lie on him?

A. No, sir.

A few minutes later Cochran asked, "Isn't it true you were expelled from the party around that time, in June of 1969?"

Without hesitation Butler answered, "No. I quit."

Cochran walked back to the defense table and scanned Butler's "insurance policy" letter. There it was, in the hairdresser's own handwriting: "First I was Relieved of all duties and offical working capacities."

Too bad I can't impeach him with this, Cochran said to himself, and show the jury what a liar he is. But it would open up the false accusations in the letter.

Butler admitted that the party newspaper had run an item about his expulsion, "but I had quit before they wrote . . . this newspaper article."

Cochran said, "Well, the party, at the time that they indicated that you'd been expelled, they gave as reasons for your expulsion the fact of your involvement in the death of Franco [Diggs], the fact that you were a police agent, the fact that they felt you had been a traitor?"

Butler admitted that "they made all those accusations."

RICHARD KALUSTIAN kept his star witness on the stand for redirect examination. As Cochran listened closely, he detected the first hint of desperation by the prosecution. Apparently it was now time to degrade the defendant's image with anecdotal evidence unrelated to the murder case. He leaned forward as Kalustian said, "Tell us of the gun incident involving Long John Washington and Elmer Pratt."

Butler needed no urging. "I was arguing with someone else that was with Geronimo about some of his behavior, particularly he'd pulled his wife's hair out and I had to do her hair that day, and I told him there was no cause for him abusing her in this manner, that he was being stupid, and at that time all three of them went in a tirade on me, and then Long John picked up a gun, and Geronimo said, 'Shoot him.' "

Kalustian said, "Tell us exactly what did he do with the gun?"

"He cocked it full cock."[21]

Q. What did he do with it?

A. He held it on my head from across the table . . . at which time I told him he had no cause for shooting me, but if he did, he had to deal with these other people that were in the room. . . .

Q. Did Mr. Pratt say anything with regard to the gun at your head?

A. He said, "Shoot him!"

Q. To who?

A. To Long John Washington.

Q. What happened after that?

---

[21] Ready to fire with a light pull on the trigger.

A. Pratt took the gun from him and held it to my head and told me he ought to kill me.

Q. Pratt took the gun and *what*?

At the defense table Cochran was recalling some simplistic advice he'd heard about driving points home to a jury: tell 'em what you're gonna tell 'em, then tell 'em, then tell 'em what you told 'em. Kalustian must have had the same teacher. But what was the relevance of this Wild West story that was being pounded into the jury's consciousness as though it were a passage from Blackstone? He decided not to object for the moment. The more stories Butler told, the sooner he would give himself up as a consummate perjurer.

Butler was saying, "He held it to my head."

"Who was he talking to?" the prosecutor asked.

"He was talking to me. Directly to me."

"What exactly did he do?"

Butler blurted out, "He said, 'I ought to kill you.'"

"Object to that!" Cochran said, springing to his feet. "That has been answered three or four times."

"The answer is in," Judge Parker said. "It may remain."

The dogged Kalustian dragged out more testimony as Cochran wondered how long the judge would continue to rule for the prosecution. This peripheral issue had no bearing on the tennis court shootings, but it did have the effect of making his client look like a murderous thug.

"Do you recall the exact words at this time?" Butler was asked again.

"He said, 'I ought to kill you.'"

The questioning circled back to the beating of Ollie Taylor. Butler testified that the incident had begun when Pratt "jumped on him," after which Roger "Blue" Lewis hit the boy in the mouth with a gun. "Ollie Taylor was sitting in the middle of the room, and I was sitting next to Ollie Taylor, and I was trying to talk to Ollie Taylor on the basis of 'Give as much information about yourself to clear yourself,' and Geronimo stated to me that the shit he was talking was a bunch of bullshit, and I looked over and he cocked the hammer on the pistol."

Kalustian asked, "Where was the pistol pointed, if at all?"

"It was actually right between me and Ollie Taylor, because I was sitting side by side with Ollie Taylor. Then I noticed that Geronimo had an erection—"

Cochran's jaw dropped. In all the police reports, in the grand jury testimony, in the documents turned over to the defense in the discovery phase, neither Butler nor anyone else had made any mention of the male genitalia, priapic or otherwise. For an instant Cochran wondered if he'd misheard. He looked at the jury box and noted quizzical expressions. The judge was leaning forward and frowning. Pratt looked disgusted.

Butler continued: "—And Pratt stated, 'If you don't move, I'll blow your head off,' and he said, 'Furthermore, I think maybe you're siding with him.' . . . So he told me to slap Ollie Taylor. He say, 'You interrogate,' so I did it in the pretense of trying to—at that time I was frightened of Geronimo's behavior, very seriously frightened. I had never seen a man with an erection."

That was enough. The two defense attorneys objected simultaneously.

Kalustian forged ahead without waiting for the judge's ruling. "At any rate," he said, "you were frightened at that time. That's why you struck Ollie Taylor?"

"Yes, sir. Then I began to talk to everybody in the room, and tried to talk—"

Hollopeter interrupted. "Object to voluntary statements, Your Honor."

"Sir," the judge politely reminded Butler, "there is no question pending right now."

Cochran thought, It's about time she reminded him. This guy has spent two days answering questions that weren't asked. That isn't evidence; it's story time.

Pratt nudged him and pointed to the triumvirate of judge, prosecutor and witness. "What is this?" he asked. "The Three Stooges?"

"No," Cochran whispered. "The Stooges were funny."

The Comedians

At the afternoon session the prosecution's star witness returned to the subject of the threats that he claimed had made him pen his "insurance letter." He told of receiving five or six frightening phone calls from his former colleague Pratt and others. "I would receive phone calls, and people would be clicking guns in the telephone receiver and telling me they would get me. . . . I had things stolen out of my house." He said that someone had fired a bullet into his beauty shop window.

Kalustian began a line of questioning that appeared aimed at characterizing Julius Butler as the party's altruistic senior philosopher, more concerned with helping his people than feuding with Geronimo Pratt or breaking heads. His ultimate exit from the BPP, Butler stressed, had to do with "motives, ideology. . . . It was my attitude that the party should have represented the desires of the community and not coerce the community into thinking the way they wanted to think."

In recross-examination Cochran seized on the opportunity to remind the jury of Butler's raw animosity toward Pratt.

"These events, these threats that were made to you," Cochran said, "they made you unhappy and afraid?"

"Yes, sir," Butler answered.

"And mad?"

"Yes, sir."

"And they intensified your dislike for Mr. Pratt?"

"I think that's a correct statement, sir."

When Butler claimed that a "Mr. Colbert" and other witnesses had been present when Pratt made personal death threats, Cochran demanded specific names, and an Abbott and Costello routine followed:

A. His name is Eli. One person. I don't know where he is.

Q. Eli? Where is he?

A. Huh?

Q. Where is Eli?

A. He is in Los Angeles.

Q. Do you know his last name?

A. His last name is Eli.

Q. What is his first name?

A. Leroy.

Q. Leroy Eli?

A. Yes.

Q. What is his address, sir?

A. I don't have it with me, sir.

Q. What is Mr. Colbert's address, sir?

A. I don't have that with me.

Butler's testimony ended at 2:45 P.M. on June 21, 1972, a week after the opening day of the trial, and Judge Parker adjourned court till the next day. Pratt and the lawyers hoped that the jury perceived the witness as a vengeful man who was trying to get even with his rival, but they had to admit that at times he'd been impressive and well-spoken.

"We're not finished with him," Cochran assured Pratt. "But that's good enough for now."

"We've still got to prove he's a snitch," Pratt said.

"Don't worry," Cochran said. "It'll come out."

FOLLOWING HER relaxed timetable, the judge reconvened court the next afternoon at 2:15. DeWayne Wolfer, the controversial chief forensics chemist for the LAPD, stated his credentials and identified a .45-caliber pistol, three .45-caliber shell casings and a spent slug as items he'd examined in his laboratory. He explained that he'd been unable to make a connection between the slug and the weapon and added, "This simply means either the barrel could have been changed or the fact that the gun has been used excessively since the time of the previous firing."

He said he'd established a connection between the weapon and the shell casings by ejector and firing pin marks.

"Is that a positive opinion?" Kalustian asked.

The expert witness answered, "That's correct."

Cochran had been called from the courtroom briefly, and Hollopeter said, "We have no questions."

Perhaps because of their age difference, Pratt and Hollopeter had become slightly estranged during the ordeal of the trial. As Wolfer stalked from the courtroom without being cross-examined, Pratt exploded in the lawyer's ear. "I respected Mr. Hollopeter's ability," he explained later, "but he didn't know a thing about ballistics. Ejector and firing pin marks aren't evidence. We should've put up a fight."

After Wolfer's uncontested testimony, the judge gave the jury a long weekend. Court was reconvened at 11:25 A.M. Monday, June 26, and the prosecution rested.

OVER A working lunch, Cochran and Hollopeter considered some of the anomalies in the case against their client. All murder trials were different, but a standard prosecutorial technique was to pad the record with police evidence and official witnesses in an effort to impress the jurors with sheer bulk. But Kalustian hadn't followed that pattern. Cochran wondered why his old classmate had avoided calling the top investigators on the case. Why hadn't he taken the testimony of Sergeant Ray Callahan of the LAPD's Panther Unit, a cop who was so personally involved that he'd volunteered to fly to Texas to put the handcuffs on Pratt? Where was Sergeant John Eckstein of the Santa Monica Police Department, the first investigator on the case and one of the most outspoken about Pratt's guilt? Where were the other detectives who'd worked the case?

"I'm thinking that Kalustian is afraid to call them because of the original ID procedures," Cochran suggested. "That's their weak point."

Hollopeter said, "Something's funny, all right. Did you ever try a murder case where everybody and his cousin were put in live show-ups—but not the main suspect?"

"Nope."

The two attorneys agreed that there was an odor, but they couldn't trace its origin.

COCHRAN DROVE home to the Hollywood hills and tried to get some sleep. From his earliest days in practice, he'd become accustomed to winning; he'd sailed through the struggling-young-lawyer phase of his career in a year. He told himself that Pratt's prospects still looked good. If this was a prizefight (and in many ways it was, he said to himself, complete with rabbit punches and head butts), Geronimo would be ahead on points. Barbara Reed had come across as impressionable and manipulable. The bereaved Kenneth Olsen was a sympathetic figure, of course, but he'd seemed a little too eager to avenge his ex-wife's death. And Julio Butler had revealed himself as a resentful duplicitous partisan. Cochran wished he'd been able to nail down the beautician's activities as an informer, but at least a few hints and innuendos about his police connections had been introduced into the record, some of them from both sides of the witness's mouth.

Cochran wished he felt certain of winning, but he'd seen too many juries bite overconfident lawyers in the backside, especially in cases involving race. The defendant who bought a new suit to go home in style sometimes ended up donating it to the Goodwill.

IN THE final days of Kalustian's presentation, Cochran, Hollopeter and the Pratt defense committee stepped up their crucial search for witnesses who could place their client in Oakland at the time of the shootings. A hired investigator and a half dozen Pratt relatives and other volunteers had searched without result. Shirley Hewitt, a former legal defense secretary at Panther headquarters, admitted to Hollopeter that she and some others could confirm the visit to Oakland, but they were afraid to testify because of the split in the party. Hollopeter begged her to reconsider.

Interviews with other Panther insiders proved equally frustrating, and some of the sessions turned ugly. Huey Newton's *fatwa* against Pratt not only dissuaded many Los Angeles Panthers from becoming witnesses but also dissuaded David Hilliard, Bobby Seale, Emory Douglas and others who'd sat with Pratt at meetings at Panther headquarters in Oakland. The only remaining friendlies in the top echelons were Newton's blood enemies, the Cleavers. Eldridge couldn't return to the United States because of

his legal difficulties, but Kathleen agreed to testify. The Cleavers were living on the kindness of strangers, and it would cost $1,200 for a round-trip
between Algiers and Los Angeles. Cochran wired a check drawn on his
personal bank account.

"I REMEMBER a chick named Jacqueline, Jackie Hooton or Horton, something like that," Geronimo said at a strategy session in the cubbyhole interview room in L.A. County Jail. "Man, you got to find her. She was with me
in Oakland a lot."

The defense got an unexpected break when an ex-Panther secretary
named Linda Redd agreed to testify. "She gave me hell when I finally
reached her by phone," Pratt told Cochran and Hollopeter. "She said, 'Why
didn't you call me a long time ago? Why'd I have to read about this trial in
the *L.A. Times*?'"

Cochran added her to his witness list.

The Best Offense

The first defense witness would be hostile and Cochran reminded himself that she would have to be handled with care. Margaret Morgan, Barbara Reed's Identikit assembler, had been a loyal Santa Monica police officer for fifteen years. Cochran opened by politely asking if she'd had special training.

"I was sent to the Identikit School out in Santa Ana," the woman testified, "and I use the Identikit in the course of my job."

Cochran asked the policewoman to refer to her notes and tell the jury how Mrs. Reed had described suspect no. 2 as the two of them were preparing the composite. "Male Negro," Morgan read. "Twenty-three to twenty-nine years. Five-eight to five-nine, medium weight, 145 to 150 pounds, medium light complexion, clean looking, very trim haircut, black shoes, black or dark pants, Eisenhower-type jacket, light beige, rust or a brown-colored shirt or sweater underneath the jacket."

"In your description," Cochran asked, "I notice that she never told you anything about a moustache or a beard or goatee. Is that right?"

Morgan took a long look at her notes, then said, "Not according to this report."

"I notice she never told you anything about any scars on the face of the individual. Is that right?"

Cochran wanted an unequivocal answer, but instead she offered, "Not to my recollection."

It was a pivotal point and he returned to it. "With regard to the face, she told you the person was clean looking?"

"As I so testified from the report, yes."

In response to persistent questioning, the police technician finally agreed that Barbara Reed had selected Identikit foils depicting a clean-shaven, scarless black man with a thick mouth, thick lips, a broad nose, bushy and thick brows. Some of the jurors appeared to be studying Geronimo Pratt. Few of the characteristics seemed to apply.

On cross-examination Kalustian suggested that Officer Morgan's memory might be imperfect since she was testifying about events that had happened three and a half years earlier. The policewoman said she recalled that Mrs. Reed hadn't been happy with the finished Identikit product.

On recross Cochran asked, "If Mrs. Reed had told you about a moustache, a beard, a goatee of any kind, you would have made an effort to put that in, wouldn't you?"

A. I would have given her the book to attempt to find one.

Q. And you did have beards and moustaches and goatees in that book. Isn't that correct?

A. Yes.

Q. Just as you had noses. Isn't that correct?

A. Yes. . . . Oh, there's pages of them. . . . pages of noses. . . .

Q. If there was some scarring that she told you about, you would try to find those scars?

A. There are no scar foils. . . .

Q. Isn't it true in the past you have drawn in scar foils, or drawn in a scar at the point where the person says a scar is?

A. We have attempted that. They don't work very well. . . .

Q. Now in your discussions with Mr. Kalustian this morning, did you ever have occasion to discuss this conversation of Mrs. Reed's wherein she said she was unhappy with the person's mouth?

A. Yes. . . .

Q. You have remembered that all this time, the last three and a half years?

A. . . . I just remember that she was unhappy with the foils. . . .

Q. And you remembered that during the conversation with Mr. Kalustian?

A. Yes.

Having once again suggested careful briefing by the prosecutor, this time of a defense witness, Cochran cut the questioning short. He hoped the jury got the point. There was nothing illegal or even unethical about preparing witnesses, but overzealous "trial prep" might seem a touch inappropriate for a deputy D.A. whose first obligation was to serve the interests of justice.

THE NEXT witness for the defense, the former secretary Linda Redd, said she'd been in high school in 1968 when Geronimo Pratt had worked with her and others to set up a black studies program. At the time, he'd had "a beard, full moustache and beard."

Cochran focused on the period around December 18, 1968, the date of the tennis court shootings. The young woman told of talking to Pratt in the Los Angeles Panther office sometime between December 13 and 15, then said she didn't see him until two days after Christmas.

"How do you recall the date that you next saw him, December 27?" Cochran asked.

"That was my birthday."

Later she testified, "I never forgot about December of '68 because that's when, like, the first person I knew, actually, in the party to get killed, and that was Captain Franco."

The former Panther secretary helped Cochran bolster an important point about Pratt's Pontiac convertible. "Everybody drove the GTO," she told the jury. "It was sort of like a community car. Anybody needed transportation, they would drive it if it was available." She confirmed Julius Butler's testimony that he'd been one of the drivers.

Soon after Richard Kalustian began his attack on the witness's credibility, Cochran objected to one of her questions.

"I didn't ask that question," the prosecutor snapped. "I never intended it. I have been a lawyer long enough to stay away from that kind of question. . . . I may be a little slow, John, but I'm not stupid."

The judge sustained Cochran's objection. It was a rare procedural victory for the defense.

SHIRLEY HEWITT, the former Panther who'd told Hollopeter that she was afraid to testify, changed her mind and told the jury that she remembered Pratt's extended stay in Oakland in December 1968. She said she'd first sighted him in midmonth, just after she'd joined the party, and noticed that "he dresses very nicely, and he had a powder-blue suit on, two-piece suit, and the thing that stuck in my mind was he had some blue suede shoes on."[22]

Cochran said, "Blue suede shoes?"

"Yes. Because it was known people who were in Los Angeles would dress sharp."

"Everybody in Los Angeles dresses sharply," Cochran said, producing smiles in the jury box.

Hewitt testified that the modishly dressed Angeleno had attended a session of the Central Committee along with David Hilliard, Bobby Seale, Kathleen Cleaver and other prominent Panthers. The meeting, she said, had begun around 6:00 P.M. on December 18 and lasted till dawn.

Cochran appreciated the woman's voluntary testimony, but he also recognized the beginnings of a problem. If the jurors kept hearing that Pratt had been at executive meetings in Oakland at the time of the shootings in Los Angeles, they would begin to wonder why Panther executives weren't in court saying so. He kept hoping for a last-minute call from Hilliard, Seale, Emory Douglas[23] or even Huey P. Newton. *The feud's over. Tell Geronimo we're on our way!* But he feared it wouldn't happen. Word from Oakland was that Newton was still adding names to his enemies list. He wasn't likely to provide an amnesty for the "jackanape" Pratt.

Cochran took a stab at elucidating the problem to the jury by asking Shirley Hewitt, "Mr. Hollopeter asked you about finding some witnesses or locating some witnesses, is that correct, in the Bay Area?"

Kalustian objected. "Apparently they are trying to bring in the testimony of other witnesses through this witness," he told the judge. "It would be hearsay. . . ."

Judge Parker agreed. "It is hearsay. It is also leading."

The fact that Panther leaders were afraid to testify was too important a point to be dropped without a fight, and Cochran tried another approach. "Did you talk to people in Northern California?" he asked.

---

[22] Regularly borrowed from Bunchy Carter.

[23] Years later Douglas explained, "We couldn't say anything because we had orders from Huey." He doubted that his testimony would have mattered. "I don't think we could have saved him. With all that disinformation that was being put out by the FBI, I don't think it would've worked."

"Yes," the legal secretary answered. "I talked to several people."

Cochran asked if other witnesses were afraid to testify.

"That's true," she replied.

"Objection!" Kalustian called out.

The judge ordered the answer stricken from the record.

Cochran didn't intend to be any less persistent than his Loyola classmate. "You are no longer a member of the Black Panther Party," he said to the witness. "Is that right?"

"That's right."

"Did you have some fear with regard to coming to testify?"

"I have some apprehensions, yes."

"Why is that?"

"Well, since I have left the party, I have been harassed myself, and I just know that my husband and the other people in the party won't relate to me coming to testify for G."

Cochran asked if there was a "split" in the party.

The witness answered, "Definitely."

It was as close to a clear depiction of the problem as Cochran would be able to provide the jurors for the rest of the trial. He hoped that at least a few got the message. In deliberations one could enlighten the others.

THE NEXT defense witness identified himself as Richard Stanley Johns, Julio Butler's former roommate and a self-described "squad leader" in the hairdresser's underground cell. Johns told of driving to a ghetto gas station to find the suspected traitor Ollie Taylor and returning him to Butler's apartment. Geronimo Pratt, the witness testified, hadn't been on the premises when Taylor was dropped off, the first of several contradictions of Butler's testimony. Johns also confirmed that many different Panthers drove the Pontiac GTO known as the Goat and that Pratt had had facial hair "as long as I have known him." He talked about Julio's assault on a Panther named Bobby for refusing to cut a dog's throat—"it was quite a few teeth that were knocked out"—and other strong-arm tactics. And he became the first witness to affirm, in contradiction to Butler's direct testimony, that Pratt had expelled Butler from the party.

AT THE morning session on Tuesday, June 27, Cochran called Dr. Robert Buckhout, a psychology professor and a pioneer in the study of eyewitness testimony. The Ohio State University Ph.D. had barely started to list his credentials when Kalustian demanded a sidebar. Out of the jury's earshot, he attacked Buckhout, his background and bona fides, and compared his field of expertise to phrenology, the ancient study of bumps on the head. After a long wrangle Judge Parker sent the jury home and approved the prosecutor's motion to hold a formal hearing to decide whether Buckhout should be permitted to testify.

The hearing droned on in an empty courtroom, and in the end the judge ruled that the psychologist could be heard. "Juries may or may not accept the testimony of an expert," she noted. "They frequently don't accept the testimony of psychiatrists." In an aside that Cochran and Hollopeter found gratifying, she added, "It is true that it is common knowledge that there are mistakes in eyewitness identification."

IN THE presence of the jury Buckhout described experiments in which staged "assaults" were committed in college classrooms and the students were asked to describe what they'd seen. In one such experiment students described the weight of the 160-pound "perpetrator" in a range from 98 to 225 pounds. The height descriptions were similarly inaccurate, "and the time estimates were the worst." The staged incident had taken thirty-four seconds; the average student guessed it had lasted three minutes. Six weeks later the test group was shown a photo lineup which included the "perpetrator" and five others. "The basic results," Buckhout recalled, "were that over sixty-five percent of the people in the classroom specifically identified the wrong man."

Cochran asked, "Based upon your experience, your background, your research, your papers that you have done, do you have an opinion as to whether or not eyewitness identification is reliable?"

"My opinion," Buckhout replied, "is that in general it is not. . . . The human perceiver in any circumstance is not a perfect recorder of what he sees." All too often, he said, preconceptions about racial characteristics weakened eyewitness testimony. "We use stereotyped judgments. 'You have seen one black person, you have seen them all.' "

With frequent objections from the prosecutor, Buckhout turned to his evaluations of the identifications of some of the prosecution's star witnesses. Sometimes he seemed to lose the jury with phrases like "proactive inhibitions," "dyadic verbal behavior" and "psychonomic perceptions," and Cochran kept forcing him to simplify. Buckhout told the jurors that he thought little of Kenneth Olsen's identification of Geronimo Pratt and less of Barbara Mary Reed's. To the psychologist, Olsen's identifications were weakened by the stress of the robbery and shooting, and Mrs. Reed's were tarnished by racial stereotyping and her "cocksureness." Nor did he agree that the memory of an eyewitness would sharpen over the years.

As to the photo selections that had been made in roundtable settings consisting of police officers, deputy district attorneys, relatives and fellow victims, Buckhout suggested that they were useless. "People have a desire to be correct," he told the jury. "A police officer or a court officer may be in the position of conveying to the person that 'I didn't bring you down here for nothing,' and the person may be saying to himself, 'I don't want to appear a fool.' " He described the photo lineup in which Pratt had been the only suspect in a bush jacket as "an unfair test."

Cochran's expert endured an intense cross-examination, his opinions and analyses challenged but unchanged, and was excused late on Friday afternoon, June 30. He'd been on the witness stand for nearly four days.

THE NEXT witness was refreshingly brief. Lamar Lyons described himself as "ex–student body president, High Potential Program, UCLA," and told the court that his classmate Geronimo Pratt wore "a light growth" of facial hair in college and never carried a gun. Then Cochran rolled the dice and called Santa Monica Detective John R. Eckstein, lead investigator on the case before it had been taken over by the LAPD's Panther Unit. Eckstein had been so emphatic about bringing Pratt to justice that he'd chauffeured Barbara Mary Reed to LAPD headquarters so she could identify the "perpetrator." Cochran had to risk the detective's adverse testimony because he wanted the jury to know exactly who had generated the two composites that bore so little resemblance to the man on trial. His first police witness, Margaret Morgan, hadn't fully answered the question.

Neither did Eckstein. He insisted that he himself had taken no part in creating the composites. He admitted that one bore the penciled inscription "M. Morgan," but "I don't know when that was put on there." He thought that the other composite might have been made by the CDC, the California Department of Corrections.

Cochran brought up the delicate matter of the suspect whom Kenneth Olsen had mistakenly identified long before he'd pointed out Geronimo Pratt. Cochran still remembered Olsen's evasiveness earlier in the trial: *I identified the person at the lineup that I had seen in the pictures, as such. And I told*

Detective Eckstein that while there was a possibility, I didn't feel I could really make an identification of that person, because I didn't feel, really, it was the person.

Cochran found it no easier to get a direct answer from Eckstein:

Q. . . . It is true, is it not, that at one point Mr. Olsen picked the pictures of two of the suspects out, didn't he?

A. I would like you to elaborate a little further, "picked you out."

Q. You showed Mr. Olsen a series of photos over a period of time?

A. Yes, sir.

Q. At some point you showed him a series of six photos on one particular date, didn't you?

A. Yes, I did.

Q. From those six photographs Mr. Olsen said two of these men looked like the men who were the attackers?

A. They looked like two of the men that could be the attackers.

Q. As such, he asked for a lineup. Isn't that correct?

A. Yes, he did. He wanted to see them in person as he couldn't identify them from pictures.

Q. You furnished him with that lineup. Isn't that correct?

A. That's correct. . . .

Q. From that particular show-up it is true, is it not, that Mr. Olsen picked one of those men out as believing that was one of the men involved in the attack?

A. He picked a man out that he had seen a picture of, and he said he thought he could be involved. But he wasn't that positive.

Q. . . . Do you have the pictures with you today of the six men in that lineup?

A. No, sir, I haven't.

Q. Where are those pictures?

A. I don't know right at this time.

Q. If we needed them later, could you get them for us?

A. It's possible . . . if I can get my hands on them.

Isn't it odd, Cochran thought in passing, how so much exculpatory evidence evaporates in police stations? He'd seen a mug shot of Ernest Perkins, the man Olsen had thought "might be involved," and he bore little resemblance to Geronimo Pratt. If Cochran could get his hands on the photo lineup from which Olsen had selected the wrong man, he could show the jury a concrete example of botched cross-racial identification. He could also show how desperate the police had been to solve the case before Julio Butler dropped Pratt in their laps.

He asked Eckstein, "Will you check for us regarding those pictures?"

"Yes," the detective promised. "I will."

OVER THE weekend Cochran drove to Los Angeles International Airport to pick up Kathleen Cleaver. The exiled Panther seemed frazzled after the long flight from North Africa but eager to testify. As Cochran steered his Cadillac onto Century Boulevard, en route to her friend's house in suburban Compton, he realized they had a tail. The pursuit driver kept his dark car a few feet from the El Dorado's bumper.

Cleaver peeked behind and said, "That's the FBI.[24] They've got their own style. They don't do surveillance. They do intimidation."

Cochran crunched the brake pedal and swerved to the curb. "Son of a gun!" he exclaimed to his passenger. "They tap my phones and tail my witnesses. What the hell kind of trial is this?"

"You were never a Panther," Cleaver said matter-of-factly.

"What do you mean?"

"You'd think this was nothing."

On the rest of the drive he kept hearing a familiar voice in his head: *This whole case is about something else. . . . You'll see. They're after me, and they're going to do whatever it takes to get me. . . .*

BEFORE TRIAL continued on Monday, July 3, Cochran and Hollopeter held a short strategy session and decided that they were still ahead. They agreed that the jury had been fed enhanced testimony, some of it downright false, and they hoped that the liars had given themselves away. Countering falsehoods was what lawyering was all about.

Then they called one witness too many.

---

[24] Years later the FBI confirmed that it had conducted surveillance on Pratt's relatives, attorneys and witnesses throughout the trial.

Overexposure

Under any conditions it would have been hard to keep Charles Emile Pratt off the witness stand. The most tightly wound Pratt had also been the most vocal about his brother's innocence. At thirty-five Charles was ten years older than Geronimo and proud to stand in loco parentis. As family pathfinder, he'd led the Pratt diaspora to the west and worked his way through UCLA. A handsome man, he'd briefly dated his classmate Johnnie Cochran's sister Pearl and earned a master's degree at USC. Along with his younger brother Jack, Charles had been in a state of rage ever since the police incursions on his sister Virginia's apartment.

"They need a warrant to search a white person's house," he complained to the defense attorneys. "But they just bust in on black folks."

The older brother claimed that he'd turned up physical evidence of Geronimo's innocence. Leafing through a family photo album, he found a Polaroid print that showed Geronimo holding an infant nephew while Charles' other three sons peeked at the camera from the bathtub. Geronimo was wearing a conspicuous moustache and a frizzy goatee. The picture had been taken during the year-end holidays in 1968, less than two weeks after the shootings.

Cochran and Hollopeter tried to decide what to do with the evidence. As students of the case would point out in future years, the introduction of the photo could produce no major gain for the defense. Five witnesses, including the archenemy Julio Butler, had already agreed that the defendant had facial hair and/or that they'd never known him without it. Other witnesses waited in the wings to say the same. Nor had Kalustian attempted to counter the damaging testimony despite the fact that the original composites plainly showed clean-shaven killers. It was the most glaring contradiction in the prosecution's case.

CHARLES PRATT, slight, wiry, with wavy hair and a neatly trimmed beard, took the witness stand on Monday morning, July 3, and immediately seemed to put Kalustian on edge. After Hollopeter asked, "How many brothers and sisters do you have?" the prosecutor called out, "Objection as immaterial!" The defense attorney withdrew the question, but when he asked, "Do you have children?" Kalustian objected again.

After the preliminary skirmishing Charles identified the Polaroid picture and said that it had been taken in his home shortly after Geronimo's return from Oakland in the final days of 1968. If he'd had facial hair at that time, he couldn't have been clean-shaven at the time of the murder two weeks earlier. Charles testified that his brother hadn't been clean-shaven since Vietnam.

Emelda Pratt Granger, married and living in Chicago, backed up her brother's testimony. The Polaroid picture had been taken December 27, 1968, she said, at a birthday party for Charles' son. She had a clear memory of Geronimo's goatee: "I was always after him to maybe cut it off because I didn't really like it."

THE QUESTIONING of the next witness, a former Black Panther and shoe salesman named Michael David Pennewell, produced an exchange that made Pratt nod knowingly at his lawyers. On direct examination Pennewell reinforced defense points about facial hair, bush jackets and the GTO's multiple drivers. On cross-examination Kalustian asked when he'd first been asked to remember the events before the court.

Pennewell began a ruminative answer, the kind that usually aggravates one lawyer or the other: "Well, the first time, going back, I got out of Biscailuz Center [jail] in July of last year, and—no, longer. I was out two weeks, and I had a visit by the FBI, and that was when the trial of the thirteen was—the Panther Thirteen was going on, and FBI told me that they was, you know, charging G with a murder."

In a stern voice Kalustian said, "What FBI agent came to you and told you that?"

"I don't know their name," Pennewell answered.

The prosecutor said, "They didn't come and tell you that, did they?" It was phrased more like a statement than a question.

"Yes, they did."

Kalustian said sharply, "The FBI's never been involved in this case, and you know it!"

Pennewell started to answer—"Well, I'"—when Cochran interrupted and said, "Object to Mr. Kalustian testifying."

"Sustained," Judge Parker said.

The deputy D.A. paused, then asked Pennewell, "The first time you remember anything about the events of December 1968 was when some people you think were the FBI came to you?"

Pennewell said, "I saw their identification, sir."

Kalustian dropped the subject. At the next recess Pratt told his attorneys, "Like I said, we're fighting the whole damn government."

"You were on track from the beginning," Cochran admitted. "You always claimed that somebody fixed this case. Wouldn't it be something if it was the FBI?"

KATHLEEN CLEAVER, an original Panther who'd once been a member of the BPP Central Committee, gave her place of residence as Algiers, Algeria. Under Cochran's questioning she testified that she had a clear recollection of Geronimo's presence in Oakland in the last half of December 1968, because a close friend had been shot on Market Street in San Francisco on December 13, "and that date sticks in my mind." She described social events, parties and meetings she'd attended with Pratt—"There was a lot of movement, a lot of flux. People were moving around, and he was there. . . ."

On cross-examination Kalustian asked about the timing of Cleaver's first awareness of the murder charges, her meetings with defense attorneys, the "importance" of the case and other marginal issues. Cleaver seemed prickly, and after a few minutes the prosecutor said, "Can I ask the questions and you answer them, perhaps?"

"Object to the lecture, Your Honor," Cochran said.

Cochran's direct examination had lasted fifteen minutes, but Kalustian kept the witness on the stand twice as long and succeeded in making her seem less certain about her timetable and more biased toward her friend Pratt.

On balance, Cochran remained happy that he'd paid Cleaver's way from Algeria. He asked a few questions on redirect examination and then induced her to repeat that "every time I have seen him, he had facial hair. I have never seen him without facial hair." He hoped he wasn't boring the jury with the heavy repetition, but it went to the heart of the case. In the deliberation room the jurors would pass Charles Pratt's Polaroid print from hand to hand, powerful physical evidence that Geronimo couldn't have been the killer. It was the best kind of proof—if it wasn't tainted.

His Own Best Witness

There'd never been a doubt that Geronimo would testify. In typical criminal trials the downside to such an appearance was that it opened up the
subject of the defendant's past life, including prior criminal activity. In
Pratt's opinion his minor criminal record was the result of a police campaign of harassment, easily countered with facts and logic, and his most
heinous offense had been breaking a high school window.

"Did you go to a hobby shop in the city of Santa Monica?" Charles
Hollopeter asked.

"No!" The answer carried to the back wall of the big courtroom. "I
didn't."

"And on the night of December 18th, 1968, did you go to any tennis
court in the city of Santa Monica?"

"No, I—did—not."

"Have you ever been in the tennis court that was described in the evidence in this case?"

"No, I haven't."

"Have you ever been in the hobby shop that was testified to?"

"No, I have not."

HOLLOPETER AND Cochran had advised their client to avoid Panther rhetoric; right or wrong, the BPP's rallying cries might annoy white jurors. As usual, Geronimo had put up an argument. "This trial's *about* the Black Panthers. This is a political trial, Cochran."

"The jury doesn't know that," Cochran had told him. "We don't want any of that 'off the pigs' stuff to slip into the record."

"The only pigs I ever wanted to off," Pratt had fired back, "were the pigs who wanted to off *me.*"

On the stand he refused to deride the organization that had shamed and expelled him. When Hollopeter asked if he'd served in the United States Army, he answered, "United States *Imperialist* Army. Correct." After that, he settled down and followed his attorneys' advice, providing direct answers and avoiding the temptation to volunteer information.

Hollopeter inquired about his relationship with the man who'd heard his repeated "confessions":

Q. . . . Did Julius Butler become a close friend of yours?
A. No. We never became close friends, no.
Q. Was there ever any time that you sought him out to ask his advice?
A. No.
Q. Was there ever a time when you looked him up in order to confide in him, tell him things?
A. No. . . .
Q. Now in around the middle of December 1968, what was your feeling and regard for Mr. Butler, if any?
A. . . . I kind of suspected the dude all along, you know? He always seemed suspicious to me. . . . After Bunchy was killed, he was coordinating some activities on the Westside and he would go to—he would pull all kinds of sadistic acts, you know, and with people who were supposed to be working with him.

Pratt testified that Butler had knocked out one young Panther's teeth and forced two brothers to their knees, "kicked one in the head because of some nickel and dime thing." He told of going to Butler's apartment and finding the high school boy Ollie Taylor "sitting down and he was bloody, his whole face was bloody . . . something was swollen on his face."

He said he had taken Butler aside, lectured him about brutality and "relieved him of his position."

"Right there?" Hollopeter asked.

"Right. He was placed on house arrest."

Pratt denied discussing the tennis court shootings with the person he'd expelled from the party. Nor had he ever introduced Butler to a man named Tyrone. He provided more detail about his Pontiac GTO, the Goat, and how it had been converted to a Panther vehicle, with the BPP making the monthly bank payments. He said the party had arranged to have the car repainted as a result of a visit by Eldridge Cleaver. "You see, he got in the car, and ever since then, it was hot and every time you'd drive even around the corner, you would get stopped by the police."

Hollopeter asked, "So the car became well-known?"

"Oh, yes, and then after [Cleaver] came down again and then at Bunchy's funeral—man, the car, it would be stopped all the time by the police and then they would kick dents in it and pull the distributor wires loose and would arrest people, you know, and it was depleting our funds, the party funds, and hardly anyone would want to ride in the car, you know, because they would get arrested by the police."

After the inevitable exchange about facial hair—"my moustache was pretty heavy"—Hollopeter turned to the subject of the .45-caliber handgun that had been recovered from the Huggins house the day of the Campbell Hall killings.

"Was that your gun?" the lawyer asked.

"No, it wasn't."

"When you went into the [Huggins] home did you see that gun there?"

"No, I didn't."

". . . Have you ever had that gun in your possession?"

"No."

Pratt reiterated that he'd been in the Bay Area at the time of the tennis court shootings, that Bunchy Carter had provided his airline ticket to San Francisco and he'd taken a taxi to a Black Panther storefront office on Fillmore Street. He'd spent the night at a nearby "Panther pad" and met a woman named Jackie Horton the next day—"I was with her most of the time I was up there." He ran down an informal list of meetings and social gatherings and said he'd joined some of the northern Panthers in selling the party newspaper on street corners. "I went to a breakfast program they had at Father Neil's church . . . and then we found out that Franco had gotten killed. . . . It was about a week or so after I had gotten up there."

"So about what date would that be?" Hollopeter asked.

"I don't know. I heard that he got killed on the nineteenth [of December 1968, the day after the tennis court incident], but I—it was about a week after I had gotten—it was a while after I'd gotten up there. . . ." He said he'd returned to Los Angeles a day or two after Christmas.

Hollopeter showed him the Polaroid photo introduced by his brother Charles, and Geronimo remembered that it had been taken at a December 1968 birthday party for his nephew—"I think it was the 27th or 28th—the 28th. It wasn't long after Christmas, you know. His birthday is on Christmas."

THE DIRECT examination was completed at 4:15 P.M. on Thursday, July 6. When trial resumed at 2:40 the next afternoon, the prosecutor set about showing the jury that Geronimo Pratt was a liar. "How tall are you?" he asked.

"Five-six."

"Have you ever been as tall as five-seven?"

"Not that I recall, no."

"What is your date of birth?"

"September 13, 1947."

"Have you ever given a different date of birth?"

Hollopeter objected—"immaterial, irrelevant."

The judge told Pratt, "You may answer the question."

"Yes," he said. "I have given other ages."

Kalustian produced a copy of Geronimo's California driver's license, showing a DOB of September 13, 1942, and asked, "Did you supply that information?"

"No. . . . I don't know where it came from." But Pratt had to affirm that the signature looked like his.

The prosecutor resumed in the same scattershot style he'd employed with other witnesses, jumping from subject to subject. Cochran remembered his opponent as one of the brightest students at Loyola Law School and presumed that the disjointedness was deliberate.

"Mr. Pratt," Kalustian said, "when you were in the service, did you ever have occasion to carry a .45 as part of your duties?"

"Yes."

Q. Are you familiar with the operation of a .45-caliber automatic?
A. Yes, I'm very familiar with a .45.

Q. . . . Do you know how to field-strip a .45, put it back together and take it apart? That kind of thing?

A. Yes.

Q. Can you interchange the barrel of a .45-caliber automatic?

A. Yes.

As Cochran watched from the defense table, he realized that his old classmate was employing the courtroom version of a basketball full-court press in an attempt to score points with the jury. "First he'd walk toward the witness," Cochran wrote later, "then move back toward the jury. He'd stand facing them, letting them read his facial expressions to Pratt's responses under attack. This created a type of split-screen effect. On one screen, the jury saw the prosecutor's face, on the other the defendant's. Each told a different story. The jury got to see both the point and the counterpoint of the hard-line questioning."

Cochran wasn't offended. He'd been taught that the ends of justice required aggressive advocacy by both sides. Besides, he was pleased to see that the ex-paratrooper who'd weathered two tours of battle seemed unfazed by the prosecution attack. "Our confidence surged," Cochran wrote later. "But 'pride goeth before a fall. . . .' "

AS THE afternoon session wore on, all parties began to show strain. Kalustian skipped back to the visit to Oakland at the time of the shootings and asked a series of questions about how much money Pratt had taken with him on the trip ("About forty or fifty dollars"), how long he'd planned to stay ("I don't think we had any pre-plans"), why he hadn't used an airport bus ("I didn't know how"), where he'd been on the evening of December 18 ("I think I was at David Hilliard's house"), what he did after the evening with Hilliard ("I was brought by this party with a sister, and we left. . . . We went to some pad, and I went to sleep"), what he did the next day ("We talked about the contradictions that was prevalent in the society") and other probings of Pratt's memory.

At an intense sidebar Cochran was making a point when Kalustian complained, "Could you talk a little softer?"

"I'm sorry," Cochran said.

Then Kalustian complained that the testimony had become "embroiled in semantics in use of terms with which I am not familiar and he [Pratt] is a lot more familiar with than I am." He accused Pratt of being vague—"he stops and starts about six times. That's my problem."

Judge Parker informed the prosecutor that he was "getting too far afield."

After the jury returned, a long colloquy ensued on the difference between "black houses" and "Panther houses." Pratt drew giggles from the spectators when he explained that "it isn't anything strict about either house, you know? Like, for instance, a Panther pad, say if Johnnie—say Johnnie Cochran would come by and wants to stay overnight, he would be welcome." He hesitated and added, "You, too, Mr. Hollopeter. Excuse me." He didn't include Kalustian.

IN PRATT'S third hour on the stand the questioning hotted up. The subject was the scene in Butler's house on the night of the Ollie Taylor beating. Pratt had testified that "Julio was drunk, you know . . . and that was a violation of the rules."

Kalustian said, "Julio couldn't even be drunk in his own home under the rules of the organization?"

"You see, man," Geronimo began, speaking slowly as though to a student, "we are socialists, you know? We relate to socialist principles. And if Julio wanted to relate to selfishness, he didn't have to join the organization. Do you understand? And—"

"No," the prosecutor said. "My only question, Mr. Pratt, was—"

"I'm *trying* to make you understand."

The judge listened to a few more acidic exchanges and said, "Mr. Kalustian, I see it is after four-thirty. We will recess until tomorrow."

ON THE next day, Friday, July 7, 1972, the prosecutor took the defendant through perfunctory questioning about his relationship with Julius Carl Butler, and Pratt seized on the opportunity to remind the jury of his sworn enemy's rage about his expulsion from the Black Panther Party. "I got a phone call at Central Headquarters after Julio was expelled in which he said he would kill my sister and my brother and my people." He accused Butler of having "a very arrogant attitude . . . like he wasn't subject to criticism. . . . that a lot of people in leadership positions weren't capable of carrying out those functions because they didn't know how to kill. . . ."

To the bafflement of the defense attorneys, Kalustian introduced the subject of the birthday party photograph. He wanted to know if Pratt had seen the picture immediately after it had been taken.

"Yes," Geronimo answered.

"Was the picture taken by your brother with a Polaroid camera?"

"I think it was with—yeah, I think so. . . . I remember seeing that picture in his album."

The prosecutor asked if Pratt had ever threatened Butler. "No," he answered. "I never did." Kalustian said he had no further questions.

THE TRIAL was winding down, and Cochran and his cocounsel were still scrabbling about for prominent Panthers who could confirm Pratt's visit to Oakland. They made contact with Jackie Horton, the woman Geronimo had described as his frequent companion during his stay in the Bay Area. Now it was time for her to testify, and she was missing. Cochran assured the judge that she "will be here sometime this afternoon."

Kalustian was surprisingly obliging about the delay and spent the remainder of the Friday session in another long plea to the judge about Julio Butler's "insurance letter." With the jury out of the courtroom he made a statement that would be quoted often in future proceedings. He spoke of the alleged confessions Pratt had made to Butler, and added, "If the jury believes Julio Butler, regardless of whether they believe or disbelieve the identification witnesses, Mr. Pratt is guilty. The case is over if they believe that."

Judge Parker adjourned court for the weekend.

ON MONDAY morning the final defense witness identified herself as Jacqueline Horton Wilcots, a former Black Panther from the San Francisco Bay Area. She could be a decisive witness if the jury believed her story, and her credibility was crucial. There'd been almost no trial preparation; she'd arrived in Los Angeles the night before. Jailers had given her three minutes with her old friend Pratt before hustling him away.

In a timid little voice the young African American told the jurors that she'd served as Pratt's driver on his December visit to Oakland and had taken him to parties and BPP meetings. At the time, she said, he'd worn a "Fu Manchu." Just after Christmas she'd driven him to the San Francisco airport for his trip home.

On cross-examination Kalustian asked how she'd first learned that Pratt was going to trial. "I ran into this sister on the street," the woman replied, "and, like, she had been down here and she told me." Wilcots admitted that she was in the courtroom "to help a brother out."

When she replied to a string of questions by nodding and saying, "Uh-huh," the prosecutor said sharply, "The reporter doesn't get your uh-huhs, Mrs. Wilcots." Her shy manner made her seem almost reluctant to testify.

After she told the jury that she'd seen Pratt in the Bay Area "twenty or thirty times," Cochran asked a few questions on redirect examination and then said he had nothing further.

"You may step down," the judge said.

The young woman got to her feet and asked, "Do I have to be sworn out?"

The courtroom erupted in laughter.

Judge Parker rapped her gavel and said, "Step down, ma'am!" Then she turned to the bailiff and said, "Will you clear the courtroom if there is going to be any further levity?"

With his climax witness reduced to the role of court jester, Johnnie Cochran announced, "The defense rests."

The Trap Springs

During the final phase of the trial Richard Kalustian called LAPD Sergeant DuWayne Rice and reestablished that Julio Butler had given him a sealed letter marked "open in event of my death." Hollopeter and Cochran were annoyed that the subject was being raised again. They still regarded it as a blatant excuse to bootstrap Butler's shaky testimony by suggesting that his charges against Pratt were supported by a written document that he'd prepared as self-protection and never intended to make public. The defense attorneys were certain that they weren't hearing the whole truth.

On cross-examination Hollopeter asked DuWayne Rice if he and Butler were personal friends.

"That's correct, sir," the sergeant answered in the crisply professional style he'd established on direct examination.

Hollopeter asked if Butler had ever named anyone "who might have threatened his life."

"No. I don't think he named any particular person."

"Well, now, as a police officer and as a friend of Julio Butler's, you wanted to protect him, didn't you?"

"I didn't want to see him killed, sir, if that's what you mean."

"Well," the lawyer said, "what did you do, if anything, to prevent his being killed?"

"Nothing, sir."

On touchier matters Hollopeter found Rice as guarded as some of the other police witnesses:

Q. Did Julio Butler give you information about the community from time to time?

A. I don't know in what context you mean that, sir.

Q. Didn't he inform on people from time to time?

A. No, sir. He didn't.

Q. Didn't he tell you about any crimes or any problems going on?

A. No, sir. We discussed some of the problems in general, but he didn't come to me as an informant.

Q. He didn't act as an informant for you?

A. Not during the time of our relationship prior to the time of my getting that letter, sir.

Q. Well, I'm not sure I understand. Did he act as an informant after he gave you the letter?

A. I would have to clarify. It is hard to answer that yes or no, sir. Because of a lot of things, I will have to qualify my answer.

Q. Let me put it this way: did he ever act as a police informant for you?

A. Yes, he did, sir.

Q. Did he do that before August 10th or after August 10th, 1969, or both before and after?

A. I would say for approximately a week or so prior, and I never saw him very much after he gave me the letter.

Q. But . . . he did give you information as a police informer?

A. Yes. I think that is a fact.

Q. Was he paid for that information?

A. No, sir.

As Kalustian stood up to begin redirect examination, Pratt whispered to Cochran, "He's not telling the whole story. Julio wasn't just a part-time snitch."

Cochran said, "I think we got as close as we could."

PRATT AND his attorneys were surprised when Kalustian called a digni-fied man who identified himself as Joseph Oldfield, a technical manager at the Polaroid plant in Waltham, Massachusetts. The prosecutor asked, "Does the Polaroid Corporation have a method of coding the film they manufacture to determine the date of its manufacture?"

"Yes, we do," Oldfield answered. He looked at the Charles Pratt photograph and identified it as "our type 107 black and white film." Then he added, "We came on the market with this in 1963."

Cochran thought, There's no contradiction; Charles took the picture at Christmastime 1968.

"Now on the picture," the prosecutor continued, "I notice there are some numbers at the bottom, E933831. . . . What do those numbers tell you?"

"The first digit refers to the month of manufacture. This is an 'E,' which would be the fifth month, which would mean that it was manufactured in May. The second digit is a '9,' which refers to the year, which means it was manufactured in 1969. . . ."

As the import of the technician's testimony began to sink in, a stunned silence came over the courtroom. If the coding was correct, the film hadn't existed until six months after the Christmas picture. In the second row Charles Pratt shook his head in vigorous denial. Virginia Pratt frowned and whispered to her brother. At the defense table Geronimo tried not to show his bewilderment.

Behind his own poker face Cochran wondered if he was hearing things. He thought, Should I have checked that coding? Three different Pratts had confirmed the date of the photo session. Each had seemed certain. The picture and the resulting testimony had added nothing crucial to the defense position. Ten witnesses—the two Pratt sisters, Charles Pratt, Julio Butler, Linda Redd, Shirley Hewitt, Lamar Lyons, Kathleen Cleaver, Michael Pennewell and Jacqueline Wilcots—had affirmed that Geronimo had facial hair at the time of the shootings. No aspect of the case had been so heavily pounded into the jury's consciousness. Now here was a Polaroid executive testifying, in effect, that the Pratts had lied in concert to buttress a point that had never been in doubt. Cochran couldn't remember a more frustrating moment in a courtroom.

The defense lawyers held a whispered conference. An intensive cross-examination might only enhance the technician's testimony. The man certainly wasn't going to do a volte-face on the witness stand and confess that he'd misinterpreted his own company's code.

Hollopeter told the judge, "We have no questions." The prosecution coup had taken less than ten minutes.

A BAILIFF escorted Kalustian's next rebuttal witness into the courtroom. For his second star turn, he was attired in slacks, dark scarf and sports jacket, a reminder that style was his profession. The prosecutor asked him to remove his dark glasses and said, "Do you know Sergeant Rice of the Los Angeles Police Department?"

"Yes," Julius Butler said. "I do."

"Is he a friend of yours?"

"Yes, he is."

Once again the subject of the letter was opened, and once again it led to a long debate out of the presence of the jury. The judge finally allowed Kalustian to ask, "Did you have a conversation with Sergeant Rice regarding opening the envelope?"

"Yes," Butler answered. "I did."

"What did you say and what did he say regarding that particular item?"

"Sergeant Rice stated to me that the Internal Affairs Bureau of the Los Angeles Police Department had instituted an investigation relevant to his being possibly subversive because of his relationship with me and the envelope, and that as a personal friend he would not open the envelope and would take his chances on being persecuted or fired if I stated so, and I told—at which time I told him he had subjected himself enough for my friendship, and to go ahead and open the envelope."

Kalustian asked the cosmetician if he'd testified truthfully before the grand jury that indicted Pratt. Hollopeter called the question "argumentative" and Cochran called it "self-serving." Hollopeter added, "You can't prove the truth of a witness's testimony by asking him if he is truthful."

Cochran took Butler on cross-examination and doubled back to the informer issue. "You'd been an informant for Sergeant Rice?" he asked.

"No."

"You never were an informant for Sergeant Rice?"

"Not an informant, no."

On redirect examination Kalustian showed his sensitivity to the issue by asking, "You have indicated that you said you never had been an informant for Sergeant Rice?"

"That's correct," Butler answered.

"Did you ever supply Sergeant Rice information?"

"You mean about the party?"

"Well, any kind of information."

"Sergeant Rice was a confidante of mine, but it was not in the sense of policeman and public relations, sir, a citizen and police relationship."

Cochran wanted to jump up and yell, *Were you an informer or not?* He listened as Kalustian asked, "Why did you use the words you'd never been an informant?"

"Well, the connotation 'informant' means a snitch, and I have never been in the world a snitch."

Cochran found it hard to conceal his contempt as he took over the questioning. He asked if Butler had ever given Sergeant Rice any information that hadn't been authorized or cleared by the Black Panther hierarchy.

Butler paused, looked at the ceiling, looked at Kalustian and finally answered, "Of what nature? Because when you are narrowing down information like that, my conversations would falsify one thing, but when you say what nature, if you specify what nature, then I'll answer you, Counsel."

Cochran considered Butler's roundabout answer almost helpful. Jurors forgave lawyers for playing word games—in a way, that was their job—but they were less likely to forgive sly witnesses. The general presumption was that evasions and tergiversations by witnesses were aimed at concealing the truth. Surely these jurors could draw their own conclusions about the proprietor of Mr. Julio's Coiffures la Dames. Hadn't they just heard Sergeant Rice testify that Butler had indeed been an informer, at least for a week or two?

Cochran decided to finish up with an ancient trick of cross-examination: simple questions in simple English. He paused to make sure that every juror was paying close attention, placed himself midway between the jury box and the witness and asked, "Did you—ever—inform—on—*anybody*?"

Butler hesitated, then said, "No."

"You *never* did that?"

"No." This time the answer was slightly more emphatic.

Cochran nodded knowingly at the jurors and said, "I have nothing further."

Later he wrote: "I looked over at our jury—nine whites and three African Americans. Some of them gazed at Butler with perplexity, some with outright loathing. None of them looked very happy."

CHARLES PRATT and his brother Jack pleaded with Cochran to let them testify in the final phase of testimony: surrebuttal. Jack now worked at Systems Development Corporation as overnight supervisor of computer operations, and he was hell-bent to educate the jury on the Polaroid matter.

"I know the whole history of that film," he told Cochran. "We buy that stuff by the case and go through it like water. Everybody takes home odds and ends. That's where this filmpack came from. I'm the one who brought it home."

"How come SDC uses so much film?" Cochran asked.

"We shoot Polaroids of all the binary numbers. The scientists come in later and study the pictures."

"What about the coding on the filmpacks?"

"They're coded in the future so the film looks fresh. Every manufacturer does that. We get packs that are months off in the coding." He paused. "I can explain all that—"

"So can I," his older brother Charles broke in. "And I'm the one they're gonna accuse of lying."

Cochran had misgivings about putting either brother on the stand. Juries were dubious about complex explanations, especially on behalf of loved ones. The best witnesses followed the old rules: Don't complain, don't explain, don't volunteer. Just . . . answer the questions.

EVENTUALLY IT was the ultradignified Charles who testified. He stared straight at the jury box and announced in ringing tones that every word of his previous testimony had been true and accurate—"no doubt at all."

Hollopeter asked if the photo could have been taken a year earlier.

"No," Charles replied. "He was in the service in Vietnam."

"Was your brother present in your home in December 1969? 1970? 1971?"

"No. He was in jail all three of those years." The inference was plain: the photograph could have been taken only at Christmastime 1968.

In response to another Hollopeter question, the oldest brother began his all-important explanation about the film and its coding: "Polaroids are used to take snapshots of the console of large computers, so that when a breakdown occurs, you can tell how core storage looked. So there was quite a supply of black and white Polaroid film at the company that I worked for for fifteen years. . . ."

Hollopeter interrupted the explanation with questions about other photographs of Charles Pratt's sons, and somehow the attorney neglected to return to the key subject of film coding. Charles was bursting to finish his explanation but was provided no opportunity.

Kalustian seemed to sense his advantage and limited his cross-examination to perfunctory questions.

Verdict

The Pratt jury began deliberations at 9:30 A.M. on Monday, July 17, 1972, the thirty-fourth day since the trial had begun. As the last juror exited, Cochran closed his briefcase with a confident snap.

"I like this jury," he told Geronimo in a soft voice. "I like the way they paid attention. I think they'll be fair."

He stuck to his practice of refusing to predict victory even when the facts seemed to favor his client. It was easier to predict frog races than jury decisions. He was concerned about the Polaroid evidence, but he kept it to himself.

TWENTY-SIX HOURS later the jury foreman sent a message to the judge asking for a rereading of the Charles Pratt testimony. "It's that damn picture again," Hollopeter said. "I wish we'd never entered it."

"We made a big mistake," Cochran admitted. "It's a hole in our case, and Kalustian ran a truck through it."

When Hollopeter complained about the prosecutor's tactics, Cochran interrupted. "I'm no Dick Kalustian fan," he said, "but the guy did his job. That's what the adversary system is all about. I'd do the same to him."

The jury also asked to hear a reading of the complete testimony of

Julius Butler, a process that took the rest of Tuesday and half of Wednesday and left the court reporter hoarse. The defense attorneys concluded that the jurors doubted Butler and wanted to confirm their doubts, or believed him and wanted to confirm their beliefs. Or, most likely, that they were split.

ON MONDAY, July 24, the sixth day of deliberations, jury foreman Dennis Romo reported that the jurors were making no progress. The judge asked him where they stood. "Ten to two," the foreman answered.

She asked if he thought there was a possibility of reaching a verdict.

"Well, Your Honor, that would be a speculation on my part, but I would have a tendency to feel that it would be more in the nature of a possibility than of a probability."

The other jurors seemed to agree. Cochran wondered if Judge Parker would be receptive to a motion for mistrial. Despite a few glitches toward the end, he'd felt confident, but he was beginning to have second thoughts. He was footing the trial expenses himself and receiving minimal wages as a court appointee, but his practice was flourishing and the potential cost of a new trial was of no concern. If we try this case again, he said to himself, we'll do a few things differently. We won't introduce the Polaroid picture. We'll make Barbara Mary Reed justify her multiple descriptions. We'll zero in on Kenneth Olsen's identification of another man and let the jury evaluate his double talk. We'll win for sure. . . .

At a bench conference he said, "Your Honor, this jury is in a hopeless deadlock."

The judge refused to declare a mistrial.

AFTER THREE more days of deliberations the count stood at eleven to one, and at 10:30 on the morning of the next day, July 28, 1972, foreman Romo sent word that a verdict had been reached. He handed several sheets of paper to the bailiff, who passed them to the judge. She perused them carefully, then handed them to the clerk, who stood up and began to read: "We the jury in the above-entitled action find the defendant Elmer G. Pratt guilty of murder in the first degree—"

Geronimo yelled, *"Guilty?"* and jumped up.

As the clerk read on, he glared at the jurors and said, "You're wrong! I didn't kill that woman. You racist dogs! I'm not gonna sit here and listen to the rest of this."

He turned toward the judge. "Your Honor," he said, his voice cracking, "can I be excused?"

She said, "Mr. Pratt, we have to conform with—"

"Your Honor," he interrupted, "I am *not* going to sit here and listen to that—me being framed for something I didn't do. Now—"

Parker tried to talk, but his outcry continued. *"May I be excused, please?"*

"You have your rights of appeal," the judge said calmly.

In the jury box twenty-two-year-old Jeanne Hamilton, one of the last holdouts, studied Pratt as she listened to his anguished words. My God, she said to herself, have we made a terrible mistake?

AFTER THE final formalities the judge thanked the jurors for being "very attentive and most conscientious. . . . You do have the satisfaction of knowing that you have made a significant contribution to the administration of justice."

Richard Kalustian told a reporter from the *Los Angeles Times* that he was elated and called the verdict "definitely in keeping with the evidence in the case."

Foreman Romo, stung by Pratt's courtroom outburst, painted a picture of a jury that had bent over backward for the defendant. "There were twelve people there that wanted to find that man not guilty, and they would have done anything. We went over the evidence excruciatingly." He scribbled an impromptu press release and passed it to reporters:

> After hearing the verdict, Mr. Pratt called us a racist jury. He will never know how difficult it was for each of us to render this decision. The evidence and the law left us no alternative. I honestly feel that this jury did its utmost to find him not guilty. Were I to stand in Mr. Pratt's place, I would want this jury for myself.

Juror Juan Santiago confirmed that Cochran had been correct about the negative effect of the absence of name-brand Panthers like Bobby Seale and David Hilliard: "If more members came in and established his alibi in Oakland that would have counted and maybe turned it around."

Juror Jesse Woods agreed: "I wondered why more people didn't come down from Oakland and testify that Pratt was there—*if* he was there." Had the Panther leaders backed their colleague's story, Woods said, he might have voted not guilty.

An upset Jeanne Hamilton told reporters that she was convinced that an appearance by Seale or Hilliard would have caused a hung jury or an acquittal. She'd originally been impressed by Julio Butler—"he seemed elegant, well-spoken, fairly credible as an ex-deputy"—but she said she would have discounted his testimony if the defense had proved that he was an informer. She'd been most impressed by the defendant himself. Not only had his story rung true, she said, but he seemed miscast in the role of mad-dog killer. Weighed against Pratt's decency and charisma, she said, Butler's unsupported testimony wouldn't have supported a guilty vote. Nor had Hamilton been impressed by the vacillating stories of Barbara Mary Reed and Kenneth Olsen, even after one of the jurors stared hard at her outside the jury room and asked, "If someone shot your husband, wouldn't you remember his face?"

Hamilton said she agreed with fellow jurors that the testimony about the Polaroid picture suggested that the Pratts and other alibi witnesses might have lied about other matters. As a strong pro-innocence juror, she'd been "devastated" by the photo. "The whole case came down to that Polaroid. I still thought he was innocent. But the people on the other side kept hammering away at me to explain the picture, *explain the picture*. They kept taking me aside privately and trying to convince me. Finally . . . I caved in."

In later years the holdout juror would express her attitude in fewer words. "They really took us," she said, "didn't they." It wasn't a question.

JOHNNIE COCHRAN worked late, combing the trial record for appeal points, but every few minutes he squeezed his eyes shut and asked himself where he and Hollopeter had gone wrong. He considered himself an upbeat person, but this . . . this was rock bottom. He thought of the way Pratt had taken his arm after court and said, "It's okay, Johnnie. It's okay," as though Cochran had been found guilty and required comforting. On his way to the holding cell to await transport to jail, Geronimo had called back, "You did your job, Johnnie. You did all you could do. Nobody could have won this thing."

In a way, Cochran wished Pratt had lost control and cussed him out. They'd been through so much together; they were bonded now, and brothers shouldn't have to suppress their feelings. He reflected on their long talks about race: the debate always came down to Martin Luther King's principles of nonviolence versus the fiery precepts of Malcolm X. Cochran was an outspoken supporter of nonviolence, thoroughly believed in the American system of justice and held that "courageous people, working within the system, can arouse the popular conscience against injustice," as he wrote later. But his friend Geronimo had been annealed in other fires: Vietnam, the LAPD cruelties, the murders of his friends, the militant teachings of Malcolm and other hard-edged black leaders. Cochran thought, There's a middle ground between Malcolm and Dr. King, a "golden mean." If Geronimo and I had talked things out, we probably would have ended up agreeing. Not that it made much difference at the moment. No amount of Aristotelian philosophizing could alter the fact that a proud young attorney named Johnnie L. Cochran Jr. had gone into court as an advocate for a good and decent and *innocent* man—and lost.

He reflected on pretrial proceedings, on Richard Kalustian's flat denial that he was withholding discovery material. He thought of his old classmate's claim in final argument that the glaring contradictions in eyewitness testimony were insignificant; all that mattered, the prosecutor had insisted, was that Barbara Reed and Kenneth Olsen had looked out over the courtroom and identified Pratt. Cochran thought of recurrent hints that the FBI had orchestrated the case, that police had put pressure on witnesses and might have suborned perjury, that key witnesses twisted information and lied. If we could have proved those points conclusively, he said to himself, I wouldn't be sitting in my office at midnight drawing up appeal points. As it was, it had taken the jurors ten days to reach a verdict.

He resolved never to trust the system again or repeat his mistakes. "I would have to be tougher, more skeptical, and, most of all, braver in the pursuit of truth," he wrote later. ". . . That's what the loss of the Geronimo Pratt case taught me: a healthier kind of paranoia."

He'd been taught valuable lessons, but his client would pay the tuition.

PRATT LAY on his side on the floor of his cell, not even trying to sleep, losing body warmth to the heat-sink effect of the damp concrete. He'd given up on his bunk; the cold metal scraped his skin. He took off his shirt and wrung out a few more drops of water. A guard had emptied a glass over his head while leading him back to the hole in chains.

His thoughts drifted to Across the Tracks, to the sound of tugboats chugging up Bayou Boeuf, to pecan trees, alligator gars, Spanish moss—and Eunice Petty Pratt. The attorneys said he had a good chance to go free on appeal, but what if they lost again? How would he tell his mother? He remembered the night she'd sat up eulogizing his father, the last time he'd seen her. He remembered her pride in everything her youngest child had done: *My little baby a soldier!*

What pride could she take in him now? Brother Timothy said she'd been busily phoning her children, quoting James 5:16, "The effectual fervent prayer of a righteous man availeth much," and ordering them to pray her son out of prison the way they'd prayed him out of the army. Geronimo wished he believed, if not in prayer, then in something. He made a solemn vow that his mother would never see him behind bars.

A Glimmer of Light

Two days after the verdict was delivered, Cochran answered a phone call from Lawrence Rivetz, a lawyer in the Santa Monica branch of the Office of the Public Defender. "I've been following the trial in the newspaper," he told Cochran. "Kenneth Olsen lied under oath."

"I thought so, Counselor," Cochran said amiably, "but how can I prove it?"

Soon he was reading a sworn declaration from the public defender:

On December 24, 1969, at approximately 10 A.M., I appeared at a lineup as attorney for Mr. Ronald Perkins, also known as Eugene [or Ernest] Perkins, who was suspected of being the gunman in the shooting of Mr. Olsen and his wife. . . .

Officer Eckstein related to me prior to the lineup that Mr. Olsen picked Mr. Perkins and another man named Vance as the men who shot him and his wife, after Mr. Olsen viewed approximately 500 mug shots over a year's period. Sgt. Eckstein informed me that these were the only ones he had picked as of December 24, 1969.

During the lineup Mr. Olsen sat in the fourth row, middle seat. I sat directly behind him in row five. After each suspect stepped forward and made statements, as ordered by Sgt. Eckstein, the statements being,

"Turn off the lights and lie on the ground," Mr. Olsen filled out a form, which he positively picked number four as one of the gunmen. . . . Mr. Olsen stated at the time, "The voice did it," a quote which I wrote down at the time he stated it. . . .

Cochran remembered how Olsen and Eckstein had danced around the subject of the mistaken identification. He thumbed through the trial transcript, a hefty four inches thick, and found Olsen's testimony about the live show-up on page 145:

A.   Well, I identified the person at the lineup that I had seen in the pictures, as such. And I told Detective Eckstein that while there was a possibility, I didn't feel I could really make an identification of that person, because I didn't feel, really, it was the person.

Then he checked Eckstein's testimony on the same subject.

Q. . . . It is true, is it not, that at one point Mr. Olsen picked the pictures of two of the suspects out, didn't he? . . .
A.   They looked like two of the men that could be the attackers.
Q. . . . Mr. Olsen picked one of those men out? . . .
A.   He picked a man out that he had seen a picture of, and he said he thought he could be involved. But he wasn't that positive.

Oh, but he *was,* Lawrence Rivetz assured Cochran. Kenneth Olsen had been dead certain.

Cochran phoned Santa Monica police headquarters to make another request for the lineup photos that Eckstein, while on the witness stand, had promised to deliver. A dispatcher reported that the detective was unavailable, and Cochran sent his own investigator to follow up in person. The agent reported from Santa Monica that the photos were missing from the police files. So was the signed lineup card.

A MONTH after the verdict Cochran was back in court with a motion for a new trial. He cited the Rivetz affidavit. He charged that the judge had erred in allowing frequent references to the Butler "insurance letter." And he argued that there'd been tampering during the jury's sequestration in a downtown hotel.

In open court Kalustian assured Judge Parker that there was "no question" that her ruling was correct.

Cochran was still pleading with the judge when all at once she waved her hand and said, "The motion for new trial is denied." She sentenced Pratt to life imprisonment and strode toward her chambers.

INTO THE new lifer's prison file went a permanent warning that he was a vicious killer and must never be released. The statement would follow him like a faithful black dog through the rest of his days behind bars. It was signed, "Richard Kalustian."

"Q"

In November 1972, a little over a year after the George Jackson massacre at San Quentin State Prison, Geronimo Pratt was delivered to the bloody war zone in handcuffs and shackles. The usual enmity between guards and inmates had metastasized into open violence as a result of the Jackson affair and other prison uprisings. At the institution known to its residents as Q, fewer than four hundred guards oversaw four thousand prisoners. The outmanned guards maintained control by pitting one racial group against another. San Quentin ran on racism and hate.

The new inmate expected to be put through the normal intake procedures—dental and medical checkup, X rays, a psychiatric interview, counseling sessions—but instead a phalanx of guards prodded him through one security door after another. He was assigned his own cell in the euphemistically named Adjustment Center, known to convicts as the hole or the bucket. The steel door slammed and he found himself alone in the light from a dim overhead bulb. When his eyes adjusted, he discerned four walls and a hole in the floor. It was the L.A. County Jail all over again, except that the toilet hole was a little bigger. He was nervous about his old medical problem. He was already bleeding.

———

EARLY ON his first night he heard someone call, "Hey, man, you know who was in your cell before you? *Dead pigs!*"

He was told that the bodies from the Jackson massacre had been stacked where he was now expected to sleep. He was sure he could smell blood. There was no sink, TV or radio. He couldn't wash or read. Meals arrived through a slot in the door—four slices of bread a day and a cut-off Purex bottle containing a few inches of water. Every few days he was fed a regular meal—"typical prison slop, barely warm," as he described it later. The young convict who'd been raised on fried catfish, shrimp, smothered chicken and *boudin* spat out his first bite. The trusty who delivered his food said the guards had sprinkled his mashed potatoes with a powdered medicine used to treat asthmatics.

"Why?" Geronimo asked. "I don't have asthma."

The trusty whispered through the slot, "Weren't you tight with George Jackson?"

"Never laid eyes on him."

"They say you were engaged to George's sister. They say you were waiting outside Q when he blew out the walls."

Pratt wondered what else was in his dossier and how it got there. He asked a counselor why he was being held in solitary confinement.

"You ran the Black Panthers, didn't you, son?" the man informed him. "We can't put a heavy dude like you with other inmates. You'd cause too many problems."

JOHNNIE COCHRAN began his first visit with misgivings. He knew from experience that meetings with solitary confinement prisoners at San Quentin were iffy propositions. You began with a long wait in the reception area. Then a sergeant might advise you to come back another day— "Sorry, visiting hours are over." "Your client's locked down." "There must be a misunderstanding." You were at the mercy of overworked, underpaid martinets in crew cuts.

This time there was a surprisingly short wait before he was led to a small interview room. He felt as though he were entering a mausoleum. Through a heavy-gauge wire grate, he watched Pratt approach in shackles. He wore a white jumpsuit with a big black X on the back.

Cochran asked the escorting guard, "What's the X for?"

"Helps us aim."

He listened as the guard warned Pratt that he would be shot if he made one false move. "You trip and fall down," the guard said, "I'll shoot you. That's my orders."

As Cochran took a seat in the metal chair, he thought, What have we wrought? He was already offering daily prayers for Geronimo. He would have to offer more.

"We'd like an extended visit," Cochran told his escort. "I'm here from L.A."

The guard told him to knock on the wall when they were finished. Cochran looked at his watch. It was a little before 10:00 A.M.

After a warm exchange of greetings Geronimo asked him to check his prison files: "I hear they got a lot of stuff about me and George Jackson. I never laid eyes on George Jackson." Cochran said he'd tried to check the jackets of other clients in the past and it was usually a waste of time. The California Department of Corrections was like the FBI: it gave out what it wanted. He promised to try again.

BY TWO o'clock, four hours into the visit, lawyer and client had exhausted the subject of future legal stratagems and were chatting about their mothers. They agreed that Hattie B. Cochran and Eunice Petty Pratt had more in common than their Louisiana roots. Cochran was reciting Lincoln's line—"All that I am or ever hope to be, I owe to my angel mother"—when Geronimo warned that he didn't want his mother to visit San Quentin. He said that he'd added other family members to his visiting list, but he would be grateful if Cochran would discourage them from making the long trip from Los Angeles.

"I understand," the lawyer said.

By 3:00 P.M. Cochran needed a bathroom break. He knocked on the wall and there was no response. Every five or ten minutes he knocked louder. By 3:45 he began to feel claustrophobic, then angry. He realized that the guards were giving him a sample taste of the hole.

At 5:00 P.M. a guard answered his knock and said, "You asked for an extended visit, didn't you?" He seemed to find humor in the situation.

Geronimo told his lawyer, "Promise you won't forget me."

"I promise."

TWO WEEKS later Cochran made the eight-hundred-mile round-trip again. This time he waited four hours in the reception area. He slid a paper under the crack at the bottom of the grate in the interview room and told his client, "Read this. It's a permanent part of your jacket."

The document was on the letterhead of the Los Angeles D.A.'s Office and appeared to be an advisory to the CDC. Pratt read:

> When Bunchy Carter was killed, Pratt assumed the leadership of the Black Panther Party . . . [as such] he was constantly in possession of bombs, dynamite, automatic weapons and hand guns. He was the instigator of an assault on Ollie Taylor who was suspected of being a member of a rival gang. . . .

Pratt looked up from his reading. "I was *acquitted* on Ollie Taylor!" he said. "Who wrote this? Kalustian?"

"Who else?" Cochran said.

Geronimo read another line and stopped. "He says that Julio said I was responsible for the death of Franco Diggs in 1968. I wasn't even in L.A. when Captain Franco was killed. That's something else that happened when I was up in Oakland. We always figured Julio did it—or the cops."

He read more, then said, "Here's some more bullshit from Julio: 'Pratt also was involved in the shootout in 1969.' You remember how I was involved, Cochran? *I was a mile away, asleep!*"

He read on:

> Julio Butler testified that during the Ollie Taylor incident while Pratt was pointing a gun at him and Ollie Taylor, Pratt had an erection. Information reveals at least one other similar occurrence wherein violence appears to generate sexual excitement.

Geronimo lowered his head. "This is sick," he said slowly. "How can I correct it?"

Cochran said, "You can't. After you're convicted of murder, you're fair game. The D.A. can say any damned thing he wants."

"What about my rights?"

"*Rights?* As far as Dick Kalustian is concerned, you have the same rights as a dog in a kennel." He paused. "Read the rest."

Geronimo read:

> Some of the jurors actually believed that Pratt set out on a mission the night of the murder with a specific intention to kill. There is no under-

estimating the danger defendant poses to others. He is coldblooded and vicious. He is capable of killing for no reason at all. . . .

At the present time he is a member of the Eldridge Cleaver faction of BPP which is violence prone. He is entirely capable of attempting to escape from prison. Information reveals that in the past he has threatened David Hilliard with death. Pratt should never be paroled. Despite any hollow words, if released, he will undoubtedly attempt to kill those who he believes put him in prison.

Cochran said, "I've heard some other stuff the D.A.'s Office is putting out about you. I'll try to track it down."

"What other stuff?" Geronimo asked.

"You led a breakout attempt. You stabbed a guard with a pencil—"

"That was another dude. Are they giving me every crime ever committed? Take a look, Cochran—does it say I shot the Kennedys?"

"They say you'll kill any guard you can reach. They say you and your relatives lied under oath. You went on crime sprees in Louisiana. You come from a crime family. You're inherently evil, you're . . . *blah blah blah.*" Cochran paused, then added, "If they wanted to get you killed in prison, they couldn't have done a better job."

"What else is in my jacket?" Geronimo asked. "I might as well hear it all."

"There's a mental evaluation. I can't tell if it's by a psychiatrist or a psychologist."

"I never talked to any shrinks. They haven't done my diagnostics."

"This guy starts off by repeating Kalustian's statement in his own words. Says it's his own professional and medical conclusion. Then he adds some propaganda."

"Like what?"

"You're a militarily trained assassin. You're a twenty-four-hour escape risk. You'll try to incite riots and take over the prison. For the safety of the institution you have to be kept in the hole."

Geronimo asked, "Is Kalustian behind that, too?"

"I wish it was that simple. I think somebody's reached the Department of Corrections. Maybe—it's the FBI."

The door opened and a guard ordered Cochran out. "I thought we had an hour," the lawyer said.

Another guard appeared behind Pratt and motioned him to his feet. "I'll be back," the lawyer said. He watched as the black X faded into the shadows.

Walking past the reception desk, Cochran said, "This was an attorney-client visit. Why'd you cut us off? You've violated my client's rights."

The guard ushered him out.

AFTER THE interview Pratt spent one of his worst nights. For weeks he'd eaten a haphazardly starchy diet that provided almost no roughage, and his intestines felt petrified. "I had to squat to go and it hurt like a son of a bitch. I asked to see a doctor and they laughed." For hours after his lawyer left, he writhed and twisted over the hole in the floor, but all he could pass was blood.

Fourth Street in Sacramento

For three months Pratt's condition worsened. Late one night he fainted. When he came to, he was lying on the floor in chains and a medical technician was jabbing at his arm. "Gimme a vein, man!" the medic muttered. "Goddamn it, wake up!"

Rivulets of blood ran down both arms. The tech tried again and missed the vein. Geronimo slipped back into unconsciousness.

When he awoke, guards were dragging him down a corridor on his back. They lifted his 170 pounds onto a gurney and rolled him to the prison hospital. In the blue glow of a treatment room he saw that both his arms were wrapped in bloody bandages.

A doctor appeared and said, "Turn him over."

Other med techs and doctors had long since abandoned examining Pratt rectally; they knew it meant a brawl. As Geronimo faded in and out of consciousness, he saw the doctor pull on a translucent glove and squeeze a lubricant from a large tube onto his fingertip. When Pratt jerked at his chains, the doctor asked, "What's *with* you, son? You trying to die?"

Geronimo felt something pierce his upper arm and blacked out again. When he revived, he was on his hands and knees. It was nighttime. He looked up and a drop of water hit his face. Through slants of rain he saw guards patrolling a gun walk with rifles. He realized he was in the prison yard.

Four guards stuffed him into a "squirrel cage," reserved for out-of-control prisoners, and trundled it to a sally port, where he was handcuffed and shackled and deposited in the back of a squad car, a guard on either side and another in the front passenger seat. The driver steered out the gates and turned onto busy Highway 101. As they sped through the rain, Geronimo saw that he was in a three-vehicle caravan: an armored van led and another followed.

Three hours later the car lurched onto the shoulder. Through the steamed-up windows he saw his first grass in three years. A guard pulled a blindfold over his eyes and the driver resumed at a slower speed, sometimes stopping and starting as though negotiating city traffic. At last Pratt was ordered out.

He had no idea how far he'd been duck-walked between two handlers before the blindfold was yanked off. He blinked in harsh light and saw that he was in a large cage with four guards and two men in civilian clothes. His restraints were removed and he was ordered to take off his clothes and bend over.

"I don't do that," he said.

He braced himself as the guards moved in. One said, "Spread your ass."

"I got shell fragments, man."

"I said—bend over!"

"You'll have to kill me first."

One of the civilians waved the guards off. Geronimo was handed a set of prison clothes and steered out the door. Along the way he saw a sign: "Abandon all hope, ye who enter here." He recognized Dante's words from his studies with Bunchy Carter. Still chained, he was led down a long corridor with cells on both sides.

"Can you tell me where we are?" he asked.

"Four-A," a guard said.

"Four-A? *Folsom?*" Cellblock 4-A was known in the underworld as Fourth Street in Sacramento, the worst hole in the California prison system. My God, he said to himself, they got me down as the baddest-ass criminal on earth.

"You're in the bucket, tough guy," another guard said. "Let's see how many revolutions you can start here."

He heard a chirpy voice cry, "Geronimo!" Charles Manson's hairy face peeked from cell no. 1. Pratt nodded. He was glad to see a familiar face even though it was ugly and scarred with a Nazi swastika. They'd been in the hole together at Los Angeles County Jail.

Manson's outcry set off other yells and shrieks: "Hey, they got *Geronimo* in here!" "It's the man!" *"Homeboy!"* A chant began: "Geronimo, *Geronimo, GERONIMO!"* He could still hear the sounds when he reached the end of the long tier. He wondered if he should feel honored.

The guards steered him through a set of sealed doors. The noises faded. At last he found himself behind heavy bars and chicken wire in a soundproof cell, the last circle of hell for uncontrollable inmates. It was the most solitary of solitary confinements, its nearest equivalent the infamous "soul breaker" in Oakland.[25]

He raised his arms and touched both walls. He didn't see a spigot or a sink, but his eyes caught a dull gleam in the back. He wondered if he was dreaming. There was no seat and no paper, but . . . it was a toilet. What a break, he said to himself. My luck must be changing . . .

A WEEK later he moved to the security cellblock to another tumultuous welcome. Via shouted introductions, he met his neighbors. "One-legged Joe Morgan, the Mexican Mafia guy, was there—they made a movie about him. I met Bulldog Ladd, the cofounder of the Aryan Brotherhood. Next to him was Kenny Como, a little-bitty escape artist, the human fly. Then came Bobby Butler, the other cofounder of the Aryan Brotherhood. Next to him was Death Row Jeff, a guy with a voice like a foghorn— *'Hey, where you at, Geronimo?'* Jeff was convicted of stealing a car in 1947 but they kept him inside for shooting a homosexual prisoner with a zip gun. At the near end there was Chili Red, a street guy out of Oakland. And, of course—Manson."

He was allowed an hour of exercise a day in a mini-yard whose concrete walls were chipped with bullet scars. Now and then he found himself sharing a mop or a scrub brush with another member of the Folsom demimonde, but most of the time the 4-A inmates were kept apart, communicating only by shouts and "kite"—bootleg letters passed by guards or other prisoners.

At first he had to deflect the jealousy of some of the older blacks. "Guys like Chili Red, Jake Louis, Death Row Jeff, all these old heavyweights had

---

[25] Eventually outlawed by the courts as cruel and unusual punishment.

been inside since the fifties. Some of 'em killed in prison; that's why they were in solitary. They were mumbling about me, all those big old studs. They were waiting to inherit the George Jackson legacy as the meanest prisoner in the CDC. It *mattered* to them. They were saying, 'Who is this asshole? How is this fool gonna take over from George? *Dude just got here!*' I put out the word: 'Hey, I lost my wife, my daddy died, the Panthers are a mess and I'm doing life. Man, I'm not trying to take over *nothin'!*' I said, 'Spread the word. People best just leave me alone. All I want to do is hit the lawbooks and work on my case.' "

He had a harder time convincing the guards of his harmlessness. In the wake of the riots at Attica and elsewhere, every action and reaction by prison staffers was rooted in paranoia, especially toward convicts who wore troublemaker tags. At first Geronimo didn't know how to handle the problem. "The hatred for militant blacks just fell on my shoulders, and I was too green to know why they were punishing me." Unlike the other residents of 4-A, he was denied radio, TV and reading matter. He remembered something that the African American novelist Richard Wright had written: "Reading kept me alive." Eunice Pratt had always taught her children that books were as necessary as food. Now Geronimo understood.

Another negative evaluation quickly followed him from San Quentin. "Mr. Pratt is a source of intrigue," a counselor wrote. "Continues to cause disruptive activities from behind scenes. Has capability and is willing to act against staff when and if staff gets careless. Needs maximum custodial controls to prevent subject gaining any advantage over his custodial supervisors. It is within the realm of possibility that subject can obtain outside assistance and gain his ends."

Geronimo didn't understand. In the time period covered by the evaluation, he'd had almost no contact with other inmates. He felt helpless against such official slander. Somewhere he'd read that innocent victims eventually feel responsible for their own suffering. He wrote to his brother Jack, "I feel depressed, oppressed and *sup*pressed." All his life he'd fought against moodiness by taking action, fighting back. Now there was nothing to fight except steel. The high-spiritedness that had made him lead his jailed Panthers against the L.A. County Jail guards had died the day he was declared a murderer by a jury of his peers. He spent hours reliving the awful moment in the courtroom, head in hands.

He slept fitfully, some nights not at all. He dreamed of being overrun by Victor Charlie. He saw himself running naked through a minefield holding loops of his own intestines. One night he watched an old woman's hair and brains burn like a Roman candle. His dreams became so violent that he was afraid he would hurt himself in his sleep. "I dreamed I was doing a blast out of a C-141. When I woke up, my head hit the ceiling so hard you could hear it at the end of the cellblock. I ripped that bunk off the wall and tore it up. Wasn't much they could do about it. I was already in the hole."

WHENEVER HE was moved, he was shackled, handcuffed and escorted by guards with ax handles, the weapon of choice among 4-A personnel. Word went out that he had led the Panthers' gun battle against the LAPD and killed three officers himself as well as members of rival black organizations. He was described as founder of the Black Guerrilla Family, the most violent black organization within the walls. "They built me up big—a captain in the Green Berets, munitions expert, armament specialist, a genius with weapons. Said I could make a zip gun out of twenty-one pieces of paper, knew how to make poison darts and fire 'em from a blowgun made from a magazine page. Said I could blow out a wall with ordinary kitchen supplies. Said I'd already sawed through two of my bars and my old Black Panther friends were gonna break me out.

"Under the strict rules on 4-A, a guard could write you up for looking at him sideways, but they were lazy about doing the paperwork. In the yard you weren't allowed to talk to other inmates, but everybody got around it. I was the exception. They wrote me up for breathing. 'Refused to shave.' 'Wouldn't stand for count.' 'Torn T-shirt.' 'Throwing apple on floor.' 'Picking up a piece of paper.' 'Talking.' Guards tried to goad me into fights. Kept saying I'd been tight with George Jackson.

"There was a permanent war between the Mexicans and the blacks, and I ended up in the cross fire. Inmates were getting shot and stabbed every other day. I was hit with a plastic bullet in the yard. It was crazy, it was madness. Some guys lost their minds, didn't even know they were in prison. You'd see 'em doing the Thorazine shuffle, had to be propped up to eat."

ONE DAY inmate B-40319 found himself talking to a convict who represented everything the black elders of Morgan City and every Pratt on earth, including Geronimo, would have despised if they'd encountered him outside the prison walls. From the moustached mouth of Wayne "Bulldog" Ladd gushed a septicemia of race hatred and violence. The cofounder of the black-hating Aryan Brotherhood had been assigned to the hole for stabbing a fellow worshiper to death in chapel. A meticulously neat man, he was built like Geronimo's stubby father.

An inmate passed word that Ladd had said, "That guy Pratt—he's a man first and a black second." In the yard Geronimo called out, "Hey, Bulldog, quit talking me up. You're killing me with the homeys."

Pratt and Ladd talked till the guard in the gun tower ordered them to separate. After that, the white racist and the Panther leader became friends.

When Ladd learned that Pratt was spending three or four hours a night straining over his cold metal toilet, he offered some medical advice.

"Avoid the prison quacks," he said. "Those fucking pills'll kill ya quicker'n a deer rifle."

"I figured that out," Geronimo said.

"First thing you gotta do is increase the flow of blood to the area. Don't jerk off. That'll redirect the flow where you need it. Quit smoking. Lay off stimulants: coffee, tea, Coke, all that shit. Eat leaves.[26] No meat. Just leaves, leaves and more fucking leaves. . . ."

With help from the trusties who ran the food carts, Geronimo went on the Bulldog Diet and lost twenty pounds in six months. He began fasting three days a month and told Ladd, "Fasting is healthy for black prisoners. Helps you to think clear through to the bottom of things. Every black man should try it."

"Haven't you noticed?" the Aryan Brotherhood leader responded. "I'm not black."

"Yeah, well, don't give up hope."

---

[26] Prison jargon for vegetables.

A Visit

On a scorching day in California's Central Valley in early March 1974, a guard came to Pratt's cell and said, "A lady outside says she's your mother."

Geronimo's heart began to pound. What on earth was his mother doing at Folsom? He managed to sputter, "Lemme, uh—lemme talk to a supervisor."

A lieutenant confirmed that the woman had signed the register as Eunice Petty Pratt.

"I'm begging you, man," Geronimo said. "My mother can*not* see me in chains." He would kill himself first. But in one full year on "Fourth Street in Sacramento" he'd never been allowed out of his cell without handcuffs and shackles. It was an unbreakable rule.

The supervisor returned in twenty minutes with a black sergeant. The two men unlocked the cell door and told him to hold out his hands. "Shut up, fool," the sergeant said. "Do what you're told."

The guards applied cuffs around his ankles, chains leading up to a belly chain, and handcuffs locked in front to the chain, the standard traveling uniform for the fractious residents of 4-A. Pratt shuffled the length of the corridor and passed under the sign from Dante. Clanking toward the visiting room, he stopped and refused to take another step. "I can't do this," he said. "I'm sorry. Maybe Mama and me can talk . . . on the intercom?"

The lieutenant started unlocking the shackles and cuffs. "Do we have your word I never took these off?" he asked.

"Yes, sir," Geronimo said.

"You have an hour."

MOTHER AND son spoke in the Security Housing visiting room while two guards hovered nearby. She called him "Gerard" and "my baby" and he called her "Mama" and "sweet Mama." She tried to comfort him, but he didn't want her to think he was suffering. He spent most of the hour telling her that life in the penitentiary wasn't bad and turning the conversation to other subjects.

"It's gonna be *okay,* Mama," he said. "I didn't kill that woman. You know that, Mama. It's a mistake. Me and Mr. Cochran, we're gonna straighten it out."

Eunice Pratt said she knew the details. "Don't you worry, baby. The Lord will provide."

Her voice was as clear and firm as ever. She was almost seventy now, but to Geronimo she didn't look much older than the woman who'd made him finish his okra.

When the hour was up, he told her, "Now, Mama, I don't want you coming back to this place. Okay?" He tried to sound stern. "I'm gonna be out real soon. I'm coming home, Mama. Please . . . *don't come back."*

They touched hands against the screen. "God watches over you, baby," his mother said. "You're *his* baby, too."

AFTER GERONIMO was returned to his cell in chains, he sat on his rack trying to remember every word his mother had said, the way she looked, everything she'd told him about his siblings, Mr. Jimmy Harris the barber, his best friend Alvin "Kaydoe" Delco, Mr. Ben the freezer owner, Morgan City's elders, teachers and preachers, the dramatis personae of the long-running drama that unreeled in his mind day and night.

The cell door rattled and a guard handed him a package clumsily wrapped in newspaper. "Sorry," he said. "We had to open and inspect it."

"I'm not allowed books," Geronimo said.

"Cap'n says you can have this one."

The Bible was in thick red leather with embossed Greek letters and a gold cross on the front. Geronimo read his mother's handwriting on the first blank page: "I am the alpha and the omega, the one who is and who was and is to come, the Almighty! Rev 1:8. Holy Bible."

"Thanks," Geronimo said, and quickly turned away.

FOR DAYS after his mother's visit he sat and stared at his new Bible. "It was so beautiful. It was, like—my only art object. But it was also . . . Mama." He was in his fourth year of solitary confinement in one jail or another and was beginning to wonder if he would ever be free. He found little comfort in the words of the Bible; never again would he be the blind believer who crawled out of bed in the dark to serve as an altar boy. But he found something talismanic about the red leather book, a reminder of his mother's love.

SEVERAL DAYS after the visit he was sitting cross-legged on his rack when he realized that he was chanting under his breath. Later he decided that it was Eunice Pratt reaching into him. He'd grown up listening to her prayers and mantras, sometimes in the Quedo tongue of her Caribbean ancestors, sometimes in the Latin of the high mass and sometimes in a mix that sounded a little like a tobacco auctioneer. Many of his fellow prisoners chanted—the unlikely Bulldog Ladd was one. At night they made 4-A hum and moan like a generator—*om om ommm, ummmmmm. . . .*

Geronimo tried to train himself to chant like the others, but after a while he realized that the process worked best if he let his mind run free. "I didn't even know what I was chanting—just words, sounds, grunts, hums, little snatches of songs. Things came into my mind, new experiences, new feelings."

After a few sessions he began to feel more relaxed, cleansed, elevated. As he chanted, he saw his mother, then Bunchy Carter, his brothers and sisters, the murdered Red, old friends in the Panthers, Sergeant Maddox and his army buddies. "I'd smoked a little dope in my life, but this was the best high in the world. I talked to Malcolm X, Martin Luther King, Medgar Evers, Stokely, Huey, the Cleavers. I had long discussions with Frederick Douglass and James Baldwin. I told off Richard Nixon. 'You sorry son of a bitch, they sent you to a mansion in San Clemente and me to a cell in San Quentin.' I talked to ants and roaches—and they talked back! I learned how to see things from other perspectives. The ants taught me that the world doesn't rotate around Geronimo Pratt. Maybe a roach was the center of the universe, maybe a fly, a mud wasp. Who knows? I thought about the collective intelligence of insects, and I learned that some things would always be beyond my grasp."

As the days passed, he realized that he'd found his daily ticket out of the hole.

Back to Q

Bulldog Ladd slipped him a work by Krishnamurti, then a pamphlet about Siddhartha. Geronimo was pleased to learn that the Hindu masters recommended techniques that were similar to the ones he'd taught himself. Ladd introduced refinements: yoga, the lotus position, astral projection, meditations, breathing exercises, other types of mantras and chants.

"Remember," the squat little racist said, "none of this shit works if you harbor bitterness. You got to get the venom off you. Start with the guards. They're just blue-collar dudes like us. Quit fightin' 'em all the time."

Geronimo pondered the advice. He'd found most of the Folsom and San Quentin guards to be as callous as the deputies who ran the Los Angeles County Jail, but in a subtly different way. The L.A. jail personnel were part of a hierarchy that included the LAPD, which Geronimo and other African Americans regarded as the most corrupt and bigoted police agency outside the Deep South. State prison personnel seemed less prejudiced against blacks but more prejudiced against criminals in general. Both Q and Folsom were grossly understaffed and full of shadowy blind spots where prisoners could do as they pleased. The guards kept order by utilizing inmate muscle. Geronimo had seen a few murderous setups in the L.A.

County Jail and had almost been killed himself at Tracy, but setups were commonplace at Folsom.

ONE DAY he was pondering the wit and wisdom of Bulldog Ladd when a medical assistant arrived with his daily allotment of laxatives. Geronimo chased them with a glass of water.

After a while he fell sideways. The next thing he knew, a guard was slapping his face and yelling in his ear, "Wake up, goddamn it! *Wake up!*" Pratt found out later that other inmates had produced such a clamor when he failed to respond to their calls that the guards had no choice but to check on him. For ten or fifteen minutes he could barely speak. The medical assistant admitted that he hadn't dispensed laxatives but a double dose of Thorazine, a tranquilizer that was usually reserved for extreme disciplinary cases.

"Why?" Geronimo asked after he'd revived. "You give me laxatives all the time. Why'd you change?"

The med tech said he'd made a mistake. The pills looked alike.

The next morning Geronimo was still groggy when a kite arrived from Charles Manson via the breakfast cart: "You been set up. Stay out of yard today man."

It was mid-March 1974; the heiress Patricia Hearst had been kidnapped a month earlier by a fanatical group that called itself the Symbionese Liberation Army. Pratt learned later that Manson had been lying awake in his cell adjacent to a guard post when he'd overheard words like "nigger," "setup," "Pratt" and "Hearst." Geronimo had heard rumors that he was a suspect but laughed them off.

He decided to ignore Manson's kite. Yard time was precious, an hour at most, twice a week. The small 4-A yard provided a view of the sky and a chance to move a few extra feet in one direction. As soon as he stepped into the sunlight, an inmate shuffled from a small group in the corner and began walking the perimeter, getting a little closer to Geronimo with each circuit. He recognized Humberto Flores,[27] a hit man for the Mexican Mafia, the power group that acted as prison enforcers. Flores stopped near Geronimo and faced away from the gun deck.

"Listen, man," he said, "I'm supposed to punch you in sight of the

---

[27] Pseudonym.

guards. That gives 'em an excuse to shoot. I'm getting a transfer out of it. Why don't you go back inside and say you're sick?"

"Why're you telling me?" Pratt asked. Blacks and Latino prisoners were mortal enemies. He didn't understand what a torpedo like Flores was doing in the yard at all. Hispanic yard time was over for the day.

"I heard about you, man," Flores said. "You taught my cousin in County."[28]

Geronimo didn't dare leave the yard right away. Any sign of weakness could be fatal in the prison society. "Do what you gotta do," he told Flores. "I'm not going anywhere." It would be better to die now from a .30-30 slug than a sharpened toothbrush later.

Flores unleashed a muffled torrent of Spanish. Then he said, "C'mon, man, *por favor.* Give it up!"

"Fuck it," Pratt said. "I ain't leaving."

A voice came down from a gun walk: "Break it up!"

Flores shuffled away.[29]

WHEN YARD time was over, a pair of guards handcuffed Geronimo and manhandled him into a side room. He was confused by their openness. Guards seldom bloodied their own hands. His personal belongings, including his Bible and the Krishnamurti, lay on a table next to a pillow slip.

"Stand still, asshole," a guard said. "You're going bye-bye."

"For what?"

"For threatening our kids."

"What?"

Geronimo's mind raced as the guards shackled him and prodded him toward the sally port. He thought about the warning kite from Manson and the scene with Humberto Flores. Was there a connection? Sometimes his most surreal dreams didn't match everyday events behind these walls.

He was shoved into the back of a red station wagon. En route in a westerly direction, he asked, "What's this all about?"

---

[28] Los Angeles County Jail.

[29] Later Pratt heard that Flores had been transferred to another prison for botching the setup. His punishment time was doubled.

One of the transport guards responded. "All's I know, man—your grave's already dug."

THE HOMECOMING ceremonies at San Quentin included a welcome by a four-man wrecking crew of guards. After a thorough beating, they lifted him to his feet, and one asked, "Kidnapped any kids lately, scuzzball?" Geronimo thought, *Kids?*

He was escorted to Sixth Floor North Block Segregation Unit, the old death row hole. The death penalty had been ruled unconstitutional, and the cells were now used for extreme disciplinary cases.

"Welcome home," a guard said as the door slid shut with a clank. "We'll be watching."

The door was a slab of steel with a peephole. He realized that he'd been put in a "quiet cell," reserved for the worst of the worst. There was no bed, but he'd been sleeping on concrete for a year and preferred it.

He wondered what had happened to his books. He was sitting on the floor when the door slid open and a pillow slip with his personal possessions was slung inside.

At dawn he discovered a kite. He read: "Your here to die, fool. Thats why they call it Death Row." It wasn't signed.

That afternoon a white prisoner was strangled to death. "A brother named Larry 'Gig' Justice and I were up front getting toothpaste and other supplies when the cop on the gun rail found the body. He came running toward us with his shotgun out, pulled the trigger on me and Gig, and it misfired. Six-foot range. I heard the hammer. I thought the gun might be empty, but it wasn't—he shucked out a dud round. Gig was screaming at him, 'Go on, motherfucker. Kill us!' The goon squad put us in cat cages, the ones used for strip searches."

Geronimo was in the middle of a bloody race war that showed no signs of ending.

NOW THAT he was back in San Quentin, negative evaluations were added to his central file. One report noted that he'd been placed in solitary confinement "because of information . . . concerning possible jailbreak," and concluded: "Subject is seen as a cold calculating individual who is a known organizer and leader of a section of the militant Black Panther Party under the direct leadership of Huey Newton in Southern California. At present time he claims he has broken off his affiliation with BPP but according to information received from FBI sources this has not been so."

He was denied yard privileges, a violation of CDC regulations. He didn't protest. Until he figured out what was going on, the yard might be dangerous. The overhead light remained on; he slept with a shirt over his face. Every now and then he heard uproars from the corridor. He decided that he'd finally reached the hot core of California prison violence. One day he felt a thud against his door and looked out his peephole to see a white inmate stab another in the eye with a sharpened pencil. He heard later that the victim, "Lacy the Killer," had been put on life support, but the pencil had penetrated his brain and he died.

AFTER A week of isolation Geronimo was escorted to the hospital ward for a physical examination. While there, another prisoner warned him that his murder had been scheduled. The tip-off was the location of his cell. The death row hole consisted of some fourteen cells divided into two sections. The rear section housed mostly African Americans. The front section, known as the front bar, was packed with members of the Aryan Brotherhood. Pratt's cell was square in the middle of the bigots. The friendly inmate advised him to do his sleeping by day.

Two nights later he was meditating when his electrically operated door unlocked with a click. As he jumped up, he heard a clamor from the cells in back. Black inmates yelled that two ABs were headed for his cell. By the time he staggered into the corridor to meet the threat head-on, no one was in sight except a guard with a shotgun.

Until his transfer from the death row hole to the Adjustment Center six weeks later, Pratt hardly slept. A prison psychiatrist examined him and reported that he was suffering "marked schizophrenia with anxiety reactions. . . ." After the inmate declined another examination, he was described as "obviously paranoid schizophrenic and defiant, angry and suspicious of everyone. . . ."

BIT BY BIT Pratt solved the mystery of the abrupt transfer from Folsom. The first clue came from a San Quentin counselor who told him that he'd been consigned to the death row hole for his part in "the hijack plot."

Geronimo said, "Hijack? What hijack?"

The counselor, a recently promoted guard, sighed and said, "You never heard a word about hijacking the Folsom school bus, right?"

"Look, man, I didn't even know there *was* a school bus. I've been in the hole for three years."

The counselor wondered aloud how any decent human being could threaten the lives of innocent schoolchildren, then walked out.

More information seeped in from guards and staff, from fellow inmates and from a Sacramento newspaper, which gratuitously added that the hostage-takers had planned to decapitate their victims. Johnnie Cochran pried out the final details with a formal demand to view CDC files.

The scenario had begun with an urgent tip-off to Folsom lieutenant L. S. Wham, who reported that his information had come from "an informant to the FBI who has proven reliable in the past." The informant warned that a female (whose name was blacked out in the copies provided to Pratt's lawyer) was "attempting to influence Mr. [Randolph] Hearst into providing money for an appeal bond for our inmate B-40319, PRATT. If this fails, and/or any other authority refuses to comply; she, with five (5) other people will hijack the school bus servicing the reservation, carrying guards and employees children, as hostages for PRATT's release. They will execute one (1) child per day unless their demands are met. States that she has already mapped details of schedule, mentions thirty-five (35) children specifically. FBI Special Agent Earl Knudsen is in charge of the case."

Lieutenant Wham noted that the threats had been made by a woman who "visits PRATT regularly."

As soon as Geronimo read the report, he knew who the woman was. Theresa Black,[30] a former Panther, had visited him at San Quentin and Folsom and showered him with cards and letters. She was young, shapely, personable and an ideal subject for midnight fantasies, but Geronimo had too many personal problems to become involved emotionally, and he'd told her so.

She'd replied that she could wait. Apparently she decided to hurry the process on her own.

---

[30] Pseudonym.

A CONFIDENTAL memo from an associate warden to Warden J. B. Gunn showed how seriously the prison officials had regarded the kidnap-hostage scenario. The memo confirmed that the children of prison personnel were to be "taken as hostages in return for the release of a Folsom inmate B-40319, PRATT." The memo described frantic meetings with city and school district officials to develop "a plan of action . . . to ensure the safety of the children." Armed officers rode the school buses, with squad cars following. Travel routes were kept under surveillance even in nonschool hours.

After two days without incident, another Folsom administrator had reported receiving "very, very reliable information" that "Geronimo Pratt, B-40319 would be involved in much violence within the next two weeks."

Three more days had passed. Then the FBI reactivated the hysteria with a report that "a car load of five people left Los Angeles . . . these people were identified as ————, ————, ————, ———— and an unidentified Black Panther of the Eldridge Cleaver faction."

At that point, the files disclosed, inmate Pratt had been rushed to San Quentin for everyone's safety. Weeks passed before the authorities learned that the kidnap-hostage plot had existed entirely in the mind of a love-struck young woman.

FOR MONTHS Geronimo continued to pay a high price for Theresa Black's impetuosity. He was assigned a counselor whose idea of therapy seemed to be to rattle the bars on his cell and keep on walking. Guards hurled insults. Tower sharpshooters sighted on him when he was allowed in the yard.

"Eventually we're gonna kill all you boys," a guard told him as he was finishing his five hundred sit-ups one night. "I think you're nigger of the day tomorrow."

Three guards dragged him into the unused gas chamber, strip-searched him and locked him in. It was a popular disciplinary technique and he'd been forewarned. He was expected to beg for his life, but he was freed in a few minutes when he failed to react.

The next day he was riding in the prison elevator with two guards when it stopped between floors. Tom Haggar,[31] one of the strongest officers in the penitentiary, said, "I hear you're bad."

---

[31] Pseudonym.

Geronimo was in a foul mood. He'd just had to tell one more prison medic that he would never submit to a rectal search. "Take off these handcuffs," he told Haggar. "I'll show you how bad I am."

He slipped the guard's first punch, did a whirl-around and kicked him in the belly with the side of his foot. The other guard tried to apply a choke hold, but Geronimo provided too small a target—in army judo classes he'd been taught to keep his chin pressed to his chest. Haggar hit him in the stomach and knocked him flat. He scrambled up and fought off the two men for two or three minutes before he was staggered again. This time he stayed down. As they were reattaching the handcuffs, Haggar said, "Where you from, Pratt?"

"Louisiana," Geronimo gasped.

"They make 'em tough down there."

PRATT HAD hardly recovered from the beating when he was told he had visitors. "The FBI's out there," the guard said as he unlocked the cell door.

Geronimo had an idea of what his visitors wanted. The nationwide hunt for heiress Patricia Hearst and her Symbionese Liberation Army kidnappers was in full cry and the authorities were frantic. Pratt had a black revolutionary's attitude about the case: if Patricia Hearst had been a janitor's daughter from the ghetto, the cops would have listed her as a missing person, worked the case for a few days, then turned to other matters. Since she was rich, famous and white, lawmen were scrambling to find her. Geronimo was aware that he was suspected of complicity in the affair, even though he'd never heard of the SLA and had been in solitary confinement.

He had other reasons to be wary of FBI agents. During his trial there'd been suggestions of FBI involvement ranging all the way up to J. Edgar Hoover's office. Geronimo and his lawyers suspected that Julio Butler, Cotton Smith and several other prosecution witnesses had been programmed by the FBI. News arrived late in the Adjustment Center, but word of a nationwide campaign of FBI "dirty tricks" against black leaders had begun to trickle in.

"Take a hike," Geronimo said to the guard. "Tell the FBI not to bother me again."

ON A chilly morning in late 1974, with the fog thick off San Francisco Bay, he'd just finished running his daily ten miles in tight circles in the yard when he was told to prepare for an attorney visit. He was shackled and led to a small room. "Your visitors will be here in a minute," the guard said.

Geronimo thought, *My visitors?* I wonder who Johnnie brought. Maybe one of his law clerks. His staff was growing.

The door opened on the other side of the metal screen and two men in dark suits appeared. One flashed a card and said, "FBI."

"I don't talk to the FBI," Pratt said.

One said, "You want out of here, don't you?"

Geronimo called for the guard.

The agent said, "We know the whole story, Pratt. Tell us where your people are keeping Patty Hearst."

A FEW days later Johnnie Cochran arrived with bad news. The State Court of Appeal had denied his petition for review.

"We're not dead yet, Geronimo," the lawyer said. "Judge Parker is hearing our resentencing motion. I think she'll listen this time."

Another Journey

Elmer Gerard Pratt's term in solitary confinement was interrupted by a plane ride to Los Angeles for the resentencing hearing. He was awakened at 3:00 A.M. by Mike Jones,[32] a San Quentin transport officer who was usually drunk or hungover and made no secret of his contempt for the race he called "spades." Jones ordered Geronimo to strip, then flung an orange jumpsuit into his cell.

Pratt dressed and said he was ready. Jones said, "Take off the shoes."

A guard held out handcuffs and shackles and cinched them tight. Jones and three guards escorted the prisoner to the sally port. Geronimo winced as the beefy transport officer settled next to him in the squad car. A torrent of trash talk and spittle humidified the drive to the airport at Napa. As the CDC's ancient aircraft bucked and shuddered along the California coast, Geronimo could see the wingtips quivering. He was sure the plane would crash.[33] He was glad that his stomach was empty.

The fat transportation officer seemed energized by the roller-coaster ride. "You gonna go after my kid?" Jones asked. "Cut off his head? Huh? *Huh?*"

---

[32] Pseudonym.

[33] It crashed two years later.

As they were flying over Santa Barbara, he asked, "Hey, what'd you think of those crispy critters?," a reference to Symbionese Liberation Army members who were incinerated when police torched their house. The ugly question reminded Geronimo of charred bodies in Vietnam.

"You're tight with them cocksuckers, aren't you, Pratt?" Jones said in another beery outburst. "I hear you're one of the big honchos. You like barbecue? I like my ribs a little charred myself."

It was impossible to ignore the man. He seemed to know every detail of the bus kidnap story and still blamed the affair on Pratt. He kept firing questions: "Where were you gonna hijack our bus?" "How the fuck were you gonna kill all our kids?"

The ordeal was nearly three hours old when the plane rumbled to a landing at an airport in Long Beach. Still barefoot, Pratt was transferred to a helicopter and flown to the Los Angeles County Jail. A black sergeant from the County Sheriff's Office took him to a visiting room where two white men in suits were waiting.

"FBI," one said as they showed their ID.

Geronimo ignored his outstretched hand. The agents talked fast; clearly they'd heard about his reaction to earlier approaches. It seemed like less than a minute before they'd offered him a half million dollars, a passport and free passage to Algiers "to join your pal Eldridge." All Pratt had to do was give up the location of the kidnapped Patty Hearst.

Behind the bonhomie, Geronimo thought he detected desperation. He asked, "What happened to that other little matter? The, uh—the lady I supposedly killed?"

"Oh, everybody knows you're clean," one of the agents replied with a grin. Pratt was astonished at his openness. Two sheriff's deputies were within earshot.[34]

Back in the hole, he was exhausted and skipped his cellisthenics. He sat on his rack thinking, How many times do I have to hear this Patty Hearst bullshit before I begin to believe it myself?

---

[34] When Cochran attempted to interview them later, one confirmed Pratt's version of the conversation on "condition that you leave me out of this," and the other refused to discuss the subject.

THE NEXT morning he had a brief meeting with Cochran. The lawyer said, "This resentencing hearing doesn't look good. We couldn't get a single declaration of support. Seems like everybody goes into a dead faint when your name comes up."

"What kind of argument can we make?"

"Mostly technical—the sentencing code, judicial overreaching, points like that. Judge Parker will turn us down, but we're making a record for appeal. Hey, how you feeling?"

"Like maybe I'm losing it."

"When you're surrounded by crazy people," Cochran responded, "that's a sign of sanity."

WAITING IN his metal restraints just before the hearing opened, Pratt saw that armed deputies lined the walls and huddled below the bench. A guard took him by the arm and led him into the courtroom. "What about these?" Geronimo said, rattling his shackles. He was embarrassed to be fettered in public.

"They stay on," the deputy said. "Judge's orders."

After Kathleen Parker's familiar face appeared, Deputy D.A. Richard Kalustian argued against any shortening of the life sentence, repeating his earlier accusations against Pratt and adding a few new charges. The prosecutor noted that the prisoner had accumulated fifteen disciplinary slips in prison and had been involved in attacks on guards and breakout attempts. One of the attempts, he said, involved a kidnap-hostage scheme in which children would be beheaded. For the record he read aloud from a CDC warning that had been delivered to the judge's office the day before the hearing: "If Elmer Pratt is brought to the court there will be some escape attempt or attempt to take even Your Honor as a hostage."

Cochran tried to hold his temper as he stood up to counter his old classmate's arguments. He referred to "all these charges that haven't been proven" and said, "Your Honor, this man has been in lockdown because of the influence he might have over inmates. I think that is part and parcel of a kind of paranoia that has gone on with regard to this man throughout his incarceration. His reputation has preceded him wherever he has gone. No matter what he does, he is kept in lockdown."

An orchestrated campaign to demonize his client, Cochran went on, had destroyed Pratt's reputation with fellow inmates and staffers and caused potential witnesses to refuse to testify. "Geronimo Pratt is simply too hot a potato. When I go to the prison to interview witnesses who can tell us good things about Mr. Pratt, the inmates won't cooperate because they fear they'll be in danger from the guards. When I try to talk to prison personnel, they don't cooperate. So I end up talking to nobody. In all matters pertaining to my client, San Quentin just stalls and stalls. The last time I was there, I waited from 8:00 A.M. till 3:00 P.M. to see Mr. Pratt and never got in. This is not justice, Your Honor. This is malfeasance. Somebody from the Department of Corrections ought to go to jail for this."

He beckoned toward his client and observed that most other prisoners would have broken down by now. "I think it bespeaks this man's composure, his violence threshold, that in the face of all this obvious injustice, he has been able to maintain himself, to come to court in the face of all these things, and yet try to assist us in preparing this case." He described Pratt's behavior as all the more remarkable in that "he has never had an opportunity to set his mind to anything. He has just been housed in a completely segregated unit, always in chains, always trying to ensure that he is going to be alive the next day."

Judge Parker reinstated the life sentence without comment. Cochran walked past her in the parking lot en route to his Silver Shadow. "We'll see you soon, Judge," he said pleasantly.

"Yes," she said. "I'm sure I will."

PRATT'S SIX siblings were upset by the brusque resentencing. They'd followed the prison situation closely, making calls to counselors and administrators whenever there was reason to believe their brother had been mistreated. Timothy found a single bright spot in the oppressive pattern. "All of this attention on Gerard," he wrote, "made it difficult for the authorities to murder him."

The family's bewilderment and bitterness about the Polaroid photo faded soon after the trial. Virginia, Charles, Emelda and Jack cross-checked their memories, studied the family albums and loose pictures and agreed that their testimony had been accurate: the photo had been shot at Christmastime 1968, and indeed could not have been taken at any other time. Each member had a theory about the Polaroid executive's devastating testimony. Ginny suspected that the man had made a plain old-fashioned mistake. Jack continued to insist that the codings were deliberately misdated. Charles agreed with Jack but also complained that Charles Hollopeter "asked me the wrong questions or I could've cleared up the whole mess on the witness stand." As for Geronimo, he suspected that one arm of the law or another—the LAPD, the Los Angeles D.A.'s Office, the FBI—had used technical resources to corrupt the evidence.

THE INDEFATIGABLE Virginia drove north to visit her brother, and this time she was granted an hour. Geronimo was excited to hear firsthand that their mother was doing well in her little house in Across the Tracks. "That's the toughest thing, Ginny," he told his big sister. "Not being able to see Mama."

Virginia reported that brothers Jack and Charles had endured their own hard times but were surviving back in Morgan City. Charles, who now preferred to be called Rasuli,[35] was scratching out a living counseling and teaching. He'd erected a geodesic dome in the backyard that once had been filled with scrap and junk. In an effort to understand the family's ordeal, he'd become a self-designated "Pythagorean transcendental astrologer," and the dome was designed to focus his thoughts. Brother Jack, the family's football star before Geronimo broke his high school records, was struggling with the notoriety of being a killer's brother. He was studying parapsychology and planning a new career as a counselor and minister.

As Virginia made her progress reports, Geronimo noticed that she didn't seem to be her usual sunny self. From behind the steel mesh, her liquid brown eyes looked teary. That was another reason he'd never wanted his family to visit. Virginia was a hardy specimen, but the prison environment, even in the visiting areas, had a tendency to grind outsiders down.

"What's the matter, Ginny?" Geronimo asked.

"Nothing's the matter."

"I want to hear what the hell's bothering my big sister."

Virginia insisted that she was fine. When the guard came to lead her away, she seemed to shrink from his touch.

A FEW days later Geronimo learned the truth. "After Ginny made her appointment to visit you, the cops came to her house," a friend wrote. "Told her they had a tip she was running drugs. Threw her on the floor and stuck guns in her face. They went through every drawer, ripped up the rugs, took the toilet apart, left the place a mess. No explanation, no apology."

---

[35] "Messenger of love and harmony," a name bestowed on him by Jomo Kenyatta two weeks before the Kenya leader and his wife were massacred.

At San Quentin Virginia had had to wait three hours before being taken into a side room and ordered to strip. Every part of her body was prodded and probed before she was allowed to dress and go to the visiting room.

When Geronimo got the news, he kicked the wall and yelled, *"Fuck!"* Cochran's words came back: *You have the same rights as a dog in a kennel.* His pencil stub tore the paper as he wrote to Virginia: "Don't come back to any of these prisons. No matter where I am, no matter what you hear about me, KEEP AWAY. If you show up, I'm gonna refuse to see you." He signed "Love, G" and instructed his sister to pass the word to every family member.

That night he sent a note to the visiting room guard: "Don't any of you son of a bitches ever disrespect my sister again. Or *any* black woman. Do NOT forget. Because I won't."

FROM HIS old Panther colleague Long John Washington, Geronimo finally learned why he'd been kept in restraints on the flight to Los Angeles. Washington explained that FBI agents had designed a plan to break Pratt out of the Los Angeles County Jail and follow him to Patricia Hearst.[36] The operation would be led by an African American mole named Darthard Perry, the same double agent who'd torched black radical Angela Davis' lifetime files, then fire-bombed the Watts Writers Workshop at the FBI's direction. Long John described how Perry had enlisted him and three others in the escape operation. The FBI provided them with information on the escape route, pictures of the breakout site, an untraceable gun and a fake driver's license for the escapee. Washington was to be the driver, but the operation was canceled. Among other problems, the conspirators didn't trust the FBI or Darthard Perry. But word of the escape plan leaked to the L.A. County Sheriff's Office. Hence the barefoot flight, the shackles in court and the extra security in the courtroom.

When Geronimo related the scenario to Johnnie Cochran in an attorney-client call, the lawyer commented, "If you told me that story five years ago, I'd have sent you and John Washington to a psychiatrist. Doesn't it make you wonder what else the FBI is up to?"

Pratt said he'd been wondering for years.

---

[36] The plan was developed under the direction of Charles W. Bates, special agent in charge of the San Francisco FBI office. Bates simultaneously directed the search for Patty Hearst and the ongoing Bay Area campaign to "neutralize" the Black Panthers.

Enter Hanlon

The law student Stuart Hanlon and his haystack "Jewfro" paid their first visit to Geronimo Pratt three weeks after the inmate's barefoot flight to Los Angeles. The young radical could hardly wait to wade into the case. At first, his prospective client sounded friendly but guarded. "I don't know, man," Pratt said through the grille. "That Theresa Black lady that sent you here, she's flaky as hell. She almost got me killed at Folsom."

Hanlon refused to be dismissed. The more he learned about the case, the more angry he became. He wondered why a hotshot black lawyer in Los Angeles was the only person standing up for Pratt. Where was the American Civil Liberties Union? The National Lawyers Guild? Where were the Bay Area rainmakers who were supposed to do a little pro bono work in between their six-figure billings?

Hanlon realized that there was no money in the case, but he retained his flower child's nonchalance about such matters. He lived alone in a ratty apartment that rented for $100 a month and looked like a sanitary landfill. His idea of a social evening was a walk in Golden Gate Park with his girlfriend, a slice of pizza and a few tokes. "Sooner or later I'll get busy and make some bucks," he promised his parents in New York. "Probably later. It's not a priority."

Five months after he first met Geronimo Pratt at San Quentin and viewed the knifing of a guard, Hanlon was admitted to the California Bar. At first he practiced "in-your-face" law, striding into courtrooms with youthful arrogance, convinced that jury boxes were full of fools who lacked his vision of truth and righteousness. "I considered them tight-ass and narrow-minded, and the jurors picked up on that and didn't like it. I was confrontational with judges, witnesses, other lawyers. I was often held in contempt but talked my way out of it. I never got in a courtroom fight, but it was close. I made one cop so mad, he told me, 'If being ugly was a felony, you'd be doing life.' After a while I began to realize that the rest of the world wasn't as stupid as I thought. Jurors wanted to do the right thing. All I had to do was help 'em a little. After that I began to win."

BY THE end of 1976 Hanlon's charter client was back in San Quentin's Adjustment Center, a minor improvement over the death row hole, and the young lawyer found himself heading north across the Golden Gate Bridge several times a week. Injustice had obsessed him since childhood, but he was also motivated by admiration for his client. "Pratt was quick, he was smart, he had a sense of humor and irony. He didn't waste time feeling sorry for himself. And he was a tough son of a bitch. If we weren't working on his case together, I'd've gone to see him just as a friend. We had a huge amount in common, which was pretty amazing considering that he was a war hero from Louisiana and I was a 4-F slacker from Westchester County, New York. He always said, 'It's because we're both Virgos.' I'd laugh and say, 'Yeah, sure, right on, that explains it all.' We talked women, sex, football— we were both high school jocks. We had the same political views. I think he was an anarchist at heart.

"I learned an odd thing—he really wasn't a Panther. He'd never officially joined because he hated the idea of leadership. So did I. He was a dictionary junkie. He was copying *Webster's*, one word at a time. He said that's how Malcolm X served his time. He figured it would take five years to finish and then he'd start on a new dictionary. He had the whole Adjustment Center playing Scrabble, yelling out their plays, threatening to cut each other over words like 'syzygy' and 'helicon.' After they allowed him books, it seemed like he read a different one every night, cover to cover. He had Krishnamurti cold. We'd spend a whole session discussing something by Michael Harrington or Dwight Macdonald, Carey McWilliams, Herbert Marcuse, all the old lefties. Marcuse was one of my professors at Columbia.

I had the best education in the world and Geronimo went to Morgan City Colored High, but he beat my ass on a lot of subjects. We talked about ideologies, about Shylock and Portia, Socrates and Plato, the LAPD and the Panthers' ten-point program. He was into etymology, the meaning of meaning, philology, a bunch of abstractions. He'd say, 'I'll never understand how someone gets in a position to say, "This is green," when it could just as easily be called purple or chartreuse.' He'd say, 'It's green because someone *says* it's green, and he has the power to enforce what he says. So then, green stays green for centuries!' It pissed him off that so many things were defined by powerful people who were often wrong. He pronounced 'hyperbole' and 'epitome' as three-syllable words. He only knew them from books. I never corrected him; he was a little wiggy about being corrected. He was a little wiggy about a lot of things."

Hanlon and Geronimo agreed that their first priority was to get him out of the hole and onto the mainline.

"He says he can handle whatever they dish out," Hanlon told Johnnie Cochran in one of their telephone conferences, "but nobody can survive in solitary for long."

Cochran said, "I've tried everything short of calling Governor Reagan. Keeping the man in the hole is against CDC policy, against public policy, against *human* policy. It's cruel and unusual punishment."

Hanlon said, "G's a lucky guy. For him they waive the rules."

CERTAIN MAD-DOG prisoners appeared to be housed in the Adjustment Center semipermanently, but the main purpose of the prison within a prison was immediate control of the general population. Sentences to the hole were not intended as holiday visits or pleasant sojourns, nor was the place designed as a regular residence. Dining hall misbehavior might bring a mainline prisoner a three-day sentence, possession of drugs a week, an attempted stabbing a month or two. Problem inmates served their sentences and left, presumably chastened. But Pratt was under an additional three-year sentence in solitary confinement after two years in other holes—Dallas, Los Angeles, Folsom, Tracy. A counselor testified later: "I told him face-to-face that he would never get out of the Adjustment Center. That was the information I received. I heard it at a full classification hearing."

Hanlon was disturbed that Pratt had been denied any opportunity to prove that he could behave on the prison's mainline. He'd been stuck in his dungeon, his only recreation two or three trips a week to the yard. He was in constant pain from his wounds, but he avoided treatment because he distrusted prison medics and drugs.

FOR A year after the resentencing nightmare in Los Angeles, Hanlon and the small Pratt support team engaged in a campaign of letter-writing to civil rights groups, prison officials, politicians and other public figures. The fledgling lawyer filed copies in cardboard boxes that lined the asbestos walls of the furnace room that he laughingly called his law office. The letters produced expressions of sympathy but no action.

"All prisoners claim they're innocent," Geronimo told Hanlon. "All prisoners write letters. People have their own lives to live. They don't want to hear about me."

The Pratt correspondents decided to concentrate their fire on prison officials. Johnnie Cochran wrote to Ed George, administrator of San Quentin's Security Housing Unit:

> It has come to my attention that the alleged "Folsom School Bus" incident is still a part of Mr. Pratt's central file. . . . These charges were thoroughly discredited. . . . If these charges are in any way causing Mr. Pratt to remain in the Adjustment Center, this is indeed unfair and an injustice. May I ask that these charges be stricken from Mr. Pratt's file and that immediate consideration be given to his joining the regular prison population.

Hanlon was enraged when he took his first look at his client's prison jacket. According to the records, Pratt was a cop killer ("responsible for the murders of three officers") and a racial agitator. He made poison darts to shoot at guards. He was a "high escape risk" who spent most of his time planning jailbreaks. One memo referred to him as "a two-time escapee." He was said to be plotting an Attica-style bloodbath. A prison psychiatrist verified that he intended "violence to everyone." He was blamed for a riot on the mainline, a world away from the Adjustment Center, that resulted in the death of one Hispanic and the stabbings of five others. A counselor warned the warden's office that "other inmates readily rally to him for leadership." Even after Patricia Hearst was captured in September 1975, and the full details of the case became known, Pratt was listed as a participant in the scheme. He was described as an "important" member of the Symbionese

Liberation Army and as "the most influential member" of the Black Liberation Army ("and the BLA has made no secret of the fact that they intend to rescue Pratt from prison by any means necessary"). He was also described as a "general" in the ultraviolent Black Guerrilla Family.

When prison officials refused to correct their records, Stuart Hanlon turned to the laborious appeals procedure known as a 602. The documents required information from outside sources, necessitating long waits for replies. As a resident of the hole, Geronimo was denied access to the law library; his formal requests for legal material were usually acknowledged four or five weeks after filing and often stamped "denied."

Lawyer and client decided to expand their net by requesting federal files on Pratt via the Freedom of Information Act. The first three items dribbled in from Washington under the letterhead "United States Department of Justice, Federal Bureau of Investigation." The text was blacked out. Various reasons were cited for the redactions: national security, protection of informants' identities, jeopardy to ongoing investigations, violation of attorney-client privilege and the all-purpose explanation: "Not relevant to the matters at issue in this matter."

Geronimo told Hanlon, "The FBI should list 'CYA,' too."

"CYA?"

"Cover your ass."

In such pursuits, another year was lost.

AT SAN Quentin a new counselor prepared a surprising report. According to A. W. Gerritsen, Pratt was "very outspoken, but in a carefully thought-out articulate way. . . . He has a deep intellectual understanding." The counselor added, "It is noted that during his first years in prison, while he was in the Security Housing Unit up until late 1974, he accumulated a large number of disciplinary reports. Based on this writer's experience (and subject tended to agree with this), they seemed to be a reflection of his frustration and boredom over being continually locked up. Since that time he has had some disciplinary reports, usually not of a terribly serious nature. . . . These seem more of a reflection of his process of readjustment . . . and possibly, as he claims, his negative reputation and notoriety."

Thus Gerritsen became the first in a long line of lower-level prison officials who seemed to sense that Pratt was miscast as a monster. Gerritsen's was a minority opinion, and it wasn't widely accepted. Some who spoke up for Pratt were later transferred or fired. But a momentum had begun to build.

EARLY IN his sixth year in his steel cage, Geronimo told Hanlon, "We're wasting time. We're trying to convince guys who'll never be convinced. Let's file a civil rights suit." He told his young lawyer about a little-known federal statute that gave prisoners the right to sue for state violations of their civil rights. He'd read the statute in a "Jailhouse Manual" provided by the National Lawyers Guild. Such actions were popular but seldom successful in the wake of the prison riots of the 1960s and 1970s.

On May 26, 1976, Hanlon filed suit against the California Department of Corrections, charging violations of Pratt's constitutional rights under the First and Fourteenth Amendments. The complaint alleged that the inmate was being held in solitary confinement on the basis of fabricated reports about his misconduct and was being punished for his political beliefs. Before the U.S. District Court in San Francisco, Hanlon argued that Pratt was being kept in the hole "for reasons that shock the general conscience and are intolerable to fundamental fairness." He asked the judge to implement Pratt's right "not to have his life endangered and put in jeopardy because of the hatred, disdain and scorn" of prison officials.

"I was flying blind," Hanlon admitted later. "If I'd had any idea how hard it was to prove a civil rights case against the government, I might never have filed. I wasn't making much money as a lawyer. In those days my middle name was pro bono. I think I grossed $1,200 my first year. I spent most of my time with G at San Quentin and representing the poor in court.

"For a while, my biggest job was keeping him calm. Once we got started on the case, he drove the guards crazy with demands for lawbooks. He went through the federal statutes and the California civil code like a logger with a chain saw. Mama Pratt did not raise her son to be a helper. He had his own opinion about everything, and it seldom agreed with mine or the court's or anybody else's. He turned up case law and citations and obscure legal bullshit that nobody knew existed. He tried to convert me into his law partner, clerk, runner and therapist; I was already his gofer and crony. He was a lawyer's dream when he wasn't being a pain in the ass."

HANLON WAS disturbed when the civil rights case was assigned to U.S. District Judge Samuel Conti, renowned for his fiery antics. "He was an extreme right-winger, and of course I came across as a dangerous radical. They called him Slammin' Sammy because every now and then he would hold an attorney in contempt and throw him in jail. Other lawyers warned me, Take your toothbrush to court. People actually wet their pants in front of him. But he had integrity. He was fair. He could be reasoned with. He wasn't inflexible like Judge Parker and some of the others. And he knew the law. Right off, he made it plain that he didn't have a high regard for prison civil rights cases. But he gave us one little window of opportunity. We had to prove that the violations of G's constitutional rights were intentional and based on his political beliefs. In other words, a guard could get away with testifying under oath, 'I beat Pratt with an ax handle, I kicked him in the nuts, I put him on bread and water and Thorazine, I strip-searched his lawyer and his mother and his sister, but *not* because he's a radical.' The burden was on us to show otherwise."

HANLON'S IDEALISTIC friends flocked to the office that he now shared with eight struggling lawyers in a Victorian house on Duboce Avenue in the Haight. The struggle to extricate Pratt from the hole was the kind of antiestablishment action that the left-wing hotbloods lived for. "Everybody worked for free. Just a bunch of cool people—lawyers, law students, writers, artists. We didn't ask about their politics as long as they worked. We had no computers, no copiers, no printers. We passed the hat to pay court fees—I collected six bucks at a Japanese restaurant while I was waiting for my sushi."

On a whim, Hanlon made a cold call to the office of U.S. Representative Paul N. "Pete" McCloskey and was told that his fellow Californian would be pleased to see him. McCloskey, an ex-marine and maverick Republican, served on the House Oversight Committee. His congressional colleague, U.S. Representative Don Edwards, a California Democrat, had already spoken out against clandestine FBI programs aimed at harassing the Black Panther Party.[37]

---

[37] "Regardless of the unattractiveness or noisy militancy of some private citizens or organizations, the Constitution does not permit federal interference with their activities except through the criminal justice system, armed with its ancient safeguards. There are no exceptions. No federal agency, the CIA, the IRS, or the FBI, can be at the same time policeman, prosecutor, judge and jury. That is what constitutionally guaranteed due process is all about. It may sometimes be disorderly and unsatisfactory to some, but it is the essence of freedom."

Hanlon drove his consumptive Toyota south to McCloskey's Palo Alto office and was ushered into the presence of a robust-looking man with reddish cheeks, a shock of salt-and-pepper hair and eyebrows thick enough to comb. Hanlon's briefing lasted till late in the evening. It might have gone all night, but the enthralled McCloskey had to catch a plane back to Washington.

Two days later Hanlon took a long-distance call. "You're right about Pratt," the hoarse voice said over the phone. "I've done some more snooping. What can I do to help?"

Hanlon said, "You can put your name on our brief and help us dig up some FBI records."

McCloskey promised to get to work.

IN LATER years the Geronimo Pratt ad hoc legal staff would grow to include the veteran civil rights attorneys Leonard Weinglass and Robert Bloom and the astute California politician Willie Brown Jr., but the earliest heavy lifting was done by a tight little group of energetic nobodies, some of them highly eccentric.

Hanlon recalled, "David Bernstein was our legal genius, a brilliant guy, lived with his mother in the San Bernardino Valley. Whatever he did, his normal speed was three hundred miles an hour. You could give David a problem that would take most lawyers a week and he'd figure it out over a beer."

To Hanlon's joy, a virtuoso legal duo from Stanford University joined up—John Mitchell and Margaret Ryan. "Johnnie and Marnie handled the first depositions, and they were brilliant. They got help from Cheryl Kessler, who was going to the University of San Francisco and working in our law office as a student. Marnie's sister Kathleen and I started dating. Kathy was working at a day-care center, but she was so disturbed by the Pratt case that she quit her job to study law. Two terrific black attorneys joined up: Sharon Meadows and Cheyenne Bell. A group called Prairie Fire sent us a worker crew. We got major help from Dennis Cunningham and Brian Glick from Students for a Democratic Society. Pete McCloskey's staff turned up classified information and helped with our briefs. Other lawyers came and went. Very few stayed to the end—we all had to make a living, and this case just wore people down, no matter how dedicated they were."

PRATT'S OWN personal love affair grew out of the legal battle and started as a simple financial convenience. "We were always trying to raise money to cover our expenses and one of the sisters came up with the idea that it would be easier for me to get my disability money out of the V.A. if I was married. A college student named Linda Session was a volunteer on my case. Her father was an African American in prison in Texas and her mother was a Japanese war bride. Linda was young, shy, quiet, smart—and beautiful. Went to school all day, worked at Kaiser Hospital at night. She lived in a housing project in Marin City, not far from Q, and she was pretty much a social outcast. The blacks didn't like her because she was half Japanese, and she didn't look Asian enough to suit the Japanese. I didn't think much about it when she started showing up at the prison; I needed legal runners anyway. One day she said some of the troops had been discussing strategy at Stu's office and they figured it would make sense for her and me to do the marriage thing since she lived so close to the prison. I said, 'Look, sister Linda, I don't relate to marriage. I don't relate to monogamy. I want you to know in front. Seems like I don't have the capacity to love. It's, like, burnt out of me.' I told her I'd already lost one wife and wasn't even sure I'd loved *her*.

"Linda said it didn't matter, it was just a formality, so we signed the marriage papers. What the hell, I was never gonna be a free man anyway."

TOWARD THE end of 1976, ominous news began to trickle out of Washington. The key word was "COINTELPRO." As Hanlon said later, "We didn't know it at the time, but without COINTELPRO, Geronimo would never have gone to prison. He and I were sitting in the attorney's visiting room and he flashed this thick green paperback report and asked if I'd been keeping up on the Church Committee hearings in Washington. He said there was a lot of stuff about the FBI and minorities. So I sent for my own copy. It was called 'The Report of the Senate Select Committee to Study Governmental Operations with Respect to Intelligence Activities' and it weighed about nine pounds. I opened it up and the first thing I read was that the FBI's COINTELPRO agents routinely interfered in judicial proceedings. I thought, *Huh?* I read the page again and it was still there. You can imagine my reaction to lines like this: 'When a target appeared before a judge, a jury, or probation board, he sometimes carried an unknown burden—the FBI had gotten there first.' Then they listed a bunch of horrible examples. I thought, Jesus Christ, this sounds familiar."

FLASHBACK: COINTELPRO

On the night of March 8, 1971, a month after Geronimo Pratt had been extradited from Dallas to Los Angeles to face murder charges, raiders had broken into an FBI satellite office in the leafy little town of Media, Pennsylvania, and hauled off a carload of secret documents.[38] Soon photostatic copies began showing up in media mailboxes.

The purloined documents revealed that the agency had been snooping on individuals and organizations without authorization of Congress or the president or due process of law. The targets included African Americans, white student groups, antiwar organizations, Communists, unions, workers' committees and anyone regarded by Director J. Edgar Hoover as subversive. In one of the memos Hoover had written, "The Negro youth and moderates must be made to understand that if they succumb to revolutionary teachings, they will be *dead* revolutionaries." For years the Director's pet hate had been Martin Luther King Jr., whom he tagged "the most dangerous and effective Negro leader in the

---

[38] The intruders were never officially identified. Some believed the burglars were associated with the Berrigan brothers, radical Catholic priests who had led protests against the Vietnam War.

country,"[39] and much of the stolen material concerned illicit activities aimed at bringing down the civil rights leader, including years of bedroom bugging, attempts to disgrace him and a concerted effort to drive him to suicide in the month before he was scheduled to accept the Nobel Peace Prize in 1964.

The capitalized word "COINTELPRO" was sprinkled throughout the stolen files but at first was taken by the media to be harmless bureaucratese. Carl Stern, a reporter for NBC News, became puzzled over the acronym and other arcane aspects of the confidential files. The Justice Department ignored his first requests under the 1966 Freedom of Information Act, then denied that COINTELPRO files existed, but was forced to begin releasing documents after NBC filed suit in federal court. The earliest releases were squeezed out with aggravating slowness; like the first few copies of FBI documents provided to Hanlon and Pratt, they were so thoroughly censored as to be useless. Investigators finally learned that "COINTELPRO" stood for "Counter-Intelligence Program," but letterheads, addresses, signatures and whole pages of text were covered with thick blobs of India ink. After more complaints a few open files were released, and a pattern began to emerge.

COINTELPRO PROVED to be a collection of domestic espionage programs that were breathtaking in their sweep, ingenuity and illegality. Given J. Edgar Hoover's lifelong contempt for African Americans and his stubborn refusal to integrate his own agency,[40] the enemies list inevitably included black organizations of all types, from the Urban League, the Congress of

---

[39] Hoover's preoccupation with African American leaders went back to 1919, five years before he became director of the "Bureau of Investigation," when he warned the U.S. attorney general about Marcus Garvey, "a West Indian negro [who] has also been particularly active among the radical elements in New York City in agitating the negro movements." Since Garvey had broken no laws, Hoover suggested that "some proceeding against him for fraud" could be drummed up.

[40] Marilyn Bardsley, journalist and student of the FBI, wrote: "Many have alleged that Hoover was against African-Americans, but that is not true. His housekeeper was black and five employees of the Bureau who attended to Hoover's personal needs were also black. Hoover just did not see an expanded role for people of color beyond waiting on white people. Naturally, this bigotry, like all of Hoover's other beliefs, became part of the entrenched culture of the Bureau."

Racial Equality and the NAACP to violent street gangs like Chicago's Blackstone Rangers and the West Coast's Crips and Bloods. Hoover personally mandated COINTELPRO to "prevent the coalition of militant black nationalist groups" and "prevent the rise of a black messiah who could unify, and electrify, the movement."

From its creation in 1957, the supersecret program was driven by race. Agents were specifically ordered to "weaken [black] groups by setting members against each other, or to separate groups which might otherwise be allies, and convert them into mutual enemies." Informers and provocateurs, many with felony records, were recruited as moles. Individual black leaders were singled out for "neutralization."

Outcries over the public revelations resulted in the naming of a select Senate committee under Frank Church of Utah. Its members included political warhorses of left and right: Barry Goldwater, Walter Mondale, Philip Hart, Howard Baker, Richard Schweiker. After studying some twenty thousand documents, the committee produced the book-length report that intrigued Geronimo Pratt and Stuart Hanlon. The introduction set the tone:

> In these programs, the Bureau went beyond the collection of intelligence to secret action designed to "disrupt" and "neutralize" target groups and individuals. The techniques . . . ranged from the trivial (mailing reprints of *Reader's Digest* articles to college administrators) to the degrading (sending anonymous poison-pen letters intended to break up marriages) and the dangerous (encouraging gang warfare and falsely labeling members of a violent group as police informers). . . . The cases demonstrate the consequences of a Government agency's decision to take the law into its own hands for the "greater good" of the country.

The introduction included pejoratives like "vigilante operation," "intolerable," "forbidden," "abhorrent," "repellent" and "silly," and credited William C. Sullivan, former assistant to J. Edgar Hoover, with a succinct characterization of the Director's programs: "This is a rough, tough, dirty business, and dangerous. . . . No holds were barred. . . . We have used [these techniques] against Soviet agents. . . ."

The lengthy introduction contained many passages about the FBI's campaign against the Black Panthers:

The Bureau approved 2,370 separate counterintelligence operations. Their techniques ranged from anonymously mailing reprints of newspaper and magazine articles (sometimes Bureau-authored or planted) to group members or supporters . . . to mailing anonymous letters to a member's spouse accusing the target of infidelity; from using informants to raise controversial issues at meetings in order to cause dissent, to the "snitch jacket" (falsely labeling a group member as an informant), and encouraging street warfare between violent groups; from contacting members of a legitimate group to expose the alleged subversive background of a fellow member, to contacting an employer to get a target fired; from attempting to arrange for reporters to interview targets with planted questions, to trying to stop targets from speaking at all. . . .

A typical attempt to fit a Black Panther for a "snitch jacket" took the form of a forged note sent by the FBI's Newark field office to another member of the party:

Brother: Jimmie was sold out by Sister ——— for some pig money to pay her rent. When she don't get it that way she takes Panther money. How come her kid sells the [Black Panther] paper in his school and no one bothers him? How come Tyler got busted up by the pigs and her kid didn't. How comes the FBI pig fascists knew where to bust Lonnie and Minnie way out where they were. Think baby.

A COINTELPRO administrator reminded his operatives in a May 1970 directive that truth was irrelevant in the campaign. "Purpose of counterintelligence action is to disrupt BPP," he wrote, "and it is immaterial whether facts exist to substantiate the charge." In testimony before the Church Committee, George C. Moore, chief of the FBI's Racial Intelligence Section, described his own policy about falsification: "You have to be able to make decisions and I am sure that labeling somebody as an informant, that you'd want to make certain that it served a good purpose. . . . As far as I am aware, in the black extremist area, by using that technique, no one was killed."

A SECTION of the select committee's report was titled "The FBI's Covert Action Program to Destroy the Black Panther Party." Not even Hanlon and Pratt expected to see so many illegal acts chronicled by a Senate committee whose members seemed appalled at their own discoveries. The BPP hadn't appeared on COINTELPRO's original target list, which consisted of the Southern Christian Leadership Conference, the Student Nonviolent Coordinating Committee, the Revolutionary Action Movement and the Nation of Islam, plus such figures as Martin Luther King Jr., Stokely Carmichael, H. "Rap" Brown, Roy Wilkins, Whitney Young and Elijah Muhammad. But in September 1968, the month Geronimo Pratt and his sister Emelda arrived in Los Angeles from Morgan City, J. Edgar Hoover had reordered his priorities and described the Panthers as "the greatest threat to the internal security of the country."

By July of 1969, several weeks before FBI agents first journeyed to the Atchafalaya Basin to begin their quiet workup on Elmer Gerard Pratt, the Panthers had become COINTELPRO's primary target.[41] As in all programs bearing the Hoover imprimatur, fine distinctions of legality were blurred in the rush to do the Director's bidding. In Chicago FBI agents sent a forged letter to the leader of the Blackstone Rangers informing him that the Panthers had taken out a contract on his life. The purpose, according to agency files, was "to intensify the degree of animosity" between the two violent organizations. In Southern California, according to the Church report, "the FBI launched a covert effort to 'create further dissension in the ranks of the BPP.' This effort included mailing anonymous letters and caricatures to BPP members ridiculing the local and national BPP leadership for the express purpose of exacerbating an existing gang war between the BPP and an organization called the United Slaves (US). This gang war resulted in the killings of four BPP members by members of US and in numerous beatings and shootings."

On November 29, 1968, the Los Angeles COINTELPRO office memoed Washington that its members were "currently preparing an anonymous letter for Bureau approval which will be sent to the Los Angeles Black Panther Party supposedly from a member of the US organization in which it will be stated that the youth group of the US organization is aware of the BPP 'contract' to kill Ron Karenga, leader of US, and they, US members, in retaliation, have made plans to ambush leaders of the BPP in Los Angeles." Two months later Bunchy Carter and John Huggins died in the shoot-out with Karenga's comrades.

---

[41] As of the committee hearings in early 1976, 233 specific COINTELPRO actions had been directed against the Panthers.

"Take a look at this," Hanlon told Pratt, pointing to a report from the Los Angeles field office to FBI headquarters dated May 26, 1970, sixteen months after the killings of Carter and Huggins. Geronimo read:

> Information received from local sources indicate that, in general, the membership of the Los Angeles BPP is physically afraid of US members and take premeditated precautions to avoid confrontations. . . . The Los Angeles Division is aware of the mutually hostile feelings harbored between the organizations and the first opportunity to capitalize on the situation will be maximized. It is intended that US Inc. will be appropriately and discreetly advised of the time and location of BPP activities *in order that the two organizations might be brought together and thus grant nature the opportunity to take her due course.*[42]

"In other words," Hanlon said, "let's keep the black dudes fighting. Two dead citizens weren't enough."

Geronimo looked up from the report. "We weren't citizens," he said slowly. "We were niggers."

The Church Committee was almost as blunt: "This report does demonstrate that the chief investigative branch of the Federal Government . . . engaged in lawless tactics and responded to deep-seated social problems by fomenting violence and unrest. . . . Equally disturbing is the pride which those officials took in claiming credit for the bloodshed that occurred."

According to the report, it was J. Edgar Hoover himself who'd first fired up the West Coast hostility between the Panthers and the United Slaves. "In order to fully capitalize upon BPP and US differences as well as to exploit all avenues of creating further dissension in the ranks of the BPP," the Director had instructed fourteen field offices "to submit imaginative and hard-hitting counterintelligence measures aimed at crippling the BPP."

The reaction of COINTELPRO agents to the UCLA deaths had been to step up the provocations. In their zeal they lost some finesse, and members of US and the Panthers began to realize that their passions were being inflamed by obviously bogus documents. For several months in early 1969 the rival black groups engaged in conciliatory talks. "I remember that pe-

---

[42] Italics added by the Church Committee.

riod," Geronimo told Hanlon. "We were naive but we weren't totally stupid. So we sat down together."

Through informers, COINTELPRO agents learned of the rapprochement and created new provocations by distributing cartoons lampooning leaders of both sides. Thus the fragile peace ended almost before it began. Aggravated Panthers chased US members from one of their public meetings, and US members retaliated by beating up a female BPP member. The FBI agent who engineered the ghetto cartoon program modestly took credit. "[Informant] has advised on several occasions that the cartoons are 'really shaking up the BPP,' " he memoed the Director.

Six weeks later open warfare resumed with the killing of Panther John Savage by a member of US.

IN SAN DIEGO, as a result of the FBI's provocations, the BPP and US devoted the summer of 1969 to amassing ordnance. On August 14 a US gunman wounded two Panthers. The next day a Panther named Sylvester Bell was killed by another US member. As the Senate committee report observed, "The FBI viewed this carnage as a positive development and informed headquarters: 'Efforts are being made to determine how this situation can be capitalized upon for the benefit of the Counterintelligence Program. . . . In view of the recent killing of BPP member Sylvester Bell, a new cartoon is being considered in the hopes that it will assist in the continuance of the rift between the BPP and US.' "

Another proud progress report went out to Hoover: "Shootings, beatings, and a high degree of unrest continues to prevail in the ghetto area. . . . Although no specific counterintelligence action can be credited with contributing to this overall situation, *it is felt that a substantial amount of the unrest is directly attributable to this program.*" The shocked authors of the Senate report provided the added emphasis.

AFTER SEPTEMBER 1969, COINTELPRO agents concentrated on tightening the pressure on Pratt. According to the Church Committee report, "One of the caricatures was designed to attack the Los Angeles Panther leader as an overpowering individual 'who has the BPP completely at his mercy. . . .' "

A fake letter to a Panther leader, ostensibly written by a US supporter, warned that "Karenga's coming!" From start to finish, the bogus note was intended to enrage:

> I would like to say that you and the rest of you black racists can go to hell! I got my ass whipped by a Newark pig all for the cause of the wineheads like you and the rest of the black pussycats that call themselves Panthers. Big deal: you have to have a three-hour educational session just to teach those motherfuckers (you all know what that means, don't you? It's the first words your handkerchief head mamma teaches you) how to spell it. . . .
>
> Why, I read an article in the Panther paper where a California Panther sat in his car and watched his friend get shot by Karenga's group and what did he do? He run back and write a full page story about how tough the Panthers are and what they're going to do. Ha Ha—Bull Shit. Goodbye, baby—and watch out. "Right on" as they say.[43]

The Church report included page after page of quotations from provocative letters and phone calls long after FBI tactics had resulted in murder and bloodshed. A tip to Stokely Carmichael's mother informed her that BPP members planned to kill her son; a bureau memo observed with satisfaction that Carmichael fled to Africa the next day. Landlords who were renting to Panthers and interracial couples were advised to evict them or face trouble. Lawyers who expressed sympathy with Panther goals were dropped from their firms over "irregularities" revealed by COINTELPRO agents. Police were tipped to imaginary sex orgies and pot parties, and more than one Panther business meeting was interrupted by local raiders acting on anonymous complaints. White parents were warned that Panthers had impregnated their daughters and corrupted their sons. Marriages were destroyed by false reports of infidelity backed up by photographs doctored in FBI labs. A typical poison-pen letter was sent to the husband of a white

---

[43] Beyond its obvious inauthenticity (few militant blacks would disparage African American motherhood or refer to a fellow black as "handkerchief head"), the letter was noteworthy for the problem of delicacy it created in the originating office. To spare bureau stenographers from the strong language, the letter was typed outside the office. The sensibilities of J. Edgar Hoover, well known for his devotion to his mother, were similarly respected. In his personal copy, as the field report solicitously pointed out, asterisks were used in place of what was described as "that colloquial phrase which implies an unnatural physical relationship with a maternal parent."

woman who worked in the St. Louis office of ACTION, a spin-off of CORE:

> Dear Mr. B: Look man I guess your old lady doesn't get enough at home or she wouldn't be shucking and jiving with our Black Men in ACTION, you dig? Like all she wants to integrate is the bed room and we Black Sisters ain't gonna take no second best from our men. So lay it on her, man—or get her the hell out! A Soul Sister.

A follow-up memo crowed about the couple's separation. The St. Louis COINTELPRO agent reported to the Director, "This matrimonial stress and strain should cause her to function much less effectively in ACTION. While our letter was probably not the sole cause of this separation, it certainly contributed very strongly."

AFTER J. Edgar Hoover was shown his first copies of the *Black Panther,* the party newspaper, he dubbed it "one of the most effective propaganda operations of the BPP" and ordered an immediate COINTELPRO response. According to the Senate report, the Internal Revenue Service was urged to open tax cases against the newspaper. Fake warnings from violent organizations like the Minutemen were sent to the editorial offices in Oakland, all containing "the common theme of warning the Black Panthers to cease publication or drastic measures would be taken. . . ." Airlines were pressured to increase freight rates on shipments of the Panther newspapers. Union members were urged to reject the cargo. In a memo to Hoover the San Diego field office suggested that "the Bureau may also wish to consider the utilization of Skatol, which is a chemical agent in powdered form and when applied to a particular surface emits an extremely noxious odor rendering the premises surrounding the point of application uninhabitable. Utilization of such a chemical of course would be dependent upon whether an entry could be achieved into the area which is utilized for the production of 'The Black Panther.' "

AFTER COINTELPRO widened the rift between Eldridge Cleaver and Huey P. Newton with a barrage of anonymous calls and letters, Hoover seemed to smell blood and issued a memo to field offices:

The present chaotic situation within the BPP must be exploited and recipients must maintain the present high level of counterintelligence activity. You should each give this matter priority attention and immediately furnish Bureau recommendations . . . designed to further aggravate the dissention within BPP leadership and to fan the apparent distrust by Newton of anyone who questions his wishes.

In response, the chief recommendation was to inundate the Panthers with more calls and letters. In a bogus note, Newton's brother Melvin was warned that Cleaver and his followers intended to kill both brothers. The snitch-jacket technique was also employed: when Newton was released from prison after the reversal of his manslaughter conviction, COINTELPRO produced a mailing:

Brothers: I am employed by the State of California and have been close to Huey Newton while he was in jail. Let me warn you that this pretty nigger may very well be working for pig Reagon. I don't know why he was set free but I am suspicious. I got this idea because he had privileges in jail like the trustees get. He had a lot of privacy most prisoners don't get. I don't think all his private meetings were for sex. I am suspicious of him. Don't tell Newton too much if he starts asking you questions—it may go right back to the pigs. Power to the People!

Another letter resulted in a transatlantic phone call from Cleaver to Newton from which wiretapping FBI agents were able to learn more details about Geronimo Pratt. The Church report quoted a memo confirming that the phone call "resulted in our being able to place in proper perspective the relationship of Newton and Cleaver to obtain the details of the Geronimo (Elmer Pratt) Group." A forged letter to Newton described how Pratt had "brutalized" and "mistreated" party members while Newton was incarcerated. The chief COINTELPRO agent in Los Angeles told his superiors in Washington that the letter was designed to open a serious breach between the paranoid Newton and his subordinate. Similar disinformation resulted in Newton's public charges that Pratt was a "jackanapes," "pig," "renegade" and "snake."

In another bogus letter Cleaver was warned not to allow his wife Kathleen to travel to the United States "because of the possibility of violence." Authentic-looking memos warned other Panthers that they were marked for death. By the use of informers and phone taps, the agents provided convincingly realistic touches. Thus the already frightened Newton came to believe that Cleaver was plotting his murder. A COINTELPRO letter from a "hit man" to Panther Chief of Staff David Hilliard warned:

> I have an "unscheduled appointment" with your leader (?) Huey P. Newton and for $3,000 I will keep any appointment. I am writing to tell you that I admired your leadership, taking the Party from nothing to something and was disappointed when I read that Huey, a pigpen graduate and queer, now, as supreme commander, outranks you. I may contact you later to see if you have a better offer, if not then maybe your on his side and I can get the ante upped. Anyway, I only hope that when I have my "meet" and believe me I will, that your not around or if you are, you won't get in my way.

Exiled in Africa, Cleaver received other divisive letters that had been generated at FBI headquarters in Washington, some in Hoover's personal office. One letter observed, "We feel Huey's recent behavior is irrational and will only further factionalize an already disorganized party." Hoover took pen in hand to add a literary touch: "As the leading theoritician of the party's philosophy and as brother among brothers, we urge you to make your influence felt. We think that the Rage [Cleaver's nickname] is the only person strong enough to pull this factionalized party back together." Hoover explained to his underlings that the added wording was aimed at creating "as much dissension as possible within the BPP. . . ."

EVENTUALLY THE COINTELPRO provocations stretched Newton's cocaine-driven paranoia beyond the limit and he formally expelled Cleaver, Pratt and their associates from the party. A bewildered Kathleen Cleaver later reported, "We did not know who to believe about what, so the general effect, not only of the letters but the whole situation in which the letters were part, was creating uncertainty. It was a very bizarre feeling."

A month after the formal expulsions the FBI declared its campaign against top Panther leadership a success. "Since the differences between Newton and Cleaver now appear to be irreconcilable, no further counterintelligence activity in this regard will be undertaken at this time and now new targets must be established."

WITH THE BPP leadership split, busy COINTELPRO agents turned to undermining Panther financial support. Wealthy Jewish backers were warned that the Panthers were a bastion of anti-Semitism.[44] Guests at a Panther fund-raiser in the New York home of composer Leonard Bernstein received fake letters describing the organization as pro-Arab. A planted item in the *Los Angeles Times* informed readers that a famous Hollywood actress was pregnant with a Panther's child; the item sent BPP financial backer Jean Seberg into a downward spiral, and her French husband, the novelist Romain Gary, blamed the FBI for her eventual suicide. The outspoken Jane Fonda drew her usual lightning. Hoover personally approved[45] a letter signed "Morris," complimenting *Daily Variety* columnist Army Archerd for publicizing Fonda's appearance at a BPP rally. The fraudulent note added:

> I hadn't been confronted by the Panther phenomenon before but we were searched upon entering Embassy Auditorium, encouraged in revival-like fashion to contribute to defend Black Panther leaders and buy guns for "the coming revolution," and led by Jane and one of the Panther chaps in a "We will kill Richard Nixon, and any other M-F-er who stands in our way" refrain (which was shocking to say the least!). I think Jane has gotten in over her head as the whole atmosphere had the 1930's Munich beer hall aura.

Other Panther supporters, including studio executives, producers and directors, found their reputations damaged by blind items in gossip columns. BPP contributors became the subject of letters to their employers, resulting in demotions and firings. Preachers who allowed their churches to be used in the free breakfast program were targeted. Bogus complaints to the San Diego Catholic Diocese, ostensibly from parishioners, resulted in the transfer of a priest to New Mexico and the termination of the breakfast program in his church.[46] Impassioned writings from

---

[44] The Director had previously authorized the mailing of a series of "Irving" letters, a bureau device in which a "disgruntled Jewish ex-Communist," wholly fictional, sent provocative letters in heavy Yiddish dialect to journalists and public figures.

[45] After emphasizing "that the mailing cannot be traced to the Bureau."

[46] Perhaps remembering the wording of the original COINTELPRO mandate from the Director, the agent reported to Washington that the priest had been "neutralized."

"parishioners" were sent to religious leaders nationwide; a typical letter warned a church administrator in Connecticut that a Hartford minister "is a revolutionist who advocates overthrowing the Government of the United States and . . . has turned over a sizable sum of money to the Panthers." A religious commentator on a Cincinnati radio station lost his job after an anonymous COINTELPRO letter complained that he'd praised a black nationalist leader.

SPRINKLED THROUGHOUT the select committee report, Geronimo Pratt and Stuart Hanlon found repeated confirmation of their long-held suspicion that local police agencies had cooperated enthusiastically with COINTELPRO and its programs. The Oakland Police Department performed espionage operations at the behest of the FBI. The Chicago Police Department's files were "open to the bureau," according to one memo. San Diego COINTELPRO agents admitted conducting "racial briefing sessions" for the local police. And most relevant to the Pratt case, a report advised Hoover that "the Los Angeles office [of the FBI] is furnishing on a daily basis information to the Los Angeles County Sheriff's Office Intelligence Division and the Los Angeles Police Department Intelligence and Criminal Conspiracy Divisions concerning the activities of the black nationalist groups in the anticipation that such information might lead to the arrest of these militants."

AFTER HANLON and Pratt digested the Church report, Geronimo reminded the lawyer of the scoreboard that a BPP member had spotted in a Los Angeles police station: "PIGS 11–PANTHERS 0."

"No wonder," Pratt said. "The game was fixed."

Original Anal-Retentives

Armed with the information from the Senate committee, Hanlon decided to apply heat to the FBI with increased use of the Freedom of Information Act. In response, the agency retreated into a familiar pattern of denial. Its customary reply to each specific request was that "BUFILES" contained nothing relevant on the subject. After more pressure, agents would admit that they'd found an item or two. Then they would produce a few pages, mostly blacked out. Kathy Ryan, Hanlon's young girlfriend, began referring to the FBI as "the original anal-retentives."

U.S. Representative Pete McCloskey had better luck at extricating documents. One FBI memo showed that immediately after Pratt turned down an attempt to interview him in 1970, a COINTELPRO agent reported: "In view of PRATT's adamant expression of hatred toward law enforcement personnel in general, no consideration is being given to reinterview PRATT for the purpose of development as a PRI [informer]. It is noted, however, that constant consideration is given to the possibility of the utilization of counterintelligence measures with efforts being directed toward neutralizing PRATT as an effective BPP functionary. . . ." Five months later Pratt had been neutralized by a charge of murder.

Documents bearing the name "Julius Butler" were forwarded from McCloskey's congressional offices to Stuart Hanlon, but most of the contents had been blacked out. Other redacted files suggested a close liaison between COINTELPRO and the LAPD, which had shanghaied the tennis court murder case from Santa Monica detectives.

The LAPD produced a few documents on demand, but the chief's office reported that "a tremendous amount of files" had been shredded.[47] The California attorney general claimed to have no paperwork relating to Pratt.

THE CIVIL rights attorney Leonard Weinglass, lending his assistance to Hanlon and the Pratt defense committee, was shocked to turn up documents confirming the existence of forty thousand pages of summary logs of round-the-clock FBI phone surveillance on Panther headquarters in Oakland. "I needn't tell you how chilling the experience is to see the Panthers laid bare and totally vulnerable over a four-year period to such total and complete surveillance," he wrote. Other FBI records confirmed Pratt's appearance in Oakland on December 20, 1968, but the agency claimed to have no wiretap logs for the date of the Santa Monica shootings, two days earlier.

UNDER THE rusty ducts and peeling insulation in Stuart Hanlon's basement war room, a dozen unsalaried volunteers bumped sweaty knees and elbows amid screaming arguments about politics, law and Hanlon's refusal to install air-conditioning. With Pratt's civil rights case still pending in the courtroom of U.S. District Judge Slammin' Sammy Conti, it was time to collect evidence, prepare briefs, dig up legal citations and get down to the pick-and-shovel work of trial preparation, but Hanlon found too much valuable time being wasted on personal disagreements and ego wars. "Everything we did was so *charged*. We had a pitched battle over the first brief. Some of our people hated a draft that was written by me and Marnie Ryan and Johnnie Mitchell, two hundred pages of sweat and tears in six-point type. Some of the other guys wanted a diatribe against the federal government; we wanted logic and law. I said, 'Goddamn it, you can't win a legal argument by calling your opponent an asshole!' I said, 'When are you

---

[47] A police source later reported that the LAPD's written reports to the FBI about the Pratt case had occupied a bookcase twelve feet wide by seven feet high.

fucking prima donnas gonna stop calling names and do some of the legal work?' They thought the brief should start with Marcus Garvey, continue through Frederick Douglass and Toussaint L'Ouverture and wind up with Martin Luther King and Malcolm X. I told 'em Judge Conti would read the first six pages and throw me in jail. One night six of us got into a free-for-all. I threw one guy into a bookshelf across the room and took a swing at Dennis Cunningham. I *loved* Dennis Cunningham. He was a big Johnny Appleseed of a guy, a typical hippie lawyer, worked his ass off and never took a fee. When it was over, I felt sick. I thought, Why am I fighting my own people?"

FROM SAN Quentin Geronimo insisted on second-guessing every decision, which meant dispatching daily runners across the Golden Gate Bridge and up Highway 101. Sometimes Hanlon found it simpler to make the half-hour drive himself. "Geronimo considered all of us to be his legal aides. A couple of Jailhouse Annies had started to visit him and he put 'em to work digging up evidence. I brought him legal papers and books and reports, which was cool, but he also insisted that I bring goodies, which wasn't so cool. They were always the wrong amount, the wrong flavor or brand. He'd say, 'What the fuck's the matter with you? Can't you do anything right?' Well, we were all under stress, and he was in solitary."

PRETRIAL DEPOSITIONS with prison officials and CDC administrators turned into slugging matches, producing hundreds of pages that had to be transcribed by court reporters at two dollars per page. Hanlon, known to his colleagues as "the king of the schmooze," solved the financial problem by making a poverty plea to Judge Conti, who surprised both sides by issuing an order permitting the complainants to tape-record depositions and do their own transcribing. "We'd take the tapes back to the Haight, and our volunteers, Nancy Jacot and Michael Bumblebee, would type 'em overnight. Nancy was my secretary and she was eight months pregnant. Michael was a San Francisco original. He was hired as a temp, but he ended up working on the Geronimo case and stayed till he died of AIDS. Sometimes he showed up in dresses, sometimes in a Girl Scout uniform. The office was so hot you'd jerk your hand back from the door knob. One night I went to the basement and Nancy and Michael were typing away in their

Radio Shack headsets. I talked to 'em for a few minutes before I realized they were naked. Nancy looked like Namu the whale. I said, 'Hey, what—?' Nancy said, 'Stuart, are you *ever* gonna put in air-conditioning?' "

IN JANUARY 1978, with the civil rights lawsuit gaining momentum, Johnnie Cochran phoned to tell Hanlon that he'd been offered the post of assistant district attorney under his old friend John Van de Kamp, a Democrat who was shaking up the country's biggest law office. Cochran would be the number three man, generally responsible for six hundred prosecutors[48] and specifically responsible for eighty-five deputies in four divisions, including the division that handled governmental corruption. It seemed like a strange flip-flop for a lawyer who'd built a successful practice partially by representing victims of municipal high-handedness. He'd just won the Jerry Giesler Award, the highest honor of the Los Angeles Criminal Courts Bar Association. He was earning $300,000 a year. Van de Kamp was offering $49,000.

"It's a chance to make a difference," Cochran informed Hanlon over the phone. "I'd be the first African American ADA in L.A."

"I hope Van de Kamp isn't looking for a token black," Hanlon said. "I don't think you qualify."

Cochran flew up to San Francisco and told his young colleague that he'd already discussed the offer with old friends like Tom Bradley, the first African American mayor in Los Angeles history. "Tom told me, 'There's no decision here. Take the damn job and enjoy it.' "

Others had offered the same advice, but the strongest influence had come from Johnnie L. Cochran Sr. "Dad said this was my opportunity to help others."

"How long is your appointment?" Hanlon asked.

"Three years. Which creates one serious problem."

"Don't worry about it. Pratt'll be out of the hole long before your term's over. Then we'll work on sending him back to Morgan City. Put him out of your mind."

"I'll never put him out of my mind," Cochran replied.

---

[48] Including the Manson prosecutor Vincent Bugliosi and three young deputies who would later become involved in the O. J. Simpson murder trial: Gil Garcetti, Lance Ito and William Hodgman.

GERONIMO WAS happy to be summoned to the visiting room, but he was surprised to see the look on his old friend's face. "Johnnie!" he said. "What's wrong?"

Cochran told him about the job offer and said, "I couldn't accept it in good conscience without talking to you. I know how you feel about law enforcement and the judicial system, and—I don't blame you."

Only one question came to Geronimo's mind: "Would it help your career?"

"I could have an effect."

"Go for it, man."

Cochran grinned and said, "I knew you'd say that."

IN THE six-year interim since losing the Pratt murder case, Cochran had successfully represented dozens of clients, but he heard from only one when his appointment was officially announced. A handmade card was inscribed:

> *The news of your promotion*
> *Is a happy thing to hear*
> *Sure hope it brings you more success*
> *With every coming year.*

It was signed "G."

Dogfight

In later years the Pratt lawyers realized that they'd grossly underestimated the California Department of Corrections' obsession with keeping their prisoner caged. To Hanlon and Cochran it seemed such a simple matter to release him to the mainline, especially after prison psychiatrists stopped rubber-stamping earlier opinions and began offering positive evaluations. A report by L. G. Nuernberger, M.D., cited a diagnosis of "anxiety neurosis, chronic, mild, secondary to combat stress, and social maladjustment by history, manifested by conflict arising from loyalties divided between two cultures," but the San Quentin psychiatrist added, "Status examination reveals [that] he is alert, quick thinking and confident in his assessment of others. He shows no indication at this time of any psychotic process or organic disorder."

Under "discussion," Nuernberger wrote, "This man came to maturity in a simple constant authoritarian and racially segregated culture. He then entered military service and compiled an outstanding record while at the same time entering into a conflict of personal, racial and national values. His postwar activities brought him to a leadership post in an authoritarian black group of revolutionary organization. If, as he contends, murder charges were part of a political plot, then psychological testimony is irrelevant to that portion of his offenses." In effect, the report was a clean bill of mental health.

Soon after the Nuernberger evaluation, two high prison officials admitted in writing that the false charges about the Folsom bus scare had been retained in Pratt's jacket solely to justify his incarceration in the hole. But CDC officials in Sacramento continued to insist that they were dealing with a dangerous animal.

TWO YEARS of the civil rights case were spent on depositions. For a week in July 1978 Geronimo answered questions, and in the end he was the only combatant in the Q&A wars who didn't appear drained. As the lawsuit ground on, the Pratt legal team turned up information about measures that the CDC officials had taken to hide evidence, including the mysterious loss of hundreds of pages from Geronimo's central file. A special security squad member at the prison testified that he'd seen a sergeant removing the file from the office: "He told me he was informed to get rid of it, destroy it." A guard captain admitted that four Pratt files had been destroyed on orders of his superiors.

At a later deposition Warden George Sumner was asked to describe Pratt's influence on other prisoners. "Pratt is a leader," he testified unexpectedly, "and whether he is in the community or in prison he is always a leader, and it's obvious to see him react with other inmates that he is a very influential leader. . . . My feeling is that he has attempted to use it positively."

Hanlon asked, "Since you've been warden of San Quentin, has Mr. Pratt done anything that would make you believe he's a security risk to the prison or an escape risk?"

"No."

The warden introduced a document that seemed to contradict the official CDC position that it was necessary to separate Pratt from other black inmates. The report, from the prison's general subclassification committee, said that the inmate had influence, but it "has proven to be beneficial to the operation of the unit rather than disruptive as many people would like you to believe."

But a major blemish remained on Pratt's record: the attack on guard Michael Imm, which Hanlon had witnessed from a front-row seat. Imm's original report glossed over Pratt's participation, but two other guards had claimed that he played an active role.

Hanlon approached Imm for a written declaration. In his statement the Asian American correctional officer, a Vietnam veteran himself, acknowledged that he'd been well acquainted with Pratt since 1974:

> In fact, Mr. Pratt saved me from serious injury at one time. . . . I was physically assaulted by three black inmates (one of which had a prison made knife) in the San Quentin visiting room. Mr. Pratt participated in the attack on me. He made it look like he was helping the other inmates but kept getting in the way of the inmate with the knife. So that I only received a few minor scratches. I have never been able to tell anyone about this or put it in writing . . . for fear that Mr. Pratt might have a contract put out on him or be retaliated against by the other inmates for helping me. In my opinion, Mr. Pratt is neither a threat to staff, the security of the institution, nor an unusual escape risk.

Another blemish in the Pratt jacket, that he'd led escape attempts at Los Angeles County Jail, was erased in a note from the L.A. County sheriff. "It is not true," Peter Pitchess wrote. "A fracas in the courtroom between co-defendants was [not] considered to be an escape attempt. . . . While housed in the Hall of Justice Jail Mr. Pratt was very cooperative and was a calming influence on the others housed in this area."

AS DEPOSITIONS ended and pretrial hearings began, Slammin' Sammy Conti lived up to his billing. The judge held a California assistant attorney general in contempt for failing to reveal some documents and sentenced him to sixty days in jail.[49] The judge scoffed at CDC officials who claimed that they'd accidentally mislaid files—"You gentlemen had better find those 'mislaid' files or you gentlemen are gonna go to jail hand in hand."

When Hanlon informed Conti that his client had been unfairly singled out in a training manual for guards, one of the state lawyers swore that no such document existed. The next morning Hanlon found a copy in his mailbox. He opened it to find that guard trainees at Modesto Junior College were being warned about the Black Liberation Army and advised that "in early 1974 [the BLA] began moving into West Coast areas. . . . This is considered to be due to the fact that Elmer Geronimo Pratt is presently

---

[49] Overturned on appeal.

confined at San Quentin. Pratt is probably the most influential leader of the BLA at this time, with Cleaver in self-imposed exile. The BLA has made no secret of the fact that they intend to rescue Pratt from prison by any means necessary."

Hanlon introduced the manual into evidence, and Conti bawled out the state lawyers, suggesting that they start bringing a change of underwear to court. The irascible judge took special delight in twitting an assistant attorney general who had a shy manner and a small voice. As she stood before him twisting her hands, he would yell, "If you can't talk loud enough for me to hear, then don't talk at all! *Write me a brief!*" Sometimes the lawyer was so intimidated that she just stopped talking and sat.

WITH THE civil rights case in its third year, the judge issued a preliminary order that Geronimo be transferred to San Quentin's general population until the proceedings ended. Shocked CDC officials held emergency meetings in Sacramento. Tentative plans were made to transfer the prisoner to Vacaville, Folsom, Tehachapi or other prisons, but the individual wardens resisted. Pratt's reputation had preceded him, and his jacket still contained Richard Kalustian's persistent warnings about future bloodbaths.

At San Quentin the prison's first reaction to Conti's order was to ignore it. But after the judge threatened contempt action, Geronimo was told to prepare for transfer to the mainline. Then four white inmates were killed in a racial incident and the prison was locked down. Weeks later he was looking out his peephole when the newest deputy warden, an African American named Reginald Pulley,[50] visited his cell.

"I've been hearing about you, Mr. Pratt," Pulley said. "You've got a lot of folks pulling for you."

"Then why am I still in the hole?" Geronimo asked.

A few days later Pulley signed his transfer to the mainline. It took only two days for the administration to learn that the Pratt truculence about social injustice remained unchanged. He was assigned to work in the furniture factory but refused the job on the grounds that a salary of ten cents an hour was tantamount to slavery. "Haven't you heard about the Emancipation Proclamation?" he asked the furniture shop foreman.

---

[50] Later promoted to warden.

The next day he got a ducat (written order) to report to the factory early in the morning. He checked out the conditions, examined the equipment and concluded that it was a sweatshop. He was agitating the workers to strike when the prison "goon squad" returned him to his cell.

DAYS BEFORE the hearing on the prison lawsuit was finally due to open, Stuart Hanlon was still drawing up plans for a prop that would focus the jurors' attention. He'd used what he called "demonstrative evidence" in other cases and found that it impressed juries. He decided that his current show-'n'-tell project would be a life-size replica of Pratt's first (and worst) cell in the hole at San Quentin. It would be made of heavy cardboard, with a barred front door, walls, a "toilet hole" in the floor and a rack with no mattress.

The California Department of Corrections cried foul when Hanlon showed up at the prison to measure the cells in the Adjustment Center. The dimensions, he was told, were confidential. "They don't want the public to know how small those cells are," Hanlon explained to Pratt in the visiting room.

Geronimo estimated the dimensions at six by seven feet, but Hanlon wanted precise figures. Legal graphics expert Steven Morris, a courtroom veteran, was also turned away by the Q administrators.

Frustrated, Hanlon took the problem to Judge Conti. "By that time, the A.G.'s Office had thoroughly pissed off the judge. He ordered San Quentin to let us in and said if they didn't, he'd jail the whole damned administration. That's when I fully realized that a federal judge has powers next to God. We went in and took measurements and photographs and came back to my office and built our model."

AT THE trial in the fall of 1978, Hanlon trundled his creation into court and, with Morris' assistance, erected it square in front of the jury box, where it resembled a storage closet. When the assistant attorney general objected to the display, Hanlon asked, "Are you trying to suppress evidence the same way you suppressed my client's civil rights?" The judge allowed the exhibit to stand.

Hanlon introduced documentary evidence about the caging of human beings. "I don't think a place more destructive of a man's mental health could be devised if we tried," Soledad Prison's chief psychiatrist had said in 1971. Another prison psychiatrist had called the San Quentin hole "so bad that corporal punishment or old fashioned third-degree methods would be preferable."

IN THE days before closing arguments Hanlon rehearsed so long and hard that he almost lost his voice. "This was the most important case of my life, in an area I really cared about—inmates' rights—and we were up against the whole damn state of California. The night before closing arguments, I told my girlfriend Kathy: 'I can't do it. My voice is gone. I'm too keyed up.' She drove me out to Ocean Beach to calm me down. She said, 'Hear the seals?' I said, 'Yeah, that's what I'll sound like tomorrow.' "

He addressed the jury for three hours. Remembering Judge Conti's original orders, he concentrated on showing that Pratt had been victimized for his political beliefs. Then he threw in an appeal to each juror's conscience. "You can't let the Department of Corrections get away with this. These people feel impervious to the rest of us. They feel they can do whatever they want—to me, to you, to the judge, to Geronimo Pratt. They feel they can come into this courtroom and lie, cheat, fabricate evidence and break the law the same way they broke it when they threw this man into his cage for offenses that he could not, would not and *did* not commit."

He gestured toward his client, then lowered his voice and said, "This case isn't about money. This case is about the torture of a fellow human being, a wounded war hero, a man with terrible injuries to mind and body. Imagine a man in such pain that he prefers to curl up on a concrete floor. Imagine needle fragments of steel irritating your bowels night after night. Imagine having to use a hole in the floor for a toilet. Imagine sleeping in your own body waste."

He pointed to the mock-up. "I hope each of you will step inside," he croaked. "See how it feels. Reach out and touch the walls. Then imagine what it's like to live in something like this—twenty-three hours a day for eight—straight—*years.* "

AN HOUR after the jury went out, the foreman sent a note asking that the cardboard cell be moved to the deliberation room. Hanlon was encouraged. "They want to go inside that thing," he told Pratt. "They're getting our point."

After a short deliberation the jury ruled that the CDC had violated Elmer Gerard Pratt's rights under the First and Fourteenth Amendments and awarded him a dollar in damages. "This was the only civil case I'd ever done in my life, and I should never have emphasized that it wasn't about money," Hanlon said ruefully, "but . . . it wasn't. We interviewed jurors, and they said the reason they didn't award a million bucks in damages was because G was the healthiest person in the courtroom. Even after solitary confinement, he was in better shape than the rest of us."

The judge awarded $125,000 in attorneys' fees. At a tequila party in his basement office, Hanlon asked each member of the defense committee to jot down a fee for services. "I know you'll be fair," he said.

Pratt and his new wife Linda Session[51] were allotted $35,000. Hanlon, Marnie Ryan, John Mitchell and the other lawyers ended up with $10,000 each. The naked office staffers, Nancy Jacot and Michael Bumblebee, were awarded $1,000 and instructed to buy clothes.

Hanlon came out of the trial exhausted. "That civil rights case was like a prizefight that went on for six years, ten thousand rounds, and you're knocked on your ass fifty times before you start doing a little counterpunching of your own, and then you're knocked on your ass again. For a while I slipped into cocaine—'the trial lawyer's best friend.' At San Francisco parties they gave it out like M&M's. It came between me and Kathy. I figured she was just being uptight and I was hip—it took me a while to find out how wrong I was. Her sister Marnie worked herself numb on the Pratt case and went into exile in Cambodia to counsel the poor. Johnnie Mitchell must've put in a thousand billable hours, with nobody to bill. He finally gave up his practice and became a law professor at the University of Puget Sound. Nobody involved in defending Geronimo was ever the same again. With one exception."

---

[51] Who now went under the Africanized name "Ashaki Pratt" and would later become "Ashaki ji Jaga."

MAINLINE

By the time Geronimo Pratt was transferred from solitary confinement to the general population in 1978, his name had become known in every cell-block in the California penal system. In CDC administrative and political circles he was still regarded as a potential Nat Turner who could stir up the slaves with a few sharp words. "The day I finally got out the hole, rumors were flying. I was gonna set up a black assault unit and kill the Mexicans and guards. I was gonna turn the Aryan Brotherhood against the Mexican Mafia so the blacks could take over the prison. I was gonna lead a mass breakout, and we were all gonna sail across the ocean and set up a new society. I mean, it was *crazy!* Man, I wasn't gonna do *nothin'*. I was just happy to get out the hole!"

Now that he could mingle with other prisoners, Pratt learned that the African Americans regarded him as a leader, a figure of myth. A fellow inmate described the move to the mainline as "Nelson Mandela returning to South Africa."

After Geronimo had eaten his last soggy sandwich in the Adjustment Center, the steel door slid open and two smiling inmates appeared with an empty flatbed cart. "One of 'em says, 'San Quentin Worldwide Movers!' The black prisoners that ran the mainline had sent Little John Willie and Henry Aldridge to help me move. They took me to D section, Second Tier.

I couldn't believe that trip: no guards, no escort, no shackles. Just me, Willie and Henry. They told me I had one hundred percent support from black prisoners, but best to stay cool for a day or two. The Aryan Brotherhood was restless, and some of the Mexicans wondered about my intentions. When we reached the tier, every eye was watching, everybody ready for action. If anybody even *looked* like he was gonna raise a hand, blood was gonna flow. I had total protection: disciplined black youngsters, some of 'em ex-Panthers, directed by elders like Trooper Webb. He was sixty, out of the old L.A. gangs that used to fight the pachucos. High Society Red gave me a big handshake. He was a pimp and a hustler out of Oakland, a high yella—I mean a *high* yella, about six-nine. Turned out he came from Meadow Forks Bottom, Louisiana. I saw a few guys I'd known in the hole and some other homeys and another guy who was so quiet you could barely hear him talk—turned out he was a multiple rapist. These dudes *ran* the mainline. Never mind the prison manual. These were the *capi di tutti capi*. The guards had nothin' to do with nothin'."

For several days Geronimo endured culture shock. He now enjoyed a toilet, sink, cot and mattress. His cell door was usually unlocked. He made his first visit to the mess hall in a time warp. "I hadn't seen a real dish or eaten with a metal spoon for eight years. In the hole you eat off paper plates with your fingers or a soft plastic spoon that you can't turn into a shank. I was warned to stay away from the mess hall—that's where the shit jumps off—but I didn't want to look like a pussy on my first day. The Muslims sent an escort, treated me like a Masai king. I'm saying, 'Look, fellas, I don't *need* no bodyguards.' I said, '*Shalom aleichem,* my brothers, but *please*—let me walk in by myself.' They finally said, 'Yes, sir,' and backed off. In the mess hall I met some homeys—Cole, Lebeau, Junie Boy, Hairon Thatch, Louisiana Blackie. I look around and see chairs, tables, spoons, trays and a hot food line. Everything tasted like a Howard Johnson's—so *good!* One of the Mexicans I taught at L.A. County Jail came over and told me I was cool with the Hispanics.

"After that first day my food was specially prepared. All the prison elite ate in their cells. Trooper Webb hadn't been inside the mess hall in three years. Every morning the guys from Culinary brought us grits, eggs, toast, fried chicken, coffee, juice, all prepared by professional cooks. Later on I started kicking 'em something down—a few bucks here and there."

Within a few weeks his new "house" had been transformed by his acolytes. "They gave me a gilded cage. Fixed me up with tile floors and a washbowl from the ceramic shop. Papered my walls and carpeted my floor.

In the carpentry shop they made a beautiful wooden headboard for my bed with remote buttons for my TV and radio. Somebody brought me a hot plate and skillet and a little refrigerator. They put curtains across my bars and a pulley system so I could open and shut 'em with a cord while I was in bed. They lifted my bunk high off the floor to give me more living space underneath, and they made me a ladder to climb up. I kept telling 'em, 'No, no, thanks a lot. You're focusing too much attention on me.' But I didn't want to hurt their feelings."

In the big mainline yard he learned that he was a prison hero. "I tried to figure out why. One of the old-timers told me it was for the things I *didn't* do when I was in the hole. Didn't turn snitch. Didn't turn punk.[52] Didn't take sides. Didn't suck up to the guards or the staff. Ran my laps in the yard, did my cellisthenics, kept up my body, read my books and kept my mouth shut. I didn't do none of those things to be a hero—it was just my way, and they respected it. Q was like a township in those days, run by the prisoners. The wardens and the guards stayed back, except that a few of 'em brought in weed, heroin, cocaine, meth, sleeping pills, uppers. I didn't touch the hard stuff, but sometimes I smoked weed for calmness. Guards would come by when you were smoking and pass right on. The only thing that scared them was prune liquor—jake, pruno, raisin jack. That stuff could tear you up. A Mexican got drunk on pruno and killed one of the nicest guards with a forty-pound weight, splattered his brains all over the laundry. When the Mexican sobered up, he cried and cried, and after a while he killed himself."

GERONIMO ENJOYED his gilded cage for a year, until the *Los Angeles Times* ran an exposé about coddled prisoners. "We went back to bare cells. That was cool with me, as long as they let me keep my little desk. I was studying anthropology, geology, behavioral science, chemistry, philosophy, subjects they didn't teach at Morgan City Colored High. I had access to the law library. Couldn't complain. We had movies on the mainline, professional entertainers. And conjugal visits. That's when Ashaki and I got close."

The couple had been married for a year when a counselor informed Pratt that he was eligible for a forty-eight-hour family visit. The accommodations consisted of an oversize trailer with a bedroom view of San

---

[52] Homosexual.

Francisco Bay—"the most expensive real estate in California," Geronimo told Ashaki as a smiling guard escorted them into the visiting area. No walls or barbed wire could be seen from the trailer. Everyone involved in the visit was kind and helpful. "I think they're trying to make up for my years in the hole," he told Ashaki. "They know. They know."

He told her about the neighborhood called Across the Tracks and she told him about life in a nearby housing project where some of the other black residents were as bigoted as any grand kleagle. Ashaki said she would like to have children someday, "but in a nice home, in a normal setting."

Geronimo got the point.

When it was time to say good-bye, Ashaki shyly told her husband that she loved him. Geronimo was embarrassed. "Look, baby," he said, "something kills your emotions in prison."

"You mean . . . love?"

He nodded.

She said she would take her chances.

"Find the Rats"

The Pratt shock troopers regrouped to prepare for his scheduled appearance before the California Community Release Board in January 1979. After eight years it was his first realistic chance at parole, and Hanlon and the other attorneys had no trouble collecting letters and affidavits of support.

A petition signed by U.S. Representative Ron Dellums and other prominent Californians called for immediate release. "The notoriety of the case should not cause the case to be judged more harshly nor less harshly than normal," Dellums wrote. "Mr. Pratt is an individual who has served a considerable amount of hard time. You should take into account the mood of the country and of the correctional community at the time Mr. Pratt was convicted."

The Southern Africa Solidarity Committee questioned the original verdict: "It is clear that Mr. Pratt has been the victim of an elaborate frame-up as part of the government's COINTELPRO program to crush the black liberation movement."

Timothy Pratt, an assistant professor of political science at the University of the District of Columbia, wrote that his brother should be paroled to his custody, "enjoying the things that we did as children: fishing and enjoying the outdoors. This country out here is beautiful during this time of year and I know he will enjoy it."

AT THE parole hearing the latest warnings by Richard Kalustian were read into the record. The deputy D.A. charged that Pratt had committed other crimes and should never be paroled—"Despite any hollow words, if released, he will undoubtedly attempt to kill those who he believes put him in prison. . . ."

Hanlon characterized Kalustian's remarks as the unsupported ravings of "a mind so totally biased and/or unbalanced as to warrant little weight or consideration. That the district attorney would have the unbelievable temerity to also make accusations regarding several unproven assaults and murders unrelated to the present charge . . . bespeaks the magnitude of his bias and his total lack of commitment to making any fair presentation."

Hanlon introduced a statement by San Quentin Warden George Sumner: "Mr. Pratt relates well with staff and inmates of all ethnic backgrounds, has a good attitude, is helpful in internal relations with other blacks, and resisted efforts to become involved in incidents and has helped forestall potential incidents."

"Most remarkably," Hanlon told the parole board members, "Mr. Pratt is a man who has maintained his decency and his congenial way of dealing with people throughout a hellish nightmare pervaded by his persistent stance that he was framed for murder by the FBI, haunted by the murder of his first wife and unborn child and tormented by over seven years of unjust segregation in the hole."

The young attorney's protestations were lost in a broadside of accusations, some entirely new and original, that were fired by anti-Pratt witnesses. LAPD Sergeant W. C. Heins echoed Kalustian's description of the cruelty of the tennis court shootings and added, "In the opinion of Los Angeles law enforcement officers, this defendant, if released, would become a rallying point for a long-defunct Black Panther organization in Los Angeles. . . . We urge you to not release him to prey on the citizens of Los Angeles again."

Kenneth Olsen, now physically recovered, made a passionate statement: "I received several phone threats on my life during the trial. This caused added tension and fear in me and concern for the safety of my minor children. I cannot believe that any individual that would place an unarmed man and woman facedown on a tennis court and then attempt to execute them by shooting them in the head would be allowed his freedom to kill someone else's wife and deprive his children of their mother."

George Tielsch, Santa Monica chief of police, offered color photos of the bleeding Caroline Olsen lying on the tennis court. Tielsch told the board that the pictures were the best evidence that parole should be denied.

The members agreed unanimously. The inmate could apply again in two years.

HANLON AND Pratt had expected a turndown for political reasons, as manifested in the LAPD's comment about the potential revival of the Black Panthers. Meanwhile, more exculpatory evidence was being turned up by Freedom of Information requests and the continuous pressure from Geronimo and his volunteers. By the time of the parole board's turndown, FOI demands had produced a statement by the FBI that Julius Carl Butler "supplied no information" but that COINTELPRO moles might have been present at defense strategy sessions during the murder trial. Hanlon was enthusiastic. Even without proof of Butler's complicity, this was potential grounds for a new trial.

"I knew it!" Johnnie Cochran said when he heard the news. By virtue of his job as assistant district attorney, he was nominally divorced from the case, but he remained an interested observer. He told Hanlon, "Now we gotta find the rats."

A FEW days after the FBI distanced itself from Julius Butler, it reversed its field again. Cornered by still more FOI demands, the agency was forced to admit that its operatives had held thirty-three meetings with Butler before and after the tennis court shootings.

The latest admission was diluted by a strained discussion about the definition of "informant." Any confusion about Julius Butler's status with the FBI, a memo argued, was "understandable in light of the contrast between the broad dictionary definition of informant and the precise law enforcement usage of that term." Under the dictionary definition "Butler would be considered an informant, for he supplied information to the FBI." But under the definition in the FBI manual the beautician would be merely a "probationary informant"—someone who was being "cultivated as an informant." The memo added that questions about definitions were "not enlightening—certainly, FBI labels are not critical." What mattered, the agency argued, "is whether Pratt was denied a fair trial because the jury was not told Butler supplied information to the FBI."

For his part the hairstylist denied the sophistry and added the FBI to the list of those who were lying about him.

ENERGIZED BY the latest FBI admissions, Pratt's investigators reinterviewed LAPD Sergeant DuWayne Rice about the mysterious "insurance letter." Rice, retired from the force and working security for the entertainer Sammy Davis Jr., told them that Butler had handed him the letter at a street-corner rendezvous, extracted a promise that it be kept sealed until his death, then turned to walk away. Butler had taken a few steps when two FBI men approached and demanded that Rice give up the letter. The sergeant told them to ask permission from Butler, still within earshot. One of the agents yelled, "Julius!," but Butler kept walking. Rice said it had seemed to him that Butler and the FBI agents enjoyed "a familiarity." The sergeant's refusal to break his promise was all that had kept the letter private for fourteen months, despite FBI threats to indict him for obstruction of justice. He seemed annoyed that Butler and the FBI had put him in the middle.

"I CAN'T WAIT to get Butler back on the stand," Hanlon told Geronimo. "I want to see his face when I ask him to explain why the FBI was a few feet away when he handed over the envelope. That's a hell of a coincidence."

"They knew what was inside, too," Geronimo said. "Man, those dudes sure know how to follow orders."

"Whose orders?"

"J. Edgar Hoover. *Neutralize him.*"

Hanlon was quiet for a moment, then said, "All that bullshit about the letter was to keep the snitch jacket off Julio. They didn't want him to testify as an FBI informer. They wanted him to testify as a poor frightened guy who tried to keep his letter secret. That way, the jury is sympathetic. He's a victim. He's . . . a hero."

ATTORNEY MARGARET "Marnie" Ryan checked into the basement command post with new information on the state's star forensics witness, DeWayne Wolfer, who'd made a crucial identification of the murder weapon based on nicks on the shell casings. Ryan confirmed reports that

Wolfer had a record of professional difficulties and had been disqualified from serving on civil service interview boards. She'd solicited the expertise of Lindberg B. Miller, a former supervising criminalist for the LAPD, and asked him to review Wolfer's procedures. The UCLA lecturer on forensics responded that "the accuracy of the shell casings comparison test is absolutely dependent on the integrity of the tester." Ryan prepared an affidavit noting that a state Court of Appeal had charged Wolfer with testimony "bordering on the perjurious" in a recent case and that he'd resigned from the California Association of Criminalists and the American Academy of Forensic Science while under investigation for gross incompetence in the Sirhan Sirhan murder case and unethical conduct in another murder case.

Armed with the new information, Hanlon began drafting a motion for a writ of habeas corpus, a legal device variously described by criminal defense lawyers as "the great writ" and "the safeguard and palladium of our liberties." Habeas corpus was the safety net that gave prisoners an ongoing opportunity to prove that they were imprisoned unlawfully. Hanlon reported back to Geronimo that "our young lawyers are really starting to kick ass. We've got enough evidence to overturn five convictions."

PRATT WAS so encouraged that he turned his attention to his future outside the walls. He bore down on his studies in behavioral science, anthropology, philosophy and geology. He enrolled in a class in public speaking but dropped out when he realized that his Louisiana accent was no more adjustable than his bowlegs. It didn't matter. Soon he would be rescuing Ashaki from her ratty housing project and taking her home to Morgan City to start a family. "It's okay, darlin'," he told her on their next conjugal visit. "I'm coming out of this place. You want a baby? Come on. We'll have our own little planned parenthood thing."

Two months later she told him she was pregnant.

Judge Parker Redux

In November 1979 Superior Court Judge Kathleen Parker found herself looking down at the faces of Elmer Gerard Pratt and Stuart Douglas Hanlon and not enjoying the view. Seven years had passed since she'd sentenced Pratt to life imprisonment. In this habeas corpus action she wasn't being asked to rule on guilt or innocence but on whether there was sufficient cause for an evidentiary hearing at which Pratt could attempt to prove that he'd been tried unfairly. Since Parker had presided at the proceedings in question, she was sitting in judgment on herself.

In court she did little to conceal her sentiments. When Hanlon suggested that the original trial had been close, as shown by the jury's ten days of deliberation, Parker broke in and said, "I think maybe I can shorten this. I do *not* agree with the defense this was a weak case. . . . Now proceed from there."

The judge complained that she'd been swamped with letters attempting to coerce her into favoring Pratt and that some two dozen prominent groups and citizens, including California Assembly members Willie Brown, Maxine Waters and Gwen Moore, seven preachers, a rabbi and several labor leaders had filed as amici curiae. Forty of the letters, she pointed out, were identically worded, bore out-of-town postmarks and appeared to be the result of a coordinated pressure campaign. She declined comment on Hanlon's suggestion that it was unfair to hold the enthusiasm of Pratt's backers against his client.

IN HIS arguments for an evidentiary hearing, Hanlon charged that Pratt's constitutional rights had been thrice violated: by Julius Butler's perjury in denying his role as an informer, by the planting of spies in the defense environs, and by Richard Kalustian's withholding of evidence.

In response, Kalustian took his usual firm stance. After sixteen years of service to the D.A.'s Office, Johnnie Cochran's old classmate had risen to the rank of head deputy and was believed to be in line for a judgeship. In a declaration filed with the court, he denied that he'd known of any connections between the FBI and Julius Butler at the time of trial. "I was not contacted by the FBI nor did I contact the FBI regarding this case or the Black Panther Party. No information was supplied to me by the FBI concerning this case. . . . I was unaware of the FBI's COINTELPRO program during this period of time, and I believe did not know anything about it until reading about it in the newspapers. . . . During the trial and continuing to this day, I have had no reason to believe Julius Butler ever was an informant for any agency. . . ."

Geronimo Pratt's nemesis also denied that he'd known of the existence of informers in the defense camp until he was advised by the FBI long after Pratt was sent to prison. He confirmed that his star witness had fared well in the interim and admitted that he, Kalustian, had "eventually asked the court to reduce Julius Butler's convictions [in the Ollie Taylor assault case] to misdemeanors" for several reasons, including the fact that Butler was no longer a Black Panther, "appeared to have stabilized his life" and had "assisted law enforcement by testifying in the murder trial."

WITH THE hearing in progress the FBI coughed up another surprising tidbit. Wiretap transcripts showed that Panther leaders Bobby Seale and/or Kathleen Cleaver had picked up "some [unknown] persons" at the Oakland airport on the exact date of the tennis court murder and that Geronimo Pratt was spotted in Oakland two days later. Even more surprising was a positive confirmation of FBI Director William Webster's previous suggestion that a COINTELPRO agent had infiltrated the Pratt legal defense team. Indeed, the "mole" had taken part in four of the team's strategy sessions.[53]

"Wait till the judge hears this," Hanlon said. "It's absolute grounds for a new trial. I could cite a hundred cases."

KATHLEEN PARKER listened impassively as Hanlon read the FBI revelations and some of the Church Committee's findings about COINTELPRO. He reminded her that Director Webster, himself a former federal appeals judge, had declared that Pratt deserved a new trial if it could be shown that Butler was an informer. When Hanlon attempted to cast doubt on one of the FBI's claims, the judge appeared shocked. "But, Mr. Hanlon," she declared, "it's the FBI!"

AFTER FOUR days of courtroom acrimony Parker issued her ruling. She admonished the Pratt lawyers for trying to "step from one point to another by speculation." An evidentiary hearing would serve no useful purpose since she didn't see "sufficient evidence that Mr. Pratt was framed and that he did not have a fair trial." The prisoner would be returned to San Quentin.

Sitting at the petitioner's table, Geronimo rocked back in his chair and shut his eyes. Hanlon felt poleaxed, confused and then angry. Every member of the Pratt team had agreed that their three constitutional claims were strong, and Kathleen Parker had discounted them like a student judge at a moot court.

Hanlon stood up and looked directly at the judge. "Your Honor," he said, selecting his words carefully, "this case has been, since its inception, a cover-up. What the court has just said has implicated itself in this cover-up. The court is the only thing in this system of law—"

Loud applause interrupted. As the judge grabbed her gavel, Hanlon said, "The court is the only thing in this system of law that separates the prosecution, the state, from framing people. It is what separated Watergate from having to become more of a national disgrace than it was. And people turn to the courts to keep the government in line."

He looked at Geronimo and fought for composure. "And this court," he went on, "this court, *this court* has said, We will not deal with it, we will

---

[53] Later the FBI amended its admission. It had had *two* informants in the defense camp.

side with the state." He looked straight at the judge. "And that makes this court part of the cover-up."

It was a brazen accusation to make to a judge's face. He knew he was risking a contempt citation and figured it was worth it. Her Honor walked off the bench without comment.

In the corridor an irate Hanlon told a reporter: "They ought to rename this place the Hall of Injustice. Judge Parker is a nice old lady but she's intimidated by the FBI. We gave her evidence and she called it speculation. We gave her facts and she called them wishful thinking. We'll see what the appellate court thinks of her reasoning."

JOHNNIE COCHRAN, sidelined by his official job in Los Angeles, offered solace on the phone. "Stu," he said, "I don't think it would've mattered what you did in court. Somebody else is calling the shots. My bet is it's the FBI. I hate all this ex parte[54] stuff. It's terrible. It could destroy our justice system."

Hanlon said, "Our system was destroyed a long time ago, Johnnie." The two lawyers had never agreed on the subject. Cochran accepted the system and tried to work within it; Hanlon felt that the system was corrupt and attempted to expose it. Both attorneys won most of their cases, achieving the same goal with different approaches.

Cochran ignored Hanlon's pessimism and asked how soon he planned to file an appeal. Hanlon said he was working on it.

"Just hope they assign Bernie Jefferson," Cochran said. "He's the man."

Hanlon agreed. Justice Bernard Jefferson of California's Second District Court of Appeal was a nationally respected African American jurist. His scholarly decisions had influenced racial jurisprudence, and many felt that he would be sitting on the U.S. Supreme Court if conservatives weren't in power in Washington.

"Keep me informed, Stu," Cochran was saying. "I wish I could jump in and help, but—you know the rules."

A FEW days later Cochran risked his prestigious new role as assistant D.A. by writing a letter to the California Community Release Board asserting

---

[54] Essentially, information that is communicated to judges privately and not shared with opposing attorneys or included in the court record.

his belief that Geronimo Pratt was innocent. His boss, D.A. John Van de Kamp, slapped Cochran on the wrist in a follow-up letter to the parole board: "It is disconcerting to me that apparently competent professionals are considering the possibility of Mr. Pratt's innocence . . . I wish to make it clear that this office does not concur in Mr. Cochran's personal views in this matter. On the contrary, we are of the firm belief that Mr. Pratt should not be released."

At a rancorous session in the D.A.'s sanctum Van de Kamp accused Cochran of creating problems. Cochran told him, "You can take this job and shove it. I know this man is innocent."

Van de Kamp said he was entitled to his opinion.

"You're darned right I am," Cochran said. "It's what I said before I took this job, it's what I'm saying now, and it's what I'll be saying long after I'm gone."

Some time later, Cochran arrived at his office to find his rare fire eel dead on the floor. The lid of the fish tank was firmly in place. "He couldn't jump out by himself," Cochran told a colleague. "I did the right thing, so somebody killed my fire eel. He wasn't just another pet. We had a friendship." Later he wrote, "There was a lot of snickering around the office about 'Cochran's dead eel.' I never saw the joke, but I got the point."

Footnote Warfare

Hanlon filed a petition for appellate review on April 10, 1980. He was joined by his young colleagues Margaret Ryan and John Mitchell, Mark Rosenbaum of the American Civil Liberties Union, the Civil Rights stalwarts Leonard Weinglass, Victor Goode and Jonathan Lubell, U.S. Representative Pete McCloskey and several others. As attorney of record at the original murder trial, Cochran filed a declaration of support.

"WELL, WE got lucky," Hanlon told Pratt in a phone call just before the first scheduled appearance in the appeals court. "Bernie Jefferson's been named to the panel along with a Superior Court judge. The third justice is L. Thaxton Hanson."

"Who's he?" Pratt asked.

"Bad news."

"We still cool?"

"As long as Bernie Jefferson stays healthy."

IN A 2–1 ruling, with L. Thaxton Hanson dissenting, the tribunal ordered the state to show cause why the prisoner shouldn't be released. It was a preliminary victory for the defense and had the effect of shifting the burden of proof to the prosecution.

The jubilant Hanlon and his associates returned to court for oral arguments. They'd barely settled in their seats when Justice Jefferson announced, "I'm taking myself off this case. This panel is dissolved." Seemingly annoyed and even angry, the most respected African American jurist in California stalked toward the exit.

"Your Honor," Hanlon called out, "could you tell us why?"

"No!" Jefferson said over his shoulder.

The Pratt attorneys were speechless. Then Hanlon muttered, "This is my worst moment as a lawyer." He wondered how many times he would have to start the same case from scratch.

WITH HELP from friends in the legal community, Hanlon and Cochran took pains to solve the mystery of Jefferson's abrupt withdrawal, but the reasons accompanied the black jurist to the grave. "It was an anomaly on top of anomalies," Cochran reminisced years later. "Was somebody making ex parte phone calls? I wouldn't be surprised. This was a highly political case. Jefferson could've been warned, 'If you want to be appointed to a higher court, you'll do so-and-so.' Stranger things have happened. He was a righteous guy, but everybody has his threshold of intimidation."

Hanlon heard other theories. "The main speculation was that the FBI threatened to expose something about Jefferson's personal life or make something up. Blackmail was a standard FBI technique. If they used it on Martin Luther King, why wouldn't they use it on Bernie Jefferson? Whatever the reason, they weren't gonna let anybody turn Geronimo loose. That was their agenda from the beginning—get the son of a bitch off the streets, and *keep* the son of a bitch off the streets. They were never gonna let up."

THE REPLACEMENT triumvirate consisted of Justices L. Thaxton Hanson and Mildred Lillie and Long Beach Municipal Court Judge George William Dunn, sitting pro tem. Hanlon felt sick when he read the list. He knew nothing about Judge Dunn except that he was black. But Mildred Lillie, like Kathleen Parker, had been appointed by ultraconservative Governor Goodwin Knight, and Hanson was a flag-waving self-avowed "patriot" who was famous for peppering his decisions with footnote warfare in which he took gratuitous potshots at his enemies.[55]

When Hanlon recounted the biographical information, Geronimo said, "Stu, is this the best panel we can get?"

Hanlon said he was afraid so.

L. THAXTON Hanson wrote the majority decision, 2–1 against Pratt, Judge Dunn dissenting. In the ruling Hanson described the prosecution's failure to disclose the FBI's thirty-three contacts with Julius Carl Butler as "nonprejudicial and harmless beyond a reasonable doubt." He defined an informant as someone who "informs or prefers an accusation against another, whom he suspects of the violation of some penal statute." Butler didn't meet the definition, the court ruled.

Hanson dispensed with Pratt's claim that the government had planted spies by observing that "the record indicates that the presence of COIN-TELPRO informants . . . had as much effect on whether or not Pratt was afforded a fair trial . . . as did the furniture in the areas where the discussions were conducted." He and Justice Lillie accepted at face value the FBI's claim that it had gleaned nothing of value from its moles. The justices also accepted allegations that Pratt had engaged in a series of robberies and other offenses in the Los Angeles area.[56]

The 130-page ruling was highly critical of Hanlon and his colleagues. The attempt to win a new trial, Hanson wrote, "follows the too often typical pattern in today's upside-down system of criminal justice where a defendant, himself charged with or convicted of such illegal acts as murder, attempted murder and robbery . . . seeks to focus attention on the alleged 'illegal acts' of law-enforcement officers." Hanson expressed his disdain for Hanlon's blunt charge of "complicity" against Judge Parker and described her as "one of the fairest and most competent and experienced trial judges

---

[55] He was once targeted in kind by Justice Lillie and another judge in a dissenting footnote of their own. The first letters of the first lines were "S-C-H-M-U-C-K."

[56] Information that the justices had gleaned while examining fifteen hundred "secret" documents provided by the FBI and the Los Angeles D.A.'s Office in a closed-door ex parte session from which the Pratt lawyers were excluded.

in the state." Repeating a judicial rationalization that always elevated Hanlon's blood pressure, Justice Hanson observed: "Defendant Pratt was only entitled to a fair trial, not a perfect trial."

The defense was also stung by a finding that seemed to penalize Pratt for witnesses who hadn't testified, a potential problem that Cochran had foreseen at the 1972 murder trial. "Conspicuously absent from defense alibi witnesses, at time of trial, and affidavits subsequent to trial," Hanson wrote, "is the testimony of the hosts at whose homes defendant Pratt and defense witnesses say he was at the time the 'tennis court murder' occurred. . . . Also absent is the testimony of the numerous other persons who allegedly were present at those meetings on the night of the murder of Caroline Olsen." Pratt was still being punished for the rifts that COINTELPRO had opened in its campaign of disinformation.

IN A strong dissent Municipal Judge George Dunn charged that his senior jurists had misperceived the issues. "Whether or not the evidence which was presented at the trial points unerringly to the defendant's guilt is not the fundamental issue, because in any trial if an effective defense is throttled there can be no conclusion other than one of guilt. . . . A trial which is not fundamentally fair is no trial at all."

Dunn argued that a full evidentiary hearing was required on the subjects of government moles in Cochran's office, the identity of any informants, the nature of any exchanged information, whether Butler had been an FBI informant and lied under oath about his status, whether Pratt had been singled out for "neutralization" by COINTELPRO, whether state and federal agencies connived at his prosecution, why insufficient action had been taken to find Pratt's alleged partner in the killing, whether Kenneth Olsen had identified someone else before he identified Pratt, and whether the government had knowledge of Pratt's whereabouts on the night of the crimes and withheld it from the defense. Failure to resolve such fundamental issues, Dunn argued, would result in a clear denial of due process and would be "more costly than we may surmise: the loss of the foundation of any free society: untarnished administration of justice."

In one of his typical footnote attacks Justice Hanson accused the temporary appellate judge from Long Beach of breaching an FBI confidence by revealing that the agency had infiltrated the defense. When Dunn read the footnote, he accused his colleague of slander, and Hanson removed the offending passage. But in the remainder of Hanson's five-page response to

Dunn's dissent, the justice ridiculed the African American judge's reasoning powers. "The dissenting opinion," Hanson wrote, "has bought hook-line-and-sinker defendant's arguments in his petition which when dissected and analyzed have as little substance as a handful of fog."[57]

GERONIMO PRATT was returned to San Quentin in a desperate mood. The next time he met with Hanlon, he complained so vociferously about the appellate decision that a guard rushed into the interview room to make sure no one was being hurt. "Those judges disregarded the evidence," Pratt yelled, "and now I'm stuck with a woman and a baby on the outside and that's the *worst* thing I ever wanted!"

It took an hour to placate him, and in the end he was comforting Hanlon. "It's okay, Stu. We'll find other issues. If you're righteous, you gotta win in the long run, don't you?"

"That's what I was taught," Hanlon said. He didn't say he believed it.

---

[57] Apparently Hanson had the last word. The record showed no dissent by Dunn from Hanson's dissent from Dunn's dissent. Dunn's rapid rise in the judicial system came to an end with his Pratt decision, but he continued to speak out about the case. In 1994 he told *California Lawyer* magazine that L. Thaxton Hanson had been guilty of fundamental error. "He says, 'This guy's guilty, look at all the evidence.' But if you don't give a person a chance to establish that there were irregularities and that the evidence is unreliable, hell, you'd never have any acquittals. Everybody would be guilty. I certainly don't know whether Pratt is guilty or not. He may well be. But he should have a chance to prove he isn't."

Moving Time

On May 10, 1980, a pacifist named Edwin Drummond climbed the Statue of Liberty and unfurled a red and white banner: LIBERTY WAS FRAMED— FREE GERONIMO PRATT. The incident was reported worldwide and the repercussions reached San Quentin. "The warden came to me and said, 'Hey, Pratt, you got to stop grandstand stunts like that.' I met Drummond later. He's such a beautiful man, you just want to hug him. But he messed up the statue—somebody said $80,000 worth—and I got moved to the California Men's Colony in San Luis Obispo. It was a big change, not as uptight as Q. No walls, lots of freedom. I saw guys walking hand in hand, tongue-kissing. It was hard for me to adjust after ten years in hard places like San Quentin and Folsom. But it was cool seeing the sun and the green grass every day."

He turned back to schoolbooks, became interested in plate tectonics and read everything he could find on oceanography. He dreamed of working as an engineer on an oil rig in the Gulf of Mexico, fishing every night and gorging himself on soft-shelled "buster" crabs and "swimp." By 1981 he had accumulated twenty-nine college credits.

Amnesty International declared him a "prisoner of conscience," and ABC's *20/20* news show did a sympathetic segment. His thoughts turned again to presiding over a family of his own on the outside. He stepped up his cellisthenics, ran twelve miles a day and lifted weights.

His sister Jacqueline rode the Blue Dog from Morgan City to visit, and his first question was, "How's Mama?"

The church organist said their mother spent most of her time on her knees, chanting and praying for her son's freedom. "She might as well pack up and live in church," his sister said. "She's so sure God will bring you back."

"That's Mama," Geronimo said.

"Don't *you* think God will bring you back?"

"Right now I'm counting on the Holy Trinity," he said. "God, Stu and Johnnie Cochran."

His oldest sister chided him for blasphemy. After the long visit, she reported to the other Pratts that the baby of the family had never looked better—"good complexion, no wrinkles, walked strong and straight. It was exalting to see him, except for the location." She told her sister Virginia, "Our prayers are working. It's the power of the presence of God, the power of prayer. It's Mama's chants."

GERONIMO BEGAN to miss his rap sessions with Hanlon and found himself resenting his best friend's absence. San Luis Obispo was halfway between San Francisco and Los Angeles, a long drive for the busy lawyer.

When Hanlon showed up, he seldom brought good news. The California Supreme Court affirmed the Court of Appeal's ruling against Pratt with only one dissent: from the controversial Chief Justice Rose Bird. Once again Pratt and Hanlon turned their hopes to the Board of Prison Terms, but the next parole hearing began with another shocking escalation by Kenneth Olsen: "Through intermediaries, Mr. Pratt has consistently threatened revenge on my family. This was particularly responsible for my recent divorce, my continuing nightmares, and my decision to abandon a successful career in education and leave Los Angeles." Olsen claimed that his daughter, a college sophomore, was "transferring universities to be safe."

In an anteroom conference Hanlon and Geronimo agreed that the grieving Olsen must have decided to avenge his wife's death by whatever means. "Hard to blame him," Geronimo said, "after what he went through."

The board listened to Olsen. Parole was denied.

BY THIS tenth year of Pratt's incarceration, Hanlon had come to realize that he made up almost all of his friend's social life. "He didn't want his brothers and sisters to visit, and Ashaki couldn't get to San Luis Obispo. She had no money, and Shona was still a baby. So the responsibility fell on me. I would lug these huge files on his case, but G wanted to talk politics, philosophy, dialectical materialism or pantheistic hedonism or something else he'd come across in the prison library. He had an opinion about everything. If I let out a little yawn, he'd yell, 'Goddamn it, Stu, pay attention. *This is heavy stuff!*' "

The young attorney's visits to San Luis Obispo seldom lasted less than four hours. "At the end he would always say, 'You're leaving already?' I'd drive home and feel guilty for days."

The Right Thing

In January 1981 Johnnie Cochran concluded his three-year assignment as assistant D.A. with a reminder to Hanlon that he was now available for duty in the matter of *People of California* v. *Elmer Gerard Pratt*. Hanlon asked, "Do you think we could ever get your boss to change his mind about the case?"

"Van de Kamp?" Cochran said. "No way." He paused, then said, "But . . . we can try."

The result was an informal meeting with District Attorney John Van de Kamp, Cochran, Hanlon and Mark Rosenbaum of the American Civil Liberties Union. U.S. Representative Pete McCloskey joined in by speakerphone.

From the outset Cochran dominated. He outlined the holes in the state's case and promised that two dozen angry attorneys and thousands of unhappy citizens would never rest till the miscarriage was corrected. "And that includes me, John," he added. "I'm your friend, but I'll never agree with you on this one."

The D.A. said that he admired Cochran "but you're dead wrong this time, Johnnie."

"You're the one that's dead wrong, John," Cochran said softly. "You and your whole office. Somebody led you guys up the garden path."

Cochran launched into a cheeky peroration on the responsibilities of a prosecutor. "I've worked in your office for three years now, John. I know what your duties are. You're supposed to further the cause of justice. You're supposed to *do the right thing.*"

Van de Kamp said that he was well aware of his responsibilities.

"For God's sake, John," Cochran said, using a rare biblical expletive, "get your people to carry them out."

Toward the end the discussion teetered between tension and forced cordiality. As it broke up, Cochran told his old boss, "This is wrong, John. This case is a disgrace. This is not the kind of case you want to stand behind."

Van de Kamp smiled, shook hands and ushered the delegation out.

TWO MONTHS later, in March 1981, a parole hearing at the California Men's Colony opened with the reading of a statement explaining why Pratt and his attorneys intended to boycott all such proceedings: "Mr. Pratt believes, based on what has taken place at the past few lifer hearings, that the decision to keep him in prison has been based not on his record while in prison . . . but on other factors. These other factors are political and not legal in nature. He therefore feels nothing will be gained at his lifer hearing. He believes that if he is released from prison it would be due to the courts and not the Board of Prison Terms."

The event provided an opportunity for another star turn by Richard Kalustian. The assistant D.A. informed the board that the subject of releasing Pratt had been discussed "ad nauseam" and that the D.A.'s Office remained opposed. "Let me make a couple of observations. . . . There was absolutely no reason for killing Mrs. Olsen. . . . It was almost as an afterthought that they turned around and shot. There's nothing about the crime that offers any mitigation for Mr. Pratt."

He criticized the inmate's behavior and attitude. "He has been disciplinary free for the last year or year and a half, but that's not really a very long time when you consider that he's been continuously in jail since December of 1970. . . . I see Mr. Pratt as a man who has very little if any patience with this entire system. He views the whole thing as a farce, a charade. . . . I see Mr. Pratt as more of a time bomb kind of waiting to go off than I do a man who is motivated by leadership and a desire to help. . . .

"I see Mr. Pratt as a man still motivated by the same forces that motivated him in the early seventies and the late sixties. He has this fixation with the fact that the FBI framed him. He can't seem to get that out of his mind. I think that single factor is one of the things that's going to prevent him from ever assimilating his role in society. I think he simply is not able to put that behind him. . . . Everything that I have seen tells me in my gut that you have a man who is so unhappy, who is so mad, who is so upset at the system—and he is just waiting for the time when he can get out and do something about it."

After a short deliberation the board concluded that the prisoner presented an unreasonable risk of danger to society.

BACK IN San Francisco, Stuart Hanlon heard from Charles Garry, attorney for the Black Panther Party and a flamboyant advocate of left-wing causes. He said he wanted Hanlon to meet M. Wesley Swearingen, a retired FBI agent. The talk session left Hanlon's head spinning.

In 1951 Swearingen had gone to work in the FBI's Chicago bureau, where he was assigned to surveillance on the wives of Communist Party leaders. For the next quarter century, he participated in disinformation campaigns, burglaries (so-called black bag jobs), wiretaps, buggings and other FBI activities. He told Hanlon that COINTELPRO agents had orchestrated the Chicago killings of Black Panther leaders Fred Hampton and Mark Clark. And he confirmed that his fellow COINTELPRO agents had dutifully carried out the orders of the Director to neutralize Geronimo Pratt. As a result, Swearingen claimed, Pratt had been framed for an unsolved killing.

The retired lawman told Hanlon that he'd shared a desk in the Los Angeles FBI office with Special Agent B. O. Cleary, who worked as Pratt's case agent under direction of the local COINTELPRO chief, Richard Wallace Held.[58] Held was believed to be one of the agents who stepped up to LAPD Sergeant DuWayne Rice on a Los Angeles street corner and demanded the letter from "Julius." According to Swearingen, the FBI had been aware of Pratt's innocence from the beginning. During the Pratt trial, he said, he overheard Cleary complain to another agent that on the night of the tennis court shootings, "the son of a bitch was in Oakland."

---

[58] Richard W. Held, J. Edgar Hoover's point man in the campaign to "neutralize" Pratt, was the son of Richard G. Held, an associate FBI director who was accused of helping to cover up the agency's role in the 1969 killings of Hampton and Clark in Chicago. With permission from Hoover, the younger Held orchestrated the campaign against the actress Jean Seberg.

Swearingen told Hanlon that agents in the Los Angeles office of the FBI had wiretapped the Panther headquarters on Central Avenue from November 15 to December 20, 1968, bracketing the murder night, but that he'd searched without success for the logs. "That was incredible," he swore in an affidavit. "There was no document to reflect that the materials had been destroyed pursuant to any FBI authorization. . . . [This] is the only time such an event ever happened that I know of. In my opinion, one or more persons in the FBI Los Angeles office deliberately saw to it that these materials were not available."

U.S. REPRESENTATIVE Don Edwards of California turned up an FBI document verifying that an informant had reported in 1971 that "Julius Butler is said to be trying to frame Elmer Pratt on the murder charge regarding the Santa Monica shooting." The information had been kept from Johnnie Cochran and Charles Hollopeter, who could have used it to their client's advantage at the 1972 trial. Evidently, the earliest clandestine meetings between the hairdresser and the FBI had led to a common goal.

Hanlon weighed the information from Swearingen and Edwards and told his client, "Grab your socks, Geronimo. We're headed back to court." Before he could file his latest petition, fresh information arrived about Butler. The former Panther had been arrested for kicking a citizen and threatening him with a gun. After he pleaded no contest to charges of carrying a loaded weapon and driving under the influence of alcohol, he was put on probation and fined. The next time the hairstylist appears in court, Hanlon said to himself, he won't look so cool.

The Kronenberg Maneuver

Armed with the new evidence, the Pratt lawyers bypassed the California justice system and filed a petition for writ of habeas corpus in the U.S. District Court in Los Angeles on July 9, 1981, the eleventh year of Pratt's ordeal. The case was assigned to a magistrate, lowest rank in the federal judiciary. Magistrates handled mundane chores like the showers of habeas corpus petitions filed by restless prisoners. This one was portly, white-haired, clean-shaven, an affable man in his middle years. To Hanlon, John Kronenberg resembled a Rotary Club sergeant at arms. Still, his overall impression was favorable.

"The guy's no Kathleen Parker," he told Geronimo. "He's got no record to protect. He isn't part of the state system. And the new stuff from Swearingen and Don Edwards should have a hell of an effect. At the least, I think he'll give us an evidentiary hearing."

Neither lawyer nor client was yet aware of a Kronenberg trait. The magistrate was so deliberate and slow as to be almost stationary. Hanlon told Pratt to expect an evidentiary hearing within a year. He wasn't even close.

THREE WEEKS after the filing of the latest petition, Geronimo got into a fight with a white inmate over the word "nigger." After the brawl he was ordered to pack for a return trip to San Quentin. The punitive transfer had a beneficial effect; now he could consult with Hanlon regularly and resume his conjugal visits with Ashaki. He was assigned to work as a visiting room attendant and made up his mind that if he had to be in prison, it might as well be on the shores of San Francisco Bay.

MONTHS PASSED without word from Judge Kronenberg, and Geronimo decided to put the downtime to use. He enrolled in more courses at UC Berkeley, joined a group called Self-Advancement Through Education (and was elected vice-president) and began informal meetings with other Vietnam veterans. He also joined a substance abuse group, explaining to his counselor: "There've been times when marijuana kept me sane in here, but I'm getting out pretty soon and I don't want to be on dope the rest of my life."

He won another upbeat evaluation from a prison psychiatrist: "There is no evidence to sustain the personality disorder diagnosis of 1973, and the post-traumatic stress disorder has apparently resolved."

In November 1981 he was transferred to the Honor Unit and began a series of coveted assignments: education department clerk, block attendant, hospital aide, dining room attendant. When rains flooded the prison grounds and work details were assembled, Lieutenant Tom Haggar, once his opponent in a one-sided fistfight, said, "Pratt, one of your paratrooper buddies thinks we should give you a chance. How about it? If I let you work outside, are you gonna run?"

Geronimo said, "I ain't gonna run on you, man."

With another lifer, Dip McRea, he helped to build retaining walls around the warden's house. The pelting rain took him back to the Gulf storms of his childhood. Sometimes he paused to let a plump drop roll down his forehead and into his eye. One day Ashaki arrived to visit and spotted him. "Look, Shona," she said to their baby, "there's your daddy! He's looking at the rain again."

After the job was completed, Tom Haggar inserted a notation in Pratt's jacket: "Inmate Pratt has always maintained an excellent attitude toward work and has been very helpful to both staff and fellow inmate workers on the crew."

GERONIMO AND Hanlon absented themselves from the next hearing of the parole board in February 1982, but the dogged Richard Kalustian spoke against Pratt once again. This time parole was denied without comment.

Soon after the hearing, Hanlon arrived at San Quentin with better news. A San Francisco private investigator, Melody Ermachild, a Pratt volunteer in her spare time, had followed a sinuous trail to a skinny black man named William Tyrone Hutchinson who nervously affirmed that he'd once been accused of being Pratt's accomplice in the tennis court shootings. Hutchinson told the investigator that he'd given police the names of the real killers: Larry Hatter and Herbert Swilley, heroin addicts from the South-Central ghetto.

"Do those names mean anything to you?" Hanlon asked Geronimo.

"I think they might have worked in Julio's cell," Pratt replied. "I never knew 'em personally. To me they were just kids."

Ermachild reported that the LAPD had arrested Hutchinson on investigation of 187 P.C., homicide, then released him with a warning to keep his mouth shut.

"How come we didn't know about this when I went to trial?" Geronimo asked.

"The cops buried it," Hanlon said. "They were after you. They weren't after Swilley and Hatter."

"Stu," Geronimo said, "I'm doing their time!"

A few days later Hanlon received a follow-up report from the energetic Ermachild. Herbert Swilley had been shot dead in 1972 in a gambling argument near Eightieth and Broadway. His arm was a road map of heroin tracks. Six years later Larry Hatter impaled himself on a steel rod while fleeing from the scene of a robbery. His body was found by workers the next morning. The location was a public tennis court in Santa Monica.

"The Lincoln Park courts?" Geronimo asked when Hanlon told him the news.

"About a mile away."

Hanlon promised to bring the information to the attention of the U.S. magistrate.

IN MID-MARCH 1983, twenty months after Hanlon had filed for a writ of habeas corpus, John Kronenberg finally granted an evidentiary hearing. But before Hanlon could pass the encouraging word to his client, he learned that the judge had added crippling conditions. The hearing would be limited to the Hutchinson information that had been withheld from the defense, the links between the FBI and the LAPD, and wiretap surveillance of the Black Panther Party. Under this order, Hanlon would be forbidden to call Julius Butler as a witness or to challenge his letter implicating Pratt. He couldn't question Richard Kalustian or any other member of the Los Angeles D.A.'s Office. He couldn't call LAPD Sergeant DuWayne Rice, his boss, Captain Ed Henry, or any other police officer. Nor would Kronenberg permit interrogation about COINTELPRO files except the ones that specifically mentioned Pratt.

TWO MORE years of wrangling ensued as Hanlon unsuccessfully fought the emasculation of his case. At last, in May 1985, a limited evidentiary hearing opened. For three days Hanlon was forced to prove almost every element of his case through hostile witnesses like former Los Angeles COINTELPRO chief Richard Wallace Held; Pratt's FBI trackers, Theodore Gardner and his successor, B. O. Cleary; Supervising Agent Richard Bloeser, and former sergeant Raymond Callahan, the retired LAPD Panther Unit officer. Each of the witnesses had a personal investment in keeping the convicted man behind bars, and their memories, even about documents bearing their signatures, proved as limited as their heavily censored files. The only exception was Gardner, who confirmed under oath that Butler had revealed the toxic contents of his "secret" insurance letter only three days after it was written.

Richard Held proved the most adroit of the FBI witnesses. He'd already testified in deposition that "I don't recall really knowing much about the [Pratt] case at all anyway," despite the fact that he'd directed the COINTELPRO operation in Los Angeles. On the witness stand he seemed to take the lofty position that he'd been summoned to court to interpret the meaning of his old memos rather than to confirm authorship or take responsibility.

Hanlon read aloud from Held's memorandum of January 28, 1970, to "The Director," a lengthy order of battle that described how the COINTELPRO agents intended to "attack, expose, and ridicule the image of the BPP" and create fake documents and leaflets "designed to challenge the legitimacy of the authority exercised by ELMER GERARD PRATT."

Hanlon asked if Held was familiar with the contents.

The agent peered at his initials in the corner and said, "I don't recall it, but I—but this would indicate that I dictated it."

When Hanlon asked why Pratt had been singled out in the memo, one of Held's attorneys jumped up to object. The indulgent Kronenberg waived normal courtroom procedure to allow Held to step into the corridor and confer with his lawyers and two FBI agents before deciding on an answer.

Back on the stand, the COINTELPRO expert asked that the question be rephrased. Hanlon said, "My question was basically what type of activities discussed in this memo . . . exposing, attacking, and ridiculing. . . . Why does Mr. Pratt's name appear among others on that document?"

Held turned toward the judge and said, "Your Honor, I don't know."

Kronenberg appeared perplexed. *"You don't know?"*

"No, sir."

The magistrate asked if it was fair to say that the memo proposed "certain activities against certain people."

"Your Honor," Held said, "I would say that I dictated this. Now, whether I dictated this based strictly on something I did or with input for others—from others—or not, I don't know. I don't recall the document, so I am really not in a position to say other than I dictated it. What the overall role I played in it, I really don't know."

Hanlon considered impeaching the reluctant witness on his conveniently poor memory. The memo in question had set the tone for the entire COINTELPRO operation in Los Angeles. It was inconceivable to Hanlon that its author recognized his handiwork only by his initials on the bottom. Hanlon remembered Judge Kathleen Parker's earlier comment: "But, Mr. Hanlon, it's the FBI!" No law shielded federal agents from difficult questions, but as a practical matter they usually testified *de minimis.* Judges seemed to consider them exalted figures, flying above and below the law at the same time. To Hanlon this was the same slavish obsequiousness that was responsible for the excesses of J. Edgar Hoover and COINTELPRO in the first place.

The lawyer produced documents showing that Held and Julio Butler had conferred, and asked the witness, "What conversations did you have with Mr. Butler . . . that led you to believe he was willing to cooperate, that he would have some kind of information to give you?"

Held answered, "I have no idea."

In an hour on the witness stand, much of it devoted to byplay between judge and lawyers, the COINTELPRO case agent answered "I don't know," "I don't recall" or close variations forty-eight times.

Seated at the petitioner's table, Hanlon muttered to his colleague Paul "Pete" McCloskey that FBI agents must study "Evasiveness 101" at the academy in Quantico, Virginia. Witnesses couldn't be charged with perjury for not knowing or remembering. To Hanlon it seemed that Held had sworn to tell the whole truth and clearly hadn't, a less than honorable stance for a public servant. But at least one fellow federal employee was impressed. After the witness was excused, John Kronenberg observed, "Mr. Held's testimony was straightforward and thoroughly credible."

Except for retired Agent M. Wesley Swearingen, the other FBI personnel followed Held's lead on the witness stand. On behalf of Pratt, Swearingen testified about missing wiretap records and other FBI discrepancies. He seemed intimidated by the presence of his old colleagues and a little less certain of his facts than he'd been at pretrial conferences, but he was the only witness who wasn't openly hostile.

THE MAGISTRATE took the case under advisement while Pratt and Hanlon waited with low spirits. Geronimo now presided over a family of four; his son Hiroji had been born in December 1982. On the phone he kept telling his lawyer, "Goddamn it, Stu, I got to get out and raise my family."

Hanlon and Kathy Ryan had married, and both agreed that this habeas corpus petition would mark her exit from the field of criminal law. "Kathy was a lot more upbeat than I was," Hanlon explained. "I always had a dark attitude—the world is screwed—but she was optimistic. She didn't like dealing with the criminal element or the ethical issues that kept coming up in a criminal practice. So she started a family practice and ended up representing rich assholes who were divorcing each other. She traded one moral issue for another."

ON MARCH 7, 1986, four years and eight months after the filing of the latest habeas corpus petition, Judge Kronenberg ruled against Pratt. The magistrate said he'd found "no regular liaison between the LAPD and the FBI" and no evidence that relevant documents had been removed from the files ("Documents apparently missing never existed"). He deftly removed the snitch jacket from Julius Butler—"the evidence indicates that he was a contact and nothing more. The definition of 'informant' is not precise." He held that Tyrone Hutchinson's arrest was unconnected to the case and that no conspiracy against Geronimo Pratt had ever existed. Nor had Pratt's attorneys presented credible proof that their client had been in Oakland earlier than December 20, two nights after the murder. Kronenberg concluded his forty-one-page finding with a firm declaration that the petitioner's constitutional rights had been zealously observed.

"PRATT IS innocent," Hanlon told a reporter for the *Los Angeles Times,* "but the judicial system is petrified by him and what he stands for and is unwilling to let him out under any circumstances."

Asked about the elephantine pace of the hearing, he said, "It's a vicious way to handle it. Why wait so long if you aren't going to do anything?"

He said he would file an appeal, of course. He didn't say what he felt: that another appeal would almost certainly produce another rubber-stamp denial.

Johnnie Cochran was also quoted in the newspapers. "I was deceived," he said. "Pratt was deceived. The whole system was deceived by the government."

Hard Time

Now in his sixteenth year in prison, a disheartened Geronimo Pratt retreated deep into himself. He told a reporter he wasn't surprised by the ruling: "I never expected justice from the criminal justice system."

To Hanlon he said simply, "Man, I just keep packing and unpacking. Every other month, I'm getting out. This is a hard way to do time."

Sitting in his cell, he faced the probability that he would die behind bars. He remembered a crazy old lifer, a former stagecoach robber, who was released from Q after forty years, took a few steps outside the gate, fell on his face and refused to move till they let him back in. For years Geronimo had lived from hope to hope, but now he faced a metallic future—doors clanking, trays rattling, keys jingling, tin cups, steel bars, metal toilets and benches and bunks and chairs. He'd never been able to escape the fear that he was doing penance for waging war against innocent Vietnamese, but thoughts of his new family made him yearn for a normal life.

"The worst thing about it," his best friend told him, "is that John Kronenberg cost us four years. Wait, wait, wait, wait—that's all we seem to do."

"It's okay, Stu," Geronimo said. "I know how to wait."

IN CONJUGAL visits after the latest setback, Ashaki was now accompanied by Shona, seven years old, and Hiroji, nearly four. Geronimo's new family lived on welfare in a drug-drenched project a few miles from the prison. Every few months he slipped into the role of husband and father pro tem and found the two-day family visits warm, touching and traumatic. Partings were always painful. "The kids screamed and hollered. They were too little to understand why they had to leave their daddy. We'd have to pry 'em off my leg. Shona was always saying, 'I want to stay with Daddy.' So we worked it out that as soon as the three of them left the trailer, they would hurry around to the visiting room. Pretty soon I'd come in and Ashaki would say, 'See, kids? Daddy's still here.' And we'd have another few minutes together."

PRATT ALSO enjoyed visits from his corps of volunteers—mostly females whom he called his runners. Sue Gegner, a paralegal at a San Francisco law firm, had read about his case in *New Times* magazine and become a friend. "I'll always be grateful to her," he said later. "She told me she would be happy for the rest of her life if she could just help to get me out of prison, not for her but for me and Ashaki and our family."

On Geronimo's behalf the petite paralegal kept in close touch with the Pratts of Morgan City and corresponded with journalists and others who might help bring the case to public attention. She contacted Centurion Ministries in Princeton, New Jersey, an organization dedicated to freeing the imprisoned innocent, but a secretary wrote that the agency received eight hundred requests a year and was hopelessly overbooked. Gegner told Geronimo not to give up hope—she was working on other ideas.

PRATT BECAME concerned about Ashaki after she missed a scheduled prison visit and didn't answer his collect phone calls. At his direction his wife and children were sharing quarters with his old friend and fellow Panther Afeni Shakur and her children,[59] and he wondered if the arrangement was working out. He was teaching a class in African culture when a new inmate from Marin County took him aside and said he'd heard that Ashaki had an alcohol problem and was dabbling in drugs. Geronimo asked one of

---

[59] A son, Tupac, an actor and rap music star, was murdered in 1996 in Las Vegas.

his runners to make a spot visit to the Marin City housing project. The next day the helper confirmed the report.

Pratt had no tolerance for abusers of alcohol and hard drugs and ordered Hanlon to begin divorce proceedings, but the lawyer counseled delay. Ashaki needed time to work out problems that were not of her making. "Your wife is *no* junkie," he said, "and you're not gonna treat her like one. She's a single mother, she's raising your kids, she's brought stability into your life. She's a wonderful woman, goddamn it, and she loves you. And you're a difficult man. You've got so many women waiting in the reception room, they oughta take a number. It's like a butcher shop out there! Don't you think that bothers Ashaki? She's stressed-out, man, that's all. It could happen to anybody."

To himself Hanlon said that the trouble with Geronimo was that he had no real feel for ghetto life, no deep understanding in his bones. A happy childhood in Morgan City hadn't prepared him for the realities of life in black urban America. Injustice, suffering, temptation, Hanlon said to himself, *that's* what this is about. Ashaki isn't the first good woman to falter.

Hanlon found his client unforgiving. After the divorce was granted, Ashaki kicked her habit, went to work for the Head Start program in Marin County and soon became director. She improved her family's quality of life by convincing a private Catholic school to grant scholarships to Shona and Hiroji. Now Geronimo's beloved children were removed from ghetto drugs and violence, at least on school days. He was impressed and grateful, and the conjugal visits resumed.

HANLON'S OWN flirtation with recreational cocaine was brought to an abrupt end by an ultimatum from his wife. His courtroom victory list was growing, but he still tended to define his career by the Pratt failures. Now and then a gentlemanly snort was a comfort.

For a while Kathy Ryan had watched silently. Hanlon knew that she disapproved, and one night he tried to explain that he needed an escape from the pressures of work.

"Get another escape," she said.

Soon afterward she said, "I found more bindles, Stu. Knock it off or get out. I hope I make myself clear."

"What the hell brought this on?"

"You're not gonna do drugs with a baby in the house."

"You're—"

"Yes. I am."

King of the Hill

By the late 1980s Geronimo Pratt was settling into a new prison routine. "I had a lot of juice. Trooper Webb had gone home, High Society Red was getting tired of responsibility and I kinda rose to the top. It wasn't anything I planned or anything I wanted, but I woke up one day and it seemed like I was running San Quentin. Every night except Sunday I led cellisthenics. I did five hundred push-ups and a thousand sit-ups and another thousand back-arms off the cell bar. I could bench-press three hundred pounds and run twenty miles around the yard without a deep breath. The guards never spiked[60] my cell door. I came out at night, moved around, had extra phone calls and family visits. The same guards that used to kick my ass turned nice as soon as they found out I wasn't gonna kidnap their kids or blow the place up. Deputy Warden Nyberg apologized to me for the past. Deputy Warden Weber said, 'I didn't know you, Geronimo. All those years I thought you were dangerous.' Warden Sumner told the *Los Angeles Times* a lot of good things about me. I thanked 'em all and turned away. This was still prison."

---

[60] Electrically locked to the floor or ceiling.

EARLY IN 1987 a newly assigned counselor told him that she'd been pe-
rusing his central file and noticed that he was boycotting parole hearings.
"What the hell's going on?" she asked. "You've got a hearing coming up
and we have to prepare for it."

Geronimo didn't know what to make of this blonde-haired woman
who looked more like a dancer in a chorus line than someone who spent
her days counseling murderers, rapists and kidnappers. He'd heard that
she talked louder and acted tougher than any of the male guards and
that she never backed down to anyone, including the warden. He'd
heard that she consistently outshot others on the firing range. He'd heard
that every guard and prisoner in San Quentin dreamed of getting her
alone in the laundry room. He'd heard that none ever had.

"My case is political," he explained. "The parole board couldn't let me
out if they wanted to."

"Oh? Then who can?"

"I dunno. The courts. The governor. The . . . World Court." He smiled
to show her he wasn't serious.

She didn't seem to get the joke. "Let's see," she said, riffling some papers on her clipboard. "You've been inside for how long?"

"I'm in my seventeenth year in captivity. Just like an orangutan in the
zoo."

"And—let's see—you've been back to court four times? Five? Just
when are you expecting the courts to let you out?"

Geronimo didn't have an answer.

"Mr. Pratt," she said, "I thought you were smarter than that."

He was glad to see her leave.

TWO DAYS later she was back. "I've got to write a report about you," she
said, "so I've been reading your file again. I see you've never told any counselor your side of the story. My classification manual says that the counselor
has to ask the prisoner his version of the event."

"I appreciate your concern," Geronimo said, "but you don't know what
you're getting into."

"Listen, Pratt," she said, her voice rising, "if the manual says I have to
do this, and if I'm willing to go to the trouble, what's *your* problem with
it?" She turned shrill. "Are you as guilty as the rest of these assholes? *Is that
why you don't want to talk?*"

She returned the next day. "Look," he told her, "I'm not gonna put no time and energy into this. I need every minute to work on my legal case."

"Mister," she said, "you're a fucking idiot."

The running argument continued for weeks. One day he said, "Please, stop wasting your time. You could be helping somebody that *wants* help. I can take care of myself."

At their next meeting she told him that she'd interviewed several of his closest friends. "I've heard most of your story now. If it's true, you're here because you were a Black Panther leader. If it's true, you *are* a political prisoner. Prove it to me and I'll get off your case."

Geronimo finally decided that it would be easier to tell his story than to be insulted and abused three times a day before lunch.

A Model Guard

Her name was A. Lynne Atkinson, self-described as an "overeducated farm girl from the Illinois cornfields." She was thirty-nine years old, five feet five inches tall, barely a hundredweight, with long blond hair that she tucked under her uniform cap, pale skin, green eyes and a nose as straight as the barrel of her target pistol. She was of mixed ancestry, mostly English, and had about as much Indian blood as Pratt. She enjoyed cats, flowers, opera, antiques and cooking. When she was in her twenties, she'd modeled for San Francisco Shirtworks and Byer of California till she learned that size fives never made the cover of *Sports Illustrated*. She quit modeling and signed on as a parole agent, but resigned after seven years "because I couldn't go into one more stinking room in one more flea-bitten hotel."

With a master's degree in administration of justice from Southern Illinois University but no prison or custodial experience, she somehow caught on as a sergeant of guards at San Quentin, where her coloratura giggles and bugle-call laughs could be heard from one end of the mainline to the other, except when she was cut down by an attack of asthma and couldn't talk. She was abrasive, profane, combative, uncompromising and popular, even with the men she'd sent to the hole. She was famous for her handling of a unique disciplinary problem in her second month on the job. "An inmate in our temporary tent city was using the rear flap of his tent for a—what's the word? *Pissoir.* Then everybody followed his act—monkey see, monkey do. Tent City reeked. I ordered him to get some soap and a toothbrush and wash every rock by hand. He said, 'Who the fuck are you?' I pointed to my stripes and said, 'That's who the fuck I am.' He said, 'You done flipped, girl.' I said, '*Sergeant* Atkinson to you, dickhead. Now wash the fucking rocks!' He washed the fucking rocks. That ended the outdoor pissing problem."

SHORTLY AFTER Atkinson was promoted to guard lieutenant and part-time counselor, she was confronted with a problem on her caseload. A convict named Warren Wells was demanding a transfer from Security Housing to the mainline. He'd been stabbed by the leader of the Black Guerrilla Family and didn't seem to understand that the BGF would probably finish the job if his soft body parts became accessible again.

"Mr. Wells," she told him at a counseling session, "being in the hole is keeping you alive. You wouldn't last five minutes on the mainline."

"Times change," the former Black Panther said. "Why don't you check things out with Geronimo?"

She discussed the suggestion with her supervisor. "Go ahead," he said. "If Pratt says the guy's safe on the mainline, he's safe."

In their first conversation Atkinson asked, "If I let Warren Wells go to the mainline, am I gonna be burying him later?"

Pratt took his time about answering. "I don't know, miss," he said at last. "Lemme think about it." He didn't seem disposed to conversation, unlike other prisoners who tried to suck up at every opportunity.

She used the waiting period to check Pratt's bona fides. A supervisor told her, "He's the coolest head around, an arbitrator, negotiator. He'll explain everything in clear concise terms, and both sides end up shaking hands, and a guard gets a commendation for bringing peace. Geronimo doesn't care who gets the credit. He's not bucking for big man on the mainline. He just *is.*"

Three days after Atkinson's first conversation with Pratt, he approached her on a walkway in the yard. "Wells is cool with the BGF," he said as they passed. "They already made their point."

LATER THE female counselor said that listening to Pratt recite the story of his arrest and imprisonment was like listening to Odysseus, chained to his rock. "I went from doubt to interest to fascination, and yeah—I finally wound up at obsession. Could this crazy story possibly be true? I tried all kinds of mindfucks to trip him up, but everything he said checked out and his story never varied. I said, 'Geronimo, I'm willing to put your version in my parole report, but I've got to see some documentation, because the board's gonna go ballistic when they read what I say. I want to be able to show them chapter and page, footnote, annotations, references.'

"Next thing I know, this frizzy-haired lawyer named Hanlon is hand-delivering five thousand pages of material. Geronimo said, 'Read this and you'll see why I don't go before the parole board.' I took it home and read every page—the Church Committee's findings, the FBI files, trial transcripts, parole board hearings, police reports from L.A. and Santa Monica, psych evals, *everything.* The hairs on the back of my neck stood up. I would work a ten-hour day at the prison, go home, feed the cats and study those documents for five or six hours. I sat on my couch in my little house in Petaluma and tried not to blow up. I was never so goddamn angry in my life. My cats thought I was nuts. I realized that the surest way to hurt Geronimo's cause was to lose my cool and piss off a bunch of people. He didn't need another hysterical woman running around yelling that he was innocent. I took notes, cross-references, drew up a chronology, made phone calls to his rat pack. At 6:00 A.M. I'd be at the prison—'Wake up, G. Answer me *this.'* I gave up trying to trick him, because it never worked. This went on for five weeks."

AS THE parole hearing approached, Atkinson called on her friend Associate Warden Henry Tabash and said, "Henry, my report on Pratt is gonna be a smoker. The board is gonna go nuts."

Tabash gave her the standard bureaucratic advice: watch your ass.

She said, "Oh, I *am.* I'm documenting everything. Nobody can touch me, Henry, because I'm reporting the prisoner's version, and he's required to tell it. If they get on me, I'll just quote the manual."

Tabash told her to dot her i's and cross her t's. "Trust me," she said. "I'll be cool."

Then she lost her temper and broke her own rule.

EVEN WITHOUT the hundreds of pages that had been destroyed, the Pratt central file was five inches thick, not counting two volumes of public correspondence. Atkinson noticed a sameness to a set of anonymous letters demanding that he be kept in the hole for life. Many contained the spelling "Afrika."

"Those are from the FBI," Geronimo told her. "They admitted it in one of their memos. They were under orders to keep me neutralized, even in the penitentiary."

Along with another counselor, she was leafing through files in the prison records office when she came to the most recent letter to the Board of Prison Terms. It was signed "Unfortunate to remain anonymous" and described how Pratt had willfully executed a woman. The letter closed with a suggestion that all black prisoners be shipped to "Afrika."

She yelled, "That son of a bitching FBI!," and threw the file against a wall.

An hour later she was summoned to an assistant warden's office and warned that she was overinvolved in the Pratt case.

"What's overinvolved?" she asked.

"Throwing files. Using profanity."

"Dear me," she said. "I'll have to watch that."

A few days later she noticed unusual activity in the administration offices and asked what was going on. When she found out, she rushed to tip off Pratt. Network TV was on the way.

60 Minutes

After the devastation of the Kronenberg decision, Hanlon and his volunteers had filed an appeal with the U.S. Ninth Circuit Court of Appeals, but a ruling wasn't expected for at least a year and they assumed it would be negative. Hanlon's wife suggested a media blitz, starting with network news shows. "Why not?" Kathy said. "Nothing else has worked."

With a barrage of phone calls, cards and letters, the Pratt team attracted the attention of Lowell Bergman, a West Coast producer for the CBS news program *60 Minutes*. Soon Geronimo was sitting in the San Quentin visiting room with marquee newsman Harry Reasoner. "I told him I didn't want to do the show. Mama was sick, and it would just embarrass my relatives. He wanted to cover my next parole hearing, and I explained that I wouldn't be going. I knew I couldn't win, and I couldn't stand to hear one more lie about myself. Reasoner told me him and Lowell Bergman had read my file and believed I was innocent. He said, 'Pratt, we want to tell the world what you've gone through.' "

Geronimo had a decision to make.

ON APRIL 21, 1987, two weeks before the scheduled date of the parole hearing, Counselor Lynne Atkinson finished her report. In it she pointed out that inmate Pratt had never given "a complete statement regarding his guilt or innocence in these crimes. After seventeen years of silence, he has chosen to present his story with its inherent complexities." She cited multiple errors in his jacket. She noted that the FBI had continued its campaign against him by "falsely labeling him as the leader of the Black Liberation Army and having ties to the Symbionese Liberation Army, and accusing him of being involved in an escape plot that included the kidnaping of a school busload of children. Pratt's central file reflects that the source of information regarding the kidnap plot was an FBI duty officer. Both of these actions resulted in Pratt's placement in restricted housing, thereby 'neutralizing' his influence in the prison community, as well as complicated his access to the Courts and public inquiry."

She noted that previous reports to the Board of Prison Terms inaccurately depicted Pratt as on-scene leader of the Black Panthers in their December 1969 shoot-out with the LAPD. She reported that he was "arrested simultaneously at a secondary location in bed." She detailed the "FBI's national conspiracy to disrupt the black community," which "directly resulted in the escalation of violence of Black against Black in Los Angeles." She cited the Church Committee's report on "the FBI's 'war' " and quoted from internal documents about the agency's program of "dirty tricks." She described the inmate as "conforming" and "not a management or disciplinary problem." She listed his job offers from Tarzana to Tanzania and said that he intended to unite with his wife and children and attend college when he was released. She cited 150 letters of support from individuals including Willie Brown Jr., who was the speaker of the California House of Representatives, novelist Alice Walker, Amnesty International, the NAACP, Synod of Presbyterian Churches, Jewish Rabbi Foundation and the Congressional Black Caucus—"This writer cannot remember when a prisoner has received so much support from such a broad spectrum of community, the state and the nation."

The blonde-haired farm girl's report characterized Pratt as "remarkably free of rancor, bitterness and self-pity. He has shown absolutely no hint of racial hatred attributed to him by the various law enforcement personnel responsible for his apprehension and prosecution. Pratt holds no animosity toward those individuals that contributed to his incarceration and states that they were as much a target and a victim of the situation as was he."

She concluded that "Pratt poses little risk to the community if released from prison at this time."

THE DAY after she filed her report, Atkinson dropped into the visiting room to hand Pratt his copy. He was being pre-interviewed for *60 Minutes*. Geronimo asked why she couldn't appear on the TV program. "Direct order from the warden's office," she said. "The administration's terrified."

"About what?" Bergman asked.

"I don't think they want the public to know we're holding an innocent man."

"The board says we can bring in video cameras."

Atkinson said, "Good. I'll try to crash the party."

On the way back to her office she was intercepted by a supervisor. He ushered her into the typing pool room of the records office, slammed a copy of her report on the desk and said, "We don't like this one bit."

She played dumb. "Isn't it terrible what they've done to that poor guy?"

"You're gonna have to change your report."

"What part of it don't you like?"

He read a passage aloud and said, "You can't prove any of this."

Atkinson said, "Sure I can."

After a hot discussion he pushed the papers aside and said, "I don't care what kind of evidence you have. You're gonna have to change your conclusions."

"I wrote a balanced report," she said. "I'm not gonna change a goddamn word."

"How do you think this is gonna play on national TV? You'll embarrass the whole Department of Corrections."

"The goddamn CDC *ought* to be embarrassed. They've kept somebody in here for seventeen years for a crime he didn't commit. That doesn't embarrass you?"

"I'm giving you a direct order," the supervisor said. "You can include all the bullshit he says about himself, but you've got to change your own conclusions."

"I'm not stupid enough to disobey a direct order," she said. "I'll write it all up in a supplemental report, including your order to lie. How do you think *that's* gonna play?"

The supervisor left and slammed the door. The next day he filed an addendum to the Atkinson report, accusing Pratt of taking "the path of least resistance" by not enrolling in correspondence courses and by choosing to remain near his wife and children instead of transferring to prisons that offered more college-level courses. The allegation, of course, was inaccurate. He took no issue with Atkinson's statement that Pratt hadn't been present at the shoot-out in Los Angeles, but pointed out that "under his leadership and direction, the headquarters building was heavily fortified and stockpiled with weapons. In essense [sic], although not physically present, he engineered the physical and organizational details that led to the four (4) hour gun battle which resulted in injuries to three (3) police officers and three (3) Black Panther members."

AT 2:45 P.M. on Tuesday, May 5, 1987, CBS-TV cameras whirred as the Board of Prison Terms convened inside a San Quentin conference room for the seventh parole hearing of inmate B-40319 PRATT. Three board members were joined by Los Angeles Deputy D.A. Diane Vezzani, standing in for Richard Kalustian, now a Superior Court judge. A team of reporters from the *San Francisco Examiner* also covered.

Lynne Atkinson was stopped at the door by a rotund staffer. Through a crack she saw Geronimo, dressed in a short-sleeved prison shirt and arranging some papers.

"What's going on?" she said. "I'm supposed to be here."

The guard didn't move.

She realized how naive she'd been. Some small part of her had hoped that the board members would be upset by her report, assign an investigator and angrily seek the truth. She'd dated one of the members and was friendly with another. Dumb me, she said to herself. I thought my friends would play it straight.

"Let me in," she begged. "I'm his counselor."

"I got my orders," the round man said.

INSIDE THE hearing room Stuart Hanlon opened the proceedings with a challenge. "What I'd like to do is ask the panel members if any of them have connections with the Los Angeles Police Department or the FBI or the law enforcement personnel, and on that basis we'll determine if we think we're getting a fair panel."

Presiding Commissioner Edmund Tong immediately ruled the question out of order.

Pratt was sworn and Hanlon demanded that his prison counselor be present. "It's my understanding that under the rules we're allowed to have her here. . . . The representative of the Board of Prison Terms informed me she would be here. And she's not."

Tong assured him that the counselor's report would be taken into consideration.

The next hour was spent in a rancorous discussion of the facts of the case. In the end, Hanlon said, "His counselor's report lays out a whole other theory of what happened in the case. I have submitted documents to you which I assume you have read about his case, and we are not going to re-litigate his murder trial in front of you. Number one, you wouldn't let us, and number two, it would be fruitless. . . ."

The lawyer who was known to some of his colleagues as Rumpled of the Bailey loosened his tie and unbuttoned his jacket. "My client denies that he committed this murder. He has always denied it, and he still denies it. . . . My client admits to fortifying that headquarters. He admits to using the techniques he was taught by our country in Vietnam in defensive measures. He admits teaching people defensive measures with guns. There is nothing illegal about fortifying one's home or office."

It grated on Hanlon that Pratt's wartime service had been used against him by public officials, and he took the opportunity to correct the record. "He had two tours in Vietnam. He was highly decorated. He received numerous war medals for saving other Americans. I think those are relevant factors that should be considered, especially when his military training is thrown back in his face. . . ."

Commissioner Maureen O'Connell, a well-nourished woman with fluffy blond hair, oversize glasses and a necklace of large beads, changed the subject. The Reagan appointee asked Pratt, "There was a warrant and hold on you from Clark County, Alabama, for robbery. Can you tell me about that?"

Geronimo seemed disconcerted as he groped for words. Hanlon felt bad for him; he knew how it disturbed him to be forced to respond to scattershot charges about which he knew nothing and against which he had no practical defense. Hanlon vaguely remembered an old Alabama case that had been included in a laundry list of unsolved crimes attributed to Pratt after he'd been arrested in Dallas in 1970. All such charges had been dropped.

Geronimo started to explain that as a result of the FBI's COINTEL-

PRO program, he'd been falsely accused of many crimes, but O'Connell cut him off at the acronym. "Just tell me about the robbery," she ordered, fidgeting at the epaulets on her military-style blouse.

Pratt said he knew nothing about it.

Hanlon was aggravated that a board member would bring up a discredited felony charge at a hearing seventeen years and three thousand miles removed. "No, he *didn't* commit the robbery," Hanlon interrupted, "and yes, the FBI *was* involved in it and that's through the FBI's own documentation, which we'd be happy to present to you if you're interested."

O'Connell thanked him politely and then quoted Justice L. Thaxton Hanson's reference to "rank speculation and sheer conjecture" in Hanlon's defense of his client. Hanlon asked if she really wanted to go into speculation and conjecture. "I would be more than happy if that's going to be an issue in this parole hearing," he said. ". . . I'd be more than happy to discuss the rank speculation that Mr. Pratt has gathered over the years about the FBI's involvement in this case."

While TV cameras rolled, Maureen O'Connell and Kalustian's representative Diane Vezzani dominated the second hour of the hearing. O'Connell questioned Pratt closely about his work record in prison, said she was awarding him a zero for his academic achievements and seemed to be trying to goad him to anger. She asked, "If you had the opportunity to do the same things today as you did in the sixties, would you do them?"

"I doubt it," Geronimo answered. "It's a whole different era . . . a whole different time."

"But do you believe in the same things?"

". . . I believed in freedom. I believed in liberation. I believed in democracy."

Vezzani, a fortyish woman wearing a frilly white blouse and a white tie bunched loosely at the neck, refreshed the board's memory about earlier anti-Pratt rulings, recited the grisly events on the Santa Monica tennis court and said, "He's guilty of the crime. He is guilty in the minds of those twelve jurors. . . . He is guilty in the minds of every reviewing court until today's date."

The deputy D.A. from Los Angeles characterized Pratt as "a walking time bomb," reprising a theme first sounded by Kalustian in 1981. She described Pratt as "still a revolutionary man" and added, "He has a network of people ready to assist him in any cause that he wishes. I think that is manifested and corroborated in the letters that are presented to this board.

. . . They all say the same thing and I think they are worthless. It does show, and I think the letters also generated by Mr. Hanlon and Mr. Pratt show, that he does have the network out there. If he chooses to set up a revolutionary organization upon release from prison, it would certainly be easy for him to do so."

Hanlon reined in his anger as he rose to respond. "I fought the parole board in prior hearings, in very angry hearings," he said. "Today that almost happened again. My job is not to come here and fight with you."

He described Vezzani's charges about a waiting revolutionary network as "ludicrous." He said, "I gather that includes Willie Brown, it includes [San Francisco Supervisor] Nancy Walker, it includes over one hundred lawyers through this country, it includes numerous doctors. . . . *There is no political group*—this is absolute garbage. What exists is a group of American citizens, some elected officials, some just regular human beings, who have analyzed his case, heard about it as a black man who's in prison, who have read the numerous articles—I mean there's articles *all the time* about his case—and they come to the conclusion that even if he's guilty, and they have questions about it, seventeen years is *enough*. . . . That's what these letters say, and yet they get twisted into talking about revolutionary groups and that he can be a revolutionary again."

He beckoned at Vezzani and said, "There's no evidence this man is a time bomb. The incident with Officer Imm is a perfect example. If he's a time bomb, he helps kill a guard. But according to the guard, he *saves* him. . . . He's been relied on by prison guards and officials to help calm the racial violence in this institution. He's *anything* but a time bomb. If he's a time bomb, he would have exploded."

At 4:57 P.M. everyone was ushered outside the room while the board deliberated. Forty-five minutes later the doors were reopened and Presiding Commissioner Tong announced a unanimous finding that the inmate could reapply for parole in a year.

Hanlon was preparing to leave when he caught the phrase "lack of remorse" from the other side of the small conference room. "How can an innocent man show remorse?" he called out. "He's not gonna say he's sorry, because he's *not* sorry. You're the ones who should be sorry. You're the ones who should show remorse."

He heard a giggle and said, "Excuse me! Is something funny? *Did anything funny happen here today?*"

Commissioner O'Connell warned that he was out of order.

"Out of order?" he yelled. *"Out of order?"* Then the words that he'd been holding back all day came out in one long gush.

The woman turned to the two guards standing along the wall. "Arrest this man!" she ordered.

Hanlon knew he was out of control and didn't care. "Fuck you, lady!" he yelled. "This is a railroad."

Geronimo grabbed Hanlon's sleeve and said, "Lighten up, Stu."

The guards approached. They were acquainted with Hanlon and Pratt and, like most of the San Quentin personnel, had seemed sympathetic. "You gotta leave now, Counselor," one of them said. "She has the right to arrest you."

As Hanlon was exiting, he yelled, "Now you know why we don't come to your fucking hearings!"

THE *60 Minutes* report opened with the sandpapery voice of Harry Reasoner: "Back in the late 1960s, while Martin Luther King was preaching nonviolence, the Black Panthers were preaching revolution. Their leaders, Huey Newton, Bobby Seale, Eldridge Cleaver, called the police racist pigs. In turn, J. Edgar Hoover called them the most dangerous group in the United States."

In the fifteen-minute segment Geronimo was defended by some of the original jurors, including Jeanne Hamilton, the woman who'd heard his anguished outburst in court and asked herself if she'd made a mistake in yielding to the majority. Through the years she'd become positive that she helped to commit an injustice. At the very least, she told the viewers of *60 Minutes,* the new information would have hung the jury. Three other jurors agreed.

Wayne Ladd's on-screen face explained his nickname. "When I look at Geronimo Pratt," the man called Bulldog said, "I don't see a black person. I see somebody that's a man. I've seen this man step in and stop any number of potential confrontations, racial confrontations. I've seen him put himself on the line. . . ."

The Aryan Brotherhood leader was asked if Pratt had saved lives in prison. "Without a doubt," Ladd replied. "Inmates, staff, everybody."

Said Reasoner, "Bulldog's evaluation was seconded by correctional officers we talked with at San Quentin."

An Inherent Kindliness

After the program aired, prison administrators removed Geronimo from Lynne Atkinson's caseload, but she continued to drop in. He always seemed the same—friendly, active, closely involved in the life of the prison. He told her that strict observance of certain personal rules was what kept him alive: avoid feuds and gangs, issue no personal challenges but never back down, and avoid close involvement in the lives of others.

Atkinson began to realize that another secret of his popularity was an inherent kindliness that she seldom saw in prisoners below the age of fifty. He professed to be irreligious but followed religious precepts. There were times when she found his generosity of spirit almost aggravating. He made excuses for the parole board, for Julio Butler and Richard Kalustian, for the FBI men whose "dirty tricks" had fomented murders, for the traitorous Melvin "Cotton" Smith and the Huey Newton sycophants who'd refused to testify on his behalf.

"Everybody's got his own story, Lynne," he told her one day. "Everybody's got his reasons. I get mad, but I can't stay mad. That only hurts *me.*"

He refused to blame Kenneth Olsen for repeatedly altering his description of the killers—"he's just a poor guy that went out to play tennis on the wrong night." He described Barbara Mary Reed as "a nice old lady that made a mistake." He was sympathetic toward his jurors, although he was pleased to see that some had changed their opinions. He was even tolerant of himself—"I was a kid in the Panthers. Didn't know nothin', never learned nothin'. I was a country boy from Louisiana. I'd probably do things different now."

She found him overly sensitive about Vietnam and dropped the subject after observing his reaction to her comment about another veteran on her caseload. "He says he's got to have tranquilizers," she told Pratt. "Every night he sees Vietnamese kids running at him. Their hands are on fire."

Geronimo lowered his head and turned away. When he looked up, his brown eyes were wet. "Whoa, Lynne, *please!*" he said. "That's too heavy. Too heavy. . . ." She'd seen similar reactions in other Vietnam veterans. She thought, They can't all be guilty, can they?

AT CHRISTMASTIME 1987, shortly after his national TV exposure, Geronimo entered his cell to find a brightly wrapped bottle of brandy, a contraband gift from a guard. Atkinson was on her night rounds when she spotted Pratt and his pal Eddie toasting the holiday season. "They looked like those cartoon characters that get thrown against a wall and slide down in two dimensions—boneless. Geronimo was the happiest drunk I ever saw. I grabbed him by the ear and took him to his cell, threw him in, locked the door and said, 'Good night, Geronimo. Sleep it off. Because we don't want you busted for booze! *Do we?* We're trying to get you out of here, asshole!' "

A FEW months later, in early 1988, Pratt and the colorful inmate James "Sneaky" White decided to form a veterans' group, and Atkinson agreed to attend their meetings as a sponsor. White had been shot down as a helicopter pilot and was serving life without parole. By day he served as clerk to an associate warden; at night he counseled war veterans. Geronimo had told her a version of his crime: "After he got rotated home, some dog raped his daughter. Sneaky put on his fatigues, drove to the city jail and bailed the guy out. Then he blew his ass away on the front steps. He walked inside and said, 'Somebody shot somebody outside.' He wouldn't lie and wouldn't cop a plea. So it was first-degree all the way. When he got here, somebody put out word that he was part Jewish, and the ABs stabbed him a couple times. We, uh—we put a stop to that."

He didn't say how, and Atkinson didn't ask.

THE VIETNAM Veterans Group of San Quentin grew too fast to survive. The front office would never allow any prison group to become influential enough to threaten the administration's sovereignty; leaders would be redistributed to Tehachapi or California Men's Colony or Folsom to start at the bottom of another peck order. Within a year the Veterans Group counted eight guards and counselors as sponsors and six dozen members from three wars. Some of the meetings turned into group therapy sessions under the direction of Atkinson, who'd studied psychology en route to her master's degree. Geronimo had become one of her prize patients. "Lynne made me feel a little better about Vietnam. I found out I wasn't the only one with guilt feelings. All us vets, we gave each other forgiveness and understanding and love. The old guys became role models for the gangbangers and the young riders. Our program was working."

An NBC camera crew filmed Pratt and White and other members of the Veterans Group raising money for charities. In two years the group collected $14,000 for the Muscular Dystrophy Association. Three members set up a clinic to assist inmates in filing claims with the Veterans Administration. Workshops and entertainments were held. Prisoners jammed into the auditorium to watch a blind veteran work with his Seeing Eye dog as part of the group's "Project for the Blind." Geronimo was exhilarated by the performance. "That dog was smarter'n most of us! Eddie the blind guy, he showed us what a dog and a man can do together. It was a beautiful experience. The Vietnam Veterans of San Quentin, we were doing good. We got so high on ourselves we forgot to watch our ass."

WITH FORMER U.S. Representative Pete McCloskey at his side, a disenchanted Stuart Hanlon argued the Kronenberg ruling before the U.S. Ninth Circuit Court of Appeals in June 1988. Hanlon was in his customary dishabille, and one of the justices peered at him over the top of his glasses and said, "What are *you* doing here?"

"Well, Your Honor," Hanlon replied, "since I've been working on this case for thirteen years and you put it on your calendar, I thought I'd show up."

The justice said, "If I wasn't in such a good mood, Counsel, I'd hold you in contempt."

The bank of judges denied the appeal, and the demoralized Hanlon filed his motion for reconsideration six days late. Such tardiness was almost always overlooked, and he was told to prepare a brief. After he'd worked on the new document for a week, the court refused to hear the motion. Hanlon was devastated. "I felt I'd let Geronimo down. I wondered if I could go on. I thought, What the hell is *next*?"

WHAT WAS next was Geronimo's eighth parole hearing. Joseph MacKenzie, his new counselor, reported: "Pratt has established himself in a highly respected position as the co-founder and co-chairman of the Vietnam Veterans Group of San Quentin. . . . In comparison with his fellow inmates, he is a man with a high degree of intelligence, a pleasing and disarming personality, and a person who, if he decides to, can make a substantial contribution to the good of society."

Parole was denied.

Old Soldiers

Through the years, Pratt had followed the erratic career of the charismatic Huey P. Newton, and he'd read enough FBI documents to understand why his fellow Louisianan had turned on him so viciously. Hanlon had shown Geronimo an FBI memo to J. Edgar Hoover after Pratt had been purged from the BPP as a "raper of black sisters."

> Huey P. Newton has recently exhibited paranoid-like responses. His Hitler-like hysterical reaction, which has very likely been aggravated by our present counterintelligence activity, has resulted in the suspension of loyal Black Panther Party workers. It appears Newton is on the brink of mental collapse. . . .

It comforted Pratt to learn that it was a temporarily crazed Huey Newton, not the idealistic leader he'd once known, who ordered him expelled. During Geronimo's years in prison Newton had been in and out of the news. After his manslaughter conviction for shooting an Oakland policeman was set aside, he exiled himself to Cuba. In 1980 he earned a Ph.D. in history at the University of California at Santa Cruz. Some ex-Panthers still considered him an FBI snitch. Others were ashamed that he'd allowed himself to be taken in by the bureau's tricks. Only a few insiders knew what Geronimo had learned from secret FBI documents: the day before Newton moved into his penthouse overlooking Lake Merritt in Oakland, FBI agents rented the adjacent apartment and installed bugs in the walls. Subsequently they recorded every word that passed his lips, every visitor, phone call, drink, food order, snore, sneeze, song, drug trip and bathroom visit.[61] With this information the disinformation specialists were able to play the Panther leader like a musical instrument. No wonder he flipped out, Geronimo said to himself. I forgave him a long time ago, but it's nice to know there really wasn't anything to forgive.

TWO WEEKS after Pratt's latest parole turndown an assistant warden asked if an incoming prisoner named Huey P. Newton would be safe on the mainline.

"Huey's coming?" Geronimo said. "What'd he do now?"

"Parole violation."

The California prison system was in transition. The CDC had built new institutions for its most dangerous criminals, and San Quentin was beginning to house a few minor felons. Newton would be serving sixty days for failing to report an arrest for drunken driving and refusing to take a drug test.

Geronimo said there was only one slight risk to assigning Newton to the mainline: "I might bear-hug him and break a few ribs."

Lynne Atkinson couldn't fathom his attitude. "If I understand the situation correctly," she argued, "Huey Fucking Newton is one of the main reasons you're here."

"The FBI convinced Huey I was destroying the party," Geronimo said. "They convinced him I was robbing and killing, bad-mouthing him, raping the sisters. He reacted to disinformation. We *all* did. Huey's a great man, Lynne. I'll introduce you."

Atkinson said she had no intention of shaking hands with any of the "dickheads" who'd helped to send Geronimo to prison. "One of these days you'll realize who your enemies are," she told him.

"I know who they are," Geronimo said. "And I know who they ain't."

---

[61] The same blanket surveillance had been directed against Martin Luther King Jr.

HE WAS shocked at the sight of his old colleague. The former minister of defense looked like a ghost in blackface. He'd once been the most energized Panther of all, a young man on a pogo stick, but now he had the slack-jawed look and cowed manner of a dedicated dope addict. Geronimo shook his head as he told Hanlon later: "The dude done lost it. I've seen that same look a thousand times. We talked for three hours. He confessed to things he didn't even do. He swore he had nothing to do with Red's death—I said, 'I already know that, man.' He kept saying how sorry he was that he expelled me from the party. I said, 'Huey, man, I *understand*.' He showed me an envelope full of FBI bullshit—cartoons showing me beating up women, anonymous letters, memos that I was trying to kill him and Bobby Seale and take over. He said he remembered my trip to Oakland and so did David Hilliard and others, but we were at war and he couldn't let 'em testify for me. I told him I understood that, too. He said he was going straight back to Oakland and make things right. Kept saying, 'I'll take care of it, my brother. I'll take care of it.' I won't get my hopes up. Huey's so wasted, I'm not sure he can take care of anything."

The Associated Press carried Newton's own version of the reunion: "I was reserved and on guard, but Geronimo welcomed me with open arms. We went through some old papers and compared notes on how we were duped by the government." He seemed exalted by the meeting.

ON THE last day of Newton's sentence, August 23, 1988, he announced to the media that Pratt's conviction was an outrage and insisted that he wouldn't leave the penitentiary without him.

Geronimo was summoned to the warden's office to arbitrate, a familiar role. When he was told what was happening, he smiled at Newton and said, "Huey, get your jive ass outa here."

"Fuck that," Newton replied. "I know what I'm doing."

Four days later, still arguing, the former minister of defense was propelled out the front gate like a drunk on a bouncer's toe. At a hurried press conference he confessed to Bay Area reporters that if he'd supported Geronimo eighteen years earlier "he wouldn't be in prison today." He seemed ashamed of himself but pleased that "Geronimo was touched by the gesture I made."

The *San Francisco Chronicle*'s article belatedly described "anonymous poison pen letters smearing Geronimo's character" and FBI agents who deliberately caused "dissension among Panther leaders." It was headlined HOW HUEY NEWTON LET A PANTHER DOWN.

The Insolence of Office

In the spring of 1989 Pratt was summoned to the warden's office and told that he'd been subpoenaed to testify at a trial in San Juan, Puerto Rico. A revolutionary member of Los Macheteros[62] was charged with shooting two FBI agents.

"They consider you an expert on governmental misconduct," an assistant warden told him. "They think you're gonna save some terrorist's ass. It's your call. You don't have to go." The man's own feelings were evident.

"I'll go," Geronimo said. Any break from the prison tedium was welcome.

Waiting for the transport crew, he was visited by A. Lynne Atkinson. "Well, well," his ex-counselor said with a big grin, "it's Mr. Lucky. You're back on my caseload."

"What?"

"Institutional fuckup. You know how the left hand doesn't know what the right hand is doing? In this lunatic asylum the left hand doesn't know what the *left* hand is doing."

She recounted a conversation she'd had with a friend on the senior

---

[62] Loosely, "the Machete Men."

staff. He'd told her that the only sensible course was to refuse the assignment. She'd replied that she'd read the transcript of the parole hearing, that it was "a pack of lies," and she intended to "put a bunch of these assholes behind bars."

When Geronimo realized that Atkinson was serious, he said, "Lynne, be cool. Don't get yourself fired on my account."

"If somebody's gonna get fired," she promised, "it won't be me."

AFTER A half dozen stops the transcontinental leg of the flight to Puerto Rico ended at a federal detention center in Miami. Overnighting in a bare holding cell, Pratt learned that he could anticipate no more gestures of support from Huey P. Newton. The former minister of defense had been shot outside a West Oakland crack house. The killer, a low-level crack peddler, told police he'd never heard of Huey P. Newton. Geronimo was saddened by the ignominious death.

At San Juan he was led from the government Learjet to find the terminal cordoned off. Soldiers with drawn side arms lined his route to an armor-plated van. "I've never seen security like this in Puerto Rico," the U.S. marshal told him.

Geronimo asked, "Who are they expecting?"

"You."

As the armored car slowed to approach the infamous "White Elephant" jail, lines of nationalist demonstrators jogged alongside, shouting and waving signs: WELCOME GERONIMO. BIENVENIDOS.

"You could run for office here," one of the escorts told him. Geronimo realized that despite the passage of almost two decades he was still considered a revolutionary. He took it as a compliment.

THE TRIAL proved anticlimactic; the defendant was freed without benefit of Geronimo's testimony. The return flight from San Juan to Miami turned into a torture test. "Having a nice spring break?" one of the marshals asked as he cinched the shackles hard. An African American guard said, "We don't like flying your ass all over the country. Who the fuck are *you?*"

In the federal detention center in Miami Pratt was assigned to a cellblock with millionaire drug lords, most of them from Colombia. After several days a counselor told him to be patient; "we lost your travel orders."

He remained for a month, incommunicado. Then he was driven to the

Miami airport and padlocked to a "black box," a block of steel that kept his handcuffed wrists apart. In his moves within the prison system Pratt had seen only one other black-boxed prisoner, an inmate from the super-maximum security facility at Marion, Illinois, who was being transferred for inciting a riot.

The device was uncomfortable at first and then downright painful. "You can't scratch your nose. It cuts into your wrist. I'll feel that pain for the rest of my life. The black box is used on the badasses. Everybody shies away from you. You're considered too dangerous."

He checked out his fellow prisoners as they boarded the shuttle. He was the only one with a black box. "Why'd you put this thing on me?" he asked a guard.

"We got word on you from the coast."

Geronimo learned later that the California Department of Corrections had transmitted a copy of his prison record showing three escapes, the attempted murder of two guards, a cop killing in Los Angeles, a failed attempt to hijack a school bus and a poison dart plot.

AIRBORNE FROM Miami in a DC-3 confiscated from drug dealers, Pratt was told that he was on a prisoner shuttle and it might take weeks to return him to San Quentin. The droopy old plane picked up and dropped inmates at various federal institutions and ran on a loose schedule. He missed Ashaki, Shona and little Hiroji. He wanted to read Lynne Atkinson's new parole report before she turned it in. He needed to talk law, politics, philosophy and sex with Stuart Hanlon. He didn't see why it should take so long to fly cross-country.

The next leg of the flight ended at Birmingham, and a bus hauled the prisoners to the federal lockup at Talladega. A white marshal said, "Who is *this* asshole?" She beckoned with her index finger and said, "C'mere, black box."

She grabbed his chain and jerked him around. The steel edges cut into his wrists. He said, "Miss, you don't even know me."

"You got a black box, man."

There was no way to resist. To the marshals he was federal number 14940054, a rogue jailbreaker and child kidnapper with fewer rights than a condemned man on death row. Keep your mouth shut, he warned himself. This is one fight you won't win. It's only for a few hours.

Three days later he was awakened at 4:00 A.M., locked into belly chains and the black box, and hauled to the airport for the next leg of the airlift. After two more weeks in the hole at a detention center in El Reno, Oklahoma, he was flown to Lexington, then to Terre Haute, then to Phoenix (where he slept in chains in a corridor because of overcrowding), and then to Denver. After a month in transit he arrived at San Quentin and was immediately thrown in the hole. He spent two days in baffled silence before being transported to New Folsom, an addition to the old penitentiary. From a trusty he learned that the CDC and its functionaries had been taking slow revenge on Lynne Atkinson. The Vietnam Veterans of San Quentin, one of her favorite projects, was on a probationary basis. Of its coleader, an assistant warden had said, "Those vets are supposed to be patriotic, but that goddamn Pratt goes all the way to Puerto Rico to testify for a terrorist."

Geronimo realized that his trip had been politically incorrect and he would have to pay. Before reaching San Juan he'd had enough influence to help the administration run the penitentiary but not enough to threaten its autonomy. The widely publicized federal trial had given him too much cachet. The hole at New Folsom was the CDC's first move in trimming him to size. He stayed awake for three days and nights, preparing to defend himself against another setup. He was forty-one now, his insides still hurt from his shrapnel wounds, and he'd almost forgotten how to chant.

"Glad to see you back with us, Mr. Geronimo," a black guard said after prodding him in the ribs with an ax handle. "We been waiting for ya. Kidnapped any kids lately?"

WHEN STUART Hanlon learned of the new developments, he sped the eighty miles to Folsom. He expected to be escorted from one wing to another, but the guards directed him to cross the open yard alone. As he took his first hesitant steps, he heard tittering behind a barrier. I'm dead meat if I go, he said to himself, and I'm dead meat if I don't.

A black inmate the size of a Volkswagen blocked his path. "Who the fuck are you, little man?"

"I'm Geronimo Pratt's attorney."

"It's Geronimo's lawyer!" the inmate yelled. "You just wait right here." An honor guard of prisoners, black and white, provided safe passage.

Pratt slapped his friend's open hand and said, "Man, you're lucky to be alive. I hear they made you walk across the yard."

Hanlon told him not to worry. "How about you? Are you in danger?"

"I don't think there's a prisoner in Folsom that would make a move on me," he replied. "But . . . the guards? I'm not so sure. They still think I tried to kill their kids."

TOGETHER WITH Valerie West, staff counsel of the Partisan Defense Committee, Hanlon filed an emergency civil rights action in federal court in San Francisco, charging that the punitive transfer to New Folsom, combined with the demonic mythology that remained in Pratt's central file, placed him in continual danger.

"We *had* to bring a lawsuit," Hanlon told reporters. "We couldn't let the CDC kill him in prison."

The defendants were State Corrections Director James Rowland, the wardens of Folsom and San Quentin, and other CDC officials. In court papers Hanlon and West pointed out that Pratt, "because of his good behavior and genial demeanor," had enjoyed low-level security status, had been allowed conjugal visits and had worked outside the walls. But now the CDC was cracking down on him again, and for spurious reasons.

At a hearing in September 1989 Pratt testified before U.S. District Judge Stanley Weigel that he'd been threatened with death by some of the older Folsom guards and would prefer the hole at San Quentin. Judge Weigel declared the transfer to Folsom retaliatory and issued a preliminary injunction. Attorneys for the state enraged Hanlon by asking for a stay while they appealed the ruling—"Just long enough to get him killed, huh?" he snapped at an assistant attorney general. The judge denied the state's request. The *Los Angeles Times* reported, "The courtroom, crowded with Pratt supporters, erupted into applause."

TWO DAYS later Geronimo was returned to San Quentin and assigned to solitary confinement. His thin mattress had been drenched with insect repellent, and he slept on the floor. In the daytime female guards trooped by to ogle him as he used the toilet. He felt like an exhibit in a zoo.

When Hanlon got word of the continuing mistreatment, he headed straight for the San Quentin administrative offices. They were off-limits to the public, but he'd never considered himself the public. "I asked 'em why Geronimo was put in solitary the day he got back from New Folsom. Nobody wanted to talk about it. Then one of the clerks handed me a slip of paper. It said that Geronimo was in the hole 'to protect the integrity of an administrative investigation.' "

Hanlon asked an assistant warden what the words meant. He was taken into a side office and informed that a major probe was in progress and that it involved the parole board, prison staff, Geronimo Pratt and a counselor. The counselor's name was A. Lynne Atkinson.

Atkinson vs. Q: Round Two

Prison officials who'd expected the red-haired counselor's second "life prisoner evaluation" of Geronimo Pratt to be a craven retreat from her first were disabused by her opening sentence: "My last report to the Bureau of Prison Terms dated 5–4–87 stands as written with no modification and should be read for complete understanding of Pratt's case."

Under a section reserved for "Offense Summary," she wrote, "Pratt states that he is innocent. See BPT report of 5–4–87 for accurate delineation of Pratt's position." In the section reserved for "Aggravating Circumstances," she wrote, "Remains unchanged from the 5–4–87 report." In the next section, marked "Mitigating Circumstances," she wrote, "See 5–4–87 report."

By the end of page one, Atkinson had made it clear that she was standing her ground. She noted that Pratt had been disciplinary-free for three years, upgraded his education and was active in self-help and therapy programming. "Pratt is the impetus behind the creation of the Vietnam Veterans Group, now over two years old. This group is the single most positive self-help program in this institution. As one of the sponsors, I have personally witnessed these men healing the psychic wounds inflicted by that war."

She quoted from his most recent psychiatric examination, by Ranald Bruce, M.D., in mid-1987:

History and test results do not support a diagnosis of antisocial personality or any other personality disorder or any form of marked psychological disturbance or any compelling indications of a high or even moderate potential for violence. . . . Mr. Pratt demonstrates no clear evidence of character pathology, neurotic symptoms, affective or cognitive disturbance or other manifest psychological difficulties. . . .

On August 17, 1989, two days after Atkinson turned in her new report, the Board of Prison Terms held a brief session, with Pratt and Hanlon absent by choice. A radio reporter and an Associated Press correspondent listened as the three commissioners dispensed with the Atkinson recommendations without comment, then read and reread the official CDC version of the tennis court murder ("The crime for which this prisoner was committed to prison exhibits a callous disregard for the lives of others and was particularly heinous, atrocious and cruel").

An emissary from the Los Angeles D.A.'s Office made the obligatory statement about the "cruel, callous and senseless murder" of Caroline Olsen. In the personal style pioneered by Richard Kalustian, Deputy D.A. Fred Horn tacked on a poignant vignette of his own:

> I had the opportunity just last week . . . to speak with the police officer who happened to be the police officer that was the first officer on the scene of this crime when it was committed, the night of the shooting. His words to me were that he remembers it distinctly as if it happened yesterday. He remembers consoling the female victim that died, actually holding her in his arms and listening to her statements being, "Why did they do it? We gave them everything they wanted." . . .

After the usual pro forma recess for deliberations, Presiding Commissioner David E. Brown announced that the board was denying Geronimo Pratt parole for two more years. Then Brown dictated an angry note to his boss, Robert Patterson, executive officer of the Board of Prison Terms:

> This is to advise you that the hearing panel of D. Brown, R. Castro, and E. Tong found the attached board record [by Lynne Atkinson] to be inappropriate and totally inadequate for the purpose for which board reports are used in life parole consideration hearings. Specifically, the board report was deficient in its failure to properly address the following issues:
> 1) Statement of Facts. (Report cited alleged facts which were not part of the record)

2) Postconviction Factors. (Cited insufficient facts and included inappropriate arguments against the recommendations of a previous hearing panel)

3) Psychiatric Issues. (Psychiatric issues should be addressed only by professional psychiatric staff and not by a lay correctional counselor)

This report was not only worthless, as far as the hearing panel was concerned, but by failing to include sufficient facts made the decision making process more difficult for the hearing panel. The panel would like for this matter to be brought to the attention of San Quentin staff.

Patterson forwarded the message to San Quentin Warden Dan Vasquez and added a comment that the Atkinson report was "deficient and biased. It appears that the correctional counselor has lost her objectivity and significantly over-identifies with the prisoner. . . . The Board believes and expects that a more balanced report will be provided for the next hearing."

THROUGH HER network of friends Atkinson learned that the CDC was irate about an op-ed column in the *San Francisco Chronicle* by Warren Hinckle, an iconoclastic Bay Area reporter who was as famous for his black eye patch as for his fierce dedication to lost causes. The column began:

> Somebody should make a movie out of the childish harassment and bureaucratic torture by the State of California of Geronimo Pratt, the last surviving prisoner of the '60s. . . . [It would be] a heroic story of Lynne Atkinson, a career counselor of the California Department of Corrections who has upset the gooney birds in charge there by giving Pratt positive evaluations. . . . She might as well have been whistling in the wind. . . . The Board of Prison Terms flat out rejected Pratt's bid for parole . . . on grounds that Pratt was a dangerous and immature fellow. . . . The board not only disregarded Atkinson's evaluation of the prisoner, but also psychiatric evaluations of Pratt prepared by state shrinks. . . . It seems that any employee of the sovereign state of California who disagrees with the fixed idea that Geronimo Pratt is a satellite of the devil will be ignored.

Atkinson looked up the article and said to herself, That's it! Geronimo will be transferred out of Quentin and I'll be fired. We might as well pack our bags.

"They didn't have the guts to fire me," she recalled later, "so they tried to administer death by gossip. They said that Geronimo and I had been having sex for years. In their pea brains, a female couldn't be motivated by truth and justice, only by sex. They tried to bribe a black inmate into saying that Geronimo and I had a relationship. They promised him a transfer to a lower security institution. He didn't take the bait. One day I was talking to a sergeant when his phone rang. I heard him say, 'Well, that's a goddamn lie! She's standing right here.' I said, 'What was *that?*' He said it was a prison official saying I was up on the fifth tier having sex with Geronimo *right now.* When I ran into the official later, I said, 'Listen, you dumb son of a bitch, any reports you hear of my heavy breathing, it's asthma.' He turned fuchsia. Next thing I knew I was assigned to an inner office with a couple of chain-smokers."

After she was demoted to guard, two ranks below counselor and one rank below her starting rank of sergeant six years earlier, she contested the action in one of the longest personnel board hearings in California history.[63] She lost her appeal and was assigned to a series of menial jobs—running the laundry, working in the gardens, escorting prisoners. For a while she was the only master's degree holder serving food. Her "outstanding" performance evaluations continued until one of her supervisors was threatened with demotion for overstating her qualities. Then the ratings began to slide.

When it appeared that she was still being welcomed in her perambulations about the prison, she was assigned a Mini-14 rifle and posted to a bubblegun, a metal shanty high up on the inside of the prison wall. She was informed that if she left the bubblegun except while going to and from duty, she would be fired.

For eight hours each day she scrunched herself into a half-sitting position and surveyed the yard below. The roof leaked in rainstorms, and the damp winds off San Francisco Bay triggered her asthma. When she used the portable toilet, she had to place flattened cardboard boxes around the lower half of the compartment for privacy.

She'd been working the bubblegun for several months when a sudden thought made her giggle. Me and Geronimo, we're some romantic couple. We're both in solitary. . . .

---

[63] She learned later that FBI files about the Pratt case had been shown to the personnel judge ex parte.

AFTER ANOTHER year of harassment the Illinois farm girl resigned her post and brought a sexual discrimination suit against the state, settling on the courthouse steps for $100,000 just before the case was scheduled for trial. She paid off her bills, bought another Siamese cat and flew to South Africa to ask Nelson Mandela to intervene for Pratt with the U.S. Department of State.

On the day scheduled for their meeting, Mandela had to make an emergency trip to the Angola-Namibia border, but his secretary assured her that he'd been following the case via her reports and backed her cause.[64]

Atkinson considered briefing Pratt on her trip, but elected to drop out of his life instead. "If I showed up in the reception area, I knew I'd be treated like a convict's floozy—strip-searched, insulted, humiliated, the whole goddamn deal. They'd already accused me of having sex with him, and I didn't want to give them a chance to lie about me again."

The plainspoken little pepper pot would see Geronimo Pratt one more time, but only from a distance.

---

[64] Later Mandela wrote letters of support for Pratt to the African National Congress and other organizations.

Exile Again

When some of the chatter and dissension began to subside inside the walls, the California Department of Corrections quietly dissolved the Vietnam Veterans of San Quentin. Pratt and the other cofounder, Sneaky White, were ordered to pack their bags.

After a wake-up call at 3:00 A.M. and a jouncing ride chained to a stanchion in the back of a van, Geronimo found himself in the company of 5,500 felons in the California Correctional Institution at Tehachapi, 350 miles southeast of San Francisco. The earthquake-shattered facility had been rebuilt, but inmates lived in a permanent haze of stone dust in the thin air of the four-thousand-foot altitude. When Geronimo began to wheeze during his cellisthenics, he realized that his new residence would take some acclimatizing.

STUART HANLON learned to dread the seven-hour drive across the dispiriting countryside, through Bakersfield with its acres of oil derricks and pumping jacks and on to the penal institution nine miles southeast of the little town of Tehachapi. The prison was set in a range of brushy hills and low granitic mountains where the locals raised daffodils, gladioli, Fuji apples, cattle, ostriches, rodeo cowboys and prison guards. Hanlon had never felt comfortable in landlocked towns, and some of the locals were a little rough-hewn for his tastes. The Tehachapi staffers seemed more openly racist than the personnel at other state prisons.

On one of his first visits he was accompanied by Valerie West of the Partisan Defense Committee, a hardworking Pratt advocate. When they joined Geronimo in an attorney's room, Hanlon bought a bag of potato chips from a dispensing machine. "No, no!" a guard called out. "The legal room's for work. You can't eat in here."

"You're full of shit," Hanlon said with his usual diplomacy. "The rules say we can share machine food."

"Give it a try. If you eat, I'll lock you up."

An hour or so later, in the middle of an intense planning session about another petition of habeas corpus, West absentmindedly picked up a potato chip. The guard terminated the visit and escorted her to a holding cell. "We drove all day to get here!" Hanlon protested.

The irate lawyers took the matter to U.S. District Judge Stanley Weigel in San Francisco, who was still considering Pratt's claim against the CDC for discriminatory practices. Once again the old judge ruled for the prisoner, castigating Tehachapi officials for violating the spirit of attorney-client visitation rules. It would always remain in Hanlon's memory as "the potato chip caper."

BY NEW YEAR'S DAY 1990 Pratt was approaching his twentieth year of incarceration and Hanlon was in his fifteenth year on the case. In the two decades since the original arrest, Geronimo had become an anachronism. Radical protest had faded from style in the Reagan era, and many of Pratt's fellow Panthers had exchanged side arms and berets for attaché cases and cell phones. The young men who'd fought alongside Columbia student Hanlon in the battle of Morningside Heights now drove BMWs and read the *Wall Street Journal*.

Geronimo had been accustomed to meeting with his lawyer three or four times a week at San Quentin, but now they seldom saw each other. Sometimes Pratt seemed resentful, and Hanlon tried to understand. "In an average year Geronimo took up a third of my practice. I was still doing too much pro bono and my annual billings were never more than $50,000. Kathy and I had two sons—Liam and Rory—and thank God she'd built up a good practice of her own. But she always had time for Geronimo. I never wrote a single pleading that she didn't improve. It was as though the Hanlon family was a cottage industry and our product was the Pratt case. I would make that long drive to Tehachapi and try to explain all this to him, but he never quite understood. He seemed to think I should visit him two or three times a week, and if I wasn't actually at his side in the visiting room, I'd abandoned him.

"At first I thought it was a problem of ego. But then I realized it was something more familiar, something common to long-term prisoners. They start getting obsessed with control—the need for it, the lack of it. They're told when to eat, sleep, shower and shave. They're told when they can have visitors and when they can't and when they can use the phone and for how long. Imagine a life where you're almost totally helpless. A lot of my problems with G came down to that, and it led to some arguments. I was happy to let him feel he was running the show, but now and then it got ugly."

HANLON KEPT in close touch with Johnnie Cochran, but neither could decide on a next step. Late at night he would phone Cochran in New York or Miami or wherever his expanding clientele had taken him.

"We spent hundreds of bucks on long distance feeling sorry for ourselves," Cochran recalled. "This case was killing us. I swear, we took it harder than Geronimo. He's the strongest man I've ever met. And Hanlon's a close second. I've never seen a lawyer fight for his client as long and as hard as Stu. We still faced the same old mystery. For years we'd been coming up with overpowering evidence and overpowering law, taking it into court—and losing."

The Pratt attorneys wondered how long their client could survive the strain without permanent psychological damage.

"I can't sleep," Geronimo complained after he'd been at his new address for two months. "The wind blows right down that valley the way it used to come off the Vietnam highlands. Every time I hear a helicopter I duck."

His lawyers arranged for an examination by a private psychologist. After one meeting Paul Koller, Ph.D., reported that the client appeared to be experiencing "dissociative experiences." In a battery of tests including the Rorschach inkblot and Minnesota Multiphasic Personality Inventory, the psychologist found "symptoms of intrusive imagery, nightmares and night terrors, amnesia for several combat experiences, a startle response and hypervigilance." They were all part of the PTSD syndrome. Koller noted that

Pratt's "intense idealism and preoccupation with justice and fairness" were common in combat veterans under stress.

"I think it's catching," Hanlon told Pratt at Tehachapi after they discussed the report. "I've been feeling depressed as hell."

"What's the matter, man?"

Hanlon said that he was beginning to doubt his own approach to the case. "I'm not sure I'm giving you the representation you deserve. I've won a string of trials, but I can't seem to win for you. Cochran thinks it's time we filed another petition for habeas corpus. Well, we already got slapped in the mouth three times. How many goddamn writs can we file? And what're we gonna use for new evidence?"

BY 1991 Hanlon had become one of the Bay Area's best-known criminal attorneys, specializing in freeing the unjustly convicted. Korean American Chol Soo Lee had been convicted of a murder he didn't commit; at a second trial Hanlon gained his release. He represented the controversial Symbionese Liberation Army leader Russell Little and other high-profile clients. The Pratt tragedy was as frustrating to him as it was to Cochran.

"I think I may be out of ideas," he confessed to Geronimo.

"We've been together a long time," Pratt said softly. "I understand, man."

"You're my number one client, G. But maybe I should take a backseat for a while."

Geronimo looked stricken. "A backseat to *who?*"

"Well, yeah, that's the problem."

Fresh Blood

Home again, Hanlon took a friendly phone call from an old New York friend, Robert Bloom, a crusading lawyer who was known for his successful defense of ex-Panther Richard Dhoruba Moore. Bloom was a hands-on operator who sometimes appeared in a "Free Nelson Mandela" T-shirt and put impassioned messages on his telephone answering machine about the sorry state of race relations in the United States. In a case with close parallels to Pratt's, Dhoruba Moore had claimed that he was set up by the New York City Police Department and COINTELPRO for shooting two officers. He'd served nineteen years in prison before he was freed.

"Where the hell are you calling from, Bobby?" Hanlon asked.

"I needed a change of scene. I moved to Berkeley."

"You're . . . across the bay?"

"Yep."

Hanlon told him to sit tight. "I'll be right over. I got something that might interest you."

WITHIN A WEEK Robert Bloom had signed onto the Pratt defense team. He hauled twenty-five boxes of legal material across the Bay Bridge and set to work with sharpened pencils and legal pads. With each promising discovery, he phoned Hanlon, only to be told that the courts had already ruled on the item and found it insufficient. "We need *new* grounds, Bobby," Hanlon reminded him.

The idealistic Bloom dug into the files for six months, then drove 280 miles north to Pelican Bay State Prison in the old logging town of Crescent City to interview William Tyrone Hutchinson. Under patient questioning the lanky former Panther revealed what he'd told police years earlier: that he'd heard his boyhood friends Swilley and Hatter admit that they'd been at the tennis court on the murder night. "They described a man and a woman shaking in fear and crying just before they were shot. They referred to the people as 'pigs.' They were laughing about it."

SLOGGING THROUGH the massive record, Bloom found some of Richard Kalustian's handwritten trial notes, subpoenaed in earlier actions but largely overlooked by the Pratt legal team. During a pretrial interview with LAPD Sergeant DuWayne Rice, Kalustian had written that Rice had been "trying to get info from JB [Julius Butler] for about 1–2 yrs." The deputy D.A.'s notes revealed that in August 1969 "JB delivered the letter. JB said 'these guys are after me and I may get killed. If something happens to me I want you to read this letter & give it to my mother.' "

Bloom wondered about the phrase "trying to get info." Did it mean that Sergeant Rice had been attempting to recruit Butler as his informer? *Did he succeed?* In Kalustian's notes the question went unanswered.

A phrase near the end seemed more promising: "It all began when FBI saw JB give letter to R[ice]. They asked for letter and R refused to give it. R told FBI they could get it by making official request from Dept. They didn't."

Bloom wondered what Kalustian meant by "it all began." The beginning of an FBI-LAPD plot to "neutralize" Pratt? The frame-up? *The whole case?*

A line from the original trial clicked in Bloom's mind, but it took him hours to relocate it in the thousands of pages of testimony he'd borrowed from Hanlon's office. In Kalustian's cross-examination of a Panther named Michael David Pennewell, the deputy D.A. had told the witness, "The FBI's never been involved in this case, and you know it."

Well, Bloom thought, if "it all began" with FBI agents observing the transfer of the letter, how could Kalustian say in court that the FBI had "never been involved"? He wondered what an impartial judge would make of the contradiction.

Bloom recalled that DuWayne Rice had spoken highly of his supervisor and fellow African American, Captain Ed Henry, whose safe had held the controversial Butler letter for more than a year. In a revealing interview Henry told Bloom that he felt "bad" about Geronimo Pratt and that the case still troubled him. The retired captain recalled that Julius "Julio" Butler had been an informant for the Los Angeles Police Department from 1966 to 1969, encompassing the years of the Bunchy Carter/John Huggins killings and the tennis court murder. Butler had provided useful information on community unrest and the Black Panthers.

Henry mentioned other activities by "the mayor of Adams Boulevard." Twice Butler had turned in illegal firearms, including two automatic rifles and a Thompson submachine gun, plus a thousand rounds of .45-caliber ammunition. Asked if Butler had acted as an agent provocateur on behalf of the LAPD, Henry said, "In effect, yes. My thoughts at the time were that I didn't think Julius Butler cared what happened to the Panthers."

Bloom left the interview session carrying a signed declaration in his briefcase. It was good evidence that Butler had lied on the witness stand, but it wasn't positive proof. He would have to keep looking.

AT A SAN FRANCISCO cocktail party the transplanted New Yorker fell into conversation with Patricia Richartz, an investigator and paralegal. Bloom told her that he was working on the Pratt case and listened politely as she recounted her own connection. Her boss, Panther attorney Charles Garry, had won a 1975 court order admitting him to the FBI's wiretap record room in San Francisco's Federal Building. Garry had sent Richartz and another investigator to peruse the logs. She told Bloom that she'd seen an entry that specifically placed Pratt in Oakland on the night of the tennis court murder.

Bloom said, "Are you sure?"

"Positive."

"My God, Pat, why didn't you tell somebody?"

Richartz said she'd been under the impression that Pratt's team already had the information. "It was in plain sight," she said.

Bloom remembered former FBI agent Wesley Swearingen's shock at finding that the wiretap logs had disappeared. "It's not in plain sight anymore," he told Richartz.

In a sworn declaration prepared for Bloom and Hanlon, the female private investigator said that she and investigator David Fechheimer had gone to the Federal Building in May 1975 and were ushered into a small room.

. . . During our examination of the wiretap logs, I observed a particular entry that reflected that at 5:30 PM on December 18, 1968, a female made a telephone call to what was known as the Santa Rosa house in Oakland, Calif., and that she had a conversation with Geronimo at that time while Geronimo was at the Santa Rosa house. . . . I recall that there was at least one FBI agent in the room with us at the time I noticed this entry. We were not permitted to remove any documents from the room and I assumed that he was present to make certain that no documents were removed. I pointed out the entry to Mr. Fechheimer and he looked at it, but we did not discuss it at that time because of the presence of the FBI agent in the room. We did discuss it later. The building that was the subject of the wiretap was known as the Santa Rosa house because it was located on Santa Rosa Street in Oakland. It was the location where Bobby Seale, one of the Black Panther leaders, was staying at that time.

In her declaration Richartz took pains to explain why she hadn't revealed the information until meeting Robert Bloom at a party:

I did not realize the importance of the log entry that I had seen because I was not aware that proof of the entries in the Los Angeles wiretap were not available during prior litigation. I had always believed that the materials had been available to Geronimo and the Courts, but that the Courts had declined to grant relief for reasons related to Geronimo's inability to prove that state authorities were aware of the federal wiretaps. That position made no sense to me, but it is the position I (mistakenly) believed that Courts had taken.

Mr. Bloom also explained to me that the main witness for the prosecution, Julius Butler, had testified that Geronimo had seen him face to face and spoken to him at his shop in central Los Angeles just prior to the crime. . . . It is clear that the wiretap log entry that I saw with Mr. Fechheimer conclusively . . . proves that Mr. Butler had to be lying about Geronimo speaking to him in central Los Angeles. . . . Had I known the true circumstances, I would have spoken to Geronimo's attorneys long ago.

Her colleague David Fechheimer's affidavit confirmed every detail of the visit.

ENCOURAGED BY the new information, Bloom sortied to the dangerous streets of the Oakland ghetto and interviewed three of the Panther leaders who'd deliberately remained silent about the Pratt case. David Hilliard, former Panther chief of staff, admitted carrying "feelings of guilt and remorse since my refusal to help Geronimo in 1972." He said he had a clear memory of Pratt's stay in Oakland. His sworn declaration verified that Geronimo had attended a party meeting on the night of the Santa Monica killing—a meeting Hilliard believed was at his home.

Bobby Seale, cofounder of the BPP, recalled the same scene: "I knew, of course, that Geronimo could not have committed this crime . . . I felt very conflicted about testifying . . . but I followed the directive of the party."

Emory Douglas, former Panther minister of culture, attributed his own long silence to Huey Newton's warning "not to associate or help Geronimo in any way."

In the next few days the busy Bloom collected three more declarations: from Seale's brother John, Landon Williams and Harvey McClendon. All confirmed Pratt's presence in Oakland on the evening of the crime.

Stuart Hanlon and Johnnie Cochran were ecstatic about Bloom's new evidence. "This is it, Stu," Cochran said in a call from Los Angeles. "This is what we need to go back to court."

"I told Geronimo we needed fresh blood," Hanlon told his colleague. "After all these years, wouldn't it be something if my biggest contribution was Bobby Bloom?"

WITH A little help from Pratt's two veteran counselors, Bloom produced a 147-page petition for writ of habeas corpus and attached 300 pages of exhibits, including the Fechheimer, Richartz and Henry statements. Bloom quoted juror Jeanne Hamilton as complaining that a member of the jury had exerted undue pressure on her and another juror outside the deliberation room, in itself an argument for a new trial. As for Julius Carl Butler, Bloom abandoned formal legalese and said simply, "Documents show that this man is a liar."

To Hanlon and Cochran the petition seemed a little long on left-wing philosophy, but that was a matter of personal style. "It wouldn't have been Bobby without the polemics," Hanlon said. "He wasn't a civil rights attorney just in the courtroom. He ate the subject, lived it and breathed it. And his record spoke for itself."

THIS TIME around, the Pratt legal team decided to bypass the Los Angeles courts and file its petition for habeas corpus in San Francisco. Cochran explained: "When you go to court in L.A., the odds are that the judge is a former deputy D.A. It's an old boys' club, and the last thing those guys are gonna do is rule against each other. Dick Kalustian was not only an ex-D.A. but a sitting judge in the same jurisdiction. How could Geronimo get justice in L.A.?"

Late on Sunday, June 2, 1991, Hanlon read the final version of the Bloom petition to his client in Tehachapi. Geronimo hadn't been enthusiastic about Bloom personally, partly because the old-school lawyer from New York didn't believe in hand-holding his clients and partly because both men were opinionated hardheads, but he was impressed by Bloom's dedication and research. "That's heavy stuff, Stu," he said. "How the hell can the courts turn this down?"

Hanlon said, "I don't know, G." He was thinking, Let me count the ways . . .

THE NEXT afternoon's *San Francisco Examiner* proclaimed, PRATT'S LAWYERS SAY THEY HAVE NEW EVIDENCE. FORMER PANTHER 'FRAMED' BY FBI, L.A. COPS IN '68 MURDER, THEY SAY. The morning *Chronicle* of June 4 headlined, LAWYER'S SURPRISE IN BLACK PANTHER CASE. NEW EVIDENCE PUTS PRATT FAR FROM MURDER SITE. Both articles ran long. California was beginning to pay attention.

TWENTY-FOUR DAYS after the habeas corpus petition was filed in San Francisco Superior Court, Hanlon and Bloom received a single typewritten page entitled "In re: Petition of Elmer 'Geronimo' Pratt, for a writ of habeas corpus: order to show cause." Their decorum slipped as they read the words:

> IT IS ORDERED that Mr. B. J. Bunnell, Warden of Tehachapi Prison of the California Department of Corrections, prepare a points and authorities to show cause before this Court . . . why the relief prayed for should not be granted. Respondent's return is to be filed on or before July 27, 1991.

At last Pratt's case would be argued before a neutral judge in a part of California where he'd received a fair press, hadn't been depicted as the prince of darkness, and was considered by many to be a living martyr. If his team prevailed, the next step would be an evidentiary hearing where the facts could be presented in their entirety, minus the restrictions that had hobbled the defense in earlier proceedings, both federal and state.

When Cochran heard the good news by phone, he told Hanlon, "You and Bloom can examine anybody you want, but Julius Butler is *mine.*"

A FEW days later the court clerk phoned the lawyers with unsettling news: the California attorney general had demanded the transfer of the petition to Los Angeles. "They're shopping for a friendly venue, of course," Cochran told Hanlon over the phone.

"How can we stop 'em?"

"It's an L.A. case, Stu. They have every right. It's up to the court."

San Francisco Superior Court judges were not unaware of the geographical issues. At their weekly procedural meeting they voted by a narrow margin to grant the attorney general's request. The case records were assembled and sent by registered mail, arriving in Los Angeles on August 14.

The next morning a Los Angeles judge delivered his ruling. In Robert Bloom's weighty collection of evidence, argument, documentation and scholarship, Superior Court Judge Gary Klausner, an alumnus of the D.A.'s Office, had found "insufficient grounds" to grant relief. Pratt and his lawyers were back where they started.

HANLON AND Bloom rushed into court in San Francisco to argue that their dire predictions had come true: once again the old-boy network in Los Angeles had denied their client due process of law. Hanlon told the court, "What we alleged would happen—that Mr. Pratt could not get a fair hearing there—actually *did* happen." His emergency petition for writ of habeas corpus was denied.

The City of Oakland responded to the dispiriting news with a proclamation declaring "Geronimo Pratt Day." Panther leaders who'd signed new affidavits for Pratt joined actor Danny Glover and other public figures at a meeting in Bethlehem Lutheran Church to denounce the latest ruling. The *Examiner* headlined its article FORMER PANTHERS SPEAK OUT FOR PRATT SUPPORTERS. SAY HIS MURDER CONVICTION WAS AN FBI SET-UP.

Encouraged by the support, Bloom, Hanlon and Cochran churned up more legal citations and references and asked the Second Appellate District Court of Appeal, the same bank of judges that had produced the L. Thaxton Hanson opinion, to order the lower court to reopen the case. The request was denied.

The Pratt team's last gasp was a petition for a writ of mandate to the friendlier First District Court of Appeal in San Francisco. Five members of the Congressional Black Caucus urged the justices to find for Pratt "on behalf of justice and equity." Coretta Scott King wrote, "Our nation cannot afford to tolerate another incident of gross racial injustice in the court system if our legal system is to have credibility for Americans of all races." The Reverend Jesse L. Jackson declared on behalf of his National Rainbow Coalition that it was an honor to join the crusade for justice for Geronimo. "I know it's dark," he wrote, "but Isaiah tells us the morning comes."

The First District Court denied the Pratt petition in a single sentence.

GERONIMO KEPT track of the losses in his cell at Tehachapi. "It's okay, Stu," he told his disconsolate lawyer by phone. But the latest courtroom setback was taken hard by every other Pratt except the matriarchal Eunice, who simply regarded the news as a suggestion from God that certain members of the family weren't praying hard enough.

Geronimo's older brother Jack had begun a new life: "teachin' and preachin'," including regular visits to the Morgan City Jail. Jack agreed with his mother and devout sister Jacqueline that "we can pray him out of prison," but the latest word from California gave him nightmares. "Suddenly I was in the hole with my brother. I couldn't take more than two or three steps. I tried to hug him but he was gone. I was locked down alone. I woke up screaming."

The Cal State graduate and computer expert confided to his mother, "I don't know if I can take it anymore. It's too hard, seeing Gerard in my dreams."

The eighty-five-year-old woman fixed her second-born son with a cold stare. *"You* don't know if *you* can take it?" she said. "Well, Gerard's taking it, isn't he? Listen to your mama: *every* great man had his time of trial, starting with Jesus. Your brother has to undergo the fire to make him strong. The Lord has *big* plans for Gerard Pratt."

Jack felt ashamed. "Yes, ma'am," he said. Even in the early stages of losing her mind, his mother made good sense.

New Centurion

The Reverend James McCloskey sat in his second-floor office above the signs for Talbot's Kids Shop and Edith's Lingerie on Nassau Street in Princeton and thought about God and Roger Keith Coleman. For fifteen years McCloskey and his Centurion Ministries had labored diligently for those he called "the imprisoned innocent." With his investigators he'd been responsible for freeing fourteen men and one woman. Roger Coleman, a dirt-poor coal miner who'd been convicted of murder in Grundy, Virginia, was one of his failures. McCloskey had battled the state of Virginia for years and was at the doomed man's side five minutes before his electrocution on May 20, 1992. The crusading minister had been so shaken that he checked himself into a retreat center in Pennsylvania to ponder the central questions: Where was God for Roger? How can there be a just and loving God when innocent men are put to death and there's so much suffering in the world?

It was an ancient religious question. Through the years theologians had labeled the paradoxical subject "theodicy" and produced libraries of answers, but none satisfied the troubled McCloskey. After a week of prayer and meditation he reached the same unsettling conclusion that he'd reached years before in Princeton Theological Seminary: the question of theodicy had no answer. "The only way Christ even touches on this subject is when he says very matter-of-factly in the Sermon on the Mount that the rain falls on the just and the unjust and the sun shines on the good and evil. Maybe that's not an answer. It's just the way it is."

Back in Centurion Ministries' office in the red brick building in New Jersey, he was just settling into his daily routine when the phone rang. A man named Robert Bloom was calling from California.

ONLY ONCE during his career had James McCloskey wasted his time and skimpy resources in an effort to free a person who later proved to be guilty. He'd resolved not to make the same mistake again and told Bloom that he wouldn't even consider the Geronimo Pratt case till he saw hard evidence. A copy of the unsuccessful petition for a writ of habeas corpus reached Princeton in two days, and the minister read it overnight in his monastic room on campus.

"It was highly polemical," he said later, "but good stuff. It definitely got my attention. I wondered what kind of judge could ignore something so persuasive."

The bulky transcript of the original 1972 trial arrived a few days later, and McCloskey read it in one gulp, his mood gradually darkening. "To me, that transcript was legal pornography. What the hell was wrong with the jury, the judge? Here you had two of the worst contaminants in our justice system: secondhand confession testimony, which usually comes from opportunists looking for a payoff, and inflated eyewitness identifications, which usually come from good people under the influence of bad cops and prosecutors. Julius Butler might as well have carried a sign: 'Snitch and Liar.' Barbara Reed and Kenneth Olsen were both dubious witnesses."

McCloskey noticed the varying physical characteristics that had been attributed to the shorter killer and drew up a list. At one time or another the shooter had been described as dark, light or medium dark. He was clean-shaven, wore a moustache and goatee or only a moustache. He had a "prominent" nose, a medium nose, a small nose or a "thin" nose. He had "normal" lips, thin lips or thick lips. He had no facial scars, one scar or two scars. His hairline was straight or he had a widow's peak. He wore an Eisenhower jacket, bush jacket, safari jacket, trench coat or sports jacket. After repeated conferences among witnesses, detectives and prosecutors, after long studies of suggestive photo lay-downs, and after a conspicuous failure to put Geronimo Pratt in a live show-up, the descriptions had blended into a homogenized finished product, suitable for courtroom use, enabling Kenneth

Olsen and Barbara Reed to point to the defense table and declare in ringing tones that the killer was the man sitting right over there.

In his work McCloskey had encountered the same phenomenon again and again. Prisons were dotted with men and women who'd been convicted after the authorities suborned perjury and distorted evidence to convict those they sincerely believed to be guilty. The more corrupt the tampering, the louder these public servants proclaimed later that they'd acted solely in the interests of justice. Sometimes McCloskey wished he'd studied more psychology.

AT THE suggestion of an old friend, CBS News producer Lowell Bergman of *60 Minutes,* the crusading minister flew to California to meet with Pratt. He was surprised at what he found. "I had this image of a fire-breathing Black Panther. But Geronimo was so moderate, so calm, so at peace with himself and the world. For the first time, I realized that the Panthers weren't really anti-white. He came across as completely non-racial. I said, 'Geronimo, how in the world did somebody like you end up in a place like this?' He told me it was because of his sins in Vietnam. He said, 'Reverend, I'm in hell because of what I did over there.' "

BEFORE MAKING a final commitment to the case, McCloskey consulted with someone he deeply respected. For three and a half years he'd worked with Los Angeles Deputy D.A. Peter Bozanich on a matter that helped to bring Centurion Ministries into national prominence. "Peter and I had met when I was looking at the case of Clarence Chance and Benny Powell, two Los Angeles African Americans who'd served seventeen years for murder. Ira Reiner was the D.A. at the time, and Peter convinced him to take another look at the case. No district attorney likes to second-guess his predecessors and run the risk of wasting the taxpayers' money. Peter laid his own job on the line and helped us convince Reiner that Benny and Clarence were innocent. Without a couple of conscientious guys like Peter Bozanich and Ira Reiner, they'd still be serving time.

"So I had lunch with Peter in L.A. He said, 'What're you working on?' I said, 'Geronimo Pratt.' His whole expression changed. He said, 'Why don't you tell that son of a bitch to serve his time and keep his damn mouth shut?' Right then and there I realized how much visceral hatred the D.A.'s bureaucracy had built up over the years. They hated Geronimo, they hated

Cochran and Hanlon, they hated *everybody* involved in that case. As close as Peter and I were, he still couldn't help reflecting that attitude. I thought, O my God, what am I getting into?"

That evening McCloskey phoned the Pratt attorneys and told them he would take the case. It was a big moment for Hanlon. "Jim McCloskey's name had come up several times. He was considered a saint by every prisoner in the country. Well, a saint was what we needed. He not only brought us new credibility, he also brought his own energy and talents. He's very strong-willed, very aggressive. Saint Jim brought us back to life."

Johnnie Cochran recalled later, "We were so grateful to Jim. I'd given it my best shot. So had Stu. And Bob Bloom added great stuff of his own—and we still got clobbered in court. Legally we had nowhere to go. Jim brought an aggressive new approach. Don't let that white collar fool you—the guy's a rottweiler. He gave us new life when we were down."

Gumshoe in a Collar

The Pratt team's ecclesiastical attack dog interviewed the three original jurors who now were convinced they'd returned the wrong verdict, then
traveled to Corcoran State Prison, near Bakersfield, where William Tyrone
Hutchinson confirmed earlier reports that his boyhood friends Hatter and
Swilley were the tennis court killers. McCloskey pressed for deep detail that
would be convincing in court. "Take me into their world, into *your* world,"
he insisted. "Tell me everything you can remember."

The skinny convict began by describing his own arrest for the shootings. He said he'd just returned to South-Central L.A. from a lengthy stay
in Seattle when a posse of ten lawmen converged on his mother's house.
Some identified themselves as members of the LAPD's Panther Unit and
some as FBI agents; it was another confirmation that the two agencies had
worked together on the case, contrary to claims at the 1972 trial and later.
Sergeant Raymond Callahan of the LAPD Criminal Conspiracy Section
seemed to be in charge of the interagency arrest team. Hutchinson remembered that the officers had treated him and his family with cold contempt. At L.A. County Jail he'd been subjected to a marathon interrogation,
and almost every question was about Geronimo Pratt. Hutchinson said that
after he'd named the real killers, Callahan warned him to "keep your mouth
shut about this if you know what's good for you." Even now, twenty-three

years after the interrogation, Hutchinson feared for his life. He told McCloskey, "Everybody in South-Central knows the LAPD can kill anybody they want and they'll never be punished. The cops squash black folks the way you and me step on ants." He said he was also afraid of reprisals from the parole board and prison officials if he cooperated with the Pratt team.

When the cleric asked for the names of others who might have been present in the Panther office the day Swilley and Hatter confessed to the tennis court shootings, Hutchinson turned reluctant. He explained that in South-Central Los Angeles the life expectancy of snitches was measured in days. Avengers had been known to strike deep inside prisons like Corcoran and Folsom. Some of Hutchinson's relatives still lived on the same block as relatives of the killers. There were gang affiliations to consider, family connections, old feuds and resentments. If inside information about the case were used indiscreetly, someone could die.

Five hours into the interview, Hutchinson finally gave up the names McCloskey needed: Harold Taylor, Thomas Holloway and William "Ying-Yang" Yankins. He also suggested that the minister pay a visit to his brother Dwight and promised to urge him to cooperate.

"In the end Tyrone Hutchinson was like a lot of other criminals I'd met," McCloskey said later. "He was basically a nice guy from a good family. Whatever crimes he'd committed, he retained some decency. Whatever beefs he had about the justice system, he still believed in justice. He wasn't especially fond of Geronimo Pratt, but he felt terrible that Pratt was doing somebody else's time. He showed a lot of courage, and so did his family. He gave me my first important affidavit."

McCLOSKEY DROVE his rental car to the South-Central ghetto to look for the men named by Hutchinson. It was a neighborhood of storefront churches, abandoned shops, stucco bungalows, burned-out shells of cars, sagging mansions, eucalyptus and ficus trees and front-porch displays of jacaranda, hibiscus and bird of paradise. At first the gumshoeing minister felt no fear. "You don't feel tension on a sunny day when you see neat houses with grass lawns and potted plants. South-Central was a battleground, but you couldn't smell the gunpowder till nighttime. I just barged right in. I never phone in advance; it's too easy to say no. I just walk up and knock. But I was careful not to wear my favorite red jacket. A few years earlier I'd knocked on a ghetto door and a woman with eyes as big as pancakes yanked me inside. 'Honey,' she says, 'don't you know where you are? You're in Crips territory—and you're dressed like a Blood!' "

The investigator cruised the battle zone known as South-Central[65] and found that few residents were willing to talk about Pratt, Swilley, Hatter, the Black Panthers or anything else. "It wasn't a case of 'Thank God you've come. We've been waiting for you.' These people had no reason to get involved with a stranger, especially a white one. Some of them had had trouble with the law or were related to criminals. They knew how politically charged the Pratt case was and how the cops and the D.A. felt about him. Their strongest instinct was fear of the LAPD. I didn't blame them for turning me away."

McCloskey phoned an interim report to the Pratt attorneys, then continued his blind canvass. "Every door and window in the ghetto had iron bars and dark heavy security grilles that you couldn't see through. You'd knock and this disembodied voice would say, 'Whattaya want?' If you said, 'I'm investigating a murder,' they'd say, 'Murder? What murder? We had four this weekend.' It was a spooky experience."

None of the locals knew the whereabouts of ex-Panther Thomas Holloway, one of the men named by Tyrone Hutchinson as a witness to the Swilley-Hatter confessions. Patient tracking led to William "Ying-Yang" Yankins and an angry rebuff. Weeks of field research produced the information that Harold Taylor now worked for an electric company in Florida. After a dozen phone calls, McCloskey connected with the Gulf Power Company and learned that a Harold Taylor was employed as a linesman in Panama City. It was a common name, but McCloskey wasted no time in booking a flight. He knocked on Taylor's apartment on Grace Avenue and was pleased to learn that the line repairman had heard about his investigation and was willing to help. McCloskey came away with his second affidavit:

> As a young teenager, I was raised on the 100 block of West 84th Street in Los Angeles. Larry "Dobey" Hatter and his family lived next door to me and my family. Larry Hatter and I grew up together and knew one another very well. I also knew Herbert Swilley extremely well. . . .
>
> Geronimo Pratt owned a 1967 Pontiac GTO red and white convertible car. The later part of 1968 and throughout 1969 this car was used

---

[65] Estimated population: 500,000, mostly African Americans and Hispanics.

by many different BPP members for whatever legitimate BPP business that needed to be done. . . . I personally saw Herbert Swilley drive this car on numerous occasions. Herbert never did have his own car.

Julio Butler liked Herbert Swilley a lot. They got along well together even though Julio was quite a bit older than Herbert. I have seen Julio and Herbert together often. I would frequently see them talking at the taco stand near the BPP headquarters on Central Avenue among other places. I remember one time when Herbert and I were selling BPP newspapers, Julio Butler drove up to us and gave a .45 automatic pistol to Herbert and told him to take it to the BPP office. No sooner had Butler driven off when police officers began approaching us. Herbert ran away in one direction, and I in another. This happened sometime shortly before Bunchy Carter's murder, probably in late December 1968.

Herbert Swilley and Larry Hatter were very close friends and criminal partners. They would do burglaries and "stick-ups" together. Herbert was what I would call a "stick up" man and Hatter's specialty was burglary. As section leader, it was my responsibility to make sure that members were performing the daily party functions. When I asked Herbert and Hatter one time when I saw them together why they weren't attending meetings and selling the party newspapers, they responded by saying, "We are working Santa Monica." I knew what they meant. They meant that they were doing their own business of burglaries and stick-ups. From my conversations with them, I know for sure that Herbert and Hatter were doing burglaries and stickups in Santa Monica for some time before the tennis court murder happened.

Herbert was the kind of person that if he stuck you up and you didn't have the kind of money he wanted, he'd shoot you out of anger. At the time of the tennis court murder in Santa Monica, I didn't put two and two together by thinking or suspecting that Hatter and Swilley might have done it. But later on at the BPP office at 84th and Broadway, I remember Herbert and Hatter talking about what happened on the tennis court in Santa Monica. All I can remember now is that they were laughing about what had happened. I don't remember specifically what they said at that time. I do remember that Thomas Holloway and Tyrone Hutchinson were with me when Swilley and Hatter were talking about it.

McCloskey flew back to Los Angeles and paid a cold call on Tyrone's brother. At forty-three Dwight Hutchinson had worked for the city of Los Angeles for almost twenty years, had a spotless record and still lived at home with his mother. After several lengthy discussions McCloskey came away with another affidavit:

> Herbert Swilley was a heavy drug user from at least 1968 until his death in 1972. . . . Part of Herbert's thing was to go around town robbing and killing drug dealers for their money. I remember one day when he wanted money so bad for dope that he attacked his own mother, broke his girlfriend's nose, and tried to drown his sister in their bathtub. I gave him $10 to quiet him down. . . .
>
> I have seen Herbert Swilley and Julio Butler together on a number of occasions before and after Bunchy Carter's murder. I remember seeing them standing together in front of the pool hall near 84th and Broadway. . . .
>
> Herbert and Dobey [Hatter] admitted to me that they shot people on a tennis court in Santa Monica. I knew that Santa Monica was a big place for Herbert and Dobey to do their thing, meaning burglaries and stick-ups. I think it was the day after those people were shot in Santa Monica when they told me this. I walked into the BPP office at 84th and Broadway. Dobey, Herbert, and Tom Holloway were talking and laughing. I asked them what was so funny.
>
> Thomas said, "These fools went out and shot and maybe killed some people."
>
> I said, "Where?"
>
> Tom said, "In Santa Monica."
>
> I said, "Where? On the beach?"
>
> Tom said, "No, on a tennis court."
>
> I turned to Herbert and Dobey and told them that what they did was bad for the Party, that it was against the Party rules. Herbert replied that "we got to liberate money somehow."

With the Swilley-Hatter connection nailed down, McCloskey turned to the matter of the mysterious FBI wiretaps. If it was true that somewhere in the agency's filing system there was a tape recording of Geronimo Pratt speaking from Oakland on the murder night, the case was won. McCloskey reread the earlier affidavits, then characteristically started at the beginning. Trustworthy police sources in Los Angeles insisted that local Panther headquarters had never been tapped. The Oakland police chief acknowledged a tap but claimed that no records were available. FBI sources continued to insist that their own bug hadn't been put in place in Oakland until after the tennis court incident.

McCloskey dug deeper and established that the Oakland P.D. had installed a telephone wiretap in the local Panther office in July 1968, two months before Pratt arrived in California, and that COINTELPRO agents had paid between $130 and $300 a month for transcripts of the conversations. The arrangement had lasted until February 1969, when the FBI put in its own wire. That meant that every key Panther conversation had been recorded. But . . . where were the tapes?

McCloskey conferred with Bloom, Cochran and Hanlon, and together they developed a new approach. They knew that the FBI was one of the most frequently sued organizations in the federal government, and in such legal proceedings, wiretap evidence was often subpoenaed. McCloskey began a broad canvass of former Panthers and their attorneys and learned of a dozen such cases. He went from city to city checking dusty old legal files but found nothing of use. Then he heard that a Connecticut lawyer named John Williams had donated a thick file of FBI wiretap records to the Yale Library for future research. With his assistant Kate Germond, McCloskey drove to New Haven and was presented with ten boxes of logs. "We dug into that stuff. It was the biggest tease in the world. We found logs from the murder night but not from Oakland. We found logs from Oakland but not from the murder night. We found taps on Panther headquarters at 3106 Shattuck in Oakland, but they began too late. We found several logs that mentioned Geronimo Pratt but they were out of context with the shooting. That cost us another two weeks."

The frustrated minister contacted the office of U.S. Senator Patrick Leahy, chairman of the committee that oversaw FBI operations, and enlisted the support of a top aide. "Leahy's office went after the FBI director with specific demands for specific records. Even under that pressure, the FBI insisted that no such records existed. We had to face reality. If there were wiretaps, the FBI was never gonna give 'em up. We'd lost that round."

BEFORE HIS investigation was completed, McCloskey traveled 150,000 miles, including a dozen round-trips between Princeton and Los Angeles. He tracked retired COINTELPRO agents in six states, gaining little for his efforts. He flew to Morgan City to see if Geronimo's relatives could dredge up helpful memories. Eunice Petty Pratt held out a warm hand but didn't seem to catch his name. She was almost ninety now and no longer recognized anyone except close relatives. She still prayed and chanted for her son's release, but she was confined to her little house in Across the Tracks. Her preacher daughter Jacqueline lived next door and did most of the care-taking.

Charles Pratt, the family's genius, insisted on guiding McCloskey through his little brother's childhood haunts, including the football field where the boy known as Elmer and Gerard had starred at quarterback for Morgan City Colored High. McCloskey thought of Geronimo in his cell at Tehachapi and felt a wave of sadness. "I couldn't help thinking about the days when he thought the most dangerous thing in the world was an open-field tackle. And how he was wounded twice in Vietnam and was lucky to get out alive. And how he came home—and fell into this deep pit."

McCLOSKEY TITLED his report "A Memo Outlining Why I Believe Elmer Pratt Is Completely Innocent." He opened by repeating remarks made by Deputy D.A. Richard Kalustian in 1972: "If the jury believes Julius Butler, regardless of whether they believe or disbelieve the identification witnesses, Mr. Pratt is guilty. The case is over if they believe that. . . . The jury must have at its disposal every fact which bears upon the worthiness of that confession; every fact which tends to show whether or not the con-fession is true; whether Elmer Pratt said these words. . . . The jury is going to have to have every piece of evidence that is relevant and material at its disposal in determining the question of who to believe, Elmer Pratt or Julius Butler."

McCloskey quoted Julius Butler's claim that he'd wanted his "insurance letter" to be kept secret. The real truth, McCloskey pointed out, was "just the opposite. . . . Only three days after he wrote and delivered it to Sergeant Rice, he told the FBI what was in it, that it contained evidence that could put members of the BPP in the gas chamber."

The minister charged that the street-corner delivery of Butler's letter was done "in concert with his handlers at the FBI. This patently artificial staging of the delivery . . . is certainly characteristic of FBI COINTEL-PRO tactics. . . . Humiliated by Pratt, Julio Butler was all too willing to help the FBI destroy him. . . . A devious device had to be created in order to give Butler's accusation an air of legitimacy. . . . Both Butler and his han-dlers wanted to destroy Pratt. And that's just what they did by concocting and staging the delivery of the letter with the smoking gun against Pratt. Not only does this offer Butler a chance for sweet revenge, but it also enabled Butler to escape prison for the felony charges hanging over his head as a result of the Ollie Taylor assault and kidnaping. Butler was putty in the FBI hands."

As for Pratt's repeated "confessions" to the beautician, McCloskey observed that "Pratt would not have gone to Butler like a ping pong ball, first announcing he was going to do something, then returning hours later to tell him he had done it, then go back the very next day to confirm that he indeed had done what was in the newspaper. . . . It defies common sense."

The Centurion Ministries' white paper came down hard on the in-court identifications. "The testimony of Mrs. Reed is one of the most blatant and shameful instances of an eyewitness filling in significant details and actually changing prior descriptions of a suspect to fit the defendant at trial. . . . It is quite obvious that the police convinced both of these witnesses that Pratt was the killer and then manipulated them into molding the suspect to fit Mr. Pratt, the chosen one."

The McCloskey report offered a logical theory of what might have happened in the twenty-four hours beginning with the tennis court shootings and ending with the execution-style murder of Bunchy Carter's confidante, the forty-year-old Captain Franco Diggs.

Prior to Captain Franco's murder on December 19, 1968, he was a captain in the BPP in charge of Bunchy's underground. . . . Four people testified at Geronimo's trial that the day Mr. Pratt left for Oakland, which was about the 14 or 15th of December 1968, Capt. Franco drove him to the airport in Pratt's 1967 GTO Pontiac. . . . Franco, after dropping Pratt off at the airport, naturally had possession of and therefore responsibility for the car and its use. Capt. Franco . . . knew full well that it was a code of Bunchy's, and therefore the BPP, that no party car must ever be used in any criminal activity, especially one that could lead to the gas chamber.

Franco also knew that if it were under his watch, when he had the car, then Bunchy would hold him accountable for such a massive screw-up, and it would be his head on the chopping block. This was told to me by a very senior L.A. BPP leader who at the time was also one of Bunchy's most senior trusted aides. . . .

Prior to meeting Franco, Tyrone [Hutchinson] told me he used to see Swilley and Franco together. . . . Tyrone also remembers seeing Herbert driving "the goat." . . . As Bunchy's former top aide told me, Franco and Swilley were both "killers." If Franco let Swilley use "the goat," and Swilley made the dumb mistake and used it for the Santa Monica murder, then it was up to Franco to somehow take care of the problem. As the aide told me, if this is what happened (Franco gave the car to Swilley), then it was simply a matter of "who was going to kill the other." Because, if Bunchy ever got wind that the goat was used in a crime of this nature, then they'd both be dead men.

. . . Franco was found dead lying on his back on a dirt strip between the pavement and a fenced business near 155th St. and Main. He had been shot three times, once in the back of his head, once in the neck under his right ear, and once in the left cheek of his face. The coroner's report indicates he was shot with a "poss 32 cal or 9 mm." He knew his killers. He would never let a stranger get that close to him. . . .

The intriguing question remains—since Franco was killed within 24 hours of the Santa Monica shooting, was his death related to the use of the BPP "goat" car in the shooting of Mrs. Olsen, given the above related Swilley circumstances?

McCloskey's twenty-thousand-word report, augmented by eighteen exhibits, concluded with a pledge that Centurion Ministries would work the case till it was solved.

Waiting Game

In mid-1993, through the good offices of TV producer Lowell Bergman, James McCloskey and Stuart Hanlon were granted an audience with the top members of the Los Angeles D.A.'s Office. Former assistant D.A. Johnnie Cochran absented himself so it wouldn't look as though he were seeking favoritism from former subordinates. The Pratt delegation arrived with armloads of documents and great expectations.

McCloskey, Hanlon and Bergman were ushered into the presence of the D.A.'s chief of staff and several of his aides, including Deputy Diane Vezzani, the matronly woman who'd been so eloquent in warning the parole board about Pratt's ability to foment revolution. After the visitors were informed that newly elected D.A. Gil Garcetti would soon join them, everyone settled into seats around a conference table. The hosts, including Vezzani, were strangely silent. After a few uncomfortable minutes, McCloskey tried to make conversation. "You know," he said, "the last time I was in this room was a year ago—the day Clarence Chance and Benny Powell were released."

Too late, he realized he'd blundered. "I could feel the frost in the room. Not a smile, not a nod—nothing. I thought, These guys didn't agree with that decision! They're career prosecutors. *They still think Clarence and Benny are guilty.*"

The loudest noise in the room was a cough. Thumbs were twiddled, coffee sipped, throats cleared. Then the stick-thin Garcetti burst through the door like a man with higher priorities, looked around and asked, "What're we here for?"

Bergman opened with a reporter's outline of the case. Now and then he turned to McCloskey or Hanlon for confirmation of a fact or date. When he was finished, the attorney and the minister added their own ringing declarations.

Garcetti appeared to pay close attention, then said, "Is this gonna cause Judge Kalustian any problems?"

McCloskey stammered, "I, uh—really don't know. We're not *after* anybody."

Hanlon said, "We just want the truth to come out." He started to ask if Kalustian's problems were more of a concern than Pratt's, but for once he held his sharp tongue.

"All right," Garcetti said. "What do you want me to do?"

McCloskey said, "We'd like your office to reexamine this conviction and whether Pratt had a fair trial."

Garcetti said he wasn't in a position to answer at the moment.

"We didn't expect a quick answer," Hanlon said. "We're just asking you to consider."

After McCloskey promised to provide a copy of his report, both sides agreed to meet again.

ON THE way to the parking lot Bergman said he was disappointed. "As soon as I saw Vezzani, I knew you were screwed," he told McCloskey. "But I expected a little more civility and respect. You've earned that, Jim."

"I don't give a damn about respect," the minister said with heat. "I can't understand Garcetti's attitude. Where's his interest in justice?"

"I think we misgauged the intensity of the symbolism," Bergman replied. "To people in law enforcement, Pratt is a test case of everything they believe in. He's a *huge* deal. I've worked with Garcetti and I know he's honest. I'm sure it galled him to be asked to reopen a case after an L.A. judge dismissed it without a hearing. Give him a little time. He'll come around."

WHEN GARCETTI still hadn't come around after six weeks, McCloskey and the Pratt attorneys asked their supporters to nudge the D.A. with letters. U.S. Representative Maxine Waters wrote Garcetti that her Los Angeles constituents "almost universally believe that [Pratt] was framed and is in prison only because he was a leader of the Black Panther Party in the late 1960s." U.S. Representative Don Edwards wrote that he was "not interested in assessing blame for anything that happened twenty years ago . . . but a person still sits in jail maintaining his innocence." Amnesty International insisted that "the interests of justice can only be served by granting him a retrial or release." Benjamin F. Chavis Jr., the new executive director of the NAACP, called the case "a glaring injustice" and said it would be "a very positive and important act for your office to join with Mr. Pratt, his attorneys and Mr. McCloskey in asking the California courts to reverse this conviction that so offends our community and so offends justice and fairness."

SIX SILENT months passed before Garcetti announced that he was commissioning a review based on the McCloskey allegations. He assigned the task to a retired deputy, Harry B. Sondheim, a pleasant, sixtyish man with frizzy moustache and goatee. The veteran prosecutor wore dark-rimmed glasses and projected the aura of a Talmudic scholar. Cochran briefed Hanlon: "Harry's an old friend and I like him, but he's an academic lawyer, not a litigator. He's honest and thorough and—well, deliberate isn't exactly the word. Slow comes closer."

Three more months passed without word from Sondheim or the D.A.'s Office. "They're certainly in no hurry," Hanlon said during a strategy session.

"That might be the plan," Cochran said. "Harry Sondheim is one way for Garcetti to deep-six this case. The thing you have to understand about Gil—he's a political animal. He started out as an idealistic young prosecutor, but somewhere along the line he turned into a politician. An old story. Now politics comes first."

"In the Pratt case," Hanlon responded, "politics has *always* come first."

Mule Creek

In the California Department of Corrections' ongoing campaign to limit Geronimo Pratt's influence on other prisoners,[66] he was transferred twice more and ended up at Mule Creek State Prison, thirty-two miles southeast of Sacramento. Once again he found himself fighting battles about toilet facilities and other matters that he thought had been settled years before. On Hanlon's first visit to Mule Creek, a two-hour drive from San Francisco, Geronimo told him, "They threw me in a cell full of shit and piss, a drunk tank kind of place, and left me there for two days."

Both Hanlon and Pratt boycotted his thirteenth parole hearing but inserted an array of psychological evaluations into the record: "Mr. Pratt's criminal history . . . is entirely associated with his political and social struggles and not with any kind of ongoing anti-social personality disorder or orientation. . . ." "Mr. Pratt has been tempered by time, maturity, introspection, a family, incarceration and a changing society. . . ." "[Mr. Pratt] has the potential to play a significant role in making positive changes in soci-

---

[66] Officially stated reason: "The high notoriety of his case factors and the safety and security of the institution."

ety. . . ." "[Mr. Pratt] does not currently pose a threat to society and he is unlikely to pose a threat to society in the future."

Geronimo was sorry to hear that one of his most faithful supporters had been barred from the latest parole board hearing. Kathleen Cleaver, a law professor at Emory University in Atlanta, had fired a parting shot as she was turned away: "You are conducting a sham."

BY NOW, Pratt had spent more of his life inside prison than out, and to Hanlon and the other members of the defense team, he seemed to be losing some of his sweet reasonableness. For weeks he'd been encouraged about Mc-Closkey's discoveries, but he seemed to expect quicker results. Robert Bloom's valuable services were lost after a heated confrontation in the prison visiting room. "That was inevitable," Hanlon explained later. "Bobby was a great legal scholar and preferred to work alone. G could never understand his attitude."

More than once Pratt hinted about firing Hanlon and handling the case pro se. A few days later he would call and apologize. Then he would erupt at their next session. The situation was wearing both men out.

THE PRATT siblings sensed a breakdown and reached out to their brother. Geronimo thanked them for their concern, returned their love, and told them he could handle his own problems. Sister Emelda, a social worker in Chicago, dispatched a bulletin:

TO THE SPIRITUAL FAMILY OF
ELMER GERARD PRATT
Every day, throughout the day and especially at 7 am,
affirm the following:
GERARD IS A PERFECT IDEA IN DIVINE MIND AND IS AWARDED DIVINELY PROTECTED FREEDOM FROM PRISONS OF ANY MAKING. GERARD IS SUR-ROUNDED BY THE LIGHT OF CHRIST AND NOTHING OPPOSES HIS GOOD!

Tanya Pratt, Geronimo's niece, his brother Jack's daughter, followed up with her own letter:

Dear Elmer "GERONIMO" Pratt family members:
This letter is going out to all of Geronimo's family members. Why? Because 1996 is the time to see GERONIMO released from bondage;

see him walking out of the court house a free man, sitting in our living rooms laughing, smiling and embracing us. I am asking each family member to take time out of their busy schedule to PRAY and FAST for the release of Geronimo Pratt in 1996.

Aware that her plea would be read by her uncle's supporters in different time zones, Tanya Pratt included a "schedule for prayer and fasting": "Pray 8:00pm (Calif) 10:00pm (Louisiana, Illinois) 11:00pm (Georgia, Indiana, Wash., D.C.) Fast 12:00am to 12:00pm."

Timothy Pratt, Ph.D., still teaching in the District of Columbia, insisted that Eunice Petty Pratt's prayers remained the family's best weapon. "Mama's teachings have taken roots," Timothy wrote, "and are being passed down to the next generations. They will set her son free." He expressed regret that Geronimo continued to shun religion, "but I light candles, have masses said for him, and say prayers every night for his safety and release."

At home in the little house that her children had built for her in Across the Tracks, Eunice knelt at her bedside and chanted words that no longer could be understood.

MORE MONTHS passed without word from the D.A.'s Office, and McCloskey and Hanlon demanded a meeting. After another strained silence McCloskey asked Sondheim, "Harry, just to get us started, could you maybe respond to some of the points I made in my report?"

Sondheim looked puzzled.

"My memo?" McCloskey said. "About the case?" This is beyond belief, he said to himself. It took me three days just to *type* the thing—and this guy doesn't remember a word?

Sondheim replied that he'd read the report but found nothing useful.

"He just literally dismissed me with a wave of the hand," McCloskey said later. "Two years of work! I did my best to keep my temper, but I was insulted and angry. Sondheim was telling us that the D.A.'s Office didn't give a damn about Geronimo Pratt. That made us twice as determined."

The crusading minister returned to the streets of South-Central, dredging up more evidence, interviewing prisoners and policemen, poring over old newspaper clippings and memos. He sent each new discovery to Sondheim and eagerly awaited replies. He offered to provide any documents that might be missing from the D.A.'s files and delivered the 2,400-page trial transcript with its voluminous exhibits. He put the offices of Hanlon, Cochran and Centurion Ministries at Sondheim's disposal.

After more months of silence the aggravated McCloskey wrote directly to Gil Garcetti. "We have provided Harry with a large amount of material on the case—whatever he asked for, we provided it to him immediately. There is absolutely nothing that I can think of that we know or have that we have not given Harry's team. . . . Other people working with me on this case have expressed concern that Mr. Sondheim and others in your office are simply stringing out this 'investigation' in the hope that we will simply give up . . . I am calling on you to reach a decision soon."

It took Garcetti two weeks to reply that his office was solely motivated by "our desire to be thorough rather than merely expeditious."

Hanlon flung the letter on the floor. "G is flipping out," he told McCloskey. "How can I show him crap like this? *What the hell can I tell him?*"

The minister shook his head.

NEARLY TWO more years of constipated communication passed before the Pratt forces came to the only possible conclusion. "The D.A. was jerking us off," Hanlon recalled later with his customary pungency. "A dozen boxes of our material disappeared down that black hole. We wasted hundreds of hours turning up new evidence, composing letters, finding new legal authorities. We should have known better. The D.A.'s Office was trapped in its own bad image. They'd blown a string of big cases—the McMartin school molestation, Rodney King, Reginald Denny, the Menendez brothers. Then along came O. J. Simpson, a case that they *couldn't* lose, and they were about to lose that one, too. They couldn't afford another public relations disaster. Justice didn't matter. G could rot in his cell."

Media Blitz

"So we were stuck in the mud," Jim McCloskey said later. "Johnnie was busy with O.J., and Stuart and I were spinning our wheels. We decided to try another media blitz for two reasons: first, there was a slim chance that Garcetti had a sense of shame, and second, we needed public support."

Before the P.R. campaign even began, the *Los Angeles Times* produced a major article. On Tuesday, May 24, 1994, the newspaper's 1,104,651 readers awoke to a page-one story about an honored institution, the first African Methodist Episcopal Church, the city's oldest and biggest black congregation with nine thousand members. The chairman of its Board of Trustees, Julius Carl "Julio" Butler, now sixty-one, was described as a native Angeleno, a wounded marine sergeant from the Korean War, a former sheriff's deputy, a campaign volunteer for former mayor Tom Bradley, a criminology alumnus of Los Angeles City College and a staff worker for Los Angeles Legal Aid. But the news hook for the long article was the picketing of the church by protesters carrying signs saying, "The snitch got to go. Free Geronimo." The *Times* headline read, A PILLAR OF FIRST A.M.E. UNDER FIRE.

The former beautician and "mayor of Adams Boulevard" was now an attorney, his image sanitized and his rap sheet laundered. The rehab project had begun three days after the Pratt conviction in 1972, when Richard

Kalustian asked the Superior Court to reduce Butler's fine in the Ollie Taylor beating case from $200 to the $80 already paid. The prosecutor also arranged to have Butler's felony convictions reduced to misdemeanors. A few stigmatizing words about Butler's use of "violence, menace, fraud and deceit" were expunged from the record on another motion by Kalustian, clearing the way for the ex-Panther's admission to law school and subsequently to the California Bar.

The same newspaper that had referred to Pratt twenty-four years earlier as "a disastrous byproduct of the Vietnam war, a black man trained as a soldier who returned home to turn his skills against the Establishment," now portrayed him as a sympathetic figure, "a decorated Vietnam veteran from Louisiana" whose supporters said that his case "symbolizes a legal system that was twisted to prosecute a political enemy." *Times* staff writer Edward J. Boyer described Butler as "the linchpin" in Pratt's controversial conviction and quoted the church leader as saying, "I still say I stand by the testimony."

Johnnie L. Cochran Jr. was also quoted: "Now he's passing himself off as this pillar of the community. An innocent man is in jail. If you're a real Christian, I don't know how you can live with that. And I don't think you can just stonewall it forever."

First AME's pastor, the Reverend Cecil L. "Chip" Murray, found himself squeezed. Years earlier he'd affixed his signature to an amicus curiae brief supporting a new trial for Pratt. Now the leaders of his 3,500-member men's group backed Butler with a strong vote of confidence. Murray chose not to comment.

THE *TIMES* article set the tone for media coverage that soon turned global. The *London Times* ran a commentary favorable to Pratt. Articles in magazines and law journals sniped at the FBI, LAPD and the district attorney. Kathleen Cleaver was widely quoted: "Pratt is a political prisoner. If he were a murderer, he would have been freed years ago." Fox-TV aired a four-part series plus follow-ups, and the *CBS Evening News* feature "Eye on America" told the Pratt story twice. Internet websites recapitulated the history of COINTELPRO and the Black Panthers and referred to "the FBI fix."

Cochran discarded his lawyerly collegiality and publicly criticized his old Loyola classmate Richard Kalustian. In a *Gentlemen's Quarterly* article entitled "The Other Case That Obsesses Johnnie Cochran," he was quoted as saying, "He shouldn't even be on the bench. He clearly knew about Julius Butler. He had to have known that. He knew the man was an informant, and he let him sit there and lie to a jury. And now there's this innocent man still sitting in prison, and Kalustian has never spoken out. I don't know if he's morally capable of being on the bench."

Pratt supporters picketed the courthouse where Cochran and the D.A.'s Office were trying the O. J. Simpson case. Placards said, UNCAGE THE PANTHER. FREE GERONIMO! . . . NO JUSTICE, NO PEACE, TILL GERONIMO'S RELEASE.

Accredited Simpson case correspondents became interested in Pratt and filed stories of their own. John Mack, head of the Los Angeles Urban League, publicly urged the D.A.'s Office to "move the case along." Jewish leader Stanley Sheinbaum, a longtime Garcetti supporter, urged him to "do the right thing." Pasadena Mayor William Paparian charged that "your office secured a conviction, but justice has not yet been done for the accused." Patrick Leahy of Vermont and other U.S. senators made personal appeals. Marlon Brando, Sean Penn and other Hollywood celebrities issued statements. Complaints reached the desk of U.S. Attorney General Janet Reno.

A reporter asked Hanlon how he and Cochran managed to keep climbing the same hill. "You know," said Rumpled of the Bailey, "Nelson Mandela's attorneys had no expectations for twenty years. But they kept going because that is what life is about. They refused to give in. And so will we. *We will not let these people break us down.*"

IN MID-1995, with Cochran and the D.A.'s Office still squared off in the Simpson murder trial, the Pratt forces decided to give up on Garcetti and make a final desperation move in the courts. "We had to do *something,*" Hanlon explained later. "Geronimo was at a low ebb. After all these years, he was losing it. He'd had his hopes dashed so many times. He'd fathered two kids in the certainty that he'd be getting out. Now Shona was sixteen and Hiroji was twelve, and he couldn't even get back to San Quentin to see them."

One afternoon McCloskey and Hanlon drove to Mule Creek for another strategy session. Pratt looked wan and downcast. Hanlon started to discuss another writ of habeas corpus and Geronimo dismissed the idea with a wave. "What's the use, man?" he said. "We'll just lose again."

McCloskey said, "You're probably right, G, but we'll generate some heat. We have plenty of legitimate issues."

"Legitimate, yeah," Pratt reminded him, "and—old."

"They may seem old to you and me," McCloskey insisted, "but they've never been addressed by the courts. Garcetti can push us around, but in court we're all equal."

Half-jokingly, Geronimo said, "Reverend, the only reason you're optimistic is because you don't have a firm grasp of the situation. Now Stu and me, we been kicked in the nuts so many times we stopped believing in Santy Claus."

"Maybe so," Hanlon said, "but we've still got options. The only one we don't have is—"

"Yeah, I know," Geronimo said. "Quitting." They'd always completed each other's sentences.

At the end of the long visit Hanlon summed up their unanimous decision: "Our chances in court are between zero and none. So—we've got to file."

THE THANKLESS job of drafting the brief for another habeas corpus petition fell to Juliana Drous, the star writer on the Pratt team. Her husband, civil rights attorney Joel Kirschenbaum, had once filed an amicus curiae brief on Geronimo's behalf and visited him at Christmastime at Folsom. Twice Julie Drous had argued before the U.S. Supreme Court, where the justices succeeded in irking her German-born mother. "There you were in that beautiful new suit," Hedy Drous complained in her thick accent. "You were gorgeous! Do you think one of those judges could have said how nize you looked?"

By October 1995 Drous was halfway through a first draft and doggedly following Hanlon's instruction: "This one has to be perfect, Julie. We can't give 'em the slightest excuse to throw us out. Because they will." He kept reminding her that Pratt's last petition, filed three years earlier by Robert Bloom, had had a shelf life of twenty-four hours.

At Thanksgiving time, a month after Drous started work on the brief, her mother suffered a severe heart attack. Drous flew to Philadelphia to be at her bedside and worked on the petition at night. Sometimes she slept as long as two or three hours.

IN EARLY December Hanlon's phone rang with a collect call from Mule Creek State Prison. His client was irate. "I thought you told me our petition would be filed this year," Pratt said.

"I did," Hanlon replied. "But Julie's mother is dying. It doesn't matter whether we file it this year or early next year."

"I'll be up front with you, Stu," Geronimo said. *"It matters.* I've got . . . commitments. You guys are making me look bad."

"Commitments? Who with?"

"My, uh—contacts. People in Asia, Africa. Man, you *got* to file that petition before the first of the year."

"Julie can't possibly get it done by then. We've gone too far to screw up now. She needs another six weeks."

"Why?"

"Didn't you hear what I just said about Julie? *Juliana Drous, attorney-at-law?* This woman who's been working for you for twenty years? For free? Her mother's dying, for Christ's sake!"

"Yeah, but—"

Hanlon lost his temper and hung up, then spent the rest of the day fighting guilt feelings. Geronimo might have waited hours for the privilege of making the call. He might not get another chance for days. Now he was back in his cell with nothing settled and another sleepless night ahead. G was serving the time, not Hanlon, not Drous or Cochran or anyone else. His lead attorney could never allow himself to forget that fact. But . . . he had.

A FEW days later Hanlon was hit by the full force of Hurricane Geronimo. "He was crazed! He tried to fire me. He phoned everybody. He sent letters, demanded meetings. He called me collect and said, 'You're off the case, asshole.' He told Jim McCloskey that I was out. I said, 'He *can't* fire me, Jim. I'm not leaving.' I told my wife, 'This is terrible. Kathy, *how can he do this to me?'* She just said, 'You're hearing twenty-four years of frustration and misery. If you don't understand that, you're not much of a friend.' She said, 'If my oldest client wanted to fire me, I certainly wouldn't be discussing it with him on the phone.' "

Hanlon arrived at the prison during nonvisiting hours. He was ushered into an empty visiting room with its steel-gray tables and coin machines. A sullen Geronimo arrived behind the sound of his own grumbling. "You and those other assholes really fucked me up with my people. I lost a lot of support. Why can't you dipshits do anything on time?"

"I'm sorry, G," Hanlon responded.

"Don't you understand, man? I'm dealing with issues, people, timing. I'm dealing with Mandela, Mobutu, Tutu."

Mandela, Mobutu, Tutu, Hanlon repeated to himself in wonderment. How come he left off King Hussein? This must be some kind of synaptic misfire. G had been having more of them lately.

"If you say you're gonna file something in 1995," Pratt went on, "then, goddamn it, file it in fucking 1995!"

Hanlon's patience was waning. "That's not the real problem, G," he said. "The real problem is you've been reading your own press."

"Fuck you, man."

Hanlon said, "Why don't you cut out the bullshit and tell me what's the real issue here?"

"The real issue is you're fired."

"I already told you twenty times. *You can't keep firing your lawyers!*"

"I want Cochran to take over the case," Geronimo said. "He'll put up a fight."

"Johnnie's a little busy."

"The O.J. case is over.[67] Now he can get back to the G.P. case."

Hanlon said, "Johnnie can't help you without me and Julie and Jim McCloskey and all the rest of us poor slobs that've been working for you for free."

"Johnnie can do anything. And he's never charged me a dime."

"Neither has anybody else. Johnnie's up to his ass. He hasn't kept track of the nuts and bolts of this case and he'd be the first to admit it."

"He'd never hang up the phone on me."

"Neither would I if you didn't act like a jerk."

Hanlon disengaged long enough to drop eight quarters into the cigarette machine. After he lit up, Geronimo said, "I thought you quit."

"I did."

"Gimme one."

"I thought *you* quit."

"Gimme a fucking cigarette, man!"

The two old friends smoked furiously against each other. After a long silence Hanlon said, "I'll talk to Johnnie for you. But I know what he'll say."

He was halfway out the door when he heard Geronimo's parting shot:

---

[67] A not guilty verdict had been returned on October 3, 1995.

"Send your wife the next time. I need a *good* lawyer. . . ." The last word he heard was "dickhead."

COCHRAN EMITTED one of his patented horse laughs when Hanlon recounted the conversation. "Is this the first time a client called you a body part?" Cochran asked. "I guess you haven't been doing your job."

On a break from the post-Simpson hubbub, Cochran flew to Sacramento and called on Pratt at Mule Creek. "Stuart's the focal point of your case, Geronimo," he said. "He's been with you for—how long?"

"Twenty, twenty-one years. *Too* fucking long."

"And you want to fire him now? Geronimo, get a grip. You can't fire your lead attorney, and you can't fire all those other folks who helped. Man, if you keep coming up with ideas like that, I'm gonna be representing you in a sanity hearing."

Pratt asked, "Will you help out?"

"Of *course* I'll help out. When did I stop? I've just been a little sidetracked, that's all."

"Substantial Issues"

The first weeks of 1996 passed with no word from the D.A.'s Office. After conferring with Hanlon, the Reverend Jim McCloskey fired a final warning shot in a thirteen-hundred-word press release that was printed in the *Los Angeles Times* and other newspapers. He affirmed Centurion Ministries' belief in Pratt's innocence, took Gil Garcetti to task for two and a half years of inaction, lambasted the FBI, LAPD, Richard Kalustian and Julius Butler, threatened a new writ of habeas corpus and charged that Pratt's conviction "was based on false testimony knowingly presented by the prosecution."

THREE DAYS later Juliana Drous delivered her brief to Hanlon's office in the Haight, then flew back to Philadelphia to be with her mother during Hedy Drous' last days. The draft contained seventy-eight pages of argument, eighty legal citations and three volumes of evidence logs. "This case," the briefing specialist had written, "represents a complete breakdown of the adversarial process . . . a travesty unworthy of our judicial system."

WITH TELEPHONE input from the client, the team of Hanlon and Cochran spent a week weaving their own ideas into the document. "This,"

Hanlon predicted, "will be the finest petition the courts have ever turned down."

Under California statutes the petition could be filed anywhere in the state. "Let's not waste time," Cochran advised. "Wherever we go, we're gonna get kicked back to L.A. Let's file there." It proved to be a brilliant decision, but for unexpected reasons.

ELMER GERARD Pratt's fifth petition for a writ of habeas corpus was hand-delivered to the Los Angeles Superior Court clerk on Monday, February 26, 1996. It charged that the prisoner had been convicted on false evidence, had been "denied material exculpatory evidence," and that "newly discovered evidence proves petitioner is innocent."

In a press conference Hanlon told a dozen reporters, "Since Mr. Pratt was imprisoned, wars have started and ended. O. J. Simpson was arrested, tried and acquitted. But Gil Garcetti has refused to act in the case." Hanlon said the defense team "has grown tired of waiting on Mr. Garcetti to make an honest decision based on evidence and justice. His decision has been to avoid this case altogether." He accused Garcetti of treating the McCloskey report as "a political thing he could play with." He said that Pratt could never be paroled "because he won't show remorse for a crime he did not commit. All he ever had to do was say: 'I did it. I'm sorry.' Geronimo has never said what the parole board wanted."

A spokesman for Garcetti said he stood by his actions.

ONCE AGAIN the L.A. courts moved swiftly, but this time in Pratt's favor. Less than seventy-two hours after the petition was filed, Supervising Judge James A. Bascue announced that he found merit in the petition and issued an order to show cause, forcing the D.A.'s Office to respond. McCloskey attributed the order to "media pressure and a little divine intervention."

When the case was assigned to Superior Court Judge Michael Cowell, Cochran advised Hanlon, "Mike was a public defender. He's a good judge, a fair guy."

"He may be a good judge and a fair guy," Hanlon reminded his colleague, "but he's an *L.A.* judge."

IN A light rain fifty demonstrators assembled outside the Criminal Courts Building to chant slogans, wave placards and catch a glimpse of the former Black Panther deputy minister of defense, now forty-eight but as light-footed as ever. He'd been brought in from Mule Creek for the first formal hearing on the order to show cause. It was Thursday, March 28, 1996, and spectators overflowed into the hall. Former juror Jeanne Hamilton confessed to a journalist, "I'm scared to death, and I want to look at him and tell him I'm sorry." Another reporter asked Cochran what had gone wrong in the first Pratt trial. Cochran replied, "I didn't know I was up against the entire government." Three Pratt siblings, Virginia, Jack and Charles, squeezed into the front row and returned their brother's smile.

With the ponderous case slowly gathering momentum, the Pratt team had been reinforced by Mark Rosenbaum of the American Civil Liberties Union, Robert Garcia of the NAACP's Legal Defense Fund and private investigator David Lynn. The usual Pratt "runners," some of them now attorneys-at-law, stood by as they'd been standing by since 1972.

When court convened, Judge Cowell acknowledged that the petitioner had raised "some very substantial issues." But so had the D.A.'s Office, he continued. Gil Garcetti asked Cowell to send the habeas corpus petition directly to the California Supreme Court. During a recess Hanlon analyzed the situation for reporters. "We put Garcetti in a tight spot with our publicity campaign. Everybody knows about the case now. If he tries to get our petition thrown out, he loses black voters. But if he doesn't take a strong position, he loses the law-and-order white voters. So he's trying to lay it off on the State Supreme Court. Then whatever happens, it's not his fault."

In the afternoon session Judge Cowell chided the D.A.'s Office for the reptilian pace of its review. Harry Sondheim explained that the delay had been necessary in the interests of truth and justice, "concepts the District Attorney's Office continues to pursue in this case."

Hanlon shot back, "We are not going to sit here and listen to people who have had this case for three years talk about truth and justice."

He ridiculed the attempt to transfer the case to the State Supreme Court. "This is a no-brainer," he told the judge. "The district attorney is engaged in a blatant attempt to shop around for the right forum. This is pure desperation."

He took his seat and whispered to Cochran, "Did you see Cowell's face? He never looked at me. *He's gonna grant this bullshit motion!*"

"He can't," Cochran said. "He's got to go by the law."

"Just watch."

For one of the few times in their relationship, Cochran was wrong.

HANLON SAT next to Julie Drous on the return trip from Los Angeles to San Francisco. "Stu felt so bad he forgot to help the pilot fly the plane," Drous said of the white-knuckle flier later. "We were sick, miserable. He said, 'What the hell is gonna happen next?' I said, 'Stu, it's something about this case. It's snakebit. Think of all the other crazy rulings.'"

Hanlon told her, "Whenever we go into court, we know we're gonna lose. But why can't we lose according to law? Why is it always something out of left field? So . . . unfair."

BY A vote of 7–0, the California Supreme Court seemed to agree with Hanlon. Less than a month after Judge Cowell had kicked the case upstairs, the high court kicked it back. Cowell was ordered to "proceed to disposition."

A jubilant Hanlon told a reporter, "This is the first time since the Republicans took over the governorship sixteen years ago that a California Supreme Court has voted seven to nothing in favor of a criminal defendant."

Jim McCloskey said, "We are all absolutely thrilled, we're delighted and we think that what this means is that finally—after twenty-four years of unjust imprisonment—Geronimo Pratt is going to get his day in court."

Cochran was coldly realistic. "I once won a murder case in Cowell's court. But he still makes me nervous."

Confidential Informant

In mid-June, Harry Sondheim filed a 113-page brief arguing that Pratt's request for a new trial was speculative, groundless and unwarranted. "Public pressure brought by uninformed citizens, celebrities, politicians and journalists," the veteran prosecutor wrote, "cannot be the basis for an evidentiary hearing when there is no credible or new evidence to support such a hearing." He accused the Pratt attorneys of offering the court a "re-hash."

While Hanlon and Drous were drafting a reply in their San Francisco office, Hanlon took a phone call from Sondheim's cocounsel, Brentford J. Ferreira. Although they were on opposite sides, the two lawyers enjoyed a casual bantering relationship. As Hanlon recalled the conversation later, Ferreira said, "We've come up with some new information, Stu. You and Cochran will try to make a big thing out of it. But in the end we'll show that it's meaningless."

Hanlon responded, "You found Dr. Mengele?"

Ferreira ignored the crack and said, "We're going to Judge Cowell to get an order to keep it in camera till we do a little more investigating."

"To keep *what* in camera?"

"The new stuff that I can't tell you about."

Hanlon was irritated. "Fuck that shit, Brent," he said. "Either you got something important or you don't, and if you got something important, we want it now."

Ferreira replied that for once in his life Rumpled of the Bailey would have to be patient.

Hanlon called Los Angeles and asked Cochran to dispatch a lawyer to Cowell's courtroom to oppose Ferreira's action, whatever it was. Cochran assigned a young associate, Shawn Chapman. On July 15 she sat outside the judge's chambers while Ferreira, Cowell and a dignified African American man of about thirty conferred in the presence of a court stenographer. At the end of the ex parte proceeding Judge Cowell advised Chapman that Ferreira's "confidential information" was indeed important and relevant. He said that he'd given the D.A.'s Office ten days to complete its own investigation and then would disclose the mystery information to the Pratt side.

Two weeks later a packet of material arrived in Hanlon's office in the Haight. He scanned the cover sheet and told his secretary to hold his calls. After reading the second page he locked his door. Then he dialed his occasional sparring partner.

"Brent," he said, "what was that remark you made about me making a big thing out of this? Brent, the whole *world's* gonna make a big thing out of this! Everybody but you and Harry Sondheim."

THE UNIDENTIFIED man whom Shawn Chapman had seen entering Judge Cowell's chambers turned out to be Brian Hale, a senior investigator for the D.A.'s Office. In May, Garcetti had assigned him and his colleague Steve De Prima to investigate all angles of the Pratt case in preparation for opposing Pratt's latest petition. One of their first acts was to reinterview Julius Butler. With Deputy D.A.'s Sondheim and Ferreira sitting in on the session, De Prima asked Butler if he'd ever been paid as an informant by any law enforcement agency. Butler admitted that several months before testifying against Pratt, someone in the D.A.'s Office had given him money to buy a gun.

At first the lawyer and churchman refused to identify his benefactor— "I don't want to get a friend in trouble"—but later he named Morris Bowles, the D.A.'s detective who'd been assigned to assist Richard Kalustian during the Pratt trial. Butler said he used the money to buy a .357 Magnum and admitted that he'd carried the weapon for the next ten years, in violation of California law.

After Butler split a few more hairs over the definition of informer—"I wasn't an informer, I was doing *liaison*"—Investigator Hale took the routine step of asking the D.A.'s Bureau of Investigation to check its informer files. A captain opened a locked drawer, looked under "B" and extracted three "Confidential Informant" cards on Julius Carl Butler. The name "Bowles" was written in ink on each.[68] The cards were dated January 27, 1972, six months before Geronimo Pratt had gone on trial for murder. The head of the D.A.'s intelligence unit said that the card file was maintained for the use of prosecutors who might need the information while trying cases.

THE DISCOVERY was a double victory for the Pratt team. It confirmed in writing what the lawyers had been saying about Butler for two decades, and it effectively swept the FBI complications from the case. Hanlon explained, "No state judge wants to hear anything about the FBI. No state judge wants to challenge the FBI. The special agents do their little song and dance in the judge's chambers, shake a little secret information out of their sleeves, and the next thing you know, you've lost your case and you don't know why. COINTELPRO agents acted like the Gestapo in the Pratt case, but every time we tried to bring this out in the courtroom, it just caused confusion and doubt. Now that we had Julius Butler dead to rights as a D.A.'s informer, the FBI stuff was out of it. We had a pure California case, with California issues and California players. It narrowed the focus."

He phoned Cochran in Los Angeles and said, "There's the smoking gun we've been looking for. I wonder why that informer information was still in the files. Why didn't they purge it?[69] Garcetti's head must be spinning."

"Brian Hale isn't the kind of guy who's gonna compromise himself," Cochran replied. "When he found those cards, he gave his superiors no

---

[68] In a statement later, Morris Bowles suggested that the former beautician was covering up for someone else. He emphatically denied that he'd prepared the C.I. cards or put them in the confidential informant file.

[69] When Ronald Maus, onetime acting chief of the D.A.'s Bureau of Investigation, was asked why Butler's card and some six hundred others hadn't been purged like thousands of other old documents in the D.A.'s records, he answered, "They were the sacred cards. They stayed there. They were very important . . . [they] pertained to people that provided information, and they [the informants] could be in jeopardy should that information get out."

choice. They had to turn 'em over or risk jail. It's nice to have a guy like Hale around."

WHEN HANLON told Mark Rosenbaum the latest news, the ACLU lawyer said, "This is it, Stu," he said. "We've won."

"Mark," Hanlon replied, "you know the history. This case is different."

"It may be different," Rosenbaum said, "but this new stuff is devastating. All these years Kalustian's been denying that Butler was an informant. How can he say he didn't know?"

"Well, that's exactly what he *is* saying."

In the California legal newspaper, the *Daily Journal,* staff writer Martin Berg quoted Kalustian: "I had no knowledge of any informant card and I had no knowledge of any gun. None. Zero." Later he amplified. "I had no knowledge that the Bureau of Investigation had a confidential informant index card file that contained a card with Julius Butler's name on it. I had no knowledge that any employee of the District Attorney's Office ever gave Julius Butler money. I never gave Julius Butler any money. I never gave Julius Butler a gun, nor did I give him any aid in obtaining a concealed weapons permit. Julius Butler never received any leniency in return for his testimony in the Pratt case. Many years after the case was over, I did help Julius Butler with a prior conviction in order to aid him in obtaining admission to law school."

A WEEK after Investigator Brian Hale's bombshell went off in the Los Angeles press, a billboard appeared above a McDonald's restaurant on Century Boulevard:

AN INNOCENT MAN IN PRISON FOR 26 YEARS.
GERONIMO PRATT.
LOS ANGELES, HOW LONG MUST HE WAIT FOR JUSTICE?

An anonymous donor had paid $60,000 to rent the space and sent along a matching check for legal expenses. Similar signs popped up at bus shelters near the Criminal Courts Building. Jim McCloskey reported from Princeton that other donors were asking how they could help.

"Don't tell me somebody's finally gonna help with the court costs,"

Hanlon said. "We'll lose our amateur standing." The contributions were set aside for legal expenses.

AT A bail hearing on August 14 Superior Court Judge Michael Cowell sent another set of mixed signals. Hanlon had argued that the smoking-gun evidence justified Pratt's release on bail, but after a long semantical argument about the difference between a snitch and an informant, the judge ruled that "Mr. Pratt is not eligible for bail. As matters now stand, he is convicted of the crime of murder."

Cowell also commented: "Mr. Butler was directly an informant to the District Attorney's Office. We also have information that Mr. Butler had indicated that either money and/or a gun was provided to him by a representative of the District Attorney's Office. He did not designate Mr. Kalustian. And while I agree with you that the question of his informant status is important, there is also an additional issue that comes into play, and that is, regardless of the impact of his testimony, to what extent is the decision of the court to be guided by the fact that money was provided to an informant without that fact in and of itself being disclosed to the defendant? In other words, even if Butler's testimony was truthful, his status as an informant is something the defendant is entitled to be notified of at the time of the trial."

Well, yes, Your Honor, Hanlon said to himself, that's exactly what we've argued for years.

FIVE WEEKS later the Pratt lawyers met for breakfast in the cafeteria of the Criminal Courts Building. When court convened, they intended to ask Cowell to stop temporizing and set a firm date for an evidentiary hearing.

After a bad night of motel sleep Hanlon arrived minutes late and said, "I got a feeling the judge is gonna throw us out of L.A." Juliana Drous agreed.

Shawn Chapman, Cochran's associate, said that she'd heard the same rumor but it couldn't be true. "Cowell's already tried to get rid of us," she said. "He wouldn't dare try again."

But none of the Pratt attorneys anticipated Judge Cowell's next step in the judicial maneuverings even after he began rationalizing his decision aloud. To another packed courtroom he explained that his judicial colleague Richard Kalustian's involvement as a possible witness had altered the tone of the case. "Why, you're attacking a sitting judge!" he told the Pratt lawyers. He held up a recent issue of *California Lawyer* magazine and read, "Cochran makes no secret of his intention to destroy Kalustian's character."

Cowell claimed that the ad hominem attack on a fellow Los Angeles judge left him no choice but to recuse himself. But he also disqualified the entire Los Angeles bench. The case would be returned to the State Judicial Council in San Francisco for reassignment, a process that could take months. A newly assigned judge might simply dismiss the petition.

Outside the courtroom Hanlon aimed a hard slap at the wall. "What rock has this judge been living under?" he raged to reporters. "We've been accusing Kalustian of putting on perjured testimony since 1977. There's nothing new about it. He's just looking for an excuse. He's afraid to make hard decisions."

Deputy D.A. Brentford Ferreira passed by, and Hanlon said, "Wipe off that grin, Brent. This might go to San Francisco. That's *my* backyard."

Ferreira commented that Bay Area hotels were expensive.

"I have a room in my basement," Hanlon said. "You can stay down there with the other rats."

The friendly enemies bantered back and forth until Ferreira said he would yield to Hanlon's expertise.

"My expertise?" Hanlon said. "On what?"

"On rats."

TWO MORE months of pachydermous waltzing passed before the Judicial Council made an unexpected announcement of its own: the Pratt matter was assigned to Orange County for a full evidentiary hearing. Hanlon felt as though he'd been blackjacked. Orange County, bordering Los Angeles to the south, was Nixon and Reagan country. It had a strong military-industrial base, a history of electing conservatives, and a diminished African American presence.

Hanlon phoned Cochran. "We got transferred to Santa Ana."

Cochran sputtered, "That's *Orange County*!"

"I don't know how they did it, but the fix is still in."

Cochran said, "I'll tell you how they did it. The D.A.'s Office has clout and we don't." He paused. "Who's gonna tell Geronimo?"

"I'd rather eat glass."

"Well, you're three hundred miles closer to Mule Creek."

Hanlon guessed that settled the argument.

HE FOUND his client oddly indifferent to the bad news. "Orange County, L.A. County, Disneyland, Yosemite Park, wherever," Geronimo said. "What's the difference?"

"I'm sorry, G," Hanlon said. "We had high hopes this time."

"Yeah. Weren't we stupid."

Geronimo said he was expecting a visit from his brother Timothy. He didn't seem excited about it. "Tim always wants to talk religion."

Driving home, Hanlon thought, My old friend is slipping. Showing signs of being beaten down. Whipped. And it only took a quarter of a century.

The Orange Curtain

Early reports about Orange County Superior Court Judge Everett Dickey were disheartening. He was described as a Reagan appointee, a right-wing Republican, ex-military, a sixty-two-year-old health freak who ran his court like a drill sergeant and sometimes jogged with his staff at lunchtime. "We've got a redneck judge in a fascist county," Hanlon protested to Julie Drous.

The only encouraging sign in Dickey's advance profile came via a friendly lawyer, Milton Grimes. "I asked Milton about Judge Dickey," Cochran told Hanlon by phone. "All he said was, 'The guy's been a judge for twenty-six years. He's a conservative, but he's got guts.' "

"Great," Hanlon said. "So did General Patton."

The two colleagues discussed another sticky problem. The Simpson case had made Cochran the most controversial lawyer in the United States. Would he be a liability in Orange County?

"It's a legitimate concern, Johnnie," Hanlon said, feeling guilty. He also suspected that Cochran might be overbooked after the "trial of the century." He was negotiating a TV deal with Court TV, publicizing his book, *Journey to Justice,* and handling his usual overload of cases.

"Of *course* it's a legitimate concern, Stu," Cochran replied, "and you'd be remiss if you didn't address it."

"You know how *I* feel," Hanlon said.

"You know how I feel, too. Why don't you guys talk it over? I don't want to do anything that would hurt Geronimo. It would break my heart to drop out. But it's your call."

AFTER JUDGE Dickey set November 22, 1996, for a status hearing, Hanlon discussed the Cochran effect with the other strategists: Jim McCloskey, Julie Drous, Mark Rosenbaum, Robert Garcia, a few of Hanlon's trusted friends and his personal adviser, his wife Kathy Ryan.

By phone from Princeton, McCloskey admitted that he saw a downside. "The judge might take the attitude 'We'll show Mr. Hotshot from L.A. who's boss around here.' But I think it's worth the risk."

Hanlon described other reactions later: "Some of our people saw Johnnie as a slick jiving guy who would bring the wrong persona to Orange County, especially if the judge turned out to be a racist. They said the judge might be intimidated or pissed and the whole hearing would focus on Johnnie. The judge might say, 'This is a guy who got a murderer off. I'll fix *his* ass.' I let all my friends have their say and then I made a little speech. I said, 'I've been dealing with Johnnie Cochran for twenty years. He has never lost interest in this case. He has never failed to do everything he promised to do. Sure, he brings some negative P.R., but he'll bring negative P.R. whether he's in court or not. The Pratt case will forever be associated with Johnnie Cochran.' I let that sink in, and then I said, 'Oh, yeah, and one other thing. He's a goddamn fine courtroom lawyer.' "

HANLON PHONED Chicago, where Cochran was in the home stretch on a forty-two-city book tour. "Johnnie," he said, "we talked it over. We need you. I know you're busy."

"You can't keep me out, Stu," Cochran said.

"You'll be cocounsel?"

"I *demand* to be cocounsel."

They decided that Hanlon and the team members would continue their work on preliminary matters and Cochran would join them for the evidentiary hearing. "I can't wait to question Julio under oath," he said.

"Get in line, Johnnie," Hanlon said. "I've wanted a piece of that guy for years."

"I've wanted a piece of him ever since he lied to me in court. You were a college kid then."

They agreed to share the questioning.

HANLON AND Julie Drous arrived in Orange County for the status hearing and were quickly reminded of their distance from the Golden Gate. The local airport was named after John Wayne, and a statue of the conservative avatar looked down on them as they disembarked.

"Welcome to Marlboro Country, Jules," Hanlon cracked. "You ain't in Haight-Ashbury no more."

Drous touched her finger to her lips. *"Sshhh.* We're behind the Orange Curtain."

That night she phoned an old friend, Don Ayoub, a local lawyer who'd provided wise counsel in the past. After the conversation, she told Hanlon, "Don says Judge Dickey might surprise us. He's a conservative, but he's one of those conservatives who actually believe in the Constitution."

Dickey had defeated a recall move for his light sentencing of two Latino killers and for nullifying the conviction of a child murderer on grounds of jury misconduct, two unlikely actions by a supposed right-winger. A prosecutor had described him as "ruthlessly fair."

"You mean we got a judge who plays it straight?" Hanlon said. "I'm not sure I'm up for anything that weird."

"Ayoub says everybody gets a fair hearing in Dickey's court."

ON HIS flight from Washington to Los Angeles Timothy Pratt offered up silent prayers of thanks that he would soon see his younger brother. A small-town California talk-show hostess had interviewed Tim by phone and learned that he seldom visited Geronimo because of the travel expense. Three days later the woman had called to inform him that her listeners had bought him the ticket.

Virginia Pratt, still teaching problem children in the ghetto, met her brother at the Los Angeles airport and drove him to the jail in Santa Ana. On the way they recalled the Halloween night when she'd sprinted through the streets of Across the Tracks to threaten Tim's attackers with a gun. "You saved my life, Ginny," he said.

"Then how come you never visit?" she joked.

Guards allowed brother and sister a two-hour meeting with Geronimo in the public visiting room. "I missed you all," he told them. "How I miss Mama."

Timothy was tempted to share his vision that God had sent him as an emissary of good news, but he held back. Geronimo didn't like to talk religion.

Enigma in Robes

After the Pratt lawyers took their first look at the imposing figure of Judge Dickey, they weren't sure what to think. His bailiff called the courtroom to order with a personalized announcement that included a paean to "the flag of our country, symbol of the Constitution." As if on cue, His Honor strode from a side door, squaring his corners and arranging himself on his high-backed leather chair with the stiffness of a West Point cadet. He had the ruddy look of someone who'd just toweled off after a swim. He wore a neatly cropped white moustache and a meticulously coiffed crown of rich wavy hair the color of mother-of-pearl. He arranged some papers and looked down his long patrician nose with an expression that suggested he was coping with an unusual smell. Hanlon asked himself, What the hell is *this?*

The proceedings had hardly begun before Dickey announced that he was fully conversant with the paperwork in the case and intended to place strict limits on the evidentiary hearing. Hanlon suppressed a groan. Ten years earlier U.S. Magistrate John Kronenberg had issued the same warning.

In an authoritarian tone Dickey made it plain that he wanted to hear all the facts from both sides but would be reluctant to listen to any testimony or argument about COINTELPRO or the FBI. The issue of informers on

Cochran's legal team in 1972 would also be taboo. Matters that had been adjudicated in other courts would *not* be remasticated. Hanlon thought, What the hell does the guy intend to hear? The answer came down from the bench: "I particularly want to deal with the informant issue. Was Mr. Butler an informant? If so, I want to find out who knew that he was an informant and when did they know it. I believe that is a main issue here."

Julie Drous passed Hanlon a note: "!!!"

The judge continued: "There has to be some clarification on what efforts were made by Mr. Kalustian on Mr. Butler's behalf. I think we have to hear from Detective Bowles." He said that the D.A.'s investigator's claim that he didn't remember how Butler's name got into the informer file "is not good enough." The judge wondered aloud why the information about the file "is only being disclosed now—twenty-four years later," and added, "It's clear that this is not a typical case. It cries out for resolution." He also reminded the lawyers that an evidentiary hearing was different from a trial, that the rules gave the judge wide latitude and that he intended to seek the truth wherever he had to look. If that entailed disregarding some of his own strictures, so be it.

When Dickey asked about potential witnesses, Hanlon announced his intention of calling Butler, several LAPD officers and Superior Court Judge Richard Kalustian. Harry Sondheim registered a strong objection, and Hanlon held his breath. In the long history of the case no court had ever permitted the Pratt team to call such key figures.

Dickey dismissed the deputy D.A.'s objection with a wave of his hand. "We're seeking the truth here, Counsel," he said. "You'll have cross-examination."

Hanlon considered the contrast between this judge and the Superior Court bench in Los Angeles. This guy could develop into a pain in the ass, he said to himself, but he's an equal-opportunity pain in the ass. He's no more impressed by these arrogant prosecutors than he is by Julie and me. This is like going to court in Lapland.

"Now as to our calendar," the judge was saying. "I would like to move this case right along." Without asking for suggestions he announced that the evidentiary hearing would open on December 16.

Sondheim argued for more time. "That's only three weeks from now, Your Honor. We have witnesses to locate. Some are missing, some are dead. This matter goes back to 1970." Hanlon got the impression that the prosecutors had been caught off guard, that they'd expected a quick win by judicial fiat or, at the least, a continuance over the holidays.

In the same flat voice Dickey informed the prosecutor that he was fully cognizant of all relevant dates in the case, and if he could be ready in three weeks, so could the litigants.

Hanlon entered a mild demurrer for the record. "Your Honor," he said, "I hate to agree with the D.A., and we would like to move this case along, too, but it's the Christmas season. Some of us have kids and family."

"I understand, Counselor," the judge said. "I also understand that you asked for a prompt hearing. Your client's been incarcerated since December 10, 1970. You claim he's being held illegally. That's what habeas corpus is all about. My calendar is open, and we will proceed as scheduled."

After a few mumbled words Hanlon backed off. The hell with it, he said to himself. I won't irritate the guy before the case even gets started. The D.A.'s been playing stallball for three years. A quick hearing will be a lot tougher on them.

Cocounsel Robert Garcia, the NAACP lawyer, made a humanitarian request. "Judge, can't the courtroom be dark on Christmas Eve?"

After some thought Dickey granted the concession. Then he gaveled the session to a close and returned to his chambers, squaring all corners as he left.

The *Los Angeles Times* quoted a pleased Jim McCloskey: "This is what we've been waiting for, to get Julius Butler on the stand. . . . This is the first time that Butler is going to be held accountable for his sins of the past."

HANLON STRODE past the statue of John Wayne and boarded an evening flight to San Francisco International Airport, where Kathy waited to drive him home. He'd felt guilty about leaving her to take care of their sons while she was also running a law practice that was every bit as stressful as his.

On the drive home he said, "It's gonna be tough over Christmas."

"As long as it helps G," she said. "He's the one—"

"Yeah, yeah, I know. He's the one doing the time." It was her regular litany. He said, "Why don't you come down to Santa Ana for the hearing? We can use another good lawyer. You can bring the kids. That'll be their Christmas vacation."

"We'll see," Kathy responded. It was her all-purpose answer to her three male dependents.

Cream Cheese and Potato Salad

O. J. Simpson's chief defense attorney terminated his book tour two weeks early and flew to Los Angeles to rejoin the Pratt team. The other members had checked into a Marriott Hotel at Irvine, convenient to the courthouse in Santa Ana and a twenty-minute freeway hop to Cochran's office on Wilshire Boulevard.

"Johnnie put his staff and his office at our disposal," Hanlon said later. "What a layout—one suite after another, two conference rooms, a big library, a kitchen, a long hall with placards and awards and pictures of him with Martin Luther King, Thurgood Marshall, three or four presidents. It was the only all-black law office I'd ever seen. From the receptionist to the other partners, every person you saw was African American. I thought, How fitting! G's in prison *because* he's black."

After several meetings in the Wilshire office, Cochran took Hanlon aside and showed him an oil painting by Andrew Loomis that hung in a place of honor on a conference room wall. It depicted a black convict sprawled inside a tiny cell, his striped shirt open, his face drawn. He was throwing pieces of bread and cheese to a rat. "I saw that painting in a judge's office and I bought it on the spot," Cochran said. "To me it was Geronimo. When we win this case and I retire, it's going home with me."

At first some of the aesthetes from Baghdad by the Bay were dismayed by Cochran's tastes in food, but the proletarian Hanlon welcomed the change. "Somebody would say, 'It's time to eat. I know a great little Moroccan joint.' Johnnie would say, 'No, no, I already sent out.' Pretty soon the delivery guys show up with cold cuts, potato salad, macaroni salad, beans, cream cheese, rice pudding, chocolate cake, banana cream pie—cartons and cartons of fattening foods. *Louisiana* food. One day Jim McCloskey said, 'Hey, Johnnie, you forgot the chitlins.' "

A FEW days into their strategy sessions the Pratt team discovered another welcome change in the atmosphere. African American lawmen who'd been avoiding them for years suddenly turned cooperative. Hanlon credited Cochran. "His influence was overwhelming. Back in the fifties and sixties, the black law enforcement circle in Los Angeles was really small. These guys knew better than to rock the boat. So for twenty years they gave us nada. Sergeant DuWayne Rice wouldn't even answer my phone calls. But when Shawn Chapman brought him in for deposition, he treated Johnnie and the rest of us like brothers."

Hanlon's biggest problem was to convince his cocounsel to pace himself. Cochran always seemed involved in a dozen matters at a time. In a police abuse case, he'd won the largest jury award in L.A. history. He'd effectively ended the use of the deadly choke hold by the LAPD, won the Simpson case and other high-profile cases and was inducted into the American College of Trial Lawyers and named Criminal Trial Lawyer of the Year. He seemed to do everything on a high-octane basis, entering the room in his own force field, jacket swirling, hand outstretched, talking fast. "Hey, great to see ya!" "I'm *so* glad you're here." "How can I help you today?" While longtime secretary Eloise McGill and special assistant Sonia Davis rolled their eyes in despair, he spent hours on the phone and gave out his personal numbers to strangers.

"He puts off *nothing,*" Hanlon recalled. "It has to be done right now. He and I worked out this delicate division of labor, and he always respected it. He'd been with G since 1972, but I was more active toward the end. So he put me in charge and kept it that way. His position was: tell me what to do and I'll do it. He kept his word."

JUST BEFORE the formal evidentiary hearing opened, the Pratt lawyers got a scare. Weeks earlier Los Angeles Superior Court Judge Michael Cowell had granted the FBI's request to present uncensored reports about Geronimo Pratt in private. Technically Cowell's ruling was still in effect. Judge Dickey seemed uncomfortable with the idea of an ex parte proceeding but even more uncomfortable about overturning a fellow jurist's standing order. Brentford Ferreira of the D.A.'s Office presented a statement that seemed aimed at reinforcing the judge's collegial instincts:

> . . . Pratt has alleged that the judge, the Honorable Kathleen Parker, now deceased, was involved in the conspiracy to convict . . . Pratt has attacked the Honorable Richard Kalustian, judge of the Los Angeles Superior Court and the prosecutor in this case, as having withheld exculpatory evidence received from the FBI. In the most recent issue of *California Lawyer,* Pratt's counsel, Mr. Johnnie Cochran, is quoted as saying, "I don't know if Kalustian is morally capable of being a judge. . . ." Pratt claims that redacted portions of FBI documents and FBI documents that simply never existed prove that Judge Kalustian put on perjured testimony. In assessing the credibility of Mr. Kalustian, a superior court judge, against the credibility of Mr. Cochran, a celebrity defense lawyer, the very least the court can do is look at the [FBI] documents which Pratt claims contain exculpatory evidence to see if, in fact, such evidence ever existed.

Hanlon bristled when he read the statement. "We've been dealing with the FBI since Coolidge was in office," he griped, "and exculpatory evidence is the *last* thing they're gonna show a judge. What they'll show him is every bit of dirt they can find, every unsubstantiated statement, every distortion, forgery and fake. They'll make Geronimo look like King Kong. The FBI has shown us as much decency and fairness as your average North Beach pimp."

IT FELL to Cochran to respond to the Ferreira statement in court. "We simply don't trust the FBI," he told the judge. He cited previous habeas corpus petitions that had been denied after cozy meetings in judicial chambers. "We're sure they'll show you disinformation and libel. At least let us look at the documents so we can point out where they're wrong."

Judge Dickey said he was bound by Cowell's ruling and denied the request. After a private huddle with an FBI investigator and lawyers from the J. Edgar Hoover FBI Building in Washington, he placed 1,511 secret documents under seal. Based on his own review of the government material, he said in open court, "there is nothing that completely decides this matter on the spot. In other words, there's nothing there that basically would be a smoking gun. . . ."

The evidentiary hearing would proceed as scheduled.

Cat and Mouse

From the Pratt team's standpoint the opening day of the hearing was memorable for a snub and a gaffe. All five lawyers—Cochran, Hanlon, Drous, Robert Garcia and Shawn Chapman—had taken extra pains with their wardrobes. Drous wore a new slate-blue suit from Saks, and Hanlon had bought a stylish tie, shined his shoes and carefully arranged the wispy remnants of his Jewfro. Cochran wore his usual gold cross in his lapel and a surreal tie with flashy yellow streaks that matched three points of a golden silk handkerchief blossoming from the breast pocket of his gray pinstripe suit.

Hanlon had developed a theory about Cochran's dress style. "After all these years, he still has no idea what a great lawyer he is," he told his wife. "He has a need to be polished, to be a fashion plate in a $5,000 suit. I think he wonders if he can do the job without all the trappings. Also, he believes in the system, and he dresses up to show his respect."

"You never had that problem," Kathy said.

AT 8:30 A.M. on Monday, December 16, 1996, the Pratt lawyers were standing in the hall with their overloaded evidence carts when a sheriff's deputy appeared at the courtroom door and instructed the swarm of spectators, "Nobody come in! Judge says we have to do this orderly."

Drous whispered, "This is definitely *not* San Francisco."

Behind them the elevator doors slid open and three deputy D.A.'s emerged: Sondheim, Ferreira and a late addition, Jodi Michelle Link.

"Right this way, Counselors," the deputy called out, his eyes on the woman's long blond hair. The three prosecutors entered the courtroom without breaking stride.

"Well!" Drous exclaimed to Shawn Chapman. "They go in and we wait."

Chapman couldn't resist. "And you're not even black," she said.

The apparent discourtesy turned out to be a simple mistake. The judge had instructed the deputies to offer equal treatment to both sides, but the deputies hadn't seen Cochran or recognized the other members of the Pratt team. Soon the five attorneys were politely ushered to their table.

Cheers bounced off the walls of the jammed courtroom as Geronimo entered through a rear door in his canary-yellow jailhouse jumpsuit with "OC" on the back. At forty-eight he'd solved the problem of his vanishing hairline by shaving his head, but he still wore a neat moustache and goatee. He smiled and waved at his supporters, including his professorial brother Tim and his sister Virginia, whose own fashion statement was a coiffure of lustrous black cornrows.[70]

Judge Dickey waited till the cheering subsided, then made his own entrance as the bailiff intoned the patriotic call to order.

THE DAY'S first witness was Clayton Anderson, former commander of the D.A.'s Intelligence Division. Early in the examination Hanlon picked up a sheet of paper and asked, "May I approach Mr. Anderson, Your Honor?"

As Hanlon stepped into the well of the court, two bailiffs rushed to head him off. In some courtrooms this area just below the bench was hallowed ground; intrusions were regarded as symbolic attacks on the judge. If a lawyer received permission to approach a witness or the bench, he was expected to walk around the well.

The Pratt lawyers realized the enormity of Hanlon's gaffe when the judge frowned and said in distinct tones, "Not. Through. *The well.*"

Cochran whispered to his colleague, "This is Southern California."

---

[70] Brothers Charles and Jack had returned to Morgan City years before and helped their sister Jacqueline care for their ailing mother. Emelda was a social worker in Chicago.

Hanlon bowed slightly toward the bench and said, "In Northern California we can do that. I won't make that mistake again, Your Honor."

The judge nodded without changing expression.

Early in Clayton Anderson's testimony it became clear why Hanlon had asked that the retired police official be designated a hostile witness. Despite a sworn declaration in which he'd repeatedly used the term "confidential informant" to describe Julius Butler, Anderson now insisted that he hadn't meant "informant" but "source." Hanlon asked if he'd discussed the matter with the D.A.'s Office, and Anderson admitted that he had. A long semantic argument ensued, with Brentford Ferreira peppering the discussion with objections. The examination turned even more contentious at the first mention of a key figure in the case.

Q. Did you ever go to Richard Kalustian, prior to or during the trial, and tell him that you had a card in your drawer, locked up, in a confidential informant index, listing Julio Butler an informant?

A. No.

Q. Okay, why not?

A. I had no—I didn't make any connection between any—

Q. . . . Were you aware that Butler was one of the key witnesses in the trial?

A. I don't recall if I was aware of that or not. . . .

Q. Did Mr. Bowles work the case with Mr. Kalustian?

A. I believe he assisted Mr. Kalustian.

Q. And Mr. Bowles worked for you?

A. That's correct.

Q. And you were the keeper of the information, right? It was in your locked desk?

A. That's correct.

Q. And were you aware that Julio Butler was a witness?

A. I don't know that I was aware. I simply don't recall. . . .

After almost an hour of jousting, Hanlon could see that Commander Clayton Anderson was unlikely to confirm any connection between Kalustian and the informant files on Butler.

Outside the courtroom after the testimony, Cochran complained to reporters that his opponents were still "playing word games to justify the result they want. We have spent twenty-five years where so-called intellectual people play word games. In many respects it's intellectually dishonest."

Hanlon told the press that he was looking forward to the next day's confrontation—"between Julio Butler, who lied on the stand, and Johnnie Cochran, who was hoodwinked."

In a page-one article in the next morning's edition of the *Los Angeles Times,* Edward J. Boyer wrote: "For almost 25 years, Johnnie L. Cochran Jr. has been waiting to get Julius Butler into a courtroom where he could be put under oath and questioned about his role as an informant for law enforcement. Cochran will get that opportunity today."

BEFORE THE BLUNT-FORCE meeting began, the judge made a short speech. "I just want to indicate to the spectators," Dickey said in an avuncular manner, "I understand that there are strong feelings about this case, and particularly with respect to Mr. Butler, and that is something that is understandable. But I cannot permit anyone in the courtroom to—by gesture or words or any other method—to convey your feelings about the witness's testimony. If you are not capable of keeping them to yourself, then you should leave the courtroom before the witness testifies. And if anyone does what I ask you not to do, and the bailiff is able to identify those persons, they will be excluded from the proceedings. . . ."

Hanlon had never heard a more artful warning to a partisan audience. For the rest of the hearing, stirrings in the crowd were put down by the merest glance from the bench. That's what they call command presence, Hanlon said to himself. The guy doesn't even have to raise his voice.

Julio Under Oath

Cochran had stayed up till 4:00 A.M. preparing questions for the witness whose testimony had doomed his client to the company of killers, roaches, rats and his own body wastes. The lawyer intended to expose former deputy sheriff Julius Butler as a liar and informer who invented an impossible scenario that dishonest law enforcement authorities were happy to embrace, since it matched their own agenda. The previous October, at the trial of another well-known African American, Cochran had asked prospective jurors: "You know, don't you, that it's possible for a peace officer to walk through these doors, take that witness stand, raise his right hand and swear to tell the truth—*and then absolutely lie?* Do you believe this happens?" Now he had to drive home the same point about a leading churchman and pillar of the black community.

Julius Carl Butler was sixty-four, his diameter and dignity expanded by ten years as a member of the Los Angeles County Bar. After he was sworn, it soon became clear how far he'd distanced himself from "Julio," the cell-leader, and "Mother," the hairstylist and cosmetician. He used lawyerly terms and emphasized his polished persona by wearing a tailored gray suit, a neatly knotted tie, black shoes and dark-rimmed glasses. His wavy hair was still full and glistening and his spade-shaped goatee was shot with gray.

Under Cochran's careful questioning, the community leader described his four years of service as a deputy sheriff, mostly involved in handling prisoners, and explained that he retired in 1960 because of domestic problems—"I wanted to leave town."

He was discussing his earliest contacts with the Black Panthers when Brentford Ferreira registered an objection that threatened to halt the proceedings on the spot. "This is history," he told the judge. "This is all in the trial transcripts. I thought we were going to limit ourselves to the issues the court wanted to hear about."

Dickey overruled the objection. At the petitioner's table Hanlon glanced at his client. He was nodding. It was always a good sign when Geronimo Pratt Esq. agreed with a ruling.

After more questions about Butler's role in the Panthers and his friendship with LAPD Sergeant DuWayne Rice, Cochran asked the witness if he knew a police captain named Ed Henry. Ferreira objected again. "At this point," he complained to the judge, "we are retrying the case."

"Your Honor, we are *not*," Cochran responded. "The trial took eight weeks."

Again the objection was overruled.

BUTLER HAD been on the witness stand for an hour when Cochran began leading up to Richard Kalustian's posttrial assistance to his star witness. Seated at their table, Cochran's colleagues studied Judge Dickey's expression. They'd been warned by insiders that he was fiercely protective of his judicial colleagues and would brook no disrespect toward any of them.

Cochran brought up Butler's convictions in the Ollie Taylor beating case and asked, "What assistance did Richard Kalustian, who you knew then to be a deputy district attorney—what assistance did he give you, if you recall?"

Butler said, "I believe—I believe when I wrote to—I went through my probation officer. I wrote to the court regarding entering law school. That is my best guesstimate of the time frame. And then I asked what . . . was my actual charges, because I didn't know the actual charges."

Q. Now, you had been a sheriff's deputy?
A. Yes.
Q. You knew that you had been charged with felonies at that point, did you not?

A. Yes. I didn't know that I was sentenced to a felony. I assumed. I wasn't sure.

Q. You found out at some point you had been sentenced on the felonies?

A. Yes, sir.

Q. Okay. Now, my question is, what, if anything, did Kalustian, a deputy district attorney, do for you regarding the reduction, if any, of these felonies?

A. I believe the aggravated assault charges were dropped. I am not sure. . . .

Q. And that he helped to have that happen?

A. I believe so.

Q. So let me see if I understand what you are telling us—that you asked Mr. Kalustian, who you had come to know, to help you get your felonies reduced, so you might be able to go off to law school? . . . Did you write Kalustian or call him?

A. I don't recall. . . .

Q. Well, let's see. Did you ask him to help you at some point, sir?

A. I just answered you.

Cochran looked at the judge. Dickey had interrupted his busy note-taking and was looking at the witness. Cochran wondered what he thought of Butler's terse answer, so he repeated the question. Ferreira began an objection, but before he'd stated his reason, the judge snapped, "Objection is overruled. You can answer the question."

A. My best recollection is that he got back to me sometime and said that—that I actually had pled to a felony and that . . . steps were made to reduce it to a misdemeanor. . . . Something to that effect. . . .

Q. Did you see Kalustian during this period of time? See each other face-to-face during these periods of time?

Ferreira. Objection. Vague as to time.

Q. I am talking about at the time when you were talking to Kalustian, and he agreed to help you get the felony reduced to a misdemeanor. . . . Did the two of you ever see each other face-to-face in 1974, during your first year of law school?

A. . . . I believe yes, sir.

Q. How many times did you see each other during this time frame?

A. I don't know. Maybe two or three. I don't know. I can't recall.

Observing his cocounsel at close range, Hanlon was impressed. "Johnnie was tough and persistent, but he was always gracious. He never said, 'Thank you'—it was always, 'Thank you very kindly.' He made people like him, but he wasn't obsequious. You could see his effect on the judge, the clerk, the bailiffs."

After Cochran had established the existence of a convivial posttrial relationship between Butler and Kalustian, he turned to the heart of the matter: whether Butler had been an informer, an informant, a source, a mediator or a liaison. He asked, "Had you ever used the word informant to describe yourself."

"Never."

"Ever used the word snitch to describe yourself?"

"No, sir."

Cochran read from a report by the D.A.'s investigator Steve De Prima in which Butler was quoted as admitting that he'd been rewarded for his work as an informant.

"It is incorrectly stated," the churchman replied. "It is not exactly what I said."

Q. . . . Weren't you given some money to buy a gun?
A. That's correct.
Q. You bought a gun, didn't you?
A. You said, "Or the gun."
Q. . . . I don't want to argue.
A. I don't either, but I want the truth to be told.
Q. Let's see if we can get it, the truth.

In a soft voice Cochran asked if Butler was familiar with the laws of perjury. "Objection," Ferreira called out. "Argumentative." Cochran dropped the question—he knew it was argumentative, maybe a touch improper, but its intent had been to remind this certified liar that perjury had consequences. Cochran asked if he'd ever informed for the FBI. Butler replied, "I don't remember any admissions of informant, no."

Q. . . . Have you seen documents which indicate that not only did you inform on but you had numerous contacts with the FBI, including informing about a Thompson machine gun?
Ferreira. Objection, as to relevance.
Dickey. Overruled.

Q. So, now, and do you recall in that same hearing, me asking you if you had ever worked for the FBI?

A. Yes, I think I do.

Cochran read from Investigator De Prima's report and stopped at the line in which Butler was quoted as saying, "I do not want to get my friend in trouble."

"I am going to ask you now," Cochran said, "who was that friend, Mr. Butler, who provided you with the money to purchase the gun?"

"It was Morrie Bowles."

Q. District Attorney's investigator?

A. Yes, sir.

Q. What date was it?

A. I believe it was somewhere in the—I think it was somewhere maybe—I am trying to think. . . . Maybe in the latter part of 1970. Somewhere in there.

Q. . . . This would be the time [when] you are on probation for a felony? And you are given money to buy a gun by a person in law enforcement in Los Angeles County? Is that what you are testifying to?

A. That is possible.

Q. . . . If that date was correct, you were on probation for the Ollie Taylor felony at that point, isn't that correct?

A. If that date was correct.

Q. As such, you would be an ex-con with a gun, isn't that right?

A. I am pretty sure I wasn't an ex-con at the time. . . .

Cochran flipped open the bound transcript of the Pratt murder trial and said, "Before we conclude for the day, I want to ask you if you re-member testifying back in 1972. . . . 'Question: did you ever inform on anybody? Answer: no. Question: you never did that? Answer: no.' Do you remember giving those answers?"

Butler said, "Probably."

Q. . . . Do you remember talking to two FBI agents on or about 9/12/69?

A. I spoke to FBI agents on several occasions. I could not give you the dates.

Q. . . . Do you remember on 12/10/69, that you telephonically furnished the following information to the FBI? You told the FBI that Elmer Pratt owned a Thompson machine gun, silver steel in color. You go on to state that the Black Panther Party in Oakland allegedly had a rocket launcher, and Eldridge Cleaver had a fifty-caliber machine gun which is mounted on a truck. Do you remember telling them that?

A.   I remember the conversation about a rocket and machine gun on a truck. Yes.

Q.   When you testified under oath after swearing to tell the truth [that] you haven't informed on anybody, you were lying, weren't you?

A.   No, sir.

AFTER THE judge's formal recessional at 4:03 P.M., Cochran, Hanlon, Drous and Chapman conferred with their client in a holding cell adjoining the courtroom. Geronimo sat on one side of the bars and the lawyers huddled together on the other. It was a sore point with Pratt that his lawyers were forced to confer with him in a sardine can. But today he seemed more concerned about his attire. *Ebony* magazine had shown its support by providing him with a blue double-breasted suit with matching accoutrements, and Geronimo despised every thread and buttonhole. "This ain't my style," he complained. "I don't wear ties. I want one of those suits like I used to wear—you know. . . ."

Drous said, "You mean like the suit you were arrested in? In Dallas?"

"That's it."

"Where the jacket looks like an open shirt? And the lapels have piping?"

"Right. A leisure suit. With that cool polyester stuff."

"Jesus Christ, Geronimo, it's not 1970," Drous reminded him. "They don't even make those suits anymore. I'd have to look in thrift shops."

Pratt seemed surprised at the news. After a discussion about style trends, he agreed to a compromise. He would wear a modified Panther outfit—dark slacks and a black outer shirt with a powder-blue shirt underneath. Anything would be better than an itchy wool suit or yellow jail clothes that made him resemble a large canary.

Hanlon asked his expert opinion of the judge. "Well, he's no Kathleen Parker," Geronimo replied. "He's no Cowell, no Kronenberg. He acts like a real judge."

Drous said, "Sometimes a true conservative can make a better judge than a half-ass liberal."

The stubborn Hanlon withheld judgment. "We've been screwed so many times," he said. "He's probably just bending over backwards so he won't be reversed."

TIMOTHY PRATT and his sister Virginia were in a good mood as they drove back to her house in Los Angeles. They'd never thought they would live to see Julius Butler struggling to answer Johnnie Cochran's pointed questions. Later Tim described his feeling in writing: "In essence, Butler was The Prince of Evil. The thought of losing in this second battle with Cochran was laughable. Butler had become so comfortable with himself that he was convinced he would beat Cochran. He'd beaten him before with lies, he would do it again. But on this day Butler got tangled in his own web of deceit and lies, and the more he attempted to extricate himself, the more tangled he got."

ON THE witness stand on Wednesday, the third day of the hearing, Butler again disputed FBI and LAPD documents about his role as a police informer. Brentford Ferreira objected to almost every item of evidence and the judge overruled almost every objection. Geronimo stared intently at the witness who'd conspired with police to put him away for life. "I just felt sorry for him," he said later. "What a poor fool he was. Worse than an Uncle Tom. Nothing I could do to Julio would be as hard as what he had to go through every time he looked in a mirror. Mother Butler. Such a sad, useless man."

Only once through the intensive questioning did Butler admit that the hated appellation "informant" might apply to him. A fired-up Cochran cited comments by Sergeant DuWayne Rice and other LAPD officers to the effect that Butler provided them with information about the Black Panthers and even led them to contraband weapons.

Q. So Sergeant Rice will know about that incident also, because he was present. Right?
A. Yes.
Q. And so will Captain Henry?
A. Possibly. Yes, I'm sure.
Q. And those two men believed that you were an informant and you helped them in recovering these weapons with information throughout the year?

A. I don't dispute their belief.

Q. Could you dispute the connotation that you were in fact an informant?

A. No, I was acting as an informant.

But later Butler scuttled back to his earlier position that he'd been a "mediator" or "liaison" between lawmen and the Panthers. He described FBI memos about his informer status as "incorrect," "false," "inaccurate," "wrong," "not true," and argued that the information he provided to police could not be described as confidential because he'd also shared it with his landlady and neighbors.

AS THE day wore on, the church leader began to revert to his old street-fighter pugnacity. He frequently said, "I've already answered that," as though he were in charge of the examination. Whenever Cochran appeared on the verge of pinning him to specifics, his memory turned hazy, or he mumbled that the question was poorly phrased. When he described Long John Washington as someone who "wouldn't have the balls . . . ," Cochran interrupted to say, "We're in court. You might want to watch your language."

Butler turned toward the bench and said, "Excuse me. I'm sorry, Judge. Forgive me."

Dickey said, "Go ahead and answer the question." A few minutes later he declared a recess.

DURING THE break an annoyed Cochran told a reporter, "Everybody— the FBI, Los Angeles police, D.A.'s investigators—believes Julio was an informant except himself. He can't bring himself to say 'informant.'" Cochran accused Butler of engaging in "semantic sophistry," and added, "This man *was* an informant. We should have been advised of that. The jury should have known that."

BACK IN the courtroom Cochran brought up the FBI's many visits to Butler and his spirit of cooperation with the agency:

Q. Mr. Butler, you know how to say no, don't you?

A. Yes.

Q. If somebody wants to talk to you, if you don't want to talk to them, you say no?

A. Yes.

Q. So when the FBI agents came on all these occasions and wanted to talk to you, you could have said no. Isn't that right?

A. That's correct. . . .

Q. You didn't say no?

A. Yes.

Q. You talked to them?

A. Yes.

Q. You informed on your colleagues, didn't you?

A. No.

When Cochran introduced the delicate question of how a pair of COINTELPRO agents happened to be a few feet away when the super-secret "insurance letter" was handed to Sergeant Rice, Butler darted from one position to another. First he claimed that no FBI agents had been present and the very idea was "ridiculous." Then he admitted that it was possible that "two white law enforcement officers" had pulled up in a car and tried to talk to him. Before he finished testifying, he'd claimed that the incident hadn't happened, might have happened, might not have happened, and that he didn't recall.

At last Cochran dropped the subject. If I can tell he's lying, he said to himself, so can this judge.

TIMOTHY PRATT watched the proceedings from a seat next to an African American who appeared deep in thought. After Pratt learned that the man was a retired law enforcement officer, he blurted out, "Sir, do you have any idea of the pain and suffering our family has endured as a result of the frame-up of our brother?"

The ex-lawman appeared disturbed by the question. "Please," he said, touching Tim's arm. "Just wait till you hear my testimony."

Timothy moved away. "The man sat alone," he wrote later, "looking like someone with a heavy weight on his shoulders."

The next morning, Thursday, December 19, the anonymous seatmate took the witness stand and wasted no time in confirming that Julius Butler had been an active informer for the Los Angeles D.A.'s Office. He identified himself as retired Lieutenant Frederic Willis and said that he'd been a

D.A.'s investigator for twenty-six years, serving as Butler's handler in 1969 and 1970. He confirmed that Butler had also informed for the FBI during that period. Willis' notebooks, showing date, time and place of his meetings with Butler, were introduced into evidence.

During the lunch break Hanlon and Cochran polished their plans for Richard Kalustian. They'd already decided that Hanlon would conduct the examination, with Cochran standing by to provide support.

"Not that you wouldn't do a great job," Hanlon told him, "but you're too angry. You might piss off the judge."

"I have no respect for Kalustian," Cochran replied, "and I've said so in print. Maybe I can examine him and not show my feelings—maybe I can't."

"Let's not take the chance."

Mister Kalustian

Just before Superior Court Judge Richard Kalustian was scheduled to take the stand, the Pratt team received a harsh reminder of Judge Dickey's protectiveness about his judicial colleagues. Cocounsel Robert Garcia stood up and said, "The next witness is Mr. Kalustian. We request that Mr. Kalustian be referred to solely as Mr. Kalustian, not as Judge Kalustian, not as Your Honor."

The request made Hanlon a little uncomfortable. Garcia was a veteran of the U.S. Attorney's Office in New York City, a Stanford professor and deep thinker, but he was taking the risk of offending Dickey over an unimportant bit of nomenclature.

"In this courtroom," Garcia plowed on, "there is only one judge. We believe that we are here in Orange County and not in Los Angeles precisely because of the concern that having Mr. Kalustian testify as a witness creates the appearance of impropriety and a potential conflict of interest."

Dickey's aquiline nose crinkled up. "Who is calling him as a witness?" he asked.

Garcia said, "We are."

In a baffled tone the judge asked, "You think I am going to give him some extra credibility because he uses his title?" Garcia started to respond, but Dickey continued, "That is ridiculous, Mr. Garcia."

The NAACP lawyer pressed on: "That is, we are concerned with the appearance of impropriety, in terms of Mr. Pratt, in terms of the public and the media."

"Your request is denied," the judge announced in the loudest voice he'd used since the hearing began. "He is a judge. He is entitled to be referred to by his title. You don't have to call him Your Honor if you don't want to."

The dogged Garcia remained on his feet. "We have been referring to *Mister* Kalustian," he insisted. "We ask that that continue."

"Denied. Call your witness."

The courtroom was silent as Kalustian was sworn in. He appeared relaxed and calm, a handsome man of about sixty, his luxuriant black wavy hair thinning and graying and his heavy moustache peppered with white. Hanlon was a little surprised at his longtime enemy's appearance. In early newspaper pictures Kalustian had put him in mind of a card shark, but now he resembled the affable uncle at a family reunion.

Judge Dickey's face gave away nothing about his own feelings. "Who is handling?" he asked.

"I am," Hanlon said.

He turned to Kalustian and asked his first question, which turned out to be a croaky "Good afternoon?" His plan was to demonize Kalustian as Kalustian had demonized Pratt, but it was difficult because the man on the witness stand looked so benign. The word that came to Hanlon's mind was "nebbish"—New York Yiddish for ineffectual, harmless, ordinary.

After the former prosecutor responded with his own pleasant "Good afternoon," Judge Dickey watched with the air of a mother hen as Hanlon launched into a staccato series of biographical questions that produced precise answers in a reasonable tone. But when Hanlon turned to the relationship between Kalustian and his trial assistant Morris Bowles, the witness began to sound slightly more tentative. He said that at the beginning of the Pratt murder trial he hadn't known that Bowles was a member of the Intelligence Division of the D.A.'s Bureau of Investigation. He'd "gradually learned" Bowles' status during the trial.

Hanlon broached the subject of the confidential informant cards:

Q. And are you now aware, asking you, now, as of today, that the D.A.'s Bureau of Investigation has confidential index cards on confidential informants?

A. I am now aware.

Q. When did you become aware of this fact?

A. When Mr. Ferreira asked me whether I knew about a bureau card.

Q. When did you leave the D.A.'s office to become a judge?

A. November 1985.

Q. And up until 1985, did you have any knowledge that the district attorney kept confidential informant cards?

A. No.

Hanlon soon realized that he was gaining no ground and switched to the subject of the Black Panthers. Kalustian admitted that the D.A.'s Office regarded the BPP as a threat to the public. When Hanlon attempted to pursue the subject, Ferreira objected again and the judge abruptly asked Hanlon, "What are you getting at?"

Hanlon made another jump-shift, this time to the Ollie Taylor case. "Mr. Butler allegedly pled to four serious felonies, without any agreement in your office?" he asked. "Just pled to the sheet and ended up with probation?"

Ferreira said, "Objection. Counsel is testifying."

"Well," the judge told Hanlon, "the problem with that question is, I don't know where it is focused."

"Let me rephrase it," Hanlon said, beginning to feel his collar tightening. "Mr. Butler, based on the records we have, pled the four felonies, involving false imprisonment and beating of Ollie Taylor, and pled to all four, without any agreement, supposedly, with your office. And my question is, in the Panther case like this, at that time, did that seem unusual to you, based on your experience?"

"Vague," Ferreira complained. "Calls for speculation. Assumes facts not in evidence. . . ."

Hanlon started to respond, but the judge interrupted him again. "It hasn't been shown that he had personal knowledge of those events. Sustain the objection."

When the chagrined Hanlon tried to go on, Dickey said impatiently, "He's already said he is not even sure he remembers. He just assumed he remembers it. So how can you get into any detail about whether he was surprised or found it unusual?"

Hanlon said, "I think he worked . . . let me try it one more time. If the court feels it is inappropriate, I will move on."

He shuffled some papers and asked himself, How'd I get off on such a wrong foot? Was it that cockamamie request to call Kalustian "Mister"?

He'd always had problems with power figures, and now he had to deal with three of them at once.

After the judge sustained another Ferreira objection, Hanlon switched to a new tack:

Q. To your knowledge, during the period of time that you knew Julius Butler, did you know that he protected himself and always carried a gun?

A. I knew that during the time around the trial, he told me he carried a gun or had one for his protection.

Q. Which one? That he always carried one or had one?

A. What I remember him saying was when he owned the beauty shop, he had one close by. He might have—that's what I remember. . . . I knew he carried a gun. I knew he had a gun. . . .

Q. And back in 1972, was it legal to carry a gun in Los Angeles County without a license, regardless of your status as a felon and non-felon?

A. I believe not. . . .

Q. Were you aware of the fact that prior to Mr. Butler's testifying for you—not you, personally, but for your office—that he was violating the law, regardless of his status of felon or non-felon by carrying a gun?

A. One has to come to that conclusion.

Q. What, if anything, did you do about that?

A. Like report it to the police?

Q. I'm asking *you*, Judge.

A. Not a thing.

Q. Okay. So you felt, and correct me if I am wrong, that under the circumstances of prosecuting the Panthers, protecting witnesses, in that light, it was acceptable, as an officer of the court, for you to let a witness break the law?

The judge sustained another Ferreira objection and Hanlon asked, "Did you believe it was all right for Mr. Butler to violate the law?"

"At the time," Kalustian testified, speaking with the calm authority of someone who wore robes on the job, "it seemed to me the man's life was in danger. . . . The man has to decide how he is going to protect himself. . . . I am not going to be the one that calls the police and tells them that he's got a gun [and] they strip him of his own protection that he thinks he needs."

Hanlon asked if this attitude wasn't "a breakdown of the law."

Judge Dickey sustained another objection and ordered, "Go on to something else."

After more questions Hanlon tried to get Kalustian to admit that he'd been aware of allegations of violence in Julius Butler's background.

Q. Were you aware that Mr. Butler owned or had control of a Thompson submachine gun as late as September of 1969?
A. I don't think so. But I don't remember, now, whether I did or not.
Q. Are you aware the number of guns that Mr. Butler possessed? . . .
A. I don't think so. I don't know.
Q. And did you consider Butler, when you knew him, to be a convicted felon or non-convicted felon?
A. I thought he was a convicted felon.
Q. So when you knew he was carrying a gun, you believed he was carrying it as an ex-felon?
Ferreira. Objection. Misstates the evidence.
Dickey. Ex-felon?
Hanlon. I am sorry. I misspoke, Your Honor. He was carrying as a felon.
Dickey. Ask another question.
Kalustian. I suppose the answer to that is, I didn't think about it at the time. The answer is, yes, I guess he was.

For the second time in the examination Hanlon addressed Kalustian as "Judge," and the witness responded, "You can call me mister. I don't mind."

Hanlon turned toward the bench, smiled and said, "I want to do what the judge wants to do."

Dickey warned, "Don't start that again."

Soon Hanlon and Ferreira were in acrimonious debate about the exact date when Kalustian had asked that Butler's fine be reduced. "Well," Judge Dickey pointedly asked Hanlon, "don't you have a calendar?"

"At the hotel," Hanlon said. "I don't have it with me. I am sorry."

The judge said, "I hope we are not going to argue about things that we can easily look up."

Hanlon asked Kalustian if he recalled making a motion "to remove certain allegations of violence, menace and fraud, deceit" from Butler's conviction record, but in his increasingly flustered state he said "1993" instead of "1973." The judge corrected him again.

Kalustian answered that he'd acted on Butler's behalf because "they wouldn't let him into law school with the allegations of force and violence remaining in the information. . . ."

Before Hanlon could frame his next question, he looked down at a note from Julie Drous: "STOP! Say you're sick."

Hanlon turned to the judge and said, "Your Honor, I know we intended to go to four-thirty. I am—I'm not feeling well and we are not going to be done at four-thirty."

The judge seemed satisfied to cut the day short. Without waiting for further explanation he said, "That is fine." Thank God, Hanlon said to himself. Now I can go back to the hotel and stick my head in the toilet.

Devil's Advocate

When Hanlon reached his suite at the Marriott, the red light was blinking on the message machine. Someone from the State Bar Association had called to suggest a referendum on Kalustian's disbarment. Hanlon returned the call and said, "For Christ's sake, wait till this case is over. You'll just piss off our judge."

The former Panther leader Kathleen Cleaver joined the other members of the team over a contentious pizza dinner in Hanlon's two-room command suite. "Everybody jumped my ass," he recalled later. "Jim McCloskey, Julie, Cleaver, Garcia, our investigator David Lynn, they all agreed I was blowing the Kalustian examination." In a situation where the lawyer must dominate the witness, Hanlon had allowed the opposite to happen. As a career prosecutor and judge, Kalustian was an expert on trial testimony. His calm judicial demeanor had carried the day.

All the pizza eaters agreed that it would be counterproductive to badger Kalustian about Julius Butler's status as an informant. Nor would the former prosecutor ever concede that there'd been anything improper about his posttrial attempts to give the hairdresser a leg up in society. Indeed, Kalustian could claim that his intercession had helped to convert a street thug into a lawyer, churchman and African American role model.

Juliana Drous advanced a devil's advocate proposition, her accustomed role. She'd been continuing her behind-scenes research, and a friend from the Los Angeles Public Defender's Office had advised her that, unlikely as it might sound, Kalustian was probably telling the truth about being kept in the dark at the time of the original Pratt trial. "He was a young D.A. in those days," she told her colleagues. "He was handed the case on short notice. He'd been working outside L.A. and this was one of his first downtown cases. They dumped it on the new kid on the block. It's quite possible that the cops and the D.A.'s investigators held out on him."

Drous said she'd also learned that Kalustian had enjoyed a good reputation as a deputy D.A. "Even defense lawyers learned to like him," she told her colleagues. "He was regarded as honorable, always opened his trial books to the defense, always provided full and fair discovery. My contact says we might be making a mistake putting horns on him."

"Do you really believe that, Julie?" Hanlon asked.

"I think it's possible."

After the last wedge of pizza had disappeared and the lawyers had drained multiple carafes of coffee, they heard from Cochran by phone. It was plain that his opinion about Kalustian was not subject to change. "The guy put on perjured testimony," he insisted again to Hanlon. "He knew Julio was a snitch from day one."

"Do you think he could've been fooled by the cops and his investigators?" Hanlon asked.

Cochran reminded him of a Julius Butler claim that he and Detective Morris Bowles had been personal friends and drinking companions. "Say Bowles knew that Julio was an informer," Cochran said. "Then he sits next to Kalustian all through the trial and never says a word? He hears Julio deny under oath that he ever snitched, and he doesn't nudge Kalustian and say, 'Hey, we got a little problem here'? *And Kalustian never asks?*" Cochran hesitated. "Maybe I'm just prejudiced, Stu. Maybe I can't get over all the years that I hated Dick Kalustian for what he did to Pratt."

Hanlon put down the phone and thought, Johnnie's a hard man, but he's usually right. Is he right this time? Geronimo's freedom could depend on the answer. He lit a forbidden cigarette and took a walk around the courtyard. He knew that he'd been bested in court and didn't intend to be bested again. This hearing is our last chance, he said to himself. We can't keep fighting the system forever. . . .

He reentered his suite just as McCloskey was saying, "Why do we have to make Kalustian admit *anything?* We don't need his testimony that Butler was an informer. We can prove it with other people, we can prove it with documents, and Julio as much as admitted it himself."

Drous said, "Stu, Judge Dickey will not let us embarrass Kalustian. And Jim's right—it isn't necessary. The real issue is, if Kalustian had known that Julio was an informer, would he and *should* he have told Johnnie in discovery? And would he and *should* he have allowed it to come out at trial?"

"And if it *had* come out," McCloskey said, "would Geronimo have been convicted? I think we know the answer to that."

Everyone except Hanlon accepted the new theory, with only minor variations. In his mind he clung to visions of a high-noon drama, with a shamefaced Kalustian forced to admit every malfeasance, real and imagined. Judge Dickey would slam down his gavel and the case would be over. But he also realized that this wasn't TV or Hollywood and it didn't matter whether Stuart Douglas Hanlon was right or wrong or whether his trial strategy was flawed or whether he looked like a hero or a fool. All that mattered was keeping Geronimo Pratt from spending the rest of his life in prison. After a while he thought, We can't win by alienating any more judges. We've made enemies all the way up to the Supreme Court. We don't need one more. . . .

Just before midnight he said, "Goddamn it, guys, you're right." He threw out the questions he'd prepared for the next day and began reworking his plan.

Kinder and Gentler

A few minutes before the start of the Friday, December 20, session, the bleary-eyed Hanlon walked into the courtroom looking even more disheveled than usual. He hadn't felt so beleaguered since the Columbia campus riots thirty years earlier. A single figure sat alone on a front bench. Hanlon had taken two or three steps past the man when he realized that it was Kalustian.

On impulse he turned. His opponent looked up and smiled. Without thinking, "the king of the schmooze" took a seat beside him.

"You know, Judge," he said, "for twenty years you've been a paper tiger to me. I never met you and I didn't know you till yesterday. We got off to a bad start. I was sullen and rude, and I apologize."

He held out his hand and Kalustian shook it. To Hanlon the ex-prosecutor looked almost relieved. He asked if he could call Hanlon "Stuart."

"Of course."

Geronimo Pratt's prosecutor sounded sincere and polite. He said he understood what had happened in the courtroom the day before and that he respected Hanlon for representing his client aggressively.

"I respect you, too," Hanlon said. "Let's get through this thing as gentlemen."

WHEN EVERETT DICKEY beckoned his judicial colleague to the stand to resume his testimony, Hanlon turned toward Kalustian and said, "Good morning, *Judge*."

After a few warm-up questions Hanlon signaled his kinder and gentler approach by asking, "I assume that as a district attorney your job was to prosecute the case in court and not necessarily to do the investigation or gather the information?"

"That's right," Kalustian replied.

Q. And you indicated yesterday that Morrie Bowles in your own office helped you in some sense in the investigation. Was that not true?

A. He was from the Bureau. He did what I asked him to do. I'm not that sure how much investigation there was left to do at that point.

Q. Okay. And do you remember which police officers of the LAPD aided you in the investigation once you got involved in the case? . . .

A. Ray Callahan.

Q. . . . Okay. I want to ask you some questions—and obviously we're going back in time. If you don't remember, you don't remember. Did you ever have any investigator or law enforcement person to check the intelligence files of the Los Angeles District Attorney's Bureau of Investigation on, first of all, any matters regarding this trial?

A. I don't remember.

Q. So if I asked if you particularly asked them about Butler, Pratt or the Party, your answer would be you don't remember also?

A. I don't remember.

Q. Okay. Did you or do you remember asking anybody to check the LAPD Criminal Conspiracy Section files, assuming they had something on Mr. Pratt, Mr. Butler or the Black Panther Party . . . ?

A. I don't remember. . . .

Q. Do you know if you instructed anybody to review the Los Angeles Sheriff's file, if any existed, on Julio Butler, former employee of the Sheriff's Department?

A. I don't think I did.

Q. Okay. Do you know if you asked anybody to run what is known as a C.I. rap sheet on Mr. Butler?

A. I didn't. I don't remember having done that. I think we may have had one.

Q. Do you have any memory of whether or not Mr. Morrie Bowles told you that he had any type of a relationship with Mr. Butler, other than as an investigator on the case for you?

A. I don't remember his telling me anything about any relationship with Butler.

By declining to challenge Kalustian's claims of lost memory, Hanlon was trying to signal to the judge on the witness stand and the judge on the bench that he was recasting himself and Kalustian as honorable men who might disagree but were trying to get at the truth. Brentford Ferreira squirmed a little more than usual, but Judge Dickey seemed pleased with the new approach. It was consistent with his original instructions.

Hanlon continued, "Did anybody in the Bureau of Investigation of the District Attorney's Office give you any information that Julio Butler was considered an informant?"

A. No.

Q. Did Clayton Anderson tell you that he believed Julio Butler to be an informant for the FBI and/or the LAPD?

A. No.

Q. Would it be fair to say that you relied on the law enforcement agencies to provide you any background information you had, other than your own interviews on Julio Butler?

A. Yes.

Q. . . . Okay. Were you aware that the Bureau of Investigation kept intelligence files back at that time period?

A. . . . I didn't think much about it. I came from Long Beach and Torrance, and there was no intelligence out there. When I got to the Bureau, I got into organized crime. There was an intelligence section of the Bureau of Investigation, but it never—the fact that it kept intelligence files wasn't part of my consciousness. I never even thought about it.

Q. Now could you tell us your procedure, if you remember it in this case or in other cases, in terms of keeping your trial notebook. . . .

A. I didn't have a procedure.

Q. Okay. Was this the first—?

A. —Probably the first case I ever tried where I didn't get the file five minutes before the trial and read the police reports on the way into court. . . .

Q. Would you like any water, Judge?

A. Do you have some?

Q. I think there's some here, yes.

The courteous colloquy occupied most of the morning session. During a discussion about Kalustian's pretrial interviews in 1972, the former prosecutor even came to Hanlon's aid. In a firm voice Judge Dickey had admonished Hanlon, "Unless this witness has some recollection of the interviews, this is wasting time."

Kalustian volunteered, "I have some recollection."

Dickey said, "Oh, well, I misunderstood."

"That's the only reason I'm asking him, Judge," Hanlon said pleasantly.

Whenever he came to a subject that might embarrass Kalustian, Hanlon tried not to word his question as a challenge. Still, there were certain matters that had to be placed on the record. It took Hanlon several minutes to lead up to asking why Kalustian had told a witness in the Pratt trial that "the FBI has never been involved in this case and you know it."

After a long intervention by Judge Dickey about whether Kalustian had intended his FBI comment as a statement or a question, Hanlon asked, "Why did you make this statement, if you remember? Do you have an independent recollection?"

Kalustian seemed to pick up on the cues from Hanlon and the judge. "I don't have any independent recollection why I made that statement. It was actually a question, I think. I intended it to be a question at the time, I'm sure."

LATE IN the morning Hanlon came to the new set of questions that he'd drawn up the night before. He began with a gentle preface: "If you can't answer these or if I can't ask a proper question, then obviously you won't have to answer them. But"—he hesitated—"*if* you had known in the period of time from when you got the case until you went to trial that Julio Butler was passing information, talking to, giving information to the FBI, is that the type of information that you would have disclosed to the defense as bearing on the credibility of Mr. Butler?"

Ferreira apparently saw where Hanlon was heading and objected. "Calls for speculation. It's vague."

Judge Dickey advised Hanlon to "break it down . . . you can ask him two questions separately."

Hanlon rephrased. "*If* you had been aware that Mr. Butler had given information about Elmer Pratt in December of 1969 about him possessing an illegal weapon [and] had passed that on to the FBI, is that information that you believe you would have disclosed to the defense?"

Without hesitation Kalustian answered, "Yes."

Hanlon continued the crucial sequence:

Q. If you had known that or if you had evidence that Julio Butler acted as a confidential informant against the Black Panther Party prior to Mr. Pratt's trial, is that information you would have disclosed to the defense?

A. Yes.

Q. If you had known that an investigator in your office, Morrie Bowles, had given Mr. Butler two hundred dollars to buy a gun prior to his testimony in this case and after grand jury testimony, would you have disclosed that evidence to the defense?

A. Assuming there was a connection between it and the case, assuming it could be inferred that it was a reward of some kind for testifying or some kind of a deal that was cut, I probably would, out of an abundance of caution.

Q. If you had knowledge that your own Bureau of Investigation maintained as of January 1972 in a confidential informant index box a confidential informant index card listing Julio Butler as a C.I. with his investigator-handler Morrie Bowles, would you have turned that information over to the defense?

A. Yes. . . .

Q. If you had known that police officer Ed Henry considered Mr. Butler an informant for him prior to the delivery of the letter in August of 1969, is that information you would have turned over to the defense?

A. . . . If I determined that he was acting as an informant for Henry, yes.

Q. . . . If you had known [Butler] was meeting with the FBI, that information alone, is that something you would have passed on to the defense?

A. Something I would have looked into to find out what the meetings were about.

Q. . . . If you had known that Sergeant Rice believed Mr. Butler to be cooperating with the LAPD in 1969, is that information you would either have investigated or turned over to the defense?

Ferreira. Objection. That's vague.

Dickey. Overruled.

A. I would have. . . .

Q. Would you, if you had known, that three days after the delivery of the letter Mr. Butler told an agent of the FBI that he had given a letter to a friend of his that could put Black Panther Party members in the gas chamber, would you have considered that an important fact in the case?

A. . . . [If] at the time . . . it appeared that he had an ax to grind, it should have been revealed.

Hanlon was more than satisfied with the testimony. The Pratt team had scored its most important points since Julius Butler's reluctant admission that he'd been a subspecies of informant. By getting Kalustian to agree that he would have provided the defense with exculpatory evidence that now was known to exist, he'd confirmed that Pratt was denied a fair trial. The man who'd sent Geronimo to prison was firmly on record that Johnnie Cochran had been denied evidence that could have led to a different verdict. In advancing his own image as an honest prosecutor who wanted to do the right thing, Kalustian had helped to make the case for a writ of habeas corpus and a new trial. And he'd made it as a sitting judge himself. But . . . would the other sitting judge see it that way?

A Lawyer's Dream

Most members of the defense team intended to spend the weekend before Christmas working on the case in the hotel in Irvine. Key witnesses remained to be examined—Morris Bowles, DuWayne Rice, Captain Ed Henry and others—and strategies had to be blocked out. All agreed that the hearing seemed to be going well, but Hanlon exhorted his colleagues, "The only way we're gonna win is if we nail down every point—no exceptions, no loopholes. Our case has to be so overwhelming that the judge and the appeals courts have no choice."

On Saturday morning, the day after the long session with Kalustian, the Marriott cashier called Hanlon to report that the rent was overdue on his suite and the single rooms of Drous, Garcia, McCloskey and Investigator Lynn. The bill was running at a thousand dollars a day, and the team's exchequer was empty. Hanlon started to call McCloskey, but Centurion Ministries ran on a tight budget and several of the lay minister's angels had already shelled out heavily for travel, legal and hotel expenses, plus the salary of the private investigator. Hanlon was reluctant to abuse their generosity.

A notorious check-grabber saved the day by volunteering his own American Express Platinum card. Hanlon paid the bill with the card and

told the cashier to retain the imprint. Before the hearing was over, Johnnie Cochran would be billed another $8,000. Everyone laughed about it later. In the defense of Geronimo Pratt, money had never been an issue.

HANLON MISSED Kathy and his sons, but he was pinned to the Marriott for the weekend. Rory and Liam were in school, and during their Christmas vacation Kathy intended to clear her court calendar and accompany them to Orange County to watch their father in action. In a way Hanlon was glad to avoid the round-trip flight to San Francisco. He was a shadow copilot who used the armrests to assist on all takeoffs and landings. In his dreams he saw great apes shaking his plane and slamming it to the ground. In lightning storms he lowered the window shades and ducked under pillows to avoid the gorillas.

JULIE DROUS, wife, mother and attorney, summed up the mood of the Pratt legal team as Christmas approached: "All we did was bitch about being away from our families. Woe is me, how'd I get into this situation, what are my poor kids doing without me? The truth was, we were thrilled and excited. The case was going well, a defense lawyer's dream. It was *Man of La Mancha, To Kill a Mockingbird.* We were righting a terrible wrong. We kept making all these noises about being stuck in Orange County with John Wayne and the Nixon sucks, but we loved every second."

EVERYONE EXCEPT the client. Separated from his supporters, Pratt felt bereft and neglected. His lawyers met with him in the holding cell whenever court recessed, but the quarters were tight and his comments tended to get lost in the legal verbiage. He wanted his friend Kathleen Cleaver, now a visiting law professor at the Cardozo School of Law in New York, to sit at the petitioner's table, but Hanlon insisted there was no room. "She's been on my side since 1970," Geronimo pleaded. "She deserves a little recognition."

"This hearing isn't about recognition," Hanlon replied. "It's about getting you out of prison. We only have so much space."

Pratt had never felt relaxed in the stiffly formal Orange County Jail. He was housed next to the multiple murderer Charles Ng, who kept explaining to anyone who would listen that it was his partner who'd committed

his crimes. "Look, man," Geronimo told him, "I don't want to hear about it, okay? I got other things on my mind."

Most of the time he was simply lonely. At the end of each courtroom day he was hustled away in handcuffs while his lawyers and friends joined together for tête-à-têtes in the hall, swims and hot tubs at the hotel, convivial meals and bull sessions. Above all else, he was a social animal, and he hated to miss the action.

He was grateful for a few touches of kindness from the judge. Despite Dickey's formal courtroom decorum, he allowed the Pratt attorneys to eat takeout food in the courtroom at lunchtime. It meant a big savings in time for the out-of-towners. Each day Robert Garcia or one of the other lawyers would carry Geronimo's portion to the holding cell alongside the courtroom and join him for a working lunch.

"When the judge let us bring food into the courtroom," Cochran said later, "I was touched. Nothing like that would ever have happened at the Simpson trial. We tried to smuggle O.J. a pastrami sandwich and the deputy acted like we were bringing in an assault rifle. We were warned if we did it again, we'd all go to jail. Folks said Judge Dickey was stiff. I just thought he was humane."

IN AN oblique way the judge's reasonableness put unexpected stress on Geronimo and his lawyers. "We were never gonna get another chance like this," said Hanlon, who found himself described in the *Los Angeles Times* as half mensch and half leprechaun. "If we lost in front of a judge who was this fair and this conscientious, we were finished. Geronimo would die in prison. He knew it and so did we. The judges who'd screwed us in the past left big openings for appeal, but Judge Dickey wasn't giving us a whiff of reversible error. We had to work our asses off to make sure we made no mistakes on our own. This didn't leave much time for schmoozing with Geronimo."

Hanlon steeled himself to take a certain amount of abuse from his old friend. "G was on edge all the time. Another guy would've cracked years earlier, knowing every hour of every day that he was innocent. I wasn't sure he was gonna make it through the hearing. He was always getting pissed at one thing or another, and I was the one he complained to. It reached the point where I didn't want to deal with him anymore. I thought, I'll fight for you, but that's it. I had to face the fact that our relationship was coming to an end. All those years! I thought, If we get him out, he'll go one way and I'll go another. It was a sad thought. I'd loved Geronimo for so long. He was never just another client to me. Thank God for Kathy. I phoned her and the boys every night, and every night she told me not to worry. She said G and I would be friends again. I asked her how she knew. She said who else would put up with such assholes?"

ON MONDAY, the eve of Christmas Eve and the sixth day of the hearing, Julius Carl Butler was ushered back to the witness stand for cross-examination by Brentford Ferreira. Cochran intended to conduct the redirect, and he filled several yellow pages with notes as it became clear that the churchman planned a major revision of his personal history. The latest version began with a setup question by Ferreira: "Last week I believe you testified to the following definition of an informant: 'someone who gives information about someone, or someone who causes another to be arrested or convicted.' Do you recall that?"

"Yes, sir."

The deputy D.A. held up a page from the trial transcript and said, "Now a question is asked: 'Could you dispute the connotation that you're in fact an informant?' And the answer states, 'No, I was acting as an informant.' Do you recall making that statement last week?"

"Yes, sir . . . it's probably a misstatement that I made it."

Cochran jumped up. "Just a moment, Your Honor. *Just a moment*. The record speaks for itself."

The judge said, "The witness can correct it if he feels that he said something erroneously last week."

After more friction between the lawyers, Ferreira asked Butler, "Did you make this statement, 'No, I was acting as an informant'?"

"If I did," Butler repeated, "it was a misstatement. . . . My intention was 'No, I was *not* an informant.' "

The bizarre cross-examination ended with Ferreira asking if the witness had ever been paid as an informant by the D.A.'s Office.

"No, sir."

"Asked and answered," Cochran said. The judge granted his motion to strike the response.

DURING A recess Cochran told a *Los Angeles Times* reporter: "Butler has this real problem with memory. He admits last week that he was an informant. He comes back and says he was wrong: 'I didn't mean to say that.' We're just trying to show just how improbable he is."

Cochran thought, Half of Geronimo's life has been stolen by lies and liars. Sensitive antennae made him suspect that Butler had been coached. There was a fine line between "trial prep" and subornation of perjury. He wondered if his old friends Ferreira and Sondheim had crossed it. Back in court, he decided to explore the possibility.

"Now, over this weekend," he asked Butler, "did you spend quite a bit of time with Mr. Ferreira and Mr. Sondheim preparing for your testimony here today?"

A. No.

Q. Well, how much time did you spend with them?

A. I spent some time this morning.

Q. . . . Did you spend any time with the prosecutors over this weekend, either over the phone or in person?

A. Over the phone, yes.

Q. What day was that?

A. Sunday.

Q. What time was it on Sunday?

A. Around five or four o'clock. . . .

Q. And where did this phone conversation take place, sir?

A. They called my home.

Q. When you say "they," who do you mean?

A. Mr. Brent—Mr. Ferreira.

Q. And also Mr. Sondheim?

A. I understand he was there.

Q. . . . And, then in the course, you had a conversation, did you?

A. It was a question and answer, not a conversation.

Judge Dickey interrupted his note-taking, turned toward Butler and said, "Wait a minute. Do you realize what you just said, sir? *He gave you the questions and the answers?*" Apparently the specter of subornation was also on the judge's mind. A prosecutor who spoon-fed a key witness specific questions and answers would be violating legal canons.

Butler quickly responded, "No."

The judge said, "I think you need to listen to the questions carefully. I don't think Mr. Cochran asked that to trick you. . . . Are you really saying that he gave you questions and answers?"

"No, sir. No."

"Well, just listen to the question."

Ferreira asked, "Could we perhaps have that part read back? I thought he said we engaged in questions and answers."

Butler said, "That's what I thought I said."

The judge said, "It's all done now. . . . Go ahead, Mr. Cochran."

Seated in the front row, the Reverend Jim McCloskey was impressed with Cochran's aplomb. "Johnnie turns every courtroom into his personal stage," he said later. "He's Leonard Bernstein conducting his orchestra."

"All right," Cochran continued in his sharp voice. "So that we're clear, nobody wanted to trick anybody here. Mr. Ferreira called you on Sunday afternoon, and the two of you then talked back and forth. Is that right?"

"Objection," the prosecutor said. "Misstates what occurred. He said Mr. Sondheim was there, too."

The judge looked impatient and asked Butler, "Did you talk to Mr. Sondheim also?"

Butler answered, "I think maybe saying hi, but I think I knew he was on the other end. That's basically all Mr. Sondheim did."

Dickey overruled Ferreira's objection and ordered Cochran to continue.

Q. Were there any questions propounded to you by Mr. Ferreira?

A. Yes, sir.

Q. He told you, did he not, what he was going to ask in court here today?

A. No, sir.

Q. . . . Did he ask you a series of questions, sir?

A. Yes, sir.

Q. And then you tried to answer those questions?

A. Yes, sir.

Q. . . . How long did this question-and-answer session go on between you and Mr. Ferreira?

A. Probably around an hour, somewhere.

Q. . . . So it felt like from four to five he was firing these questions at you, right?

Ferreira took exception to the phraseology. "Well," Cochran said, "I'll take 'firing' out."

"You know from today, Counsel," Ferreira said, "I don't fire questions."

Cochran said, "So stipulated, Your Honor."

Both lawyers apologized to the judge for the byplay. Then Cochran continued his attempt to suggest that there'd been an unusual amount of trial prep over the weekend:

Q. . . . And you answered them to the best of your ability, sir?

A. Yes, sir, I did.

Q. Did he ask you this question about page 427, where you said that you were acting as an informant?

A. Not then. No, sir.

Q. Well, did he ask you about that this morning?

A. Yes, sir.

Q. Well, we'll get to that. So, now you talked for an hour, maybe until about five o'clock. And in that period of time, how many questions would you say he asked you?

A. I don't know. He repeated the questions many times. He asked them, reframed them differently oftentimes.

Q. . . . Now, when is the next time you had occasion to speak with Mr. Ferreira or Mr. Sondheim or Miss Link prior to your testimony here this morning, sir?

A. This morning.

Q. And what time was that, sir?

A. About six-fifteen, six-thirty.

Q. Now where did that conversation take place?

A. . . . At the hotel where he was staying.

Q. . . . So the two of you have some conversation when—where just the two of you were alone?

A. Yes.

Q. And he showed you something during that time frame?

A. Yes.

Q. And what did he show you?

A. The statement there, that one that I said I was misstated. . . .

Q. He asked you whether you said, "I was acting as an informant"? Is that what he asked you?

A. Yes, sir. . . .

Cochran felt that he'd made his point. At the very least, a pair of weekend strategy sessions ending in predawn darkness on Monday suggested extraordinary dedication by the D.A.'s Office. He recalled the same anti-Pratt obsession in 1972, when witnesses like Kenneth Olsen and Barbara Reed had sounded like carefully rehearsed stage actors. It was clear that the D.A.'s Office was still bent on keeping Geronimo in his cage. In twenty-five years nothing had changed.

AS JUDGE Dickey had agreed earlier, the court in Santa Ana went dark on Christmas Eve and Christmas Day. Most of the lawyers flew home to enjoy a foreshortened holiday season and planned to return to the hotel in Irvine on Christmas night. School was out in San Francisco, and Kathy Ryan and the Hanlon sons planned to join the group in a few days, Kathy to play her old role of legal adviser and the boys to visit Disneyland and Knott's Berry Farm. It would be the beginning of a family tragedy that no one could have foreseen.

Man with a Gun

When Julius Butler returned to the witness stand at 9:00 A.M. on the day after Christmas, Cochran began his attempt to finish him off. The first area of attack would be the "secret" letter of August 10, 1969, that tipped police that Geronimo Pratt was a killer. Cochran asked, "You wrote this letter yourself?"

"Yes, sir."

"And you described last week that you didn't want to reveal the contents of this letter because you didn't want people to think you were a snitch?"

"Depending on when, the context of when, I thought I wanted to reveal it."

Q. When you wrote this letter, that was about a week after you had provided information about the weapons that you took Rice and Henry to recover. Isn't that correct?

A. I don't recall the chronology, sir.

Q. . . . How did you make arrangements to reach or talk with DuWayne Rice about this letter?

A. I don't remember whether he had called me or I had called him and I told him I wanted to talk to him and I would meet him outside.

Q. Any particular reason, Mr. Butler, that a document this important to you at that time, that you would arrange to meet DuWayne Rice outside on the street or in or about his car?

A. It wasn't the first time.

Q. . . . Did you consider this to be a very important letter?

A. Yes, sir.

Q. To be opened only in the case of your death?

A. Yes, sir.

Q. And yet you decided to make the transfer of this letter on the street to an LAPD officer. Isn't that what happened?

A. That's what happened. Yes, sir.

Q. And it's true that around that time you already told us that you heard the voice of a man calling your name that you believed was Agent [Richard Wallace] Held, the FBI agent. Right?

A. That's not accurate.

Q. Well, did you hear his voice? After the delivery?

A. After the delivery, yes.

Q. . . . So two or three minutes after you delivered this letter, you heard Agent Held's voice out there in the street calling your name. Right?

A. I heard someone that could have been Agent Held.

Q. . . . You thought it was probably Agent Held?

A. I said it *could* have been.

Q. When this person called your name, did you go back and talk to them?

A. No, I kept going.

Q. Where did you go?

A. . . . I went home to my apartment. . . .

Q. Did you ever look back and see whether or not these FBI agents encountered or appeared to be talking with DuWayne Rice?

A. No, sir. . . .

Q. How soon after the delivery of this letter . . . did you talk to DuWayne Rice next?

A. I don't recall.

Q. He told you that FBI agents immediately came over to him and said, "Give us the letter"? Didn't Rice tell you that?

Ferreira. Objection. Calls for hearsay.

Dickey. Overruled.

A. I don't recall that conversation. . . .

Q. . . . You told a number of people about this letter and its contents. Isn't that correct?

A. Yes, sir.

Q. Tell us—I want you to tell us all the people that you told about this letter and its contents, tell us their names.

A. I think that's impossible.

Q. Well, do the best you can.

A. I think I told Michael at the beauty salon. . . . I think I told the guy at the cleaners. I can't remember his name. It's been so long . . . I think I told the guy that owned the drug store next to the salon. Right now his name escapes me.

Q. Who else?

A. I think I told the people in my cadre. . . .

Q. You told pretty much all of the people close to you about this letter, this so-called insurance letter you had written?

A. I told people.

Q. You wanted to get the word out. Is that right?

A. Yes, sir.

Q. . . . What about Morrie Bowles? Did you tell him?

A. I think so.

Q. . . . You did also tell the FBI, did you not, that you had written a letter containing information relating to the involvement of Black Panther members in an affair that could put them in the gas chamber?

A. No, sir. I don't recall that.

Q. Put them in the gas chamber, quote, unquote? You didn't make that statement?

A. I've already answered you, Mr. Cochran.

For another hour the lawyers passed the witness back and forth. Then the judge had questions of his own. "I'm not going to ask you for names," he said, "but were there any other law enforcement or ex-law enforcement officers that were members of the Black Panther Party that you were aware of?"

"No, sir."

". . . Is it something that you tried to conceal or hide from members of the Black Panther Party?"

"Never, no. It was a known fact, sir."

Dickey asked a few questions about the Ollie Taylor case, then said, "When you were going to court during the trial of people vs. Pratt, I think you said earlier that Morrie Bowles was sometimes taking you to court? Was he driving you in a county vehicle?"

"I don't know whether it was an unmarked vehicle or his personal vehicle. I didn't see a red light or anything inside."

Q. Were you carrying that gun?

A. No, sir.

Q. At that time?

A. No, sir. No, sir . . . I never carried the gun to the courthouse.

Q. You weren't necessarily carrying it into the courthouse. Were you carrying at this time in your life?

A. Oh, yes, sir. Yes, sir. Yes, sir.

Q. When you arrived at court, what would you do with it then?

A. It didn't leave the house.

Q. You left it at home on those days when you were going to court?

A. Yes, sir.

Butler's third appearance at the hearing lasted two hours before he was excused for good. The first witness after the noon recess would be Morris Bowles.

The lunchtime conversation among the Pratt team members centered on the impromptu interrogation by the judge. What did it signify? Was he leaning?

"Don't anticipate," Hanlon warned his colleagues, "because you'll probably be wrong. This is the Pratt case. Nothing is what it seems."

COCHRAN HANDLED the direct examination of Morris Bowles. They'd been office acquaintances during Cochran's tenure in the Los Angeles City Attorney's Office and later as number three man in the D.A.'s Office. The seventy-five-year-old Bowles was already on record that Butler's garrulous claims about their friendship were a tapestry of lies, and in court he methodically denied Butler's claims of a relationship that dated to their days as young lawmen. The first time he ever saw "Mr. Julio," Bowles testified, was when he served him a subpoena in the Pratt murder case. He said he'd never socialized with Butler, visited his apartment or salon or gone nightclubbing with him. Nor had he given Butler a gun or the money to buy one. Bowles even contradicted Butler's testimony that he'd chauffeured the star witness during the trial. The former D.A.'s investigator acknowledged that the name "Bowles" appeared on the confidential informant cards but emphatically denied that the handwriting was his.

Despite his age, the retired investigator's voice rang loud and clear as he insisted that Julius Carl Butler was a "street thug" with whom he would

never have established a friendship. He confirmed that he'd acted as Kalustian's investigator during the Pratt murder trial but insisted that his role was limited to providing security, serving subpoenas "and making sure that all the witnesses appeared at the time they were designated to testify."

As for concealing Butler's informant status from Kalustian, Bowles emphasized that he'd possessed no such information to conceal. Nor was he aware of or involved in any favors Kalustian might have done for the hairdresser after the trial.

Cochran asked how Bowles would characterize his relationship with Butler in the years after the Pratt verdict in 1972. "Like two ships passing in the night," the old man replied, and brought a rill of laughter from the packed courtroom by adding, *"Far* at sea." He acknowledged that he and Butler were members of the First AME Church—"I see him all the time. . . . He's right up front"—but insisted that their social interactions were minimal.

The Pratt lawyers were impressed by the Bowles testimony and the firmness of his denial. Was it indeed true, as Bowles had once remarked, that Julio Butler was simply using him to cover up for someone in high places who'd been willing to buy the hairdresser a gun and favor him with other illegalities? If so, who? An LAPD administrator? An FBI official? A deputy D.A.? Every member of the Pratt team drew up mental checklists of possible conspirators.

HANLON CONDUCTED the examination of retired LAPD Captain Ed Henry, who'd already told the Reverend Jim McCloskey that Butler was his regular informant. Like Bowles, Henry took pains to distance himself from the chairman of the board of the First AME Church. He said he'd also seen indications of a connection between Butler and the FBI. He testified that he'd sometimes noticed "two male Caucasians" hanging around Butler and asked Butler who they were. "He stated that he thought they were FBI agents and that he thought they had his telephone tapped because every time he would call to meet with either me or with [Sergeant] Rice they would beat him to the location. And he says they were bugging him, and they wanted to talk to him, and he had refused to talk with them."

Q. Did you give him any advice as a police officer as to what to do?
A. Yes. I said to him, "Well, why don't you talk to them? You don't

have to tell them anything, but you can talk to them and get them off your back."

Q. Do you know if Mr. Butler ever talked to the FBI? Do you know through your own knowledge if he ever took your advice?

A. No, I do not.

Before court was shut down for the weekend, the retired police captain agreed with Hanlon that the term "agent provocateur" might well apply to Julio Butler and his activities. But Henry also seemed to feel that the cosmetician's chicaneries were of a low order of sophistication. He testified that whenever the police contacted the members of his cell, Butler would go out of his way to act more belligerent and foulmouthed than the other Panthers. It was obvious that he was acting. No one had been fooled.

Ordeal for Kathy

On Sunday Kathy Ryan flew to Orange County with her sons Rory and Liam and confided to Juliana Drous, "I don't know what's the matter with me. God, I'm so tired all the time." Her lassitude didn't keep her from escorting the boys to Disneyland and Knott's Berry Farm, as promised.

In an evening hot tub session at the Marriott, Kathy joked, "Look what Stuart's been doing to me." Faint discolorations were visible on her legs and shoulders. She thought she might be having an allergic reaction. Her fingertips had a bluish tinge. She didn't seem concerned—"that's been happening a lot lately."

"You should get that checked out," Julie told her old friend.

"No big deal," Kathy said. She'd always hated to call attention to herself.

"SHE DIDN'T like to go to doctors," Stuart Hanlon said later. "She'd been showing signs of fatigue for six months, but she figured it was natural for a working mom. I was involved in the Pratt case and didn't pay much attention. She'd always done too much. She insisted on an immaculate house, and I didn't give a damn one way or the other. She'd go around picking things up and I'd say, 'C'mon, Kath, take a break. That's ridiculous.' That was the only thing we ever disagreed about."

THE THIRD week of the evidentiary hearing began on the next-to-last day of 1996, with retired LAPD Sergeant DuWayne Rice testifying heatedly that in the street-corner letter exchange he'd been "set up" and still resented it. He said that about fifteen seconds after Butler handed him the letter, two men in business suits appeared. "They pulled out their identification and said, 'FBI. Give us the letter that Julius gave you. It's evidence.' I said, 'What do you mean?' He said, 'We're FBI agents.' He repeated again, 'We want this letter. It's evidence.' I pulled out my badge. 'I'm LAPD and it's mine.' They said, 'Well, we'll take it.' I said, 'No, you won't.' And they backed off."

Later, FBI agents approached him in the police cafeteria and threatened to have him indicted for obstruction of justice if he didn't turn over the letter. "I said, 'Why do you want the letter so bad?' and he said, 'Because it's evidence.' I said, 'What kind of evidence?' They said, 'Well, we just know it's evidence' . . . I says, 'Who told you that I had a letter in evidence?' They said, 'Well, we have information.' "

Under Cochran's close questioning, Rice told the painful story of how the letter finally came to be opened. A white policeman had been tormenting him with "pictures of gorillas, spears, comments on paper about the jungle bunnies, things like that, very racial type things, negative." In a hallway confrontation his tormentor "walked around the front of me . . . grabbed the lapel of my coat, and said, 'Boy, did you hear what I said?' "

Cochran's eyebrows shot up. "He said 'boy'?"

"Yes."

Q. When he said that, what happened next?

A. I hit him.

Q. What happened to him?

A. He went down.

Q. . . . Did some investigation start?

A. Yeah. A commander came out of the office because he wasn't moving. I thought he was injured very seriously. . . . He finally woke up and got up and wanted to fight some more. . . . An Internal Affairs investigation accused me of striking an officer, which I didn't deny. . . . And at that time I mentioned that you don't ever put your hands on a man where I came from. I was raised in Detroit. You don't put your hands on a person."

In the course of the internal investigation, Rice said, the subject of the Butler letter came up and the chief's office ordered him to turn it over. Rice refused, explaining that he'd given his word to protect the contents till Butler's death. After a supervisor threatened him with prosecution, Rice phoned Butler for permission and was told, "The FBI is jamming me, man. Give it to them."

Rice recounted his reply: "Why would you do this to me, Julius? You know, I'm willing to lose my job. I almost lost my job and gone to prison because I was keeping my word to you. In the meantime, you told people I got the letter and what's in it."

Cochran asked if he'd been upset with Butler at that point. "Yes," Rice replied. "Upset, yes, sir." He said that he'd told Butler "a few words that were not nice."

Q. Have you ever talked to him again since that, if you remember?

A. He tried to talk to me, and I looked at him and he left . . . I saw him at the chief's funeral . . . and he came over and sat in front of me and looked back. I looked at him and he got up and moved to another seat.

Q. . . . Any of those times the FBI and LAPD was asking about Butler's letter, you did not know the contents?

A. I had no idea. I didn't ask Julius.

Q. Butler never told you?

A. Never told me.

Q. . . . You said they couldn't put pressure on you. What do you mean by that?

A. Because I'm the type of person you can't bully. . . .

Q. Why didn't you want to have a confrontation with Butler after you thought he had set you up?

A. Because I would have hurt Butler, and I have a family to take care of.

On recross-examination Ferreira asked, "When you got here, did you come in and embrace Mr. Cochran and kiss his associate [Shawn] Chapman?"

"Yes, sir," Rice answered, "because we were old friends."

Cochran resented the implication. He took back his witness and said,

"Sergeant Rice, you and I have known each other since I was a young city attorney in 1963. But because you have known me for almost thirty-four years, did you ever come into court, raise your hand and swear to tell the truth—and lie?"

"No, sir."

"When you testified against Geronimo Pratt in 1972, you were testifying for the prosecution?"

"Yes."

"You did your job?"

"I did my job."

As he was about to release the witness, Cochran remembered the contradiction between the Bowles and Butler testimony about their friendship. Perhaps Rice could shed some light. He asked the retired sergeant how long he'd known Bowles.

A. Thirty years, thirty-five.

Q. Was he part of the group that you were meeting with . . . at restaurants, social activities?

A. No. Bowles lived in the [San Fernando] Valley, and I only saw him on occasion, if he happened to come into town. . . .

Q. Do you ever recall Mr. Bowles with Mr. Butler at any time?

A. No, sir.

FORMER DEPUTY D.A. Ronald "Mike" Carroll, one of the last witnesses before the year-end recess, took the stand and admitted that he'd been dubious about Kenneth Olsen's identification of his wife's alleged killer.

"I didn't like Ken Olsen," Carroll testified. "I just had a personality conflict with him. . . . I liked the woman from the hobby shop much better. She seemed to have her head screwed on better."

"Imagine that," Hanlon told reporters in a tone of heavy sarcasm. "Mike Carroll says the woman from the hobby shop had her head screwed on better. She's the one who changed her description of the killer every five minutes." He shook his head in mock disappointment. "These guys are so caught up in defending their position that they've lost the capacity to realize how ridiculous they sound to others."

Then Hanlon escorted his wife and sons home to San Francisco for the New Year's Day respite. Kathy promised to see a doctor as soon as she found the time.

GERONIMO'S BROTHER Tim was so sure of a favorable decision that he returned to his family in Washington, D.C. "I felt that my mission to California had been accomplished," he wrote later. ". . . I left knowing that Christmas of 1996 would be G's last behind bars. The judge was no Pontius Pilate."

AFTER ROUTINE testimony on Thursday, January 2, 1997, defense investigator David Lynn drove Hanlon back to his hotel in Irvine. In his suite Hanlon listened to a voice-mail message from a family friend in San Francisco. *Call me, Stu. Right away. It's important. . . .*

He returned the call, but there was no answer. He tried his home and decided that Kathy was probably running errands. She would return from her law office to put the boys to bed, make their snack and read to them, then sit up till 1:00 or 2:00 A.M. working on cases. She was tall, wide-eyed and slender and gave off a pale aura of Irish fragility, but she had the work capacity of a water buffalo. It was one of the secrets of Hanlon's success.

After another room-service dinner Drous and Robert Garcia arrived to help frame questions for the next day's witness, Brian Hale, the investigator who'd turned up the informant cards on Julius Butler.

The Pratt lawyers had just begun their homework when a call came in. After a short conversation Hanlon told Drous, "It was just my niece from Seattle." Julie felt a sense of relief and wondered what was making her so jumpy. Maybe it was the unanswered voice message earlier.

The lawyers resumed work. Around 8:00 P.M. Hanlon said, "I'm gonna call home again." He disappeared into the bedroom.

A few minutes later Drous heard him cry out, "Julie, come here. *I need you!*"

She found him sitting on the side of the bed, sobbing. "Kathy has leukemia," he said. "She's gonna die."

Drous was so shocked she couldn't speak. The Hanlons were among her oldest friends. Robert Garcia came into the room and she shooed him out. "What's going on?" he insisted.

"I don't know," she said. "Let me think."

She phoned David Lynn. The private investigator told her, "Stay cool. You and Stuart are going home on the next flight. I'll drive you to the airport."

LATE THAT night Hanlon found his wife weak but cheerful at California Pacific Hospital. An oncologist had informed her that there were essentially two kinds of leukemia: bad and terminal. She told her husband, "The doctor thinks I lucked out. He thinks I've just got the bad." Hanlon thought, It's a dark version of the doctor joke: I've got bad news—and worse news.

They comforted each other all night. Toward dawn he downed a handful of tranquilizers and nodded off in his chair.

The Just and the Unjust

At 8:00 A.M. the phone rang in Kathy's hospital room. A groggy Hanlon listened as Cochran explained that he was headed to Santa Ana to take over. "Tell Kathy we're all praying for her," he said. "Tell her we *envelop* her in our love. You too, Stu. Stay where you belong."

Before court reconvened, Cochran held a hurried conference with Shawn Chapman and Robert Garcia. "It's a sacred duty now," he said. "We've got to win."

BLOOD TRANSFUSIONS over the weekend seemed to strengthen the stricken woman. On Monday she told her husband, "You're going back to Orange County. You put half your life into this case. You're not quitting now."

"I'm not leaving this hospital," Hanlon insisted.

"I'm in good hands. Geronimo needs you."

"Geronimo hates my ass."

"That's just his way, Stu. If he didn't love you, he wouldn't get so upset."

While Kathy dozed, Hanlon drove to a tie shop on Fillmore Street. His colleagues had been kidding him about being outstyled by Cochran. He bought two garish ties, the loudest he could find. When he returned to Kathy's bedside, he checked himself out in the mirror. My God, he said to himself, the judge will hold me in contempt. His tie was the opposite of how he felt—tired, depressed, dead.

LATE ON Sunday night Hanlon and Julie Drous returned to John Wayne country. In the end the doctors had helped him to make his choice. They told him that Kathy had at least a year to live and an outside chance of full recovery. If there was a change for the worse, he could return to San Francisco on the shuttle.

As soon as Hanlon arrived in Irvine, he began berating himself for leaving his wife but also for entertaining the thought of abandoning Geronimo. He kept trying to reconcile the prospect of winning his long legal battle with the prospect of losing Kathy.

"I'm sick, Jim," he told McCloskey. "I'm lost. I don't understand."

McCloskey mentioned Christ's teaching that the rain falls on the just and the unjust.

"But why Kathy?" Hanlon asked. "Everybody loves her. *Why Kathy, of all people?*"

McCloskey said he wished he had the answer.

THE HEARING slogged on. Through the Monday sessions Hanlon willed himself to put his wife out of his mind and function as a legal technician. "I found I could focus on witnesses for five or six hours, then return to real life. It's a reflex, it's training, it's what she wanted me to do."

At the end of the day, after he'd collected his papers and snapped his briefcase shut, it hit him like a shower of ice: *Kathy has leukemia.*

On Tuesday he learned that the doctors had downgraded their diagnosis. She needed a critical bone marrow transplant. He hung up the courtroom phone in tears. The clerk and Julie Drous comforted him and he managed to tough out the session.

ON THURSDAY he lost his composure when he learned that Drous had delayed their return plane reservations by a few hours. "Who are you to change my goddamn reservations?" he yelled. "Why don't you mind your own business for once?" She fled to her room and cried.

At the first break in testimony on Friday morning, he apologized in front of the others. It was a first in his long friendship with his star brief-writer. Drous knew what he was going through and tried to comfort him. "Stu, you're my friend. I will always love you. It's okay for you to yell. It's *okay*, all right?" They both fought tears.

He turned away, then said, "But you shouldn't have changed the reservations."

WITH THE major themes of the hearing established, the Pratt team's closing strategy was to pound home the tripartite alliance of Julius Butler, the LAPD and FBI. In the end the lawyers felt they'd made their case. On Friday, January 10, Judge Dickey dismissed the final witness of the four-week hearing and gave both sides five weeks to produce written briefs. Oral argument would follow two weeks later. It was another painful delay, but Cochran urged his colleagues to be patient. "I checked this judge's record," he said. "He takes his time. That's another reason he doesn't get reversed."

REPORTER EDWARD J. Boyer of the *Los Angeles Times,* in his third year of doggedly following the case, asked Jim McCloskey how the Pratt forces had managed to come up with such a powerful presentation after so many earlier defeats. McCloskey told him it was "no great genius-derived master plan. We were in the dark bumping from wall to wall." Besides, he said, we still haven't won.

Return Fire

Another *Times,* this one published in New York, roused Stuart Hanlon to anger with an attack on his famous colleague. In the editions of January 28, 1997, columnist Maureen Dowd described Cochran as "this man who had persuaded a jury to ignore evidence and decide O. J. Simpson's fate based on racial grudges, this man who had the gall to rank the Simpson case as a civil rights struggle akin to Brown v. Board of Education. . . ." Dowd wrote that "the dark impulses have been good to Mr. Cochran" and were now paying off with *Cochran & Co.,* his show on Court TV.

At first, Hanlon regarded the column as mild, at least compared to some of the diatribes aimed at Cochran after the Simpson acquittal. But his eyebrows shot up as he read the next passage:

> Indeed, Mr. Cochran was so busy in New York this month preparing for the debut of his show that he missed most of the hearing in California to overturn the murder conviction of his client Elmer (Geronimo) Pratt, the former Black Panther leader who may have been wrongly sent to prison 25 years ago. Mr. Pratt's other lawyer, Stuart Hanlon, came from San Francisco, even though his wife had just been hospitalized with leukemia. . . .

Hanlon fired off a lengthy response, portions of which appeared under the prominent three-column overline "Cochran Did Not Abandon Geronimo Pratt." Hanlon accused the highly respected columnist of "insinuations that are not only untrue, but that I find personally offensive." He wrote:

Any conclusion that Mr. Cochran abandoned both Mr. Pratt and myself is untrue. Mr. Cochran has stood up for Mr. Pratt for over 20 years, both publicly and privately. During the evidentiary hearing he was a true co-counsel who examined half the witnesses and was involved in all aspects of the hearing. Mr. Cochran has demonstrated his commitment to Mr. Pratt by being an integral part of Mr. Pratt's legal team. For almost a month, through the Christmas holidays, Mr. Cochran worked pro bono for Mr. Pratt. . . .

Ms. Dowd's intimation that Mr. Pratt and I were abandoned is more than merely inaccurate; it suggests a cruel insensitivity toward Mr. Cochran totally unsupported by facts. In reality, Mr. Cochran is coming back to court to argue the case before the judge. If a new trial is granted, Mr. Cochran has committed to try the case with me.

Kathy Ryan read the exchange in her hospital bed and managed a weak gibe at her husband. "Let's see, Stu," she said. "You're fighting with the cops, the D.A., the LAPD and the FBI. You're fighting with Julie and you're *always* fighting with Geronimo. And now you're fighting with the *New York Times*. Who's next, Stu? Australia?"

He was glad that she was feeling better.

IN MID-FEBRUARY Deputy D.A. Brentford Ferreira suffered a mild stroke. Both sides were saddened. Like his colleague Harry Sondheim, Ferreira was more an academic lawyer than a litigator, but he brought a light touch to the courtroom and had proved to be a skilled opponent.

Back home in Washington, D.C., Timothy Pratt thought out his own reaction as a Christian and finally committed it to paper: "It was very tempting for me to pass judgement and conclude that this was an act of God's judgement against this man who deliberately kept my brother in jail for an additional three years, after he knew that he had not received a fair trial. Instead of passing judgement, I prayed for his safe recovery."

It was what Eunice Petty Pratt would have told her son to do.

FERREIRA'S ILLNESS caused the judge to postpone oral arguments until March 13. Geronimo was enraged by the latest delay. It was easy for his lawyers to point out that he'd been inside for twenty-six years, and "what's another month?" Every time he began to count the days to his release, someone rewrote the calendar. Toward the end of the evidentiary hearing, he'd begun to fantasize about a victory parade down the courthouse steps. Instead he moped in his cell and missed Ashaki and his children.

Hanlon relieved the boredom with an unexpected visit. Within minutes the two old warriors were engaged in a verbal shoot-out over a matter so petty that a few weeks later neither could remember the subject. As they argued, the visiting room guard lowered his newspaper to watch. Hanlon fired his verbal salvos from a sitting position, but Pratt circled the table, clenching and unclenching his fists. Hanlon looked up at him and said, "You want to punch me out, don't you?"

Geronimo said, "You got that right, turkey."

"Fuck you, G." He stuck out his chin. "Take your best shot."

Pratt cocked his arm, then turned away. He looked back, raised his arm again, flopped into the chair and shook his head. "What a couple of dip-shits," he said under his breath. The guard turned back to his newspaper.

After a long silence Geronimo said, "What're we gonna do about this judge?"

"You got a beef with him? The guy's just trying to do things right."

"That's because he's not serving the time. You got to push him, Stu. This isn't fair. File a motion. Get him off his ass."

"I'd file a motion if I knew what motion to file."

"Man, I thought you were a lawyer."

"I *am* a lawyer, goddamn it, and I'm telling you—if we push this judge, we'll regret it. He's not the kind of guy that yields to pressure."

"Neither am I. Where's Cochran? I need a lawyer with balls."

"Fuck you, G."

As Hanlon started to leave, he thought, Why should I even care about this asshole? I have a sick wife. I have other things to worry about. Sure, he's scared, petrified—he knows this is his last chance. It was a mistake to visit him. He relieves tension by blowing up at people. So do I. What a combination. How'd we make it this far?

When he finally stalked off, he was convinced their friendship was over.

Inside Story

The Orange County Jail was overpopulated, and three weeks before final oral arguments were to be heard, deputies chained up Geronimo for a temporary stay in a state prison. The van lurched to a halt after an hour's drive and he wondered where he was. He flashed back on the rainy night he'd been jabbed in the arm and dragooned to Folsom.

The door of the vehicle opened and he found that he was in Chino State Prison near Pomona, just outside Los Angeles. "Hey," he said, "this is a mistake. I'm supposed to go back to Mule Creek."

A black guard said, "Don't ask us, Geronimo. We just work here."

Three days later he was peering out of a cage in the infamous "Palm Hall," Chino's solitary confinement section and the locus of several bloody riots. When he demanded to know why he was once again in a hole within a hole, a counselor told him, "I guess it's your reputation."

"This isn't right!" Geronimo raged. "I've been on the mainline for years. I'm on my way out of prison. You know about it. It's been in all the papers."

"Don't worry," the counselor said. "You're going back to Mule Creek. You'll soon be on your merry way."

THAT NIGHT Geronimo heard cellblock stories about fresh blood on the walls of Palm Hall. African Americans were in the majority at Chino, as they were in the entire California prison system, but they hadn't been able to head off an atrocity by a party of young whites. A popular black correctional counselor had been sodomized, slashed to death and dumped in a garbage can. His skinhead killer was being held in another part of the prison. One of the black prisoners warned, "Watch your ass, Geronimo. The guards already put out word that you're here to do a hit on the Nazis."

"What?"

"It would make some motherfucker a big man to kill you."

Around midnight Geronimo heard his cell door lock click open. "I saw this little white face coming around the corner with a shank in his hand. The homeys had been sitting up watching, and they began rattling their bars, howling, yelling, banging the walls. They made so much noise that the guards had to come in. The little white guy slipped back in his cell."

Geronimo realized that he'd survived another assassination attempt. He didn't blame the intruder; he blamed the Chino staffers who'd spread word that he was a hit man seeking revenge. "The skinheads thought I was gonna kill them, so they were gonna kill me. That's the way it works in prison. But I didn't expect to get set up just when I'm ready to go home. I guess it went back to the poison darts, the bus kidnap, taking hostages, all that bullshit. Prison guards have a long memory for things that never happened."

He reached Hanlon by collect call and was soon transferred to Mule Creek to await the resumption of the hearing in Santa Ana.

SEVERAL DAYS after his return to the mainline, Geronimo was meditating in the sunny yard when another inmate began to talk in a confidential voice. Pratt hardly listened. He'd always provided a strong shoulder for his fellow prisoners, but recent events had redirected his mental energy inward. It was a matter of survival.

After a few minutes he heard a familiar name from his distant past. "Say what?" he asked the talkative inmate. "You said 'Captain Franco'?"

Through the years he'd often thought of his murdered colleague, Bunchy Carter's strong right arm and underground cell leader. Jim McCloskey had always suspected that there was a connection between the tennis court shootings and the execution of Franco Diggs less than twenty-four hours later.

Geronimo's last contact with the forty-year-old Diggs had been a few days before the Santa Monica shootings when the "captain" drove him to the Los Angeles airport in Pratt's red and white GTO. A week later Pratt returned from Oakland to learn that his driver had been found on a sidewalk with bullet holes in his head.

Geronimo apologized to the prison yard monologist and confessed that he'd been half listening. "Take it from the top, will ya, brother? Captain Franco was a friend of mine."

The inmate identified himself as a former resident of South-Central Los Angeles and a distant relative of Swilley or Hatter—Geronimo didn't catch the exact relationship and knew better than to pry. Within minutes he'd heard a new version of the tennis court shootings:

Herbert Swilley and Larry "Dobey" Hatter had been members of Julio Butler's cell. In an ongoing feud with Butler, Captain Franco had demeaned the hairdresser by ordering him to sell several bundles of the *Black Panther*. Butler gave his underlings the keys to the GTO and instructed the young heroin addicts to carry out the assignment on his behalf. "Mama" also reminded them that the red and white convertible was known to police as a Panther car and was not to be used in illegal activities.

Swilley and Hatter quickly gave up on the thankless job of selling the party papers and threw them away, like other young Panthers before them. They robbed the Olsens to get the money to reimburse Julio for the newspapers and to buy drugs, then fled the scene in Pratt's GTO. When they told other cell members what they'd done, they were warned that Franco Diggs knew about the newspaper transaction and might connect them with the tennis court shootings. The next night Swilley and Hatter set up a meeting with Captain Franco on the South Side and shot him dead on the sidewalk.

Geronimo relayed the story to his team members. All felt that it came as close as could be expected to solving the puzzle. The remaining question was whether the wrong man, in his fiftieth year of life, would continue to serve time for the crimes of others.

Endgame

In the nine weeks of downtime between final testimony and closing arguments, Stuart Hanlon fought off daily bouts of anguish. Aided by his precocious son Liam, he frantically searched the Internet for medical information. "We kept coming up with leukemias that had a good cure rate, but then the doctors would tell us, 'No, she has a different kind.' So I'd say, *'What* kind?,' and they'd say, 'We're still not sure.' They were only sure of one thing: if she didn't have a bone marrow transplant, she would die."

Kathy's brother John proved a perfect match, and four surgeons performed the procedure at the University of California Medical Center. Once again doctors were optimistic; one predicted that she might resume her law practice within a year. Her siblings had rushed to the Hanlon home in San Francisco: John for the transplant, Sheila to run the house, Marnie in from Cambodia to care for the boys. The Ryans of Massachusetts had always been a tight family. They made Hanlon proud to be half Irish.

ON MARCH 13, 1997, sixty-five days after the final testimony in the evidentiary hearing, the lawyers reassembled to act out their roles in the legal theatrics known as final argument. The judge would learn nothing new, having been briefed and rebriefed by both sides on what he'd already learned during testimony. Opportunities for anti-Pratt oratory would be limited; Brentford Ferreira was recuperating from his mild stroke, and the legal scholar Harry Sondheim, with backup from Deputy D.A. Jodi Michelle Link, would speak for the side euphemistically known as the people. Hanlon and Cochran would present opening statements and later rebut Sondheim's remarks, giving the Pratt team four chances, against one for the prosecutor, to influence the judge.

COCHRAN INTERRUPTED his Court TV schedule and flew in from New York. Just before the session opened, he took his former associate Sondheim by the arm and said, "C'mon, Harry, join us now. This is the time." He beckoned toward the overflowing courtroom. "Everybody here knows Geronimo didn't get a fair trial. Nothing's secret anymore, Harry. It's all out in the open. Let's stipulate and end this thing right now. Then I'll take you out for dinner. All the soul food you can eat."

Sondheim didn't seem to share Cochran's good spirits. He insisted that it didn't matter whether Julius Butler was an informant or not—Pratt would still have been found guilty.

Cochran squeezed his opponent's arm and said, "Good luck, Harry. I know you have your orders."

GERONIMO PRATT entered the courtroom in a long-sleeved oyster-white dashiki with tribal hieroglyphs on two front panels, long black sleeves and a charcoal back. A flickering rhomboid from fluorescent ceiling lights glowed on his shaved head. He wore wire-rim glasses and nervously clasped and unclasped his hands as he joined Cochran, Hanlon, Kathleen Cleaver and Robert Garcia at the petitioner's table. Garcia handed him a white plastic cup of coffee, and Geronimo bolted it down in one gulp.

Hanlon summarized the case and then yielded to Cochran, who took over the courtroom in his customary style, part formal and part florid. "Thank you very kindly, Judge Dickey. To Judge Dickey, to Ms. Link and to Mr. Sondheim. To my colleagues, Mr. Hanlon, Mrs. Cleaver, Mr. Garcia, and to my client, Mr. Elmer Pratt." As he spoke the last name, he put his hands on Geronimo's shoulders.

"Your Honor," he said, bowing slightly toward the judge, "I stand before this court as a lawyer who has now practiced for more than thirty-four years in the courts of this state. I have tried a number of cases, a lot of murder cases. This case, however, has and always has been the most important."

He apologized for being "a little more emotional than usual today." He nodded toward Hanlon and said, "It is because this has been our life's work."

Hanlon had covered the factual issues, so Cochran opened on legal morality and ethics. "Part of our life's work as lawyers is to seek the truth and justice in these cases. The prosecutor has a different burden, as the court is aware, than certainly the defense has. Their idea is to make sure the guilty are punished and the innocent go free. Our role as defense lawyers is to do the best we can for our client, to represent to the best of our abilities. In this case, as Mr. Hanlon has so correctly pointed out, we have got mixed up somewhere along the way. The search for truth has come from the defense. We are the ones asking for witnesses to be brought forward. They are the ones seeking to block it out with technicalities. They are the ones who didn't want Rice and Henry to testify. . . . They are the ones who alleged the evidence is not relevant and that there is overwhelming evidence against Mr. Pratt. . . . I hope that today, by the time Mr. Sondheim stands up, that he will review—and he is a good and honorable man—he will review in his mind the responsibility of the Los Angeles County District Attorney's Office to do the right thing in this case."

Like Hanlon before him, Cochran thanked the judge for "an opportunity to seek justice, to get the facts out. . . . They tried to block us at every turn, but you had the courage when we came down here to at least allow us to put these witnesses on and, Your Honor, out of that came information that we couldn't have dreamed of when I tried this case in 1972. Because, as a young lawyer, you see, I tried this case thinking that everything was fair, that everything was aboveboard. . . . Richard Kalustian and I went to law school together. We were in the same class, so I knew this man. I had known him for some twelve years before he walked into that courtroom. I knew him. I didn't think they would try to hide documents from me. I didn't think he was caught up in trying to win or to neutralize this man. . . ."

He reminded the judge of Kalustian's statement in 1972: "If the jury believes Julius Butler, regardless of whether they believe or disbelieve the identification of witnesses, Mr. Pratt is guilty. The case is over if they believe that." Now, Cochran pointed out, "in this revisionist history that Mr. Sondheim and the others want to do, Butler is not nearly as important. It was always that *other* evidence. They try to rewrite history."

He blasted the officials who'd helped Butler buy a gun. ". . . Public funds were given to a man who had pled nolo contendere to four felonies. Four felonies! . . . And he didn't just walk around with the gun. He used that gun to disarm people, to threaten people, until he was finally arrested in 1981, ten years later, with the same gun that they gave him. . . . They looked the other way. This is the picture of the prosecution that has emerged. . . . They made this man and put him above the law. This is about Julius Butler, and they elevate him to a status. Then, in their brief, they try to make him seem like a saint. When we finish, you are going to see he is not a saint. . . . He is not worthy of your respect. He is a lying perjurer . . . a con man . . . a conniving snake . . . a pathological liar. . . ."

For the first time in the courtroom history of the case, Cochran publicly accused the FBI of being directly involved in the creation of the "insurance letter" that had led to Geronimo Pratt's conviction and incarceration. "We see Kalustian's notes where it says this thing all started with the FBI. There's a reason for that, Judge. *This all started with the FBI!* They knew about the letter back then and they sat on it all those months. *They helped him write that letter.*"

The spectators fell silent as the significance of the accusation sank in.

Hanlon watched admiringly as his team partner dominated the courtroom. "You could see how Judge Dickey admired his lawyering skill," Hanlon said later. "I was forty-eight, but to Dickey I was still a young punk. But Cochran was . . . Cochran."

HAVING DIRECTLY accused the nation's top law enforcement agency of helping to frame an innocent man, Cochran returned to the subject of Julius Butler. "He's had a great run," he told the judge. "Here is a felon who, through survival skills, through conniving, through pretending to be someone that he isn't, parlays his four felony convictions . . . and goes off to law school. Meanwhile, this man"—he gestured toward Pratt—"this man is in a prison cell . . . the first eight years in solitary confinement. And Butler does all these things hiding behind a prosecution that's supposed to be interested in truth and justice. . . . But his great run is coming to an end."

He accused the prosecution of abandoning every principle of justice. "All the way through, it is about winning. It is almost as though the prosecution went to the Vince Lombardi school of winning—that winning is everything. They are not interested in any justice. That's what we dealt with.

And they tried to tell you they had an overwhelming case. They had no overwhelming case at all. They were here to *thwart* justice and, unfortunately, they have continued to thwart justice by their response, by their motions, by their resistance. . . ."

He turned toward the D.A.'s lawyers. "So finally," he said, "I ask my friend Harry Sondheim: will you, after seeing what we have presented at this hearing, will you join us today and stand up and agree that Geronimo Pratt was deprived of a fair trial by virtue of the evidence suppressed, not by Harry Sondheim, but by the others on the prosecution team? That's the least they should do. Because after twenty-seven years, and you believe in the system as we did, what do you say to Geronimo Pratt? What I do say to him is that there is one court who was willing to give us a hearing, and these are the fruits of that hearing, and by their fruits shall ye know them. And the fruits that we have uncovered here will lead to this man's freedom. They know it. It is unavoidable. It will not be stopped, because its time has come."

SONDHEIM OPENED on an unexpectedly waspish note. "I suppose if I were really to comply with Mr. Cochran's wishes, I wouldn't answer any questions. I would just take about half a minute, concede, and sit down, because that's what he is suggesting I do."

He looked at Cochran and said, "On the other hand I know he has reserved some time and wants to rebut whatever I am going to say, so I don't want to deprive him of that opportunity and I think I will continue."

Cochran smiled and mumbled, "It's okay. It's okay."

Sondheim hearkened back to his own three years on the case and repeated that he'd turned up nothing to suggest Pratt's innocence. Then he reprised the latest rationale for keeping Geronimo in prison: "What difference does it make whether Butler was an informant or not? There is no evidence that Julius Butler gave any evidence of value to law enforcement." He spoke of the "overwhelming" proof of Pratt's guilt, including the Barbara Mary Reed identification, and read aloud from the L. Thaxton Hanson decision:

> As a matter of practicality and probability, it would be extremely coincidental and highly improbable for any other light-complexioned male Black Panther in the Southern California chapter, or any other male

black in the greater Los Angeles area, or any place at all, to have an identically shaped and sized scar in the same position on his face, that scar in part that was used by Mrs. Reed to make her identification.

Befitting a respected legal scholar, Sondheim based many of his arguments on earlier decisions, frequently quoting judges who'd ruled against Pratt. He echoed U.S. Magistrate John Kronenberg in praising Superior Court Judge Kathleen Parker. He quoted Justice Hanson's reminder that the defendant "was only entitled to a fair trial, not a perfect trial." He accused the Pratt lawyers of "ritual incantation of prosecutorial misconduct," and added, "If you can't support your own contentions, blame the other side. And that's what we have been getting here—a lot of blame—and it isn't warranted." If Geronimo Pratt was denied a fair trial in 1972, Sondheim argued, the fault lay with Johnnie Cochran and Charles Hollopeter, not with the D.A.'s Office. If Pratt's lawyers had done their jobs, they could have found the evidence that was now being used as the basis for a new trial.

As for the defendant himself, Sondheim dismissed him with a simple phrase: "The jury concluded that Elmer Pratt was a liar."

Cochran listened impassively until he heard Sondheim refer to Pratt as "a street thug," then began scribbling on his legal pad. Judge Dickey put down his own busy pencil when Sondheim cited the length of the 1972 trial as an indication of Kathleen Parker's fairness and thoroughness. "If I can interrupt you just a moment, Mr. Sondheim?" the judge said.

"Sure."

"That raises an interesting point, because there have been several references to the trial as a protracted trial." Dickey said he'd added up the hours devoted to actual testimony and they totaled only thirty-six. Judge Parker had run a relaxed court, seldom convening before 11:00 A.M. or remaining in session beyond 4:00.

Dickey also took issue with a Sondheim claim that the evidence against Pratt had been "overwhelming." Obviously, the judge said, the original jury hadn't thought so or it wouldn't have taken ten days to deliberate. The Pratt lawyers were encouraged. Someone was paying attention. Someone was keeping score.

WHEN COCHRAN rose in rebuttal, he was still seething about Sondheim's personal slam at Pratt. "I must say I'm a little disappointed in my good friend Harry Sondheim," he began, the light glittering off the gold cross he always wore as though to counterbalance his taste in ties. "He calls Geronimo Pratt a street thug. Where does he get that from?" He glared at his former colleague. *"How could you make a slanderous statement like that?"*

Once again he put his hands on Geronimo's shoulders. "This man was a Vietnam veteran who was decorated, who got the Purple Heart, who saved a lot of men, who came home from that war a young man. He was concerned about changing things in this community to make it better."

His voice rising, Cochran said that there was "never any evidence he was a street thug. It becomes convenient to dehumanize him, to try to justify what [Sondheim] is trying to say: that he shouldn't have had a fair trial. That he could be neutralized and put out of the way. He is not a street thug! He hasn't lied. He hasn't manipulated this system for twenty-five or twenty-six years. He has been a victim. . . . I looked at him today, and he is almost fifty years of age. . . . I have been associated with this man over half of his life. More than half of his life he has been in custody—and they have the temerity to stand up here and say he is a street thug? *We know who the street thug is.*"

Before he yielded the floor, Cochran paid tribute to his colleague. "I want to say how much I respect Stuart Hanlon. The court is aware of the personal problem he has been facing of life-threatening proportions. . . . When I first met him at San Quentin, he had a lot more hair and was a lot younger and wasn't even a lawyer. . . . The fact that he is even here today lets you know how important this is to us."

Then he returned to his theme on morality: "Justice is very elusive. . . . You can try to blot it out, but it keeps coming back. As Dr. King says, injustice anywhere is the threat to justice everywhere, and that the arc of the moral universe is long, but it bends towards justice. . . . Because, you see, the same system that helped put Geronimo Pratt away is the same system that allows us this moment here in court. . . . So that same government gives us some hope. You, Your Honor, are that last and best hope, an independent person who doesn't owe anybody anything, who can say that, based upon this evidence, we have carried our burden even far beyond the preponderance of the evidence. I hope you will do that and this man will get his rightful day in court. That is all we ask."

He smiled at the judge and thanked him very kindly.

HANLON'S VOICE would be the last heard in argument, and he decided to pound home a final lesson on prosecutorial ethics. He noted that Sondheim had bestowed praise on the Los Angeles D.A.'s Office for ultimately providing key information about the confidential informant cards. Except for this extraordinary cooperation, Sondheim had argued, the Pratt team would never have seen the information that bulked so large in their case.

Hanlon turned toward the D.A.'s table and said softly, "Mr. Sondheim, that's *supposed* to be the way it works. You are the government. You have the police. You have the evidence. We find out about it as defense lawyers because it is *your job* to give it to us. There is nothing to take pride in that you do *your job* as a prosecutor."

He pointed out that the D.A.'s arguments and briefs "tried to take apart each piece of evidence and say, 'This alone would not have made a difference, this alone.' " But the law, he said, required the judge to weigh the evidence as a whole. "A gun does not stand alone. Being a felon to carry a gun does not stand alone. Clayton Anderson's belief that Mr. Butler was an informant for two other agencies did not stand alone. Mr. Willis' statement that he was an informant for the D.A. does not stand alone. Mr. Layne's statement that 'I believe he may have been an informant' does not stand alone. Captain Henry's statement that he was an agent provocateur did not stand alone. Sergeant Rice's statement does not stand alone. The fact that the FBI was present when the letter was delivered does not stand alone. . . . That the FBI at the same time were investigating Butler for a federal arms prosecution does not stand alone."

He turned to Sondheim's accusations about Cochran's lack of diligence in the 1972 trial.

"I really had a difficult time sitting there," Hanlon told the judge, "because he wants to blame Mr. Cochran for believing in the system of justice and believing in the District Attorney. . . . There is nothing wrong with a lawyer, whether he is young or old, believing that a prosecutor will give you the evidence they are supposed to."

As for the telltale scar that L. Thaxton Hanson and his fellow appellate judges had found so decisive, Hanlon said, "Mrs. Reed says that she based her identification on a scar. Well, she did say that at trial. The only problem is she didn't say it to the police department on December 19th of 1968. She didn't say it at the Grand Jury. She only said it after she sat in court and saw Mr. Pratt."

Hanlon confessed to Judge Dickey that he didn't agree with Cochran's declaration of faith in the legal system. "I started with Mr. Pratt's case. This is where I began. And I have done many trials. But my faith in this system has been tempered by seeing what has happened in his case. I have seen the machinations of the legal system, whether it be courts or district attorneys, so my belief in this legal system will always be tempered by what has gone on for him and me in the last twenty-three years in this case. I am a lawyer. I believe in the system and I try as hard as I can, but there is a part of me that questions the ability of the legal system to deal with cases like Mr. Pratt's."

He paused, then said, "And this is where I want to end, Your Honor. When I began this case, we wrote of conspiracies. You never heard that word before this court. There are many large issues that can be raised about Mr. Pratt's case, about why things happen, who did what. The answers to those large issues are not for the Court. They should not be. They don't have to be, and they will never be. There is a very small issue, and all we have to deal with here is: Did Mr. Pratt get a fair trial? And, if he didn't, should the trial be reversed? I believe that this court has heard the evidence and will finally mete out justice for Elmer Geronimo Pratt. I truly believe that as I stand before you. Thank you very much."

Whispers went through the packed courtroom like a soft breeze. It was now within the judge's authority to order a new trial, set bail and send Pratt and his new dashiki out the front door and into the arms of his well-wishers. But none of the attorneys expected an immediate decision from such a deliberate judge.

Everyone listened closely as Dickey confirmed the expectations. "The court, probably to the disappointment of most people present, is not going to make a ruling on this today." A low moan issued from the spectators. Instead of gently admonishing them as he had during the hearing, Dickey said, "I have been a judge almost twenty-seven years, and I have never had a case with so much reading involved. . . . There is just a mountain of material, and I want to make sure that I don't overlook anything, including reviewing the arguments today with the evidence which has been referred to fully. So I will submit this matter and advise you in writing of my decision . . . I will try to do this as soon as possible."

After the judge squared his shoulders and strode into his chambers, Hanlon squeezed Geronimo's arm and said, "A couple more weeks, G. That's all. You can make it."

As a bailiff started to lead Pratt toward the holding cell in the rear of the courtroom, he turned to the crowd and waved. Hanlon and his friends were pleased to see that he was smiling.

"Nervously Calm"

Back in his cell at Mule Creek after another long ride in chains, Geronimo filled his hours with chess, Scrabble, chants and meditation. In Morgan City friends and relatives added prayers, and the drone of Eunice Pratt's mantras filled the little house on Second Street. Sister Jacqueline, self-styled "prayer warrior" and minister of the gospel, urged friends and distant cousins to send up more heavenly appeals. Brother Timothy reported hearing an African American talk-show host urge his listeners to "pray for Geronimo as the judge prepares his decision." At Howard University a young law professor named Nkechi Tiefa began teaching a course on political prisoners, built around the Pratt case.

Newspapers and broadcast media carried progress reports that referred to Geronimo as "last man standing," the world's longest-held political prisoner now that Nelson Mandela had been freed. A revolutionary website headlined its coverage "From the Gulag, Geronimo Fights On." The *Los Angeles Times* informed its readers that Pratt "may be on the verge of winning a reversal of his murder conviction." A newspaper editorialist called his case "overpowering."

Hanlon read the coverage and prepared himself for another blow. "Even if we lose," he told a reporter, "I know in my heart that I've taken on these people for twenty years. They want this to go away. It's never gone away. And I can take some pride in that. Even if we lose, it's never gone away."

On doctor's orders, he prepared a sterile room at home, and Kathy was sent home by ambulance, too weak to see anyone except her immediate family. Her young sons were excited by her arrival but confused and embarrassed by the baldness caused by chemotherapy. She was in agonizing pain on Liam's tenth birthday in mid-May. Hanlon acted as master of ceremonies at the party.

The prognosis varied from day to day.

BY MAY 29, 1997, Judge Dickey had been silent for nearly three months. Nor had he sent any signals. His clerk fended off Juliana Drous' insistent calls and finally asked her to be patient—the decision would be sent to Hanlon's office when it was available. No, she didn't have the slightest idea which way the judge was leaning. All she knew was that he disappeared behind mountains of lawbooks every morning and left each afternoon with his usual crisp "Bye. Thank you." Everett Dickey would not be hurried.

The edgy players became edgier. Cochran said, "I'm still nervous. I think we've won, but I can't forget all those other decisions. There's one big unknown factor: politics. This is the most political case I've ever tried. The FBI is always lurking in the background. I have the feeling that all it would take is one call from [Director] Louie Freeh and—*phffft!* We're tubed again."

Jim McCloskey checked in by phone. He was on the road again, toiling at his appointed task of freeing the imprisoned innocent. "I'm optimistic," the lay minister kept telling his colleagues.

"I wish I was," Hanlon replied.

Pratt called often from Mule Creek. To Hanlon he sounded "nervously calm."

IN THE afternoon of May 29, 1997, the phone rang on the set of Court TV's *Cochran & Co.* It was Cochran's longtime secretary, Eloise McGill, calling from Los Angeles.

"I don't know what this is all about," she told her boss, "but Mr. Hanlon's office wants you to stand by on the speakerphone."

In the Victorian building on Duboce Avenue in San Francisco, Juliana Drous was trying to patch up a transcontinental telephone network. Just after lunchtime, Judge Dickey's clerk had called. She was preparing to fax the order to the Hanlon office. It would be released to the press thirty minutes later.

"Did we win?" Drous asked.

The clerk politely refused to answer.

Drous located Mark Rosenbaum and Robert Garcia and asked them to stand by on their phones. Jim McCloskey was out of touch. Kathy Ryan was running a high fever and Hanlon was on his way to the office by car.

Tony Tamburello, distinguished senior partner of the firm of Tamburello, Hanlon and Waggener, yelled down from the second-floor fax room: "Julie, I think it's starting!" He'd never been directly involved in the case, but for two decades his firm had backed Pratt with resources, patience and cash.

Drous rushed up the stairs, grabbed an extension phone and watched the fax machine as the words "Orange County Superior Court" inched into sight. Voices babbled in the telephone that she cradled against her ear. "Just shut up!" she yelled. "It's coming out."

She read the first few pages aloud. The words seemed encouraging. The judge cited errors by the D.A. and observed, "The evidence which was withheld about Julius Butler and his activities could have put the whole case in a different light, and failure to timely disclose it undermines confidence in the verdict." He referred to Julius Butler's "false testimony" and noted that for three years before the Pratt trial, Butler had been "providing information about the Black Panther Party and individuals associated with it to law enforcement agencies on a confidential basis." This crucial fact, the judge ruled, was "obviously relevant to his credibility as a witness" and should have been shared with the defense and the jury.

As the pages extruded from the fax machine with mouselike scratchings and squeaks, Drous began jumping up and down. She smacked Tamburello on the back, then said, "What's keeping Stu? Oh, Tony, we *need* him here."

Telephone voices in her ear ordered her to continue reading. Staffers thronged around the machine. Over the babble she heard a sharp command voice from New York: "None of this preliminary stuff matters. Read the ruling, Julie. At the end. *The end!*"

"I don't *have* the fucking end, Johnnie," she said. "I'm getting it page by page."

"Read, damn it!" a female voice ordered. It was Cochran's aide Shawn Chapman, weighing in from Los Angeles.

Drous read the judge's critical comments about the gun that had been provided to the state's star informer. Dickey observed that Richard Kalustian and various law enforcement officers "were aware that Butler was carrying the weapon without any official sanction, even though it was a violation of state law punishable by up to fifteen years in prison." He took note of the peculiarly light sentencing in the Ollie Taylor case and criticized the LAPD for allowing Butler to turn in his personal submachine gun on the pretext that it was Panther property.

As for Sondheim's attempt to blame Cochran and Hollopeter for failing to turn up exculpatory evidence, Dickey cited a 1972 U.S. Supreme Court decision: "Even without request from the defendant, either intentional or negligent suppression by the prosecution of substantial material evidence favorable to the accused denies the accused of a fair trial and requires reversal."

Drous' voice began to crack as she read and exulted and pounded on her colleagues' backs. When she paused for breath, she heard a cackling sound over the phone and realized it was Cochran, chortling. "Calm down! Julie," he was yelling, but he wasn't taking his own advice. "Hurry up. *Get to the good part!*"

She read the judge's comments about the courtroom identification of Pratt by Kenneth Olsen and Barbara Mary Reed. Dickey wrote that apart from the implausibility of such identifications after two years, "the possible unreliability of cross-racial identifications of strangers based on a brief period of observation under stressful conditions has become so well known in the years since the Pratt trial that judges now almost always specially instruct a jury on the subject."

At last Drous came to the end of the order. Her voice broke as she read the legal jargon: "Therefore, habeas corpus is granted and petitioner's conviction is reversed and remanded for further proceedings."

The phone line fell silent. She wondered if there'd been a disconnect. Then she heard Cochran's choking voice: "God bless Geronimo Pratt."

HANLON ARRIVED to chaos. Tony Tamburello had opened the liquor cabinet, and revelers dripped with champagne, beer and liqueurs of many colors. Staffers toasted Geronimo, Hanlon, Cochran, McCloskey, Bob Bloom, Drous, Judge Dickey, Orange County, John Wayne and the United States of America. Drous whirled in a victory dance, her long gray-black hair flying.

"Stu!" she yelled. "Do you believe this? Look at these pages! *Just look!*" Her face gleamed with tears and champagne. "We won, Stu!" she yelled. "We won, we won, we won. We won it all! We won in every possible way. You can't *win* a better win."

Hanlon rubbed his eyes and said softly, "It's about time. It's about fucking time."

He phoned the news to Kathy. She said, "Oh, Stu, I'm so happy." After he promised to come straight home, he retired to his inner office with Drous and Tamburello. He took a phone call from a wire service reporter who wanted to know if the good news about the ruling helped to cancel out the bad news about his wife's health. He slammed the phone down. Then it hit him: *Pratt doesn't know. We're drinking champagne, and G is locked in a cell at Mule Creek. . . .*

The law firm's phone lines were swamped by the media. When Hanlon finally got through to the prison, the operator reminded him that inmates weren't permitted to take incoming calls. Contact had to be initiated by the prisoner himself by collect call.

"Listen," Hanlon said, "I've got to talk to him. Elmer Gerard Pratt, B-40319. You've *got* to connect us."

"Sir—"

"Please. Break your rules for once. Have a heart. This is life and death."

The operator was silent and Hanlon was afraid she'd hung up. "Please," he said, "could you give me the warden's office?" Maybe a little schmooze would work.

A CBS film crew burst into Hanlon's office just as he started talking to his client. Geronimo said he was speaking on the warden's personal phone.

"Hey, G," Hanlon said, "we won! We fucking won!"

At first his client didn't seem to comprehend.

"We won," Hanlon repeated. He read the last paragraph of the order into the phone.

Geronimo said, "Say it again, Stu. Read me the end again."

When the brief conversation was over, a local reporter elbowed his way into Hanlon's office and asked for comment on a statement that had just been released by Gil Garcetti: "After an incredibly exhaustive investigation, one that I personally undertook, there is no evidence that's been brought to my attention that convinces me in any way as to the innocence of Mr. Pratt."

Hanlon grunted and said, "No evidence? Tell Garcetti to drop in on my basement. I've got twenty-five boxes he can go through."

What if the D.A. made good on his threat to appeal?

"We'd kick his ass from here to Tijuana."

While the office staff began an all-night celebration, Hanlon headed home.

AFTER JOHNNIE Cochran signed *Cochran & Co.* off the air for the day, he escorted his wife Dale to their favorite New York restaurant, the Trattoria del Arte, for a night of excess and celebration. Neither of the Cochrans had a taste for alcohol, but they took a few sips of champagne in honor of Geronimo and a few more in honor of Judge Dickey. "It was the greatest evening of my life," Cochran said later. "After that champagne I went completely out of control and ordered a second helping of penne."

TIMOTHY PRATT stayed up late, preparing an exegesis. He credited "the power of consistent collective prayer and faith" for the vindication, and likened the legal system that had imprisoned Geronimo to the systems that enslaved Daniel and Joseph. "They were released by the power of God, not man. Johnnie and Stu were God's instruments, and for that they should feel blessed. Judge Dickey felt the power of God and decided to do the right thing."

IN MORGAN City Jack Pratt broke the news to their mother. "They're gonna let Gerard out, Mama," he said, speaking slowly into her ear. *"Gerard is coming home."*

At ninety-four Eunice Petty Pratt was in the advanced stages of senile dementia and Broca's aphasia, incapable of coherent speech and almost blind, her range of vision a foot or two. No one knew how much she understood. She hadn't spoken clear English in four or five years, but sometimes she acknowledged her children by lightly squeezing their hands. She responded to the good news by chanting a little faster.

Reveille for Radicals

In the two weeks between the judge's decision and a final bail hearing, Pratt remained in bureaucratic suspension as his lawyers exchanged salvos with the Los Angeles D.A.'s Office. Gil Garcetti announced that he would appeal, "of course." He reminded the *Los Angeles Times* that the Panther leader's conviction had been upheld repeatedly by other courts.

Cochran called the D.A.'s decision sickening. "They can't retry this case for a lot of reasons because of their own impropriety," he told *Times* reporter Edward Boyer. "So why appeal it? It's an act of folly. Once again Mr. Garcetti has succumbed to people in his own office who are from a different era—maybe the Pleistocene era."

From San Francisco Hanlon issued a response to Garcetti's claim that the D.A.'s Office had "acted appropriately and ethically in this case." Hanlon called the comment "garbage" and challenged Garcetti personally: "If you're so convinced Mr. Pratt is guilty, then you get in there yourself and retry the case. Let's forget about the appeal. Let's go to trial in sixty days."

Editorialists added to the clamor. The *San Francisco Chronicle* declared that Pratt had been subjected to "a nightmare few can imagine" and suggested that his immediate release "would be a fitting rebuke to a witch-hunting era. . . ." The *Los Angeles Times* urged Garcetti to "distance his office from the improper tactics of an earlier District Attorney's Office by declining to retry a man who has already spent more than half of his life in prison." Loyola Law School Professor Laurie L. Levenson publicly urged Garcetti to "close the book."

COCHRAN AND Hanlon visited their client at Mule Creek and had to pick their way through a fan club of guards, both black and white, some of whom had rushed back to the prison on their days off. Staff members held out slips of paper for autographs.

"It was Johnnie's signature that they wanted," Hanlon said good-naturedly. "Hanging out with him was like being backstage at a rock concert."

Hanlon was pleased at the Pratt support inside the walls. "Guards asked if they could write recommendations to the judge to release G on his own recognizance. Some of them were Vietnam veterans. They wanted to provide an honor guard for the prison van on the trip back to Orange County, on their own time, at no pay."

The lawyers spent three hours with their client and listened to his travel plans. After the bail hearing he intended to fly to Marin County to attend his daughter Shona's graduation from high school and his son Hiroji's graduation from junior high. Then he would head straight for Across the Tracks and his mother. "He hadn't seen her in twenty years," Hanlon told reporters. "It was all he could talk about."

Pratt also had invitations to appear at political events and civil rights forums, at a poverty conference in the Caribbean, in African American churches, at a meeting of the National Black Leadership Forum, at the Essence Music Festival in New Orleans, at his old colleague Bobby Seale's ghetto program in Philadelphia, at a black convocation in Jamaica and at reunions with old Panther warriors. He intended to visit the Vietnam Wall in Washington to run his fingertips across the names of old comrades. He would be busy.

THE *LOS ANGELES TIMES* described the bail hearing on the morning of June 10, 1997, as "reveille for radicals, a gathering of old Panthers who have grown long in the tooth and gray at the temples." As news helicopters racketed back and forth above the courthouse, Dennis Banks and fellow members of his American Indian Movement waved placards saying "Free

Peltier"[71] and pounded on tom-toms made of buffalo skin. Somayah Kambui, the former Peaches Moore, strummed her thirty-six-string autoharp and sang, "May J. Edgar Hoover burn in fire and Geronimo walk on free soil." Eldridge Cleaver, now sixty-one, divorced, a born-again Christian dying of cancer and diabetes, arrived in a gray banker's suit with a red carnation and shook hands weakly. The Pratt juror Jeanne Hamilton, now teaching accounting in Orange County, and Wesley Swearingen, seventy and long retired from the FBI, wept openly outside the ninth-floor courtroom. Geronimo's big sister Virginia made her way to a front row, her black hair done up in tight braids that framed her pretty face and flashing teeth. It was her birthday. At her side was Geronimo's track-star son Hiroji, now fourteen, his head freshly shaved in tribute to his father.

The proceedings in Department 35 were brief. Pratt was flanked by law professor Kathleen Cleaver on his right and Cochran and Hanlon on his left. When Judge Dickey asked for bail suggestions, Garcetti's representative was silent. Cochran said, "I'd suggest $25,000, a thousand for each year Mr. Pratt spent in prison.[72] It's symbolic, Your Honor."

"All right," Judge Dickey said after a long pause. "Bail will be set at $25,000." A shriek pierced the courtroom. It came from retired prison counselor A. Lynne Atkinson.[73] Spectators yelled and cheered and stomped, and the judge made no effort to control the jubilation.

As Geronimo stood up in his saffron jumpsuit with "OC JAIL" on the back, a gray-haired black man called out, "Free at last!" Several responded, "Amen."

Pratt looked straight at the judge and said, "I want to thank you from the bottom of my heart. If there are further proceedings, I'll be the first one here. You can be assured I will adhere to any rule the court orders me to follow." He stood at attention and squared his shoulders, then tapped his fist where he'd once pounded paratrooper's wings into his bare

---

[71] Leonard Peltier, a Native American activist, was serving two life sentences for the killings of two FBI agents in South Dakota.

[72] Pratt had actually served twenty-six years and seven months, counting time served while awaiting trial.

[73] Back home in Petaluma the next day, Atkinson told a friend, "I was at Geronimo's bail hearing in Santa Ana." "I know," the friend replied. "I heard you scream on TV."

chest. "That's my word," he said in a husky voice, "as a Vietnam vet and a man."

"Today's a happy day," Ginny Pratt told a reporter on her way out of the jammed courtroom. "After all those years, all those prisons." As usual, the pragmatic schoolteacher was looking ahead. "This will be such a big change for my brother," she said. "He's not gonna fly out like a wild bird."

HANLON AND Cochran signed papers in the jail office while Geronimo changed into khaki slacks and a print shirt for a public appearance on the lawn. When he walked down the front steps just after noon, he blinked in the bright California sunshine, then thrust his fist upward in a Black Power salute. As the crowd surged forward, Hanlon told him, "Everybody wants to touch you."

Pratt walked across the lawn and touched a tree. He told Hanlon it made him weak in the knees. Rumpled of the Bailey slipped into the crowd. He was happy for his old client, but he couldn't stop thinking about the latest word from San Francisco. Kathy Ryan Hanlon had six months to live.

The TV cameras picked out Cochran and Pratt, smiling and waving and acknowledging the crowd. Cochran yelled, "He's an American hero!" Someone asked how the lawyers had managed to stay with the case for so many years. Cochran pointed to Pratt and said, "We drew our strength from him. And from the justice system. You see, it works!"

"Yeah," Hanlon whispered to himself, "after twenty-seven years."

A reporter steered Pratt to a bank of microphones that were wired up to TV satellite trucks. Eldridge Cleaver cried out, "Hey, we need some peace on those drums!," but the throbbing obbligato continued.

Above the din a Fox-TV reporter asked the freed man what he thought about Julius Carl Butler. "I wish him well," Geronimo replied, "and I hope he wakes up out of his stupor and begins telling the truth. I'm not the only victim of J. Edgar Hoover and Richard Nixon and the FBI. You have political prisoners on top of political prisoners. I'm only one of many."

"You're not upset about Butler?" another reporter asked.

"When you go through what I've gone through, you learn that bitterness has no place in the human heart." Pratt said he was incapable of harsh thoughts at the moment. He beckoned toward the crowd and said, "This is such a loving thing."

He asked his interviewers to remember the murdered Caroline Olsen in their articles. "She was an antiwar demonstrator," he said. "She was a teacher, a progressive, a good person. No one speaks up for her. She was like a comrade of ours."

A reporter asked about his plans. He smiled and said, "I need to see my mother. Every time I left home I've always gone back. I'm a mama's boy." He looked around and frowned. "Where's Stu?" he said, then yelled, *"Where's Stu?"*

A trio of husky young African Americans led Geronimo toward Hanlon and a white Jeep Cherokee, a gift from a Pratt angel. On the way through the smiles and elbows, Geronimo gently pushed aside an autograph book. "Excuse me, miss," he said softly, "I'm not a movie star. I'm a revolutionary."

At the car he hugged Hanlon and said, "Hey, bro, stay close. You scared me for a minute."

Hanlon thought, It's okay now. We're friends.

As Geronimo started to enter the station wagon, he felt a sudden apprehensiveness. "I'm thinking, Wait a minute! This can't be real. Somebody's gonna come get me. I'm gonna hear a whistle blow, hear a guard yell, *'Hold it right there!'* "

He sat on something hard. It was the first time since his arrest in Texas in 1970 that he'd entered a vehicle unshackled and uncuffed. News cameramen tightened their focus as he fiddled with the shoulder strap. Hanlon advised him to pull it across his chest.

"Don't worry," Geronimo called out with an embarrassed smile. "I'll get it. I'll learn."

As the vehicle eased away, members of the crowd shouted "Power to the people!" and tried to follow. On the lawn, old enemies Eldridge Cleaver and David Hilliard embraced. "We're all older," said Hilliard, who now conducted Black Panther bus tours in Oakland and lectured on party history. "We have kids we have to put through school. But except for Huey Newton we're all still alive. We try to keep the message alive."

Donald Freed, historian of the Panther phenomenon and a professor at the University of Southern California, told a group of his old radical friends on the lawn, "To the mainstream media, Geronimo's getting out of prison says the system works, that the bad old days are gone and this will never happen again. But what this really is all about is that a man who was buried alive in the California Department of Corrections walks out to haunt America."

A FEW hours after the last celebrant had left the courthouse, the First African Methodist Episcopal Church of Los Angeles issued an announcement. Board Chairman Julius Butler had resigned his post with a statement that "I don't want to cause any further harm or pain to my church family."

"As the door opens for Geronimo Pratt," a church leader told the media, "the door closes for Julius Butler as a leader within the First AME Church. But Julius will continue to be a member here. Now is the time for healing. . . . We invite Geronimo Pratt to come to the First AME Church and share in the glory of Jesus."

Reunion

That night Geronimo attended a jubilant foot-stomping service at the lower end of the South-Central ghetto. The parishioners of Faith United Methodist Church at 108th and Broadway had held weekly "Free Geronimo Pratt" meetings, and the church overflowed on this first night of his freedom. Pratt entered to the sound of a scratchy tenor sax blaring one of his father's favorite songs, "When the Saints Go Marchin' In." He worked the aisle slowly, smiling and shaking every hand.

The Reverend Jim McCloskey tried to catch the joyous spirit from a front pew, but his throat hurt from holding back tears. He regarded this as one of the great days of his life, but it was not without its confusions and ambiguities. Somewhere behind him sat Clarence Chance, an African American whom Centurion Ministries had freed after seventeen years of imprisonment. The minister thought of Roger Coleman, the coal miner who'd been electrocuted five minutes after their last good-bye. If the U.S. Supreme Court hadn't declared the death penalty unconstitutional in 1972, McCloskey reminded himself, Geronimo would be in the ground with Roger, his case a forgotten entry in dusty legal files. McCloskey kept remembering Christ's words in the Sermon on the Mount: *he maketh his sun to rise on the evil and on the good. . . .*

The crusading minister often explained to doubters that his job would be impossible without faith. Now he asked himself, Was it faith that won this day? Did God intervene to cause this miracle? He wanted to think so. But why was God there for Geronimo Pratt and not for Roger Coleman? It was theodicy again: . . . *and sendeth rain on the just and on the unjust.*

He watched as Pratt approached the altar in his loose ex-quarterback's stride. "I saw this dark man in his beautiful dashiki, red and black with gold highlights, his long flowing gown, his amber-tinted glasses, his shaven head and goatee that ran into his moustache. I saw him standing proud in front of hundreds of people like an ancient tribal king. He thanked them in a few graceful words, a natural orator, no more intimidated by crowds than he'd been by cops or judges or prison guards. He said, 'I want to bring back that spirit of the sixties. I am a revolutionary. We are not yet free!' I saw a proud, principled, determined man. I thought: *twenty-seven years.* That's when I broke down."

JOHNNIE COCHRAN had paid off his plundered credit card, and he booked dinner for seventy-five at the Georgia Restaurant, a West Los Angeles gourmet soul-food restaurant that was popular with the African American elite. Geronimo arrived with Ashaki and their two children. Hanlon attended with Russell Little and Bill Harris, former clients and veterans of the ill-starred Symbionese Liberation Army. Over bowls of crawfish bisque and jambalaya, gray-haired warriors traded memories. Said Clarence Chance, now in his sixth year of renewed freedom thanks to Centurion Ministries, "I feel secure now, knowing my brother Pratt is free." Wes Swearingen said he still felt ashamed of his fellow FBI agents. Dennis Banks said that the American Indian Movement had known Geronimo was framed from the beginning—"no one with such a heroic name and manner could be guilty." Eldridge Cleaver spoke of the toll of prison life, "and the reason that Geronimo was standing up so well was because of his innocence." David Hilliard said he hoped that his Panther colleague would continue to fight for the people.

Pratt assured Hilliard and the crowd that his marching orders hadn't changed in thirty years, but he let the others do most of the talking as he munched contentedly on fried catfish, brown rice, corn bread, biscuits and "leaves." He took a sip of a 1994 Clos du Bois from Sonoma County, his first taste of alcohol since he'd overindulged on brandy at San Quentin and had to be poured into his cell by Lynne Atkinson. He joked that several of his fellow prisoners had been "beefed" by guards two weeks earlier for trying to make wine from raisins and sugar. "And here I am now with a glass in front of me." He held it up like a rare jewel.

FOR THE rest of the evening the Pratt entourage was secluded at Cochran's beach house in Marina del Rey. Hanlon planned to fly home to San Francisco in the morning. Around midnight, with Ashaki and the children asleep, Pratt and Hanlon walked the sandy littoral with Russell Little and Bill Harris. Later Hanlon reflected: "Harris kidnapped Patty Hearst; I helped him get off with eight years. Little was falsely convicted of murder, and Tony Serra and I got his life sentence reversed. And G was free. It was a rare moment in the life of a criminal defense attorney, a great natural high. Somebody said, 'Who ever thought we'd live to see this day?' That said it all. I felt so grateful that Kathy lived to see the end."

Homecoming

Four days later, on the afternoon of Saturday, June 14, 1997, the little neighborhood known as Across the Tracks hummed with anticipation. Network TV trucks parked across the street from the old Pratt house, and from there to the levee the streets and lawns swarmed with people, almost all of them black. Welcome signs hung in "Death Alley," and gnarled old pecan and fruit trees bore crops of streamers and balloons. On tables set up on the lawn in front of Eunice Pratt's cinder-block cottage, mounds of corn bread and baking-soda biscuits sent up puffs of steam under metal foil. Vats of crawfish and crab warmed over portable stoves. The tails of jumbo shrimp shone pink in pails of shaved ice. Cooks stirred pots of beans and rice and flipped chicken parts and fish fillets in iron skillets. Grease dripped from ribs of beef and pork, rotating over spits. Tables sagged with buttered grits, *boudin noir,* spaghetti, garlic potato salad, spicy gumbo, okra, fresh Avoca Island greens.

Old friends clutched gifts and mementos to press on Geronimo: a "catfishing kit" from his childhood pal Alvin "Kaydoe" Delco, a "Blue Devils Forever" T-shirt from a Morgan City Colored High teammate, a box of pralines from a neighbor who'd helped to change his diapers. The Pratt siblings bustled about; not one was missing. For some the trip had been made on borrowed money. Timothy clutched a slip of paper on which he'd written a couplet from a Shakespeare sonnet:

> *Thou art thy mother's glass, and she in thee*
> *Calls back the lovely April of her prime.*

Tim intended to share the poetry with the brother he still called Gerard, who was en route from San Francisco on airline tickets that had been sent to Johnnie Cochran's office by Shaquille O'Neal, the pro basketball star. Geronimo, Ashaki, Hiroji and Shona would be escorted by retired insurance executive Johnnie L. Cochran Sr., eighty years old, and their arrival was expected any minute.

JUST AFTER 2:00 P.M. the crowd stirred as a long limousine, provided gratis by local mortician Byron Jones, bumped over the Southern Pacific track. Lights flashing, the big Lincoln rolled slowly past the Catholic church where Enoch "Jack" Pratt and Eunice Petty had been married. The celebrants yelled and clapped as the sunroof slid open and a shaved head appeared, followed by sturdy shoulders. The limousine was still in motion when the man of the hour erupted through the roof, leaped into the crowd and ran toward his mother's front door.

"I'm sorry!" he called back to the driver. "If I hurt the car, I'll pay."

Geronimo hadn't seen his mother since her bus trip from Morgan City to Folsom in 1974. As he reached the door, he lowered his voice and told a reporter, "She's an old lady now. I'm scared of making her nervous."

Jacqueline, Emelda and Virginia had brushed their mother's gray-black hair and dressed her in her favorite color. A sky-blue twist held her thick braid. She wore a simple dress of blue plaid, white socks and blue flowered slippers as she slowly rocked and chanted on her favorite chair in the tiny living room. Her daughters had told her that Gerard was coming home, but no one knew if she understood.

"WHEN GERONIMO came into the front room, he shooed everybody out," his brother Jack said later, "but I was standing in the corner and didn't move. Ain't nobody gonna keep me out after twenty-seven years. I watched him kneel by our mother. He said, 'Mama, your baby boy's home. Your baby boy made it.' Mama chanted louder. He said, 'Mama, I promised you I was coming home.' He took her hand and a surprised look came over his face. He said, 'Mama, that's the same chant I did in the hole. *That's the chant that kept me goin'!*' I was standing in the corner, tears running down my shirt. The Lord privileged me to see that scene. I know Mama recognized him. He stayed with her twenty minutes, holding her hand and listening. Then G and I walked out the door together. I said, 'Thank God, it's gone. All those years, carrying that cross.' He lowered his head and said, 'What did I put my family through?' I took him by the arm and we went outside to see our friends."

EPILOGUE: 1

After California's Second District Court of Appeal denied the D.A.'s appeal by a 3–0 vote, Gil Garcetti announced that he was dropping the case. With the last legal cloud removed, Pratt moved his mother and immediate family into a big antebellum home two miles north of the Sunset Limited tracks in Morgan City. He spent hours alone with Eunice, holding her small hands, rubbing circulation into her back, trying to teach her a word a day, helping her in and out of a therapeutic hot tub in a room that he'd tiled himself in blue.

He was in demand as a lecturer but still refused to give autographs. "Don't hero-worship me," he told his admirers on a college campus. "We all have to be our own heroes—and *act* like it. Our family structure is failing because too many young black men are in prison. Write to the brothers, help the kids on the edge. Give something back."

No longer obliged to do cellisthenics, he worked out and jogged every day, cut back on fried food after a brief hospitalization for high blood pressure, and fished for black bass, *sac-à-lait* and choupique in the Atchafalaya Swamp. "He's trying to get used to the world," Stuart Hanlon explained. "It'll take a while."

HANLON LOOKED back on the Pratt case as a mellowing experience, full of pain and tragedy, but in the end a lesson in human behavior. "When I was young, everything was a conspiracy. But I gradually came to realize that nobody sat down and said, 'Let's frame Pratt.' It was just a bunch of people making wrong decisions, and then it snowballs and others help them cover up because they're convinced the guy is guilty, so what's the difference if they bend the law to keep him locked up? It doesn't take a big plan to form a conspiracy. It started with J. Edgar Hoover telling his agents, *Get the Panthers. Neutralize Pratt.* That was an act of racial hatred, worse than the worst crimes of the Ku Klux Klan. COINTELPRO versus a bunch of black guys was a naval engagement between a battleship and a canoe. Hoover's agents knew their asses would be covered no matter how many dirty tricks they pulled and how many Panthers died. That's where the courts should have intervened. Somewhere along the line a judge should have told Richard Held and those other agents, 'Hey, I don't care if you *are* the FBI. You're breaking the law.' That's what courts are for. But I don't see the judges as a bunch of conspirators. For the most part, I see 'em as gutless."

IN HIS customary upbeat style Johnnie L. Cochran Jr. found a bright side to the Pratt story. "It taught me and a lot of other lawyers never to accept the official version of an event, never accept a lab report, a forensic finding, never take so-called expert testimony at face value. It taught me to check *everything,* then check it again. As a result, I see things I never saw before, ask questions I never asked before. I'm a better advocate for my clients. But . . . what a price Geronimo had to pay."

Unlike some of the other Pratt lawyers, Cochran never softened toward Richard Kalustian, Julius Butler, the LAPD or the Los Angeles D.A.'s Office. "After we got Geronimo out, I went to [ex-Mayor] Tom Bradley's funeral services at First AME Church, and Julio was ushering in his Sunday suit. He looked at me and I looked away. The Lord and the First AME may forgive him, but I never will. And I don't have a shred of respect left for those prosecutors. All the rapport and admiration I built up from working with them through the years, from knowing them personally, from being friends—it all disappeared in the Pratt case, with very few exceptions. Dick Kalustian and Gil Garcetti were sworn to do justice, but they turned their eyes away. They never had the courage or the integrity to set the record straight, even when we proved they were wrong. Kalustian tracked Geronimo to the parole board hearings, and at the same time he was helping Julio clean up his record so he could get into law school. I could *never* forgive Kalustian. I could *never* go into his courtroom. Superior Court judge or not, there should be some kind of penalty for what he did."

In its social implications the Pratt case struck Cochran as part of a tragic continuum that had begun when the white citizens of Los Angeles delegated their civic responsibilities to the law enforcement establishment. "Back in the fifties and sixties, whites saw the LAPD as the thin blue line protecting them from the invading masses—African Americans, Asians, pachucos, zoot-suiters, anybody that didn't have white skin and a bank account. The power structure told the cops and the D.A., 'Take care of this problem for us. Keep 'em in their place. *We don't care how you do it.*' Black folks were regarded as a nuisance at best and a menace at worst. After the Watts riot ended, Police Chief William Parker said, 'We've got 'em dancing like monkeys in a cage.' Was he fired over an insensitive remark like that? Nope. Now we have a police building named after him. Some of the chiefs that succeeded Parker believed in a proactive policy. Proactive means, *Get them before they get us.* They turned justice upside down."

KATHY RYAN died at home a month after Geronimo's release. A few nights later Hanlon took an uphill walk toward Twin Peaks, and a group of Asians snapped his picture from a tour bus. He imagined them displaying the prints when they returned home: *San Francisco man, crying in rain.*

In his grief he decided to abandon his law practice. "I'd had enough of other people's problems. I never wanted to see another court. I hated doctors. I hated lawyers. The Pratt case had been my focus for so long. Now I had to learn how to raise two boys. I told Liam and Rory, 'Let's get away from here and start over.' But they didn't want to leave their mother's house."

Honoring Kathy's last request, Hanlon and five-year-old Rory scattered her ashes in the Pacific near Mendocino. Ten-year-old Liam stayed home and kicked the TV in sorrow and rage. Then the male Hanlons tried to outrun their grief with frantic trips to Hawaii and Mexico. Stuart would put the boys to bed and sit up late at night listening to the surf and wondering how he would spend the rest of his life.

After a few tortured weeks he realized how much he missed the law. He couldn't imagine living out his years as anything but a lawyer, no matter how flawed the system or the players, himself included. There were drawbacks, but there were benefits, too.

Another Geronimo Pratt might come along.

EPILOGUE: II

In April 2000, Geronimo Pratt's lawsuit for false imprisonment and violation of civil rights was settled out of court. The City of Los Angeles agreed
to pay $2,750,000, the FBI $1,750,000. It was the first public acknowledg-
ment by the FBI of its culpability.

Author's Note

I worked very closely with Geronimo Pratt, Stuart Hanlon and Johnnie L. Cochran Jr. in researching this book, but I also received valuable assistance from Zachary Arbore, A. Lynne Atkinson, Lowell Bergman, Emily Sara Bischoff, Robert Bloom, Edward J. Boyer, Jacqueline Brown, Shawn Coyne, Sonia Davis, Alvin Delco, Juliana Drous, Reverend James McCloskey, Eloise McGill, Dolores ' Michelsen, Chris Min, Su Peterson, Ashaki Pratt, Charles Pratt, Reverend Jack Pratt, Timothy Pratt, Virginia Pratt, Linda Steinman and a small army of patient court clerks, researchers, paralegals, librarians and secretaries who made some 55,000 pages of documentary material available. In the end, however, I am solely responsible for the accuracy of the finished product, and any errors are my own.

Jack Olsen
Bainbridge Island, Washington
July 2000

INDEX

Abundant Living Magazine, 35
Across the Tracks. *See* Morgan City
Aldridge, Henry, 247–48
Amnesty International, 269
Anderson, Clayton, 392–93, 417
Appellate review, 263–67
Ashaki (Linda Session), 217, 245, 249–50, 255, 278, 286–87
Atkinson, Lynne, 290–91, 293–99, 305–6, 310, 313–14, 318–23, 471, 476
Ayoub, Don, 381

Baker, Howard, 221
Baldwin, James, 39
Banks, Dennis, 470, 476
Bardsley, Marilyn, 220n
Bascue, James A., 368
Bates, Charles W., 208n
Bell, Cheyenne, 216
Bell, Sylvester, 225
Berg, Martin, 374
Bergman, Lowell, 297, 299, 339, 351–52
Bernstein, David, 216
Bernstein, Leonard, 230
Bird, Rose, 270
Black, Theresa, 198–99, 209
Black Panther newspaper, 43, 227
Black Panther Party (BPP)

Butler expelled from, 55–56, 128–29, 143, 154–55
at Clark's funeral, 47
COINTELPRO's operation against, 222–31
headquarters raid, 46, 59, 61–62, 64, 89
Morgan City elder on, 35
police harassment of, 46, 49–52, 55, 85, 89
Pratt expelled from, 72–73, 311
Smith's characterizations of, 90–92
splinter factions within, 40–41
trizophrenic nature of, 38
United Slaves' animosity toward, 44–46, 59, 224–25
Bloeser, Richard, 280
Bloom, Robert, 216, 329–36, 356
Bond, Julian, 64
Bowles, Morris, 372–73, 399, 406, 416–17, 419, 431–33, 438
Boyer, Edward J., 360, 394, 443, 469
Bozanich, Peter, 339–40
Bradley, Tom, 484
Brando, Marlon, 361
Branton, Leo, 108
Brown, Alonzo (pseudonym), 4–5
Brown, David E., 320–21
Brown, Willie, 216, 257, 303
Bryan, Ralph, 81

Buckhout, Robert, 143–45
Bumblebee, Michael, 235–36, 245
Butler, Bobby, 185
Butler, Julius Carl (Julio or Mama or
        Mother)
    arrest of, 276
    connections to Hatter and Swilley,
        344, 450–51
    described, 53–54
    Diggs's death and, 450–51
    evidentiary hearing and, 384, 394–403,
        412–13, 416–20, 429–34, 443,
        455–57, 465
    expelled from BPP by Pratt, 55–56,
        128–29, 143, 154–55
    habeas corpus actions and, 253–54,
        258, 280–81
    informer status evidence, 25–34,
        233–34, 276, 330–31, 344,
        347–48, 372–73, 398–404
    informer status suspected, 54–56, 86,
        107–8, 126, 136, 162, 164–65,
        170, 200
    letter accusing Pratt, 76, 83–84, 110,
        124, 161, 164, 254, 275, 403, 419,
        429–31, 436–37, 456
    perjury evidence, 332
    Pratt's supposed confession to, 106,
        124–25, 348
    resignation of, 474
    rivalry with Pratt, 53–55
    sanitization of, 359–60, 395
    statements in Pratt's record by, 180
    trial testimony regarding, 154–55,
        158–59, 161–62
    on the witness stand, 86–87, 124–31,
        133–34, 165–66, 395–403,
        424–27, 429–32

California Lawyer, 376, 389
California's Second District Court of
        Appeal, 483
California Supreme Court rulings, 270, 370
Callahan, Raymond, 74, 85, 93, 135, 280,
        416
Carmichael, Stokely, 226
Carroll, Ronald "Mike," 81, 95, 97, 438
Carter, Alprentice "Bunchy," 35, 37–40,
        45, 47, 52, 93, 155, 224
Chance, Clarence, 339, 351, 475–76
Chapman, Shawn, 375, 392, 437, 465
Chavis, Benjamin F., Jr., 353
Chicago police riot (1968), 36
Christian Science Monitor, 65
Church, Frank, 221
Civil rights suit, 214–16, 233–45

Clark, Mark, 59, 275
Cleary, B. O., 275, 280
Cleaver, Eldridge, 39–40, 69, 73, 93–94,
        155, 227–29, 471, 473, 476
Cleaver, Kathleen, 53, 106, 137, 142, 147,
        151–52, 228, 356, 411, 454, 471
Cochran, Hattie B. (mother), 97, 179
Cochran, Johnnie
    as assistant district attorney, 236–37,
        260–61
    at bail hearing, 471–72
    Buckhout interrogated by, 143–45
    Butler interrogated by, 125–29,
        133–34, 164–65, 395–403
    celebrations after Pratt's release, 476–77
    Cleaver interrogated by, 151
    at conspiracy trial, 90, 92–97
    Eckstein interrogated by, 145–47
    enlisted as Pratt's lawyer, 103–4
    evidentiary hearing and, 376–77,
        379–81, 387–89, 393–404, 412,
        421–22, 424–33, 436–38, 454–59,
        465–69
    eyewitness manipulation suspected by,
        108, 112–15, 428
    FBI intimidation of, 147
    on government deception, 283
    habeas corpus actions, 333–36, 367–70
    Hanlon counseled by, 260, 365
    Hanlon's first meeting with, 8–9
    Hewitt interrogated by, 142–43
    on Lee's death announcement, 93
    lies under oath discovered by, 173–74
    on McCloskey, 340
    media blitz by, 297, 359–61
    meeting with Van de Kamp, 273–74
    Morgan interrogated by, 139–41
    motion for new trial by, 174–75
    motion to exclude witnesses, 109–10
    New York Times article and, 445–46
    post-trial reflections of, 171
    Pratt (Charles) interrogated by, 150
    Pratt's conspiracy worries and, 105,
        115–16
    on Pratt's innocence, 9
    on Pratt's prison treatment, 211
    Pratt visited in prison by, 178–82, 365
    Redd interrogated by, 141
    Reed (Barbara) interrogated by, 112–13
    Reed (Fred) interrogated by, 114–15
    reflections on Pratt case, 484–85
    at resentencing hearing, 205–6
    search for defense witnesses, 136–37, 159
    Simpson case and, 359, 361, 364, 379,
        423
    worries about Pratt, 327–28

Cochran, Johnnie, Sr., 97
COINTELPRO (Counter-Intelligence
    Program), 217, 219–31, 251,
    258–59, 265–66, 275–76
    See also Federal Bureau of Investigation
    (FBI)
Coleman, Roger, 475
Como, Kenny, 185
Conspiracy trial, 89–97
Conti, Samuel, Judge, 214–15, 241–43,
    245
Cowell, Michael, Judge, 368–70, 372,
    375–76, 388–89
Cullen, Countee, 39
Cunningham, Dennis, 216, 235

Daily Journal, 374
Davis, Angela, 108
Davis, Edward M., 63
Deacons for Defense and Justice, 26
Delco, Alvin "Kaydoe," 479
Dell, George (Judge), 89, 91, 94–97
Dellums, Ron, 251
Democratic National Convention (1968),
    36
De Prima, Steve, 372, 398–99
Dickey, Everett, Judge, 379–81, 389–90,
    392, 394, 396–98, 400–2, 405–7,
    409–10, 416–19, 423–28, 430–32,
    443, 447, 455, 458–61, 464–66,
    471
    See also Evidentiary hearing
Diggs, Captain Franco, 42, 141, 155–56,
    180, 348–49, 450–51
Dominguez, Juan, 100–1
Douglas, Emory, 136, 142, 333
Douglass, Frederick, 68, 235
Dowd, Maureen, 445–46
Driving while black (DWB), 49n, 50
Drous, Juliana, 362–63, 367, 371, 375,
    379–81, 384, 392, 400, 411–13,
    422, 435, 439, 442–43, 464–67
Drummond, Edwin, 269
Dudley, Bud, 24
Dunn, William, 264–67
Dymally, Mervyn, 63

Eckstein, John, 113, 118, 135, 145–47, 174
Edwards, Don, 215, 276, 353
Ellison, Ralph, 39
Ermachild, Melody, 279
Everett, Ron (Karenga), 44–45, 59
Evidentiary hearing
    Anderson on the stand, 392–93
    appeal actions, 469–70, 483
    Bowles on the stand, 432–33

Butler on the stand, 395–403, 424–27,
    429–32
Carroll on the stand, 438
celebrations afterward, 466–68
Cochran's participation debated,
    379–81
decision for the defense, 464–66
FBI presentation, 388–90
final argument, 453–61
final testimony, 443
Henry on the stand, 433–34
Kalustian on the stand, 405–10,
    415–20
opening day, 391–94
opening proceedings, 383–85
Orange County assignment of, 376–77
Rice on the stand, 436–38
strategy sessions, 387–88, 411–13,
    421–23
Willis on the stand, 403–4

Fanon, Frantz, 39
Farr, Mel, 36
Fechheimer, David, 331–32
Federal Bureau of Investigation (FBI)
    BPP declared security risk by, 40, 65
    BPP headquarters attacked by, 61–62
    Butler in documents of, 233–34,
        253–54, 276
    Cochran accuses of collusion, 456
    Cochran intimidated by, 147
    COINTELPRO (Counter-Intelligence
        Program), 217, 219–31, 251,
        258–59, 265–66, 275–76
    Edwards on clandestine programs, 215
    evidentiary hearing presentation,
        388–90
    "hijack plot" and, 200–1, 208
    at Huggins' funeral, 47
    informant for conspiracy trial, 90
    McCloskey's help getting records,
        215–16, 233
    Newton characterized by, 309
    parole board letters by, 295–96
    Pratt files requested, 213
    Pratt's innocence known by, 204,
        275–76
    Pratt's murder trial and, 147, 150–51,
        171
    Pratt threatened by, 44
    wiretap logs of, 276, 331, 345–46
Ferreira, Brentford J., 371–72, 376
    evidentiary hearing and, 389, 392,
        396–97, 407–9, 417–19, 424–27,
        430, 437–38, 446–47, 454
Flores, Humberto, 194–95

Fonda, Jane, 230
Footnote warfare of Hanson, 265–66, 267n
Fort Bragg, 32–35
Freed, Donald, 473
Freeman, Roland, 62, 106
Freeman, Ronald, 106

Garcetti, Gil, 351–53, 358, 367–69, 372,
    380, 467, 469–70, 484–85
Garcia, Robert, 369, 385, 405–6, 411,
    423, 454, 465
Gardner, Theodore, 280
Garry, Charles, 275, 331
Garvey, Marcus, 25, 220n, 235
Gary, Romain, 230
Gates, Daryl, 63
Gegner, Sue, 286
Gentlemen's Quarterly, 360–61
Gerritsen, A. W., 213
Glick, Brian, 216
Goldwater, Barry, 221
Goode, Victor, 263
Gordon, James, 96–97
Grand jury (tennis court murder), 86–88
Grimes, Milton, 379
Guevara, Che, 39
Gunn, J. B., 199

Habeas corpus actions
    Bloom's petition, 333–36
    in California court, 255, 257–60
    petition filed in L.A., 367–70
    in U.S. District Court, 277–83
    See also Evidentiary hearing
Haggar, Tom, 199, 278
Hale, Brian, 372–74
Hamilton, Jeanne, 169–70, 304, 471
Hampton, Fred, 59–60, 275
Hanlon, Kathy Ryan. See Ryan, Kathleen
Hanlon, Stuart
    ad hoc legal staff of, 216
    appeals procedure 602 initiated by, 213
    appellate review and, 263–65, 267
    attorney fees awarded to, 245
    authority distrusted by, 1
    at bail hearing, 471–73
    childhood of, 6
    civil rights suit, 214–16, 233–45
    cocaine habit of, 245, 287
    as defense witness at Adjustment
        Center, 3
    early law practice of, 209–10
    evidentiary hearing and, 376–77,
        379–81, 383–85, 387–89, 392–94,
        405–13, 415–24, 433–34, 438–39,
        442–43, 454–56, 459–61, 464–68

Ferreira's information for, 371–72
financial sacrifices of, 326–27
first meeting with Cochran, 8–9
first visit with Pratt, 1–8
at Folsom, 316–17
friction with Pratt, 356, 363–65,
    423–24, 447
habeas corpus actions, 255, 257–60,
    277–83, 333–36, 367–70
Hatter and Swilley learned of, 279
"Jewfro" of, 2, 7
at L.A. D.A. meeting, 351–53
letter-writing campaign, 212
marriage of, 282
on McCloskey, 340
media blitz by, 297, 359–61
New York Times article and, 445–46
at parole hearings, 252, 270, 300–4
on photo lineup rigging, 87
Pratt's release and, 472–73, 476
Pratt visited at Mule Creek by, 361–65
reflections on Pratt case, 484
San Luis Obispo visits by, 270–71
setup attempt in San Quentin, 4
Swearingen meeting, 275–76
Tehachapi prison visits by, 325–28
Van de Kamp meeting, 273–74
wife's illness and death, 435–36,
    438–42, 453, 465, 472, 485
See also Evidentiary hearing
Hanson, L. Thaxton, 263–67, 302, 457,
    460
Harris, Bill, 476–77
Harris, Jimmy, 14, 24, 26
Hart, Philip, 221
Hartman, John, 17
Hatter, Larry "Dobey," 85, 279, 330,
    341–45, 451
Hearst, Patricia, 194, 200–1, 208, 477
Hearst, Randolph, 198
Hegel, G. W. F., 39
Heins, W. C., 252
Held, Richard Wallace, 275, 280–82, 430
Henry, Ed, 280, 331, 396, 401, 419,
    433–34, 455
Hewitt, Shirley, 141–43
High Potential Program (UCLA), 39
Hilliard, David, 47, 58, 74, 106, 136, 142,
    157, 169–70, 229, 333, 473, 476
Hinckle, Warren, 321
Hollopeter, Charles
    Cochran approved by, 103–4
    eyewitness manipulation suspected by,
        104, 113, 120
    objection to Butler's voluntary
        statements, 131

objection to side arm as evidence, 124
Olsen interrogated by, 119–21
Pratt (Charles) interrogated by, 166
Pratt interrogated by, 153–56
Rice interrogated by, 161–62
search for defense witnesses, 136–37, 159
Wolfer interrogated by, 135
Holloway, Thomas, 342–43
Hoover, J. Edgar, 40, 65, 200, 254, 304, 471
    COINTELPRO and, 219–20, 224–25, 227–28, 484
Horn, Fred, 320
Horton, Jackie. *See* Wilcots, Jackie Horton
Huggins, Ericka, 45–46
Huggins, John, 41–42, 45, 47, 73, 224
Hurston, Zora Neale, 39
Hutchinson, Dwight, 344–45
Hutchinson, William Tyrone, 85, 124, 279, 282, 330, 341–42, 348

Identikit composites, 80, 87, 112–13, 139–41, 145
Imm, Michael, 2–3, 5–6, 240–41, 303
Invisible Man, 39

Jackson, George, 177–79
Jackson, Jesse L., 336
Jacot, Nancy, 235–36, 245
Jeff, Death Row, 185
Jefferson, Bernard, 260, 263–64
Johns, Richard Stanley, 143
Johnson, Lyndon, 33
Jones, Byron, 480
Jones, Mike, 203–4
Journey to Justice, 379
Justice, Larry "Gig," 196

Kalustian, Richard
    Butler interrogated by, 124–25, 129–31, 133, 164–65
    Butler sanitization and, 359–60, 409
    Butler's informer status denied by, 374
    Butler's weapons not reported by, 408–9, 466
    Cleaver interrogated by, 151–52
    Cochran's abiding enmity toward, 484–85
    Cochran's knowledge of, 104, 107
    Cochran's public criticism of, 360–61
    evidentiary hearing and, 384, 389, 393, 396–98, 404–13, 415–20, 455–56
    Garcetti's concern about, 352
    habeas corpus actions and, 258, 280

Morgan interrogated by, 140
Oldfield interrogated by, 162–63
Olsen interrogated by, 115, 118–19
opening statement by, 109–10
parole hearing warnings by, 252, 274–75, 278–79, 320
Pennewell interrogated by, 150–51
Pratt interrogated by, 156–59
Redd interrogated by, 141
Reed (Barbara) interrogated by, 110–12
Reed (Fred) interrogated by, 114
at resentencing hearing, 205
rules of discovery and, 107, 171, 258, 418–19
sidebar concerning Pratt's testimony, 158–59
statements in Pratt's record by, 175, 180–81
trial notes of, 330
Wilcots interrogated by, 159–60
Wolfer interrogated by, 134–35
Kambui, Somayah, 471
Karenga, Ron, 44–45, 59, 223–24, 226
Kessler, Cheryl, 216
King, Coretta Scott, 336
King, Martin Luther, Jr., 34, 170–71, 235, 310n, 459
Klausner, Gary, 335
Knight, Goodwin, 265
Koller, Paul, 327–28
Kronenberg, John, 277–80, 282–83, 285, 383, 458
Ku Klux Klan, 22–26

Ladd, Wayne "Bulldog," 185, 187–88, 191, 193, 304
Larsen, Nella, 39
Leahy, Patrick, 361
Lee, Chol Soo, 328
Lee, Saundra "Red," 58–59, 62–63, 73, 93–94
Legionnaires, 25
Lenin, V. I., 39
Lewis, Roger "Blue," 49–50, 84, 130
Lillie, Mildred, 264–65
Link, Jodi Michelle, 392, 427, 454
Little, Russell, 476–77
Loomis, Andrew, 387
Los Angeles Police Department (LAPD)
    blacks killed by (1967–1968), 42
    BPP harassed by, 46, 49–52, 55, 85, 89
    BPP headquarters attacked by, 61–62
    at Clark's funeral, 47
    Criminal Conspiracy Section (CCS), 74

documents shredded by, 234
photo lineup rigged by, 87, 112–13
racism in, 43–44, 46, 51
tennis court murder case taken over by, 85–86
testimony missing at trial, 135
Urban Counterinsurgency Task Force (Panther Unit), 43–44, 47
Los Angeles Times, 65–66, 70, 91, 93–94, 169, 283, 317, 359, 367, 385, 423–24, 443, 463, 469–70
Louis, Jake, 185
Lubell, Jonathan, 263
Lynn, David, 411, 421, 439
Lyons, Lamar, 145

Mack, John, 361
Maddox, Sergeant, 31
Mafia
  Folsom setup and, 194–95
  Lee's murder by, 93–94n
Malcolm X, 25, 32–33, 39, 52, 170–71, 235
Mandela, Nelson, 323, 361, 463
Manson, Charles, 184–85, 194
Mao Tse-Tung, 39
McClendon, Harvey, 333
McCloskey, James
  character of, 337–38, 340
  decision to take Pratt's case, 338–40
  evidentiary hearing and, 380, 385, 388, 411–13, 433, 443, 464
  on habeas corpus decision, 370
  investigation by, 341–47
  at L.A. D.A. meeting, 351–53
  later remarks of, 38, 56, 85–86
  media blitz by, 359–61
  Pratt's release and, 475–76
  Pratt visited at Mule Creek by, 361–62
  press release of, 367
  report by, 347–49
  Ryan's illness and, 442
  Sondheim pressured by, 357–58
McCloskey, Paul N. "Pete," 215–16, 233, 263, 273, 281, 307
McGill, Eloise, 464
McKay, Claude, 39
McKissack, Luke, 75–76
McRea, Dip, 278
Meadows, Sharon, 216
Miller, Lindberg B., 255
Mitchell, John, 216, 234, 245, 263
Mondale, Walter, 221
Moore, George C., 222
Moore, Gwen, 257
Moore, Oneal, 26
Moore, Peaches, 471

Moore, Renee, 62
Moore, Richard Dhoruba, 329
Morgan, Charles, 15
Morgan, Margaret, 139–41
Morgan, One-legged Joe, 185
Morgan City
  Across the Tracks, 13–15
  elders of, 24–26, 34–35
  McCloskey in, 346–47
  Pratt's homecoming, 479–81
  racism in, 18, 21–23, 25–26, 35
Morgan City Colored High, 24, 92
Murray, Cecil L. "Chip," 360

Newsweek, 64
New Times, 286
Newton, Huey P.
  Cleaver's split with, 69, 73, 93–94, 227–29
  decline of, 69
  Lee's murder and, 93–94
  Pratt and, 69, 72–73, 106, 123, 136, 309–11
  rallies for, 40
  in "soul breaker" cells, 42
  Texas rendezvous missed by, 71–72
New York Times, 64, 445–46
Nuernberger, L. G., 239–40
Nyberg, Deputy Warden, 289

O'Connell, Maureen, 301–2, 303
Oldfield, Joseph, 162–63
Olsen, Caroline, 78–80, 119, 253, 320
Olsen, Kenneth Crismon
  Buckhout on Pratt's identification by, 145
  early descriptions and identifications, 80–82, 145–46
  grand jury testimony of, 87–88
  Hamilton's lack of trust in, 170
  official lack of confidence in, 81, 438, 466
  parole hearing statements, 252, 270
  perjury by, 118, 173–74
  Perkins identified by, 81–82, 87, 146, 173–74
  Pratt identified by, 87, 106, 110, 115
  robbed and shot at tennis court, 78–79
  suspicion of manipulation of, 120, 427–28
  on the witness stand, 115, 117–21

Panther Unit (Urban Counterinsurgency Task Force), 43–44, 47
Paparian, William, 361
Parker, Kathleen, Judge

Buckhout's testimony and, 144
evidentiary hearing and, 458
habeas corpus action and, 257–60,
    265–66
Hanlon's condemnation of, 259–60, 389
jury congratulated by, 169
jury questioned by, 168
on Kalustian's interrogation of Pratt,
    158
on levity in the courtroom, 160
new trial motion denied by, 175
Pratt's unchaining agreed to, 109
at resentencing hearing, 205–6
at tennis court murder trial, 130
Parker, William, 485
Parole hearings, 251–53, 270, 274–75,
    278–79, 295, 308, 320–21, 355–56
60 Minutes report, 297–304
Patterson, Robert, 320
Peltier, Leonard, 471*n*
Penn, Sean, 361
Pennewell, Michael David, 150–51, 330
Perkins, Ernest James, 81–82, 87, 146
Perry, Darthard, 208
Pharr, Wayne, 62
Pitchess, Peter, 67, 241
Plasse, Richard, 79–80
Potato chip caper, 326
Powell, Benny, 339, 351
Pratt, Charles (brother), 17, 20, 24*n*, 37,
    50, 123, 347
    birthday party photo from, 149–50,
        156, 159, 162–63, 165–67, 206–7
Pratt, Elmer Gerard "Geronimo"
    accent in speech of, 39
    ad hoc legal staff of, 216
    after release from prison, 472–73,
        475–77, 479–81, 483
    as American hero, 470, 472–73
    as Amnesty International "prisoner of
        conscience," 270
    appearance of, 6–7
    appellate review of case, 263–67
    Atkinson reports on, 290–91, 293–99,
        319–21
    bail hearing, 470–72
    birth of, 16–17
    bowlegs of, 16
    in California Men's Colony (San Luis
        Obispo), 269–71, 274–75, 277–78
    California Supreme Court ruling, 270
    on Carter, 39
    charges against, 8
    in Chino State Prison, 449–50
    civil rights suit, 214–16, 233–45
    Cochran congratulated as ADA by, 237

conspiracy trial, 89–97
Dallas arrest and jailing, 72–74
early life of, 11–27
    accused by white girl, 21–22
    education, 12, 17–18, 24
    elders' graduation teachings, 24–26
    father's stroke, 19–20
    Klan attack on brother, 22–24
    rebellion against God, 16
    work, 11–14, 20–21
education in prison, 210–11, 214, 249,
    255, 269
at evidentiary hearing, 392, 396, 400,
    422–24, 454, 458–59, 461
at father's funeral, 70–71
in Folsom, 184–95
    after Puerto Rico trial, 316–17
    chanting by, 191–92
    inmates jealous of, 186–87
    Ladd's friendship with, 188–89,
        193–94
    mother's visit and, 189–92
    move from San Quentin, 183–84
    return to San Quentin, 195–96
    set up by guards, 194–95
    thorazine given to, 194
friction with Hanlon, 356, 363–65,
    423–24, 447
as Geronimo ji Jaga, 38, 99
grand jury indictment, 88
habeas corpus actions, 255, 257–60,
    277–83, 333–36, 367–70
injury from land mine, 31–32, 75
kindness of, 113, 117–18, 305–6,
    472–73
as last man standing, 463
Lee's murder and, 93–94
in Los Angeles County Jail, 12–13,
    66–68, 76, 97, 99–101, 105
with Los Angeles Panthers
    after Clark's funeral, 47–48
    arrests and charges, 46–47, 55, 62–63
    BPP headquarters fortified by, 59
    Butler expelled by, 55–56, 128–29,
        143, 154–55
    Butler's rivalry with, 53–55
    Carter's friendship, 37–38, 66–68
    decision to join, 36
    expelled by Newton, 72–73, 311
    family warnings against BPP, 41
    in L.A. County Jail, 66–68
    Lee as "wife," 58–59
    move to L.A., 36–37
    named as Carter's successor, 53
    not an official member, 210
    Panthers taught by, 40, 42, 44

police harassment of, 46, 50–51, 55
Times fake interview with, 65
in UCLA High Potential Program,
    39
marriage to Ashaki, 217
medals earned by, 30–32
in Miami detention center, 314
Morgan City elders' counseling of,
    24–26, 34–35
in Mule Creek State Prison, 355–57,
    361–65, 450–51, 467, 470
in New Orleans, 70–71
in Orange County Jail, 422–24, 447,
    449, 470–72
parole hearings, 251–53, 270, 274–75,
    278–79, 295, 297–304, 308,
    320–21, 355–56
prayers for, 336, 356–57, 463, 468, 481
prison murder attempts, 196–97, 199,
    450
Puerto Rico trial and, 313–18
in San Quentin, 177–82, 196–201
    in Adjustment Center, 210–12
    after Puerto Rico trial, 317–18
    Ashaki's family visits, 249–50, 278,
        286–87
    cell mock-up at civil rights hearing,
        243–44
    Cochran's visits, 178–82
    cruel and unusual punishment, 211
    family asked not to visit by, 208
    furniture factory job, 242–43
    Hanlon's first visit, 1–8
    Hearst case and, 200–1, 208
    as hero, 247–49
    "hijack plot" (Folsom bus scare),
        197–99, 203–4, 240
    in Honor Unit, 278
    as king of the hill, 289
    in mainline section, 242–43, 247–50
    move to Folsom, 183–84
    Newton with, 309–11
    prison guard wounding and, 2–6,
        240–41
    remembered by inmate, 68
    return from Folsom, 195–96
    sister's visit, 207–8
    sixteenth year, 285–87
    statements in record of, 175,
        180–81, 196–97, 212–13, 239–40,
        242, 278, 315
    Vietnam Veterans Group formed by,
        306–8, 319, 325
    volunteers' visits to, 286
"self-defense" defined by, 51–52
60 Minutes report on, 297, 299–304

in Tallegada federal prison, 315
in Tehachapi prison, 325–28, 336
tennis court murder and
    187 P.C. charge, 75–76
    Butler's accusations, 76, 83–84
    on Cochran after verdict, 170
    Cochran enlisted as lawyer, 103–4
    conspiracy worries, 105, 115–17
    evidence of whereabouts on night
        of murder, 331–33
    grand jury indictment, 88
    guilty verdict by jury, 168–69
    Kalustian's prison file statement, 175
    police brutality in jail, 76
    post-trial reflections, 171–72
    reactions to witnesses' identification,
        113, 117–18, 305–6
    resentencing hearing, 205–6
    Tracy penitentiary setup, 100–1, 104
    unchained in courtroom, 109
    on the witness stand, 153–59
    travels undercover, 69–70
    Vietnam tour and, 30–34, 301, 306,
        327–28
    See also Evidentiary hearing; Tennis
        court murder investigation; Tennis
        court murder trial
Pratt, Emelda (sister), 19, 23, 36–37, 50,
    150, 356
Pratt, Enoch "Jack," Sr. (father), 11–16,
    18–20, 70–71
Pratt, Eunice Petty (mother), 15–16,
    18–20, 23, 27, 32, 70–71, 127,
    179, 189–92, 480–81
    prayers for her son, 16, 336, 357, 463,
        468, 481
Pratt, Jackie (brother), 17, 20, 23, 30, 35, 37,
    41, 47, 50, 123, 207, 336, 480–81
Pratt, Jacqueline (sister), 17–18, 270, 336
Pratt, Tanya (niece), 356–57
Pratt, Timothy (brother), 17, 21–24, 29,
    33, 41, 70, 251, 357, 377, 381–82,
    392, 401, 403, 446, 468, 480
Pratt, Virginia (sister), 20, 29, 37, 50,
    123, 207–8, 381–82, 392, 401,
    471–72
Pulley, Reginald, 242–43

Racism
    of COINTELPRO, 220–21
    in conspiracy trial, 96–97
    in Folsom, 187–88
    of Hoover, 220
    in L.A. County Jail, 66
    in LAPD, 43–44, 46, 51
    in Morgan City, 18, 21–23, 25–26, 35

on paddlewheel workboats, 18–19
in Vietnam, 34
Reagan, Ronald, 63
Reasoner, Harry, 297, 304
Red, High Society, 248, 289
Redd, Linda, 137, 141
Reed, Barbara Mary
  Buckhout on Pratt's identification by, 145
  description improved during
    testimony, 111–12, 460
  early descriptions of robber, 80–81,
    112–13, 139
  evidentiary hearing and, 428, 438, 466
  grand jury testimony of, 87
  Hamilton's lack of trust in, 170
  hobby shop robbed, 77–78
  Identikit composites and, 80, 87,
    112–13, 139–40
  McCloskey on, 348
  Pratt identified by, 87, 106, 110–13,
    457–58
  suspicion of manipulation of, 104, 108,
    112–13, 427–28, 438
  on the witness stand, 110–13
Reed, Fred, 114–15
Reiner, Ira, 339
Rice, DuWayne, 124, 164–65, 254, 275,
    280, 330–31, 388, 396, 401, 419,
    429–30, 433, 436–38, 455
Richartz, Patricia, 331–32
Rivetz, Lawrence, 173–74
Rizzo, Frank, 69
Rogers, David Creed, 26
Romo, Dennis, 168–69
Rosenbaum, Mark, 263, 273, 369, 374,
    380, 465
Ruffin, Joe, 24–25
Ryan, Kathleen, 216, 233, 282, 287, 297,
    326–27, 385, 428, 446
  illness and death of, 435–36, 438–42,
    453, 465, 472, 485
Ryan, Margaret "Marnie," 216, 234, 245,
    254–55, 263

San Francisco Chronicle, 311, 321, 469
San Francisco Examiner, 300, 335
Santiago, Juan, 169
Savage, John, 225
Schweiker, Richard, 221
Seale, Bobby
  absence at Pratt's trial, 106, 136, 142,
    169–70
  Butler's letter mentioning, 83
  on Pratt's innocence, 333
  security offered Pratt by, 58
  speech after King's murder, 34

Seale, John, 333
Seberg, Jean, 230
"Self-defense," Pratt defines, 51–52
Serra, Tony, 477
Session, Linda (Ashaki), 217, 245, 249–50,
    255, 278, 286–87
Sheinbaum, Stanley, 361
Simpson, O. J., 358–59, 361, 364, 368,
    379, 423
60 Minutes report, 297, 299–304
Smith, Melvin "Cotton," 61, 71–72,
    90–92, 96, 200
Soldier's Medal, 30–31
Sondheim, Harry B., 353, 357–58, 369,
    371–72, 384, 392, 425–27,
    454–55, 457–60
"Soul breaker" cells, 42
Soul on Ice, 39
Southern Christian Leadership
    Conference, 64
Stafford, Willie, 90, 92, 95, 97, 103–4
Sullivan, William C., 221
Summer, Freedom, 25
Sumner, George, 240, 252, 289
Swearingen, M. Wesley, 275–76, 282, 331,
    471, 476
Swilley, Herbert, 85, 279, 330, 341–45,
    348–49, 451

Tabash, Henry, 295
Tamburello, Tony, 465
Taylor, Harold, 342–44
Taylor, Ollie, 55, 127–28, 130–31, 143,
    154, 158, 180, 258, 348, 396, 399
Tennis court murder investigation
  Butler's letter accusing Pratt, 76,
    83–84, 110
  grand jury regarding, 86–88
  happenings on night of crime,
    77–80
  hobby shop robbery and, 77–79
  Hutchinson arrested by LAPD, 85
  LAPD takeover of, 85–86
  187 P.C. charge, 75–76
  Pratt's grand jury indictment, 88
  suspects identified and described,
    80–82, 87
Tennis court murder trial
  appellate review, 263–67
  Buckhout on the stand, 143–45
  Butler on the stand, 124–31, 133–34,
    164–65
  Butler's letter accusing Pratt, 110, 124,
    161, 164, 254, 275, 403, 419,
    429–31, 436–37, 456
  California Supreme Court ruling, 270

Cleaver on the stand, 151–52
Cochran enlisted as Pratt's lawyer, 103–4
Eckstein on the stand, 145–47
eyewitness identification of Pratt
    bowlegs and, 16, 120
    Buckhout's testimony and, 144–45
    facial hair and, 80, 87, 112, 119, 126,
        140, 143, 149–50, 152, 155, 159,
        163
    Identikit composites, 112–13, 120,
        139–41, 145
    jacket worn and, 80, 87, 112, 114,
        119, 139, 150
    live lineup avoided, 118, 135–36
    manipulation suspected, 104, 108,
        112–15, 120, 428
    McCloskey's summary of inequities,
        338–39
    mouth and, 140–41
    mug shots (photo lineup), 87,
        112–13, 118, 145
    scars and, 80, 111–13, 119–21,
        139–40, 457–58, 460
FBI "mole" on defense team, 258–59
GTO owned by Pratt and, 106–7, 110,
    124, 141, 143, 150, 155, 348–49
guilty verdict, 168–69
habeas corpus actions, 255, 257–60,
    277–83, 333–36, 367–70
Hewitt on the stand, 141–43
Johns on the stand, 143
jurors' defense of verdict, 169–70
jury deliberations, 167–68
Kalustian's opening statement, 109–10
Lyons on the stand, 145
Morgan on the stand, 139–41
motion to exclude witnesses, 109–10
Oldfield on the stand, 162–63
Olsen on the stand, 115, 117–21
Pennewell on the stand, 150–51
police testimony missing, 135
Pratt on the stand, 153–59
Pratt (Charles) on the stand, 149–50,
    166
Pratt's birthday party photo and,
    149–50, 156, 159, 162–63,
    165–67, 206–7
Pratt to be unchained at, 109
preliminary statements and pretrial
    motions, 106–7
as protracted trial, 458
Redd on the stand, 141
Reed (Barbara) on the stand, 110–13
Reed (Fred) on the stand, 114–15
resentencing hearing, 205–6
review of anomalies, 135–36

Rice on the stand, 161–62
Rivetz affidavit on perjury and,
    173–74
search for defense witnesses, 136–37, 159
side arm as evidence, 124–25, 134–35,
    155–57, 254–55
Wilcots on the stand, 159–60
Wolfer on the stand, 134–35
Tielsch, George, 253
Time magazine, 64–65
Tong, Edmund, 300–1, 303
Toomer, Jean, 39
Tracy penitentiary setup, 100–1, 104
Trainwreck, 74

United Slaves (US), 44–45, 59, 224–25
U.S. Ninth Circuit Court of Appeals,
    297, 307–8

Vance, Stanley, 81
Van de Kamp, John, 236, 261, 273–74
Vasquez, Dan, 321
Vezzani, Diane, 300, 302–3, 351–52
Vietnam
    Pratt's experience, 30–34, 301, 306,
        327–28
    prison Veterans Group, 306–8, 319, 325

Walker, Nancy, 303
Wallace, Richard, 280
Washington, Long John, 53, 60, 73,
    83–84, 106, 129–30, 208, 402
Waters, Maxine, 257, 353
Webb, Trooper, 248, 289
Weber, Deputy Warden, 289
Webster, William, 258–59
Weigel, Stanley, 317
Weinglass, Leonard, 216, 234, 263
Wells, Warren, 294
Wham, L. S., 198
White, James "Sneaky," 306–7
Wilcots, Jackie Horton, 155, 159–60
Williams, Edward C., 61
Williams, Landon, 333
Williams, Tommye, 62
Willie, Little John, 247–48
Willis, Frederic, 403–4
Wolfer, DeWayne, 134–35, 254–55
Woods, Jesse, 169
Wright, Richard, 186
Writs of habeas corpus. *See* Habeas
    corpus actions

Yankins, William "Ying-Yang," 342–43

Zinman, Marvin, 89–92, 94, 97